PRAISE FOR JOHN KEEGAN'S

The American Civil War

"Keegan teases out the Civil War's parallels with World War I with great aplomb, from how troops were mobilized through methods of attacking enemy trenches. He also catches, quite movingly, the essential difference between these two wars."   —*The New York Times*

"[A] history that offers a thoroughly satisfying account for the general reader . . . and a multitude of intriguing insights for the Civil War buff."   —*The Boston Globe*

"A commanding history of the Civil War. . . . [Keegan] is a big picture writer. . . . The one-volume approach is refreshing."
                                                    —Bloomberg News

"Written in crisp prose and a confident, distinctive voice. . . . [Keegan] offers the kind of provocation we need to foster a thoughtful and inclusive, rather than a romantic, commemoration of the Civil War sesquicentennial. . . . When such a craftsman offers a one volume narrative account of the American Civil War, we should pay attention."
                                                        —*Slate*

"An excellent political and social history. . . . [Full of] important facets often neglected."   —*The Virginian-Pilot*

"Thoughtful, incisive. . . . [Keegan] breaks down the elements of battle in the war, noting the unusual fact that they were so frequently compared to other wars of the time . . . and ponders how a single democratic society could produce such a ferocious intensity of war against itself. . . . A cogent, well-argued and insightful book, which approaches so much of the story from a vantage different than that of most of our Civil War scholarship."
                                —William C. Davis, *The Military Book Club*

"Keegan delves into leadership, strategy and geography in his examination of this much-explored topic, bringing his remarkable knowledge of comparative military history to bear."   —*The Kansas City Star*

JOHN KEEGAN

The American Civil War

John Keegan was for many years senior lecturer in military history at the Royal Military Academy, Sandhurst, and has been a fellow at Princeton University and a visiting professor of history at Vassar College. He is the author of twenty books, including the acclaimed *The Face of Battle* and *The Second World War*. He is the defense editor of *The Daily Telegraph* (London). He lives in Wiltshire, England.

The American Civil War

A MILITARY HISTORY

JOHN KEEGAN

VINTAGE CIVIL WAR LIBRARY
VINTAGE BOOKS
A DIVISION OF RANDOM HOUSE, INC.
NEW YORK

To Lindsey Wood

FIRST VINTAGE CIVIL WAR LIBRARY EDITION, DECEMBER 2010

Copyright © 2009 by John Keegan

All rights reserved. Published in the United States by Vintage Books, a division of
Random House, Inc., New York, and in Canada by Random House of Canada
Limited, Toronto. Originally published in Great Britain by Hutchinson, the Random
House Group Ltd., London, and subsequently published in slightly different form,
in hardcover in the United States by Alfred A. Knopf, a division of
Random House, Inc., New York, in 2009.

Vintage is a registered trademark and Vintage Civil War Library and colophon
are trademarks of Random House, Inc.

Portions of this work originally appeared in *The Civil War Times* and
Military History Quarterly.

The Library of Congress has cataloged the Knopf edition as follows:
Keegan, John.
The American Civil War : a military history / by John Keegan.
p. cm.
Includes bibliographical references and index.
1. United States—History—Civil War, 1861–1865—Campaigns.   2. Military
geography—United States—History—19th century.   3. United States—
Strategic aspects.   4. United States—Geography.   I. Title.
E470.K255 2009
973.7'3—dc   2009019469

Vintage ISBN: 978-0-307-27493-9

Author photograph © Jerry Bauer
Book design by © Robert C. Olsson

www.vintagebooks.com

Printed in the United States of America
10   9   8   7   6   5   4   3   2   1

CONTENTS

Contents

MAPS

Configuration system for deployments, etc.

■	Union forces	☐	Confederate forces
→	Union advances	⇨	Confederate advances
▪▪▶	Union retreats	◻◻⇨	Confederate retreats
⚑	Union commanders	⚑	Confederate commanders
▶	Corps commanders	▷	Corps commanders
++++++ Railway	⚑ Ford	⚑ Bridge	===== Road

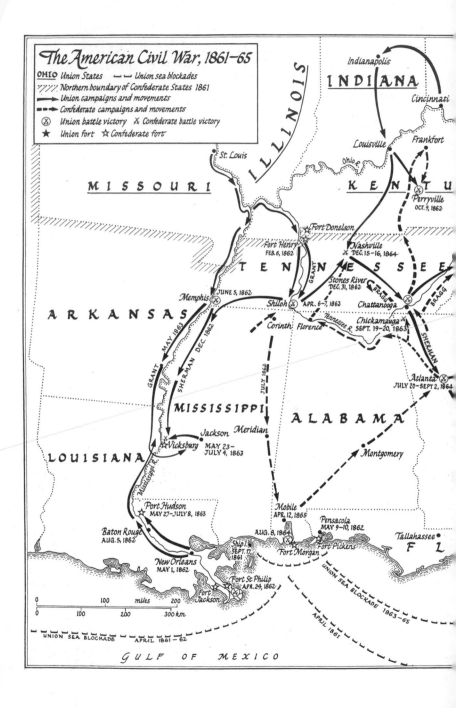

The American Civil War, 1861–65

OHIO Union States   — ·— Union sea blockades
//// Northern boundary of Confederate States 1861
⟶ Union campaigns and movements
--→ Confederate campaigns and movements
⊗ Union battle victory ✕ Confederate battle victory
★ Union fort ☆ Confederate fort

INDIANA
Indianapolis
Cincinnati
ILLINOIS
Louisville
Frankfort
St. Louis
Ohio R.
MISSOURI
KENTU
Perryville
OCT. 9, 1862
Fort Donelson
Fort Henry
FEB. 6, 1862
Nashville
✕ DEC. 15–16, 1864
TENNESSEE
GRANT
Stones River
DEC. 31, 1862
BRAGG
Memphis
JUNE 5, 1862
Shiloh ⊗ APR. 6–7, 1862
Chattanooga
BRAGG
ARKANSAS
Corinth· Florence
Tennessee R.
Chickamauga ✕
SEPT. 19–20, 1863
MAY 1863
GRANT
SHERMAN DEC. 1862
JULY 1862
SHERMAN
Atlanta ⊗
JULY 20–SEPT 2, 1864
MISSISSIPPI
ALABAMA
Jackson
Meridian
Vicksburg MAY 23–
JULY 4, 1863
Mississippi R.
LOUISIANA
Montgomery
Port Hudson
MAY 27–JULY 8, 1863
Mobile
APR. 12, 1865
Pensacola
MAY 9–10, 1862
Tallahassee
Baton Rouge
AUG. 5, 1862
AUG. 8, 1864
Fort Morgan
Fort Pickens
F L
Ship I.
SEPT. 17,
1861
New Orleans
MAY 1, 1862
Fort St Philip
APR. 24, 1862
Fort
Jackson
UNION SEA BLOCKADE 1863–65
APRIL 1861
0   100   miles   200
0 100 200 300 km
UNION SEA BLOCKADE — APRIL 1861–62
GULF OF MEXICO

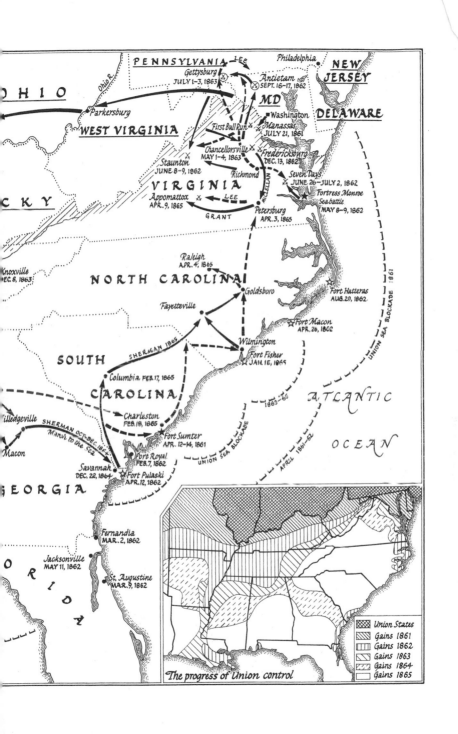

OHIO

Ohio R.

Parkersburg

WEST VIRGINIA

KCY

Knoxville
DEC. 6, 1863

PENNSYLVANIA   LEE   *Philadelphia*   NEW JERSEY

Gettysburg
JULY 1-3, 1863   ⊗   *Antietam*
SEPT. 16-17, 1862

MD   DELAWARE

■ Washington

First Bull Run   *Manassas*
JULY 21, 1861

Chancellorsville
MAY 1-4, 1863   *Fredericksburg*
DEC. 13, 1862

Staunton
JUNE 8-9, 1862   *Richmond*

VIRGINIA   *Seven Days*
JUNE 26-JULY 2, 1862

Appomattox   LEE   *Fortress Monroe
Sea battle*
MAY 8-9, 1862
APR. 9, 1865   GRANT

Petersburg
APR. 3, 1865

Raleigh
APR. 4, 1865

NORTH CAROLINA

Fayetteville   *Goldsboro*

Fort Hatteras
AUG. 29, 1862

Fort Macon
APR. 26, 1862

Wilmington

SOUTH   SHERMAN 1865   *Fort Fisher*
JAN. 15, 1865

Columbia, FEB. 17, 1865

CAROLINA

Charleston
FEB. 18, 1865

illedgeville   SHERMAN OCT.-DEC. 1864
March to the Sea   *Fort Sumter*
APR. 12-14, 1861

Macon   *Fort Royal*
FEB. 7, 1862

Savannah
DEC. 22, 1864   *Fort Pulaski*
APR. 12, 1862

GEORGIA

Fernandia
MAR. 2, 1862

Jacksonville
MAY 11, 1862

St. Augustine
MAR. 9, 1862

RIDA

UNION SEA BLOCKADE 1861

ATLANTIC

1863-64

OCEAN

UNION SEA BLOCKADE   APRIL 1861-62

▨ Union States
▧ Gains 1861
▥ Gains 1862
▨ Gains 1863
▨ Gains 1864
☐ Gains 1865

The progress of Union control

INTRODUCTION

I began an earlier book with the sentence "The First World War was a cruel and unnecessary war." The American Civil War, with which it stands comparison, was also certainly cruel, both in the suffering it inflicted on the participants and the anguish it caused to the bereaved at home. But it was not unnecessary. By 1861 the division caused by slavery, most of all among other points of division between North and South, was so acute that it could have been resolved only by some profound shift of energy, certainly from belief in slavery as the only means by which America's colour problem could be contained, probably by a permanent separation between the slave states and their sympathisers and the rest of the country, and possibly, given the ruptions such a separation would have entailed, by war. That did not mean, however, that war was unavoidable. All sorts of political and social variables might have led to a peaceful resolution. Had the North had an established instead of a newly elected president, and a president whose anti-slavery views were less provocative to the South; had the South had leaders, particularly a potential national leader, as capable and eloquent as Lincoln; had both sections, but particularly the South, been less affected by the amateur militarism of volunteer regiments and rifle clubs which swept the Anglo-Saxon world on both sides of the Atlantic in mid-century; had industrialisation not so strongly fed the North's confidence that it could face down Southern bellicosity; had Europe's appetite for Southern cotton not persuaded so many planters and producers below the Mason-Dixon line that they had the means to dictate the terms of a separatist diplomacy to the world; had so many "had nots" not clustered in the mentality of both North and South, then simple and scant regard for peace and its maintenance might have overcome the clamour of marching crowds and recruiting rallies and pointed the great republic through the turmoil of war fever to the normality of calm and compromise. Americans were great compromisers. Half a dozen major compromises had averted the crisis of division already during the nineteenth century. Indeed, a tacit resort to compromise had led the whole country to adopt compromise as the guiding principle of relations with the old colonial overlords at the beginning of the century and to forswear conflict with Britain, after the aberration of the War of 1812, in perpetuity. Unfortunately, Americans were also people of principle. They had embodied principle in the guiding preambles to their magnificent governing documents, the Declaration of Independence and the Constitution and the Bill of Rights, and, when aroused, Americans resorted to principle as their guiding light out of trouble. Even more unfortunately, the main points of difference between North and South in 1861 could be represented as principles; the indivisibility of the republic and its sovereign power and states' rights both had to do with the passions of the republic's golden age and could be invoked again when the republic's survival was under threat. They had been invoked, iterated, and reiterated throughout the political quarrels of the century's earlier decades by protagonists of great sincerity and eloquence, Henry Clay and John Calhoun. It was finally unfortunate that America produced opinion leaders of formidable persuasiveness. It was the South's ill fortune that, having dominated the debate in the first half of the century, at precisely the point when the issue of principle ceased to be a contest of words and threatened to become a call to action, the North had produced a leader who spoke better and more forcefully than any of the South's current champions.

War must have been very close beneath the surface of debate in 1861, for scarcely had the South moved to the level of organisation for secession than it was appointing not only its own Confederate president but also a secretary for war, as well as secretaries of state and of the treasury and the interior. Scarcely had President Lincoln assumed office before he was embodying the militias of the Northern states for federal service and calling for volunteers in tens of thousands. In only a few weeks one of the most peaceable polities in the civilised world was bristling with, if not armed men, then men demanding arms and marching and drilling in the manual of arms. It would take time for the arms to appear. The delay would not, however, abate the turmoil, for the challenge to the republic's integrity and authority had aroused profound popular passions. In the Old World, it had become, through struggles for national liberation, as much in the Spanish-speaking part of the continent as in the English-speaking half, the concern of populations. The Americas of 1861, North and South alike, had decided by unspoken consensus that the issues of principle the quarrel provoked by the election of Abraham Lincoln were grave enough to be fought over. The decision was to invest the coming conflict with a grim purpose. It would become a war of peoples, and those of each side, who had hitherto considered themselves one, would henceforth begin to perceive their differences and to consider their differences more important than the values that, since 1781, they had accepted as permanent and binding. The coming war would thus be a civil war, and it was quickly so called and recognised to be. In the meantime, however, the leaders of North and South turned to consider what form the war should take if war overtook their peoples. The matter, for the South, was simple. It would defend its borders and repel any invaders who appeared. For the North, things were not so simple. Any war would be a rebellion, a defiance of its authority which had to be defeated; but how and, more crucially, where should defeat be inflicted? The South formed half the national territory, an enormous area that touched the North's organised regions at only a few widely separated points. There was contact between the South and the North's region of great cities in the Atlantic coast corridor of Maryland and Pennsylvania, a region amply supplied with railroads; there were some tenuous connections between North and South in the Mississippi Valley, where there were extensive riverine links, but a dearth of cities and population. As a result, when war broke out in April 1861, it began in a haphazard, unplanned, and largely undirected form, the embryo armies falling upon each other as and when found. The first encounters would occur in what would become the state of West Virginia, minor engagements on what the correspondent of the London *Times* would dismiss as "unfought fields." It was greatly to the South's advantage that the first major battle of the war, First Manassas, or First Bull Run, resulted in a Southern victory, though it had lamentable consequences for the United States. This unexpected victory disheartened the North but persuaded the South that ultimate victory was attainable. Had the battle gone the other way, as it might so easily have done, the war might have been concluded more quickly and at much lower cost both to North and South.

As it was, after Bull Run, the war had to be fought as a major undertaking, needing the fullest commitment of resources by both sides. Yet

Bull Run did not point the way forward for either North or South. It still consigned the South to the defensive, without revealing to Lincoln and his generals how a successful offensive might be conducted. The much maligned General George McClellan, an organiser of genius but a halfhearted strategist and warrior, conceived the scheme of taking the Army of the Potomac from the environs of Washington and shipping it by water down Chesapeake Bay to the approaches to Richmond. It was a fruitful and well-reasoned conception, since it promised to avert a series of contested river crossings in northern Virginia during an approach march from one capital to the other. What it spared the Union army was demonstrated by Grant's Overland Campaign of 1864, when he did indeed have to fight every step of the way in a series of bloody battles that included Spotsylvania and Cold Harbor. The Peninsula Campaign, as McClellan's enterprise was called, deserved to yield great results, but its originator's timidity robbed it of outcome, obliging the Army of the Potomac to return to profitless frontal battles around Washington. The failure of the Peninsula Campaign also fostered the emergence of General Robert E. Lee, who was to frustrate all the Army of the Potomac's offensive efforts for three years, while leading several of his own into Union territory.

A successful Union strategy, though long debated, eventually emerged only accidentally, when General U. S. Grant's victory at Forts Henry and Donelson led him to make the first serious penetration of Confederate territory down the Tennessee River. Grant thereby inaugurated the "campaign in the West," actually the south-central United States. Grant was to inaugurate two other strategies, that of living off the country and that of inflicting casualties. Several major Union leaders, including Winfield Scott, the general in chief, and his successor, George McClellan, shrank from making the Confederacy pay in blood for its rebellion, believing that time and a milder way of making war would wean the South, which was believed to contain a large, hidden constituency of Unionists, away from war and into a mood of reconciliation. Grant took no such tepid view. Though not a bloodthirsty man, he believed that only fierce blows would bring the war to an end and, though deploring the "effusion of blood," he always fought to win. His first great battle, following Forts Henry and Donelson, at Shiloh was a ghastly bloodletting, which introduced the country to the nature of the conflict they had undertaken. The introduction was salutary, for thereafter the casualty lists rose inexorably. Thus the Civil War became unintentionally a body-count war, as the United States' later war in

Vietnam was to be a body-count war. Populous North Vietnam would be able to sustain a body-count war, in the 1960s sacrificing 50,000 of its young men each year to death at the hands of the U.S. Army and its allies and replacing them the following year without faltering in its war effort. The American South could not bear such a cost. In 1861–64, it appeared to be able to replace those lost in battle or by the diseases of war without weakening, but the appearance of invulnerability was deceptive. The war progressively bled the South to death, while the more populous North, suffering though it was, made good the numbers and continued to fight. As the North ate into the South's stock of fighting men, approximately a million strong, it was also eating into the South's landmass. The Shiloh campaign inaugurated Grant's bisection of the South, while also inflicting heavy losses. Bisection was followed by fragmentation, first when Grant cut across southern Tennessee to reach southern Georgia, then dividing the Lower South from the border states. Thereafter Grant was able to chew the South up into smaller and smaller fragments, inflicting losses all the time.

The South, or in particular the Army of Northern Virginia, under Lee's command, was not able to inflict similar damage on the North. Lee's invasions of Pennsylvania and Maryland were little more than large-scale raids. Neither secured permanent footholds, and while Lee secured large body counts, particularly at Antietam and Fredericksburg, his battles cost him dear. After the failure of his invasions, Lee no longer had a strategy in the east. He could only maintain a strong defence, while watching the North develop an increasingly effective strategy in the west.

The American Civil War is one of the most mysterious great wars of history, mysterious because unexpected, mysterious also because of the intensity with which it took fire. It was a great part of the mystery that a civil war should have broken out in a country which from its earliest times had devoted itself to peace between men, to the brotherhood of its inhabitants, as its largest city, Philadelphia, proclaimed, on the outbreak of the Civil War. The Civil War is also mysterious because of its human geography, a war which at the outset seemed rooted in the immediate locality of the two capitals, Washington and Richmond, but then, like an exotic invader from a tropical flora, sprang up at a distance from the Virginia battlefields, in Tennessee, Missouri, and Louisiana, often apparently without any cross-fertilisation. Abraham Lincoln, the new president in 1861, said that the "war was in some way about slavery," but in 1862 and 1863 it put out massive aggressive

shoots in parts of what had been the United States where slavery was a
very subordinate feature of economic and social life. Indeed, as we now
know, many Southerners had no personal connection with slavery at
all, neither as owners of slaves nor as employers of their labour. The
considerable slave owners were, indeed, often resented by their non-
slave-owning neighbours, though that did not deter them from joining
in their thousands in the new Confederate army and in fighting with
terrifying ferocity and admirable military proficiency in the battles it
conducted with the army of the Union. There was another mystery of
the war: why should men who lacked a rational interest in the war
struggle so fiercely against Northerners who, in their present circumstances, were frequently not to be distinguished from their poor
Southern opponents? In the South the lack of direct personal motivation was often apparent as a paradox, "a rich man's war, but a poor
man's fight," emphasising the undeniable fact that the gray ranks were
but sparsely populated with large slave owners or their sons, but enormously by hardscrabble farmers and often by men who owned nothing
at all.

The relative wealth of North and South also adds a mysterious
dimension to the war. In flat balance-book form, the South ought not
to have been rich enough to sustain a serious war effort against the
North. The per capita wealth of the South was greater than that of the
North but only because of the market value of slaves and the cash crops
they produced, wealth which was in private hands. The capital and revenue values of the Northern economy vastly exceeded those of the
South because they produced essential raw materials—iron, steel, non-
ferrous metals, coal, chemicals—in large quantities, and had access to
transport terminals, which the South did not. Even more deficient was
the South's output of manufactured goods. By 1861, the North had
become an exporter of coal and steel on its own account; by 1900 its
production of essential war materials would exceed that of the United
Kingdom. This reversal of commercial fortunes was already anticipated at the outbreak of the Civil War.

The ability of an enemy that was economically outclassed as well as
outnumbered by the other side, as the South was by the North, to
prosecute struggle on such a large scale compounds the mystery of
the war.

The American Civil War

CHAPTER ONE

North and South Divide

A MERICA IS DIFFERENT. Today, when American "exception-
alism," as it is called, has become the subject of academic study,
the United States, except in wealth and military power, is less
exceptional than it was in the years when it was to be reached only by
sailing ship across the Atlantic. Then, before American culture had
been universalised by Hollywood, the technology of television, and
the international music industry, America really was a different place
and society from the Old World, which had given it birth. Europeans
who made the voyage noted differences of every sort, not only political
and economic, but human and social as well. Americans were bigger
than Europeans—even their slaves were bigger than their African
forebears—thanks to the superabundance of food that American farms
produced. American parents allowed their children a freedom not
known in Europe; they shrank from punishing their sons and daughters in the ways European fathers and mothers did. Ulysses S. Grant,
the future general in chief of the Union armies and president of the
United States, recalled in his memoirs that there was "never any scold-
ing or punishment by my parents, no objection to rational enjoyments
such as fishing, going to the creek a mile away to swim in summer, taking a horse and visiting my grandparents in the adjoining county, fifteen miles off, skating on the ice in winter, taking a horse and sleigh
when there was snow on the ground."[1] It was a description of child-
hood as experienced in most prosperous country-dwelling families of
the period. The Grants were modestly well-to-do, Jesse Grant, the
future president's father, having a tanning business and also working
an extensive property of arable land and forest. But then most established American families, and the Grants had come to the New World
in 1630, were prosperous. It was prosperity that underlay their easy

3

way with their offspring, since they were not obliged to please neighbours by constraining their children. The children of the prosperous were nevertheless well-behaved because they were schooled and churchgoing. The two went together, though not in lockstep. Lincoln was a notably indulgent father though he was not a doctrinal Christian. Churchgoing America, overwhelmingly Protestant before 1850, needed to read the Bible, and north of the Mason-Dixon line, which informally divided North from South, four-fifths of Americans could read and write. Almost all American children in the North, and effectively all in New England, went to school, a far higher proportion than in Europe, where literacy even in Britain, France, and Germany lay around two-thirds. America was also becoming college-going, with the seats of higher education, Harvard, Yale, Columbia, Princeton, the College of William and Mary, established and flourishing. America could afford to fund and run colleges because it was already visibly richer than Europe, rich agriculturally, though it was not yet a food-exporting economy, and increasingly rich industrially. It was a newspaper country with a vast newspaper-reading public and a large number of local and some widely distributed city newspapers. Its medical profession was large and skilful, and the inventiveness and mechanical aptitude of its population was remarked upon by all visitors. So too was the vibrant and passionate nature of its politics. America was already a country of ideas and movements, highly conscious of its birth in freedom and its legacy of revolution; anti-imperialism had been its founding principle. During the decades before the Civil War, America was experiencing an industrial boom and its own distinctive industrial revolution. England's industrial revolution had taken its impetus from the development of steam power, fuelled by the island's abundant deposits of coal and directed to the exploitation of its large deposits of metal ores. Early-nineteenth-century America was also beginning to dig coal and iron ore, of which its soil contained enormous quantities, but at the outset it was two other sources of power which drove its proliferating factories and workshops: waterpower and wood. The rivers of New England, New York, and Pennsylvania were harnessed to turn waterwheels and its extensive forests to supply timber for burning. In Europe the days were long gone when forests could be cut down to supply heat. The Continent, outside Scandinavia and the Russian interior, was highly deforested. In America, trees were still an encumbrance which had to be felled to provide land for farming, but which also, when sawn, provided the raw material for every sort of building and manufactured item. America needed deforestation if its soils were to be farmed in the future, and in that process industrialisation and land clearing went hand in hand. During the 1830s and later, New York City consumed several million loads of wood every year, cut and stripped from Maine and New Jersey. It was only gradually that mines were dug and extended, originally by immigrants from the English coalfields and Welsh valleys, but by 1860 production in the Pennsylvanian anthracite fields had increased fortyfold in thirty years. By that date a distinctive economic geography of the United States could be discerned, with expanding industrial regions centred on New York and Philadelphia, exploited coalfields in New Jersey, Pennsylvania, and the Allegheny region of the Appalachians, a developing industrial region around Pittsburgh, and a thriving textile and engineering zone in southern New England. In the North the proportion of farmworkers in the labour force had fallen below 40 percent, while it remained above 80 percent in the South. An economic map would show that there was no industrial centre south of a line drawn from St. Louis to Louisville to Baltimore; in the South nine-tenths of the population lived in the countryside, but in the North only a quarter. Timber also provided the steam power for paddleboats, which by 1850 were to be seen on every navigable waterway, and the railway locomotives, which were becoming familiar on the tracks which were stretching out to link all the more important cities to one another and to the seaboard ports. By 1850 there were 9,000 miles of track in the United States; by 1860, 30,000. Rivers and then canals had been the means of transportation and distribution in the early stages of the boom. Canal boats and river steamers were rapidly overtaken in importance by the railroad. By 1850, America had surpassed Britain, home of the railroad revolution, in miles of operating track; indeed, American track mileage exceeded that of the rest of the world put together.

The United States was still an industrial client of Europe, particularly Britain, from which most manufactured goods came, but that was due to Britain's head start in the industrial revolution. By the end of the century this would no longer be the case. In the meantime, America was ceasing to be a predominately rural country and becoming an urban one. At the outbreak of the Civil War, America had more country-dwellers than town-dwellers, many more in the South, but the trend was for town-dwellers to outnumber country-dwellers. Cities were being founded at a breakneck rate and growing at exponential speed. The old cities of colonial settlement, Boston, New York, Philadelphia, Baltimore, retained their importance, but new cities were appearing and expanding, particularly beyond the Appalachian chain and even beyond the Mississippi; for a time Cincinnati promised to be the most important of the new metropolises, but it was rapidly over-taken by Chicago, which grew from a population of 5,000 in 1840 to 109,000 in 1860. It might be said that Chicago was only keeping pace with the United States itself, whose population increased from 5,306,000 in 1800 to 23,192,000 in 1850. Part of the increase came from migration, though the decades of mass immigration lay in the future; most of it was the result of a high birthrate. The astonishing productivity of the United States furnished work for all who chose to stay in the towns, while the abundant availability of land for settle-ment in the new states beyond the Appalachians and the Mississippi attracted would-be farmers, or employed farmers seeking better land, in large numbers. In whichever direction a visitor to the United States looked, the country was growing.

It was not that America was giving up the land. On the contrary: in the twenty years before 1860 enormous areas of the subcontinent were put under the plough; but the work was done by internal migrants who abandoned their homes on the thin, worked-out soils of New England, Virginia, and the Carolinas to trek westward into the new land in and beyond the Mississippi and Missouri valleys. Federal land policy encouraged the migrants. In 1800 public land was sold at $2 an acre, with a quarter to be paid down and four years to pay off the residue. By 1820 the price had gone down to $1.25 an acre. Land was sold in sub-divisions of a section of 640 acres. By 1832 the government accepted bids for a quarter of a quarter section, 40 acres. In 1862 Congress passed the Homestead Act, which allowed a settler free possession of 160 acres if farmed for five years. The legislation effectively trans-ferred eighty million acres of public land into private hands, and accommodated half a million people. American land policy was the making of such states as Ohio, Indiana, and Illinois, the Middle West proper. As settlement moved on to the more distant lands of the prairies in Iowa, Kansas, and Nebraska, the first comers got the best of the deal. The prairies were settled during an uncharacteristic era of moist climate, which conferred bountiful crops on the hardworking. By the twentieth century, desiccation had set in and many farms joined the dust bowl.

Settlement was not exclusively by free men. Cotton profits pulled plantation owners westward into new lands during the period 1830–

50, particularly onto the dark, rich soils of the "black belt" of Alabama and Mississippi, but even as far away as the river lands of Texas. It is calculated that 800,000 slaves were moved, by their owners, from the Atlantic coast farther inland between 1800 and 1860.

America was growing not only in population but also in wealth. Not yet an exporting country, except of cotton, its enormous internal market consumed all that could be produced. The whole of America was industrialising in the 1850s, particularly those parts settled since the eighteenth century: New England, Pennsylvania, New York, and some of Virginia. The industrialisation had its centre in Connecticut, which had both excellent river and canal connections with other parts of the region, and plentiful waterpower to drive factory machinery. Even as a pre-industrial economy, America wanted and bought the output of New England's workshops and factories, which worked by methods that would be copied all over the world. It was in Connecticut that what came to be called "the American system of manufacture" first established itself. The American system also became known as the "system of interchangeable parts," which is exactly descriptive. A well-educated and well-trained workforce learnt to make parts in metal or wood to such narrow tolerances that one manufactured item could be assembled from a random selection of parts. The American army's rifle, the Springfield, was such a product. It so impressed British visitors to the Springfield armoury that the British government bought the appropriate machinery to equip its armoury at Enfield for the Crimean War. When in 1861 the American government was gripped by demand for large quantities of rifles, the Enfield armoury supplied much of the need. Because the Springfield and Enfield products were manufactured in almost the same calibre, the Enfield being slightly larger, American cartridges fitted both quite satisfactorily, so well in fact that Union soldiers did not differentiate between Springfields and Enfields. Many good republicans thus went into battle with a weapon which bore the letters VR under a crown on the plate of the lock. The "system of interchangeable parts" also enabled the manufacture and assembly of clocks, watches, household and agricultural machinery, and the increasing number of labour-saving devices which American inventiveness brought to the world. America was chronically short of labour, both in town and country, so that any device that could multiply the work of a pair of hands was rapidly adopted. The sewing machine, which allowed housewives to dress themselves and their families at home or the local dressmaker to set up as a businesswoman, was widely adopted across America as soon as it was perfected. American farmers meanwhile were buying reaping machines, binders, and seed drills which could perform the tasks for which labour was lacking. The most significant element of mechanisation antedated the nineteenth century. It was the invention by Eli Whitney in 1793 of the cotton gin, a machine that separated the cotton fibre from the seed on which it grew, the boll. The gin revolutionised cotton production. A process which required a slave's hard labour for an hour to produce a pound of cotton could be completed by the machine in a few minutes. Little was turned into manufactured goods in the South, which, having sent raw cotton north to be spun, then had to buy it back as woven cloth or finished apparel.

The South's dependence on the industrial resources of the North underlay a visible social split. The South remained, as the North had been in the eighteenth century, agrarian and rural, with most Southerners living on the land and working as subsistence farmers, raising corn, hogs, and root crops, most of which they consumed themselves or sold locally, while the Northerners began during the nineteenth century to migrate from the land to towns in which they found wage-paying work. The readiness during the war of the two sides to fraternise at times of truce, formal and informal, and the willingness of both to be taken prisoner dispose of the idea that North and South were markedly different societies; despite the war, Americans remained American. Accent apart, and many Northerners complained they could hardly understand the way Southerners spoke, the soldiers of the two sides resembled each other much more than they differed. Both, in overwhelming majority, were country boys, in their twenties, farmers' sons who had left their land to join the army. Nevertheless, North and South were different, and the differences showed in the character of the armies.

Southerners were almost without exception small-town boys, or the sons of small farmers. Only a minority were slave owners. Of the South's white population of five million, only 48,000 were identified as planters, that is, men owning more than twenty slaves. Only 3,000 owned more than a hundred slaves, only 11 more than five hundred, truly staggering wealth in times when a fit, young field hand cost a thousand dollars. The white-pillared mansion, surrounded by shade trees and at a distance from the cabins of the field hands, existed, but more substantially in the imagination of outsiders than in reality. Of the four million slaves in the South, half belonged to men who owned fewer

than twenty. Most owned only one or two and used them to work subsistence farms on which they raised corn—maize, to Europeans—and
pigs. Most Southerners were hand-to-mouth farmers who owned no
slaves at all.

Hence the phrase, much quoted during the war, particularly at bad
times for the Confederacy, of "a rich man's war, but a poor man's fight."
Most Confederate soldiers were poor men from harsh circumstances, a
circumstance which has caused a question to be constantly raised: "If
so, why did the Southerners fight so long and so well?" Part of the
answer is that most Southerners were attached to the institutions of
slavery and aspired to slave ownership, which was the mark of Southern prosperity and success. Slave owners dominated Southern politics,
and it was by buying slaves that a Southerner moved up the social tree,
went from being a small to a large farmer and perhaps eventually a
plantation owner. More than that, slavery was the system on which the
foundations of Southern society rested. As slaves outnumbered whites
in several areas of the South, constituting the majority in South Carolina and Alabama and outnumbering whites in many other local areas,
slavery was felt to be a guarantee of social control.

Even though the planters were often resented as a class by the
classes below, they remained objects of envy and jealousy. The sentiments were not unrealistic, since many Southerners did make the transition from yeoman farmer to planter. It is doubtful, however, if many
successful social migrants were found in the ranks of the Confederate
army, which was disproportionately enlisted from the inhabitants of
the upland South, the piney, hilly regions of inland Georgia, the Carolinas, and Virginia; the Southern soldier's legendary toughness was a
product of hard upbringing in surroundings unsuitable for cotton
planting.

The typical Northern soldier also came from the farm, a farm
owned and run by his father which he expected in time to inherit.
Unlike the Southerner with his unspoken but persistent hopes of social
advancement by graduation to slave owning, the Northerner could not
harbour the same hope of elevation unless he abandoned the land,
moved to the town, and undertook work as a wage earner. Lives were
transformed by leaving the land for the town and in nineteenth-
century America much more quickly than they could be in Europe. It
was the hope of economic liberation which drew in the thousands
arriving as immigrants from the Old World, in numbers that the outbreak of the Civil War diminished but did not staunch. The Northern

recruit would almost certainly have been to school for several years and was probably a member of one of the large Protestant denominations, Methodist, Presbyterian, or Baptist. Religious belief and practice characterised a minority in most Northern regiments. It was usually an influential minority however. Captain John Gould of the 10th Maine recorded that it was "painful to know how few profound Christians there were in our large regiment—the number was under fifty—but beyond controversy the regiment was better in every way for the presence of this little handful. Their example was good, for they were good soldiers—a Christian soldier fighting for the right is always the model soldier. In every time of trial the regiment was always the stronger for having its few Christian men."[2] Confederate regiments also usually contained a Christian nucleus which was of equal importance, but with this difference. Southern Christianity was compromised by involvement with slavery, which had led to the pre-war split in the Baptist and Methodist churches. Even devout Confederate soldiers could harbour violently unchristian feelings as a result, applauding the killing of black Union soldiers at the Battle of the Crater in 1864 and the killing of individual black prisoners. The morals of plantation society also compromised Southern Christianity. In an America that had conferred the highest value on the family and on the sacred bond between the mother of the family and her husband, the sexual use of slave women by the planter and his sons, and the presence of mixed-blood cousins in the slave quarters of plantations, was a constant affront to Southern planter wives and daughters. Nothing similar happened in Northern society, which practised what it preached. The Christian family was a reality in the North, and its strength helped to make the Christian woman, exemplified by Harriet Beecher Stowe, author of *Uncle Tom's Cabin*, the formidable exponent of abolitionism she so often became.

Once the Northern soldier began to see the Southland for himself, as he did from 1863 onwards, he was confirmed in his critical opinions. Southerners, except for the truly poor whites of the poorest subsistence farms, were per capita richer than Northerners. This situation was brought about because the capital value of slaves was very high, but slave ownership was patchy. To Northern eyes, however, they looked poor. That had to do with the Southern way of life. Southerners did not care for their houses as Northerners cared for theirs, nor keep the gardens and surroundings as neat and tidy. Elegant Southern women allowed themselves to be accompanied by black servants in rags.

Northerners also tended to judge Southerners by the condition of their blacks. If the blacks were badly spoken and ignorant, Northern soldiers concluded that this was because of the example given them by their masters and mistresses.

Yet despite the real differences between Northern and Southern societies, the soldiers of the two sides shared many similarities. As the war drew out, and its harshness and ordeals bore down on the men in the ranks, that was not in the least surprising. They were the subjects of a common experience, and soldiers came to recognise the fact. Northern soldiers, better fed and better supplied than their opponents, were to form an admiration for Johnny Reb. He had "grit." He kept going in circumstances that tried the endurance of the hardest men. Johnny Reb commonly thought himself the better man than Billy Yank, an opinion that was to persist long into the war. The result of the first battle, First Manassas, or First Bull Run, seemed to confirm it. Until the exchange of the first shots, the differences between North and South were not that substantial. Once blood had been drawn, they came to seem so. What confirmed the difference was the war itself, a self-fulfilling judgement.

Dixie—the region of the continental United States lying south of the Mason-Dixon line—was becoming a distinct entity before 1860. It had not so been historically. Indeed, even under the Confederacy Dixie was never "the Solid South." Its territory and economy were too varied, its people too diverse, to form a cohesive unity. Moreover, "Southernness" drifted, as it does today. It overlapped the Mason-Dixon line to run into southern Illinois and parts of New Jersey, so that Princeton was regarded as a Southern university. Although the majority of Southerners in 1860 were of old English stock, or Scotch-Irish, as Americans denominate settlers from Ulster, there were important elements of the population which came from other directions. The citizens of Charleston and Savannah originated in many cases in Barbados, while the ancestors of those of New Orleans had in many cases made their way down the Mississippi from New France in Canada, staging via such other Frenchified cities as St. Louis, Missouri, and Louisville, Kentucky. Nor was the South solid in terms of how it made its wealth. The South was wealthy. The individual value of its free inhabitants was calculated to be twice that of their equivalents in the North. Not all their money, however, had come from cotton. Cotton was a picky crop. It did well only on certain soils and under particular climatic conditions. Thus it flourished in the "black belt," so called after the colour of the soil, in the Lower South, in the Sea Islands off the coast of Georgia and the Carolinas, and certain strains had adapted well to the wetter parts of Texas. It was scarcely grown in Virginia, where the staple remained tobacco. In the Mississippi delta the predominant crop was sugar; in the Carolinas and Georgia low country, rice.

Slave population and slave ownership correlated with the pattern of staple production. The densest areas of slave population were in South Carolina and along the Mississippi River, in Alabama and Mississippi, and in north-central Virginia; slaves formed the majority of the population in South Carolina, and not only there. They formed almost half the population of the whole South, more in the Old South. Slave ownership was a minority occupation, but those owning twenty or more slaves formed the Southern ruling class, dominating both its economy and its politics. In the Confederacy's first Congress 40 percent of members belonged to the more-than-twenty-slaves ownership group. Very few owned none at all. Slave ownership was the measure of all that was important in the antebellum South: not only wealth—twenty healthy slaves would fetch $20,000—but social position, local authority, and domestic ease and comfort. Financial surplus in the pre-war South almost always went into buying more slaves or more land, which then required more slaves to work. Very big landowners might own a hundred slaves or more. The big holdings were organised as plantations, with a colony of slave cabins near the big house, usually built in neoclassical style with a pillared portico, stables, and nearby accommodation for a slave overseer. A vision, crystallised in the enormously successful novel *Gone with the Wind* and the Hollywood film made from it, was transmitted, a vision of big plantation life which captured the American and European imagination; a vision of untitled aristocracy, leisured living, peremptory squires, high-spirited, commanding women, waited upon by privileged house slaves, with the liberty conferred by long association with the family to speak their minds to their grown-up former infant charges, living conducted in the context of ample meals, frequent social entertainments, and unworried prosperity. The *Gone with the Wind* world existed in few places; but exist it certainly did, and it set a model to which lesser planters aspired and, below them, the prosperous farmers also. The wealth of the South was increasing during the 1850s, if only because the price of slaves was rising. The market price of cotton had doubled since 1845 and big producers earned huge profits, as much as 20 percent on their capital, and spent much of it on the luxuries of plantation life, European fashions, fine horseflesh, and French wine. Many big planters did not live on the land at all but left overseers in charge and spent their days in state capitals or country seats, particularly at places like Charleston, South Carolina; Natchez, Mississippi; or the new Garden District of New Orleans.

Southern towns, or "cities" in American parlance, were, however, all small by comparison with their Northern counterparts. New Orleans was four times larger than any other. Montgomery, Alabama, the Confederacy's first capital, was the fastest growing but had only 36,000 people at secession, at a time when Chicago had grown to 109,000 in twenty years and both St. Louis and Cincinnati exceeded 160,000. The population of Richmond and Petersburg combined amounted to only 56,000 at secession, and there were no big towns at all between the lower Mississippi and the Atlantic coast; Charleston actually lost population in the years before the Civil War. The South made a virtue of its rurality, emphasising the pastoral nature of founding-father America, but it was in truth an index of the South's loss of competitiveness with the North and of relative decline. Industrially it could not compare. At the time of independence half the population of the United States lived south of the Mason-Dixon line. By 1860 half of the population lived west of the Appalachians, the majority in the Mississippi Valley.

The South's ability to compete economically with the North was limited by educational backwardness. Twenty percent of its white population was illiterate while 95 percent of New Englanders could read and write, and one third of Southern children went to school against three-quarters in New England and nearly as many in the Atlantic states and the Midwest.

Illiteracy keeps people poor, and Southerners were poor. Half the population of the United States in 1860 owned only one percent of the national wealth, but Northerners with the initiative to take a risk could and did increase their wealth by migrating from farm to city. Cotton was not the dominant crop of the South, but corn, ground to make coarse flour for corn bread or grits, i.e., porridge, or fed to pigs. The staple diet of the South, outside the big plantation houses, was corn bread, grits, and pork. The same food was eaten in the slave quarters, though more corn and less pork.

Plantation life formed most Americans' picture of slavery. It was on the plantation that slaves were found in the largest concentrations and

that the distinctive features of slave existence, repressive and enchanting alike, were to be observed. That there were enchanting features all
but the bitterest opponents of the slave system conceded. Masters and
mistresses commonly, out of self-interest, but also out of humanity and
affection, cared for their slaves' welfare, even happiness, arranging hol-
idays and festivals, giving treats and presents, and celebrating notable
events, births, and marriages (though legal marriage between slaves
was not recognised in the slave states, nor could it be, since a planter's
solvency ultimately depended on his freedom to liquefy capital by selling his slaves in the market). Good times always alternated, even on the
most benevolently run plantations, with harsh; slaves were regularly
whipped for misbehaviour or laziness. The plantation was an intrinsically repressive society. Even the good master so often identified by
slaves and ex-slaves presided at the apex of a disciplinary system, in
which the overseer, if one was employed, as was generally the case,
gave orders, to be imposed if necessary by force, through a layer of
foremen, or "drivers," who reported faults. Overseers were often the
sons of planters, learning the business or working to accumulate the
purchase price of land or slaves for themselves. There was also a class
of professional overseers, earning to support themselves but perhaps
also with the hope of accumulating capital; these were typically an
insecure group who were frequently dismissed, either for inefficiency
or because change of personnel was thought desirable to keep field
hands sweet.

    Self-interest prompted slave owners to see to the welfare of their
slaves, and most were well-fed. They were not, however, well-housed,
the one-room slave cabin being cold in winter and malodorous in summer and infested with parasites and germs at all times. Disease was
endemic in the slave quarters; very few slaves lived beyond the age of
sixty. The real threat to their well-being, however, was not disease but
social instability. There was no legal redress, because American law did
not recognise marriage between slaves, even though it was recognised
by the slaves themselves and by some masters. Under benevolent masters, weddings would be formally celebrated, performed by a preacher,
black or white, though in an edited form, since the parties could not or
would not swear fidelity "till death do us part." Many slave families'
circumstances were lifelong. But not even the best masters could guarantee that financial circumstances would not force slave sales at times
of stringency. Prudently, therefore, sometimes slaves swore "till death
or distance do us part." Equally, some masters did not permit religious

formalities for that reason but presided at what were called broomstick weddings, where groom and bride signalled their commitment by jumping together over a broomstick.

Some slave owners encouraged black "marriage" because it made for contentment and stability on the plantations and formed black community. They supported it, by helping the slaves to build their living quarters, the "cabins" of plantation literature, and by allotting acreage for the slave gardens, chicken runs, and pigsties. On a prosperous and properly run plantation, the slaves could live quite well: the master distributed rations at set times of the week, flour, pork, and cornmeal; the slave added potatoes, peas, and turnips which he grew himself. If the master allowed the slaves to hunt, as was the usual case, he also added possum, raccoon, rabbit, and squirrel.

The plantation day was a harsh one, working time typically running to twelve hours, though the slaves themselves reckoned more like fifteen. Work normally stopped at dusk. Sunday was a day of rest as, quite often, was Saturday afternoon. At harvesttime, the day would lengthen, though so too would work breaks. Different crops had different timetables. The sugar plantations of southern Louisiana imposed long days during the sugar harvest. Corn shucking, a regular feature of work on most plantations, required intense and prolonged labour but was enjoyed by the slaves because it was dedicated to providing their diet and could be lightened by games and competitions. Almost everywhere, however, on good plantations and bad, under kind and harsh masters, work progressed by the regular application of the whip, twenty, sometimes thirty-nine lashes, inflicted by the overseer or driver, sometimes by the master himself or, in the house, the mistress. The whip was part of slave life. Its use was regulated by public opinion. Cruel masters suffered the disapproval of their neighbours; nevertheless, whipping went on. Some masters prided themselves on never whipping, but they were a minority. Some slaves, notably privileged house slaves, were never whipped, but they were a minority also. An overseer on one plantation, who took the whip to a mammy—the senior house slave, usually a former nurse to the mistress, who traditionally enjoyed the status of a constitutional monarch, to be consulted in all matters of family importance, to advise and to warn—was discharged and sent from the plantation with his family that very day. But his offence was unusual, as was the penalty.

This daily routine required the slaves to fit personal pursuits into the timetable of the fields, a requirement which fell heavily on the slave wife, since cooking had to be done at the end of a day's hard work. Masters might frequently report finding their contented field hands chatting or singing around the cabin fireplace as the night fell, but there was little free time in the slaves' working week. The slaves could, however, usually count on the free Sunday, since the South was God-fearing and churchgoing and the Sabbath had to be respected. By the nineteenth century, moreover, America's black population was universally Christian. Elements of African religion remained, particularly strongly in the Gullah regions of the Georgia coast, and black Christianity had incorporated African features, including dancing during church singing and the loud affirmatory cries of worshippers uttered during sermons. The two churches which slaves most often joined were the Baptist and the Methodist, probably because of their informality of organisation and the inspirational nature of their services. Until the end of the eighteenth century, however, white churches did not welcome black membership. Black Christianity was correctly suspected by whites who were involved in any way in the slave system as being subversive of the slave order by its message of equality between all human beings and its celebration of poverty and powerlessness. During the seventeenth and early eighteenth centuries, devoted white Christians found that part of Christian teaching difficult to reconcile with the picture of slavery, so that both Baptists and Methodists began in America as anti-slavery organisations, as the Quakers would remain throughout. Progressively, however, the churches, particularly those with numerous slave-owning adherents, such as the Episcopalians and Presbyterians, began to justify slavery on doctrinal grounds. As a result, the Episcopal Church lost almost all its black members. Meanwhile slaves were finding their own way to reconcile their Christian beliefs with church organisation, and hence the rise of black churches, beginning with the appearance of black preachers. At first forbidden by law to practise, slaves, as well as freedmen, soon appeared as preachers in several churches, notably the Baptist and Methodist, though often they had to do so in the guise of "assistants" to white clergymen. The black liberation movement was later to condemn the black churches for the effect they had of reconciling blacks to their deprivations and of seeking consolation in prayer and Christian practice instead of seeking objective advance by political activity. At a time when political opportunities were not open to blacks, let alone slaves, religion offered the only opportunity for subjective solace, besides bringing undoubted richness and even happiness into the lives of the oppressed. Religion also brought objective advantages, since by a well-known process it opened avenues to literacy. In many states, laws were introduced from the seventeenth century onwards, with increasing severity during the nineteenth, particularly in the Lower South, against teaching slaves to read. Many slaves learnt nonetheless: perhaps as many as 5 percent of the slaves were literate by 1860, in the calculation of the famous black scholar W. E. B. Du Bois. Some were taught by masters and mistresses who had an aristocratic disdain for small-minded laws, some by white playmates, but many were taught by white Christians seeking to transmit the Bible's message. Slave literacy nonetheless aroused alarm among slave owners and for a strictly practical reason. Slaves were only allowed off the plantation if equipped with a written pass, and the pass system was policed by the "patrols," gangs of white slave owners or their minions, who literally patrolled the roads, stopping blacks to see their passes and beating slaves who could not produce the necessary card.

The patrol regime was intermittent, since rich slave owners disliked the duty, generally leaving it to poor whites acting on their behalf or on their own account. Nevertheless, patrolling, if sometimes lax, never lapsed altogether, because it was animated by white fears of slave revolt, which all entertained, more or less regularly and with better or worse reason. Slave revolt was a reality, though more frequent and on a larger scale in the West Indies, Guiana, and Brazil than in America. There were slave revolts in New York in the seventeenth century, in Florida and Louisiana in the nineteenth, but most memorably in Virginia in 1831, when Nat Turner led an uprising that killed nearly a hundred whites. The Nat Turner revolt terrified the South and led to repercussion in many forms, practical and legislative. Fear of slave revolt underlay much of the support for secession. The emancipation campaign, simply a moral issue to Northern emancipationists, speaking, writing, and organising in states with small black populations, was a life-and-death issue in whites' estimation in states where blacks coexisted with whites and often outnumbered them. Harping on the dangers of slave revolt of course undermined and invalidated the populist defence of slavery, that it suited blacks, that it was their natural condition, that it cared for their welfare and provided for their old age and so on, arguments endlessly rehearsed and as familiar to Southern whites as the celebration of America's founding freedoms. However illogical, the slave revolt fear was taken seriously by Southerners and particularly by the spokesmen for "the peculiar institution."

The economics of slavery required the sale of individuals to supply labour needs elsewhere in the cotton kingdom, and slave sales inevitably broke up some slave families; perhaps as many as one in four sales entailed the separation of husband and wife, parents and children. Slaves sold away would rarely meet again, which made for functional orphanage and divorce. Masters of any decency normally sought to keep families together, because separation caused disabling heartbreak, but it occurred and it was sometimes deliberately done to discipline a fractious slave. It was this feature of slavery that principally drove the humanitarian motive behind abolitionism, particularly among evangelical Christians, since American blacks were often devout Baptists or Methodists. The tragedy of separation supplied Harriet Beecher Stowe with her most powerful theme in *Uncle Tom's Cabin*. Tom wept for his children left behind in Kentucky when he was sold south and millions of Mrs. Stowe's readers wept with him. When she was introduced to President Lincoln, he supposedly greeted her with the words "So, this is the little lady who wrote the big book that made this great war. . . ." He was as near to the truth as it was possible to get.

The early 1830s was a critical moment in the history of American slavery. It was the moment when the attack on slavery became a national movement, and one to be forbidden or silenced. Until 1831, or thereabouts, it was possible to shelter from the ongoing debate by adhering to the fashionable view that slavery would wither away, a view widely held as much within the South as the North. The grounds for so believing were manifold, but had much to do with the abolition of the slave trade by Congress and enforcement of its abolition by the British Parliament through the use of the Royal Navy. The suppression of the international trade in slaves was counterbalanced, however, by the meteoric rise of the international trade in cotton, which by 1840–50 had transformed the economy of the South and made many planters rich men. The rise of Southern fortunes encouraged Southern politicians and writers to find words in defence of slavery and Northern writers and politicians to articulate an intellectual attack on it. In 1831 William Lloyd Garrison founded his newspaper, *The Liberator*, which was to be the mouthpiece of the abolition movement. In 1837 Garrison joined the Tappan brothers of New York in founding the Anti-Slavery Society, which quickly attracted the support of churches, schools, and colleges, notably Oberlin College in Ohio. What lent substance to the anti-slavery movement, however, were the fugitive slave cases that occupied so much newspaper space in the decade before the Civil War broke out. In 1793, Congress had passed a fugitive slave law, giving owners the right to repossess, and to be assisted in repossessing, their runaway slaves, wherever found. In 1850 an even more rigorous Fugitive Slave Act was enacted by Congress, and its passage inaugurated a flurry of cases in which runaways who had found sanctuary in the North were pursued by owners, sometimes assisted by law officers, to be confronted by local anti-slavery activists, often acting with the support of a personal liberty law, passed by several states after 1850.

By 1860, and despite lulls and Northern retreats from the issue, slavery had got a thoroughly bad name in the North. Most Northerners, despite their undoubted Negrophobia, were ashamed that their country, alone among the great constitutional polities of the Western world, continued to allow the practice of slavery and, without agreeing in any way about how the end was to be achieved, wished to see the institution disappear. Many Southerners, though trapped by the economics of slavery, in which their world and livelihoods were embroiled, deduced, with some sincerity, that slavery was a burden to them and that, paradoxically, slave owners were themselves the slaves of the system, committed by it to a way of life that monopolised all their time and attention. Even some among them who would fight most energetically for the Confederacy, or support their husbands in so doing, were frequent complainers of the loss of liberty that their performance of slave-owning duty imposed on them. They held that the peculiar institution was the hardest of taskmasters. Nevertheless, a majority of Southerners were prepared to fight to defend it. The question was, how many Northerners were prepared to fight them over the issue?

At the beginning, after the first clashes of 1861, the soldiers who were to fight the Civil War began to demonise each other. To Southerners, the men in the Union ranks were, of course, Yankees, but also "mercenaries" or "Hessians" or "regulars," terms of abuse descended from the War of Independence against the British. To Northerners the men of the South were "secesh" but also "savages" and "brutes" as well as "traitors" and "rebels." "Rebel" was of course an accurate description and quite quickly the Confederates became Johnny Reb to the Union soldier, who became Billy Yank in return. "Yankee" had a qualitative as well as geographical meaning to Southerners. It implied a cold, narrow-minded Puritan, everything that the Southerner held himself not to be. Well-educated Southerners preferred to think of themselves as cavaliers, figures from a novel by Walter Scott, the writer whom Mark Twain, only half jokingly, identified as having caused the Civil War.

The spectre of slave uprising was constantly raised by alarmists and by die-hard defenders of slavery. Nevertheless, for all the searching for motives that occupied minds on both sides once the fighting had begun, it remained, as it still remains, difficult to explain why the Civil War became a war as opposed to a continuation of a long-running dispute over slavery which had occupied minds, North and South, for the previous forty years. Yanks were given to asking Rebs why they were fighting. One Reb, captured in Virginia early on, answered, "Because you are here." It was, and remains, as good an answer as any.

It is often suggested that the war was a conflict between two Americas, an older, agricultural South and a newer, industrial North that was coming into being. There is something, if very little, in that.

With fewer places in which to find industrial employment, more Southerners than Northerners were country-dwellers and farmworkers. Nevertheless, both armies were predominantly raised from farming communities, and the list of soldiers' occupations was closely similar. Bell Irvin Wiley, in his study of Johnny Reb, found that of 9,000 soldiers in twenty-eight Confederate regiments, although half described themselves as farmers, 474 entered themselves as students, perhaps school as well as university pupils, since it is known that at least one teacher closed down his school on the outbreak of war and marched his class off to enlist. There were also 472 labourers in Wiley's sample, 321 clerks and 318 mechanics, 222 carpenters, 138 merchants, and 116 blacksmiths. Other occupations showing more than 50 enlistees were sailors, doctors (most of whom must have served as surgeons), painters, teachers, shoemakers, and lawyers.[3] Some described themselves as gentlemen, no doubt from the planter class, whom the elected officers often found difficult to handle. Professor Wiley's examination of the rolls of 12,000 Union soldiers disclosed an almost exactly similar set of occupations and numbers of those practising them with the difference that more of the Northerners were teachers or printers, evidence of the higher degree of literacy in the Northern ranks.[4]

Another category better represented in the North than the South was the foreign-born. In 1860 there were a million Germans living in the Northern states, most of them immigrants from the repression following the 1848 revolution. They and their native-born descendants, who might still be German-speaking, numbered 200,000 of the Union army's two million members. The next largest foreign-born contingent was the Irish, with 150,000. The Irish were, of course, English-speaking, as were the 45,000 English-born and most of the 50,000 Canadians. The Confederate equivalent numbers were not separately counted, but it is known the Irish, Germans, Italians, and Poles totalled tens of thousands. However, the typical Confederate soldier, if such a being can be isolated, was English-speaking and of British ancestry, English or Scotch-Irish. Many immigrants were to prove violently opposed to conscription when it was introduced in 1863. Most of the New Yorkers who looted and burnt and fought in the streets during the infamous draft riots of that year were Irish, who equated military service with British oppression.

The soldiers of the two sides were alike enough to fraternise readily when opportunity offered, to their officers' great disapproval. A common pretext was the exchange of Reb tobacco for Yankee coffee. At Kennesaw Mountain in 1864 one of Sherman's soldiers recorded that "we made a bargain with them that we would not fire on them, if they would not fire on us, and they were as good as their word. It seems too bad that we had to fight men that we like. Now these Southern soldiers seem just like our own boys. They talk about their mothers and fathers and their sweethearts just as we do. Both sides did a lot of talking but there was no shooting until I came off duty in the morning." Not all contestants were so easygoing. Sergeant Day Elmore wrote from near Atlanta in July 1864, "The Boys have been to gather a number of times . . . traiding coffee for tobacco, but I do not love them so I could not take them by the hand as some of the Boys did."[5]

Earlier in the war, Billy Yank commonly execrated Johnny Reb, cursing him as the blackest of enemies and as a foe of the liberty that the Founding Fathers and their men had won from the British. What can we tell about the United States at mid–nineteenth century from the sentiments of the men who wore the blue or the gray? The enormous extent of the United States was still more unsettled than not. Many of the modern states had not yet come into being, so that there was no Idaho, no Wyoming, no Washington State, no Oklahoma, while Utah and New Mexico were territories and included land that would eventually belong to states later admitted to the Union. Many familiar cities were as yet simply unbuilt landscape, Bismarck and Pierre, Omaha, Helena. Most of the vast plains stretching from the Mississippi to the Rocky Mountains was still the preserve of the buffalo and the Indians who hunted it and, so unpromising did it appear for settlement, that it was known to early American geographers as the Great American Desert, though in time it would prove, given adequate irrigation, abundantly fertile. What both Billy Yank and Johnny Reb noticed about each other's landscapes was the difference in appearance that their different styles of farming imposed on the land. At dividing lines like the Tennessee River, Northerners noted that the northern shore ran down to the water like a garden, while below the southern shore looked unkempt. Northern soldiers were also deeply critical of the condition of the landscape in Virginia, writing home to say that "if in Northern hands, it would have been far more productive than it was." Jesse Wilson, a soldier in a Maine regiment, wrote to his mother in 1862 from Virginia, "In the hands of New England people, this country might be created into a garden." Southern farming methods probably did differ from Northern, since Northern farms were usually small family enterprises, raising cash crops, while Southern farms were either subsistence holdings or else slave labour properties. In either case, the Southerners did not expend the care on them that Northern proprietors did on their cherished acres. Northerners were also often contemptuous of Southern towns, which they found small, poky, and ill-built. They often complained that the streets were dirty and the general air "old-fashioned," a common term of criticism in Northerners' letters home. They also criticised Southerners themselves, finding them badly educated and badly spoken.

Bell Irvin Wiley, who read many thousands of soldiers' letters and hundreds of diaries in compiling his wonderful profiles of the common soldiers, North and South, formed the impression of a spiritual and temperamental difference between Yank and Reb, reflecting differences in the two societies. Johnny Reb was a lighter-hearted correspondent, passing on jokes and comic incidents to the folk at home more frequently than Billy Yank. He was more heartfelt in expressions of affection and more graphic in his descriptions of battle. Billy Yank was more political, expressing views about forthcoming elections, which the Southerner lacked the opportunity to do, since the Confederacy held only one presidential election during 1861–65, and he was generally less given to stating his views about the conduct of the war and government. He was also more businesslike, demanding news about the family fortunes and management, typically of the farm. Whatever the pattern of difference, however, soldiers with paper and pen in hand revealed more similarities than differences. Analysis of soldiers' letters emphasises the tragedy of the war and raises questions about how and why enmities were so long sustained.[6]

In the years before 1860 North and South, not seriously dissimilar at the time of independence, had drifted far apart. It was not simply economic difference, the industrialisation of the North and its extension westward into the new farming lands beyond the Appalachian Mountains, and the South's persisting otherness. It was the social difference between a wholly free region and a partially unfree one. That was Lincoln's point in his famous remarks about "a house divided." A country which in 1781 had been united by its origins in British, largely English culture, by its common practice of English-speaking Protestantism, by its acceptance of British legal and political forms, had by 1861 become separated by the features that the practice of slavery had inflicted on its southern half.

CHAPTER TWO

Will There Be a War?

I N DECEMBER 1860 the United States of America trembled on the brink of . . . what? Disunion certainly. But civil war? Violent language filled the columns of newspapers, North and South, and the air of debating chambers in state and the national legislatures. How far would violent language lead those who spoke with passion? On December 20, a convention in South Carolina declared its secession from the United States, created by the thirteen British colonies' declaration of independence and their subsequent promulgation of a common constitution eighty years earlier. South Carolina's secession was swiftly followed by that of Mississippi, Florida, Alabama, Georgia, Louisiana, and Texas. The occasion of secession was the election of Abraham Lincoln as the new president of the United States. He and his Republican Party had won on a platform that opposed slavery, and many in the South had concluded that his presidency threatened an end to the "peculiar institution," which for them defined their way of life and underpinned their prosperity. Secession secured the means to preserve both. Secession did not, however, imply war, nor did the South, or the North for that matter, proceed from secession to undertake any preparation for fighting.

Moreover, as cooler heads in the South recognised, neither Lincoln himself nor his Republican Party proposed abolition, the legal ending of slavery by an amendment of the Constitution, which indirectly permitted slavery while not positively endorsing it. What Lincoln and the Republicans and indeed a very large number of Northerners insisted upon was that slavery should not be extended into the "territories," the vast tracts of North America belonging to the Union but not yet organised as states. Unfortunately, many in the South had persuaded themselves that slavery and a South dependent on slavery could only survive if slavery was extended into the territories. The issue had already caused a great deal of trouble within the United States, legal, political, and constitutional, and in some of the territories, notably Kansas, was provoking bitter and violent conflict. Pro-slavery parties were prepared to tolerate the violence, or the passions that underlay it, if that was the price of carrying slavery westward. The anti-slavery parties foresaw that the extension of slavery would strengthen Southern power in Congress and, they believed, undermine the principles of political and economic liberty on which the United States had been founded. In December 1860 the implications of the crisis were yet to be perceived. While there was talk of war by some, it was still only as an eventuality, not an inevitability.

Sixty years earlier few would have been found who believed that slavery could cause a crisis threatening the domestic peace of the nation. The South's attachment to slavery in 1860 was explained by the slaves' role in cultivating and preparing raw cotton. In 1800 only 70,000 bales of cotton fibre had been produced, in 1860 over four million bales. The number of slaves had increased proportionately, from 700,000 at the time of the first census in 1790 to four million in 1860, exclusively the result of births, since the slave trade had been abolished in 1807. The rise in output had a number of causes, including the invention of the cotton gin, which separated fibre from the hard cotton boll much more quickly and less laboriously than it could be done by hand. Rich land in Alabama, Mississippi, and Louisiana also yielded much larger crops, at a time when the traditional growing areas in Virginia and the Carolinas were losing their fertility. The development of "short staple" cottons also opened up regions unsuitable for the planting of long staple varieties. The expansion of planting was driven by rising demand from Europe, where in Britain, Belgium, and France the industrial revolution was bringing a mechanised textile spinning and weaving industry into being. Rising demand for cotton generated rising demand for slave labour, supplied by slave owners who were also slave breeders in the South and who despite the prohibition of slave imports made large profits by selling American-born slaves on the domestic market at prices that rose throughout the century's first half. Rising slave numbers heightened the South's attachment to slavery, since the institution had sound social as well as economic functions, assuring control of an unfree population, which in some areas of the Deep South exceeded in number that of the free, slave-owning white population.

During the 1850s, as the population of the United States was swelled by the immigration of millions of European settlers, many of whom joined native-born Americans in moving west into the fertile farmlands of the Midwest, slavery acquired a critical political importance. Southerners sought to have the legality of slavery established in the new areas of settlement not only because they wished to profit by the spread of slave owning, but also because territories, once settled, were destined to become states and so to alter the balance of power in Congress. Thitherto, the balance between slave and free states had been maintained with remarkable equilibrium; in 1847 there were fifteen slave and fourteen free states. The balance was crucial to the South, since though it could not hope to limit numbers of voters in states, their electoral weight counted only in the House of Representatives. In the Senate, by contrast, each state controlled two votes. As long, therefore, as territories were admitted to Congress as states in which slavery was permitted, and slavery was accepted in the federal Constitution, slavery was safe within the South, since anti-slavery legislation passed by the House of Representatives could be voted down in the Senate. Much of the political business of the United States during the first half of the nineteenth century was concerned with the creation of new states, carefully supervised by the South to assure that the balance was maintained. The process was delicate. In 1787 Congress had by ordinance banned slavery in the Northwest, territory that became the states of Ohio, Illinois, Indiana, Michigan, and Wisconsin, then only beginning to be settled. In 1820, when the question of admitting Missouri arose, the North agreed to a compromise, accepting Missouri as a slave state on condition that Maine, the northern part of Massachusetts, was admitted as a free state, thus maintaining the balance. The Missouri Compromise also excluded slavery from those territories forming part of the Louisiana Purchase, north of 36°30′, the largest remaining tract of federal territory within the United States. The South did not quibble because the excluded territory was recognised to be unsuitable for slave agriculture, in that neither its climate nor its soil was fitted for the intensive cultivation of cotton or tobacco.

In 1820 it seemed unlikely that more land would be added to the territory of the United States. Though there was agitation to adjust the frontier with British Canada, the issue was muted. The vast Southwest, today California, Texas, Arizona, Nevada, Utah, and New Mexico, was being infiltrated by American settlers, but was the property of the sovereign country of Mexico and so apparently inviolable. That nevertheless was where the penultimate crisis over slavery would arise. In 1836 the American population of Texas rebelled against Mexico and declared itself an independent republic. It soon became obvious that it would seek to accede to the United States, as it did in 1845. Mexico accepted the loss with ill grace but showed itself determined to resist over the incorporation into the new state of large Texan territories to the west. The dispute led rapidly to war. Though the Mexicans outnumbered their American invaders several times, the invaders—many Southern volunteers—were hardy and excellent marksmen. In sixteen months of fighting in 1846–47, the Americans won all the battles and arrived in Mexico City on September 14, 1847, to impose a peace. It robbed the Mexican republic of nearly half its territory, an indignity only softened by President Santa Anna's acceptance of a large sum in dollars in return for territory and the United States' acceptance of Texan debt.

The first legacy of the Mexican War, however, was the opportunity it gave to free settlers to form new non-slave states from the surplus of Texan territory. The probability appeared even before the Mexican War was over. In 1846 an anti-slavery congressman, David Wilmot, introduced in the House of Representatives a measure outlawing slavery in all territory conquered from Mexico. Southern congressmen at once recognised that the Wilmot Proviso spelt doom to the slave system, since captured Mexican territory was likely to give rise to sufficient new states to endow the anti-slave factions with an undefeatable majority in both the House and Senate. Using their current equal representation in the Senate, the Southern politicians worked to annul the Wilmot Proviso. But they could not prevent its reappearance in some form in the future. It reappeared in 1850, when Congress was forced to consider legislating for the future status of California, former Mexican territory which had overnight acquired a surge of population because of the discovery of gold within its borders. The gold-rushers were overwhelmingly Northerners and, as pioneers out to make private fortunes, adamantly opposed to the legalisation of slavery on soil they were determined to exploit by free labour. Complex debate in Congress eventually yielded a second compromise, which admitted California as a free state, and allowed the territories of New Mexico and Utah to settle the slavery issue by popular vote. Both territories legalised slavery, though the institution in practice did not take root there. The really baleful consequence of the Compromise of 1850 was the inclusion, among other legislation, of the Fugitive Slave Act, which allowed slave owners to enter free states to recover runaways and obliged both federal and state jurisdictions to assist them. The re-enslavement of fugitives outraged many in the North, where it was seen as a violation of the laws of liberty guaranteed in the Constitution and by the struggle for freedom against British colonialism. Attempts to frustrate recapture of fugitives equally enraged many Southerners, who saw repossession of runaways as an exercise of the right of property, a principle equally dear to Americans. The issue was inflamed by the publication in 1852 of *Uncle Tom's Cabin*, a depiction of the practice of slavery that blackened the South in Northern eyes, and enraged Southerners, all the more by the enormous scale on which it sold.

The political leaders of the South correctly recognised that the tide of opinion in a country in which they represented a minority was moving against them. They might have moderated their position and sought common ground. It would have been difficult to find. Not only was the South indeed different from the North, with the difference founded on an institution that could not be disguised or easily altered; as the dispute with the North dragged on, Southerners had begun to make a virtue of the difference, by inventing a creed of Southern nationalism which eventually committed them to confrontation. Mid-century Southerners proclaimed themselves to be a superior breed to Northerners, preserving the agrarian way of life on which the republic had been founded at the Revolution and led by a breed of cultivated gentlemen who better resembled the Founding Fathers than the money-grubbing capitalists who dominated public life in the North. The South's poorer classes, too, sons of the soil and outdoorsmen, were held to be superior to their equivalents in the North, whose lives were confined by factory walls and who were often not native-born but immigrants, sometimes not English-speaking, and Catholic rather than Protestant. Southern nationalism had impressive ideologues as its own founding fathers, John C. Calhoun and Henry Clay, and it even had its own lyceum, the University of the South, founded at Sewanee, Tennessee, to train Southern scholars who could debate on equal terms with men from Harvard. The North took it seriously enough to destroy its buildings, down to the foundation stone, soon after the Civil War began.

Faced by growing Northern hostility and fired by an impassioned belief in the rightness of their cause, the Southern political class, in the aftermath of the Compromise of 1850, deliberately sought to challenge the North over the issue of slavery. In 1854, Jefferson Davis, secretary of war in the cabinet of Franklin Pierce, persuaded the president to support the repeal of the Missouri Compromise, which in 1820 had banned slavery in the territories north of 36°30′. He was backed by the great orator Stephen Douglas, a rational moderate who was hungry for presidential power and saw the chance to gain Southern votes by endorsing a Southern measure. The measure was the Kansas-Nebraska Act, which would admit both territories as states, though both were north of 36°30′, but the first allowing slavery, the second free. The act was bound to cause trouble. Though Kansas bordered Missouri, a slave state, its population was strongly divided between Southerners and Northerners and its internal affairs were already sinking into the violence that would disfigure it in the years before the Civil War. The act not only disturbed the domestic peace of Kansas. It also enraged opinion in the North generally but particularly within the Democratic Party. The Democrats were, with the Whigs, one of America's historic political parties. The Whig Party was already in decline by the 1850s; the Democratic Party, though still a vigorous and important medium of political activity in national and regional politics, was badly split over slavery. Stephen Douglas, its most important national figure, exhausted his considerable intellect during the debate by seeking a formula by which both sides could get what they wanted: the South extension of slavery into the territories, the North the popular right in the territories to make laws excluding slavery. The two positions were, of course, irreconcilable, and the Kansas-Nebraska Act, which attempted to fudge the issue, was rapidly recognised in the North and particularly by Northern Democrats as a false compromise. As Stephen Douglas was its author, and the Democratic Party his seat of power, Northern Democrats reacted by leaving the party in droves and joining the new Republican Party, which, without being markedly abolitionist, was doctrinally anti-slavery. In the presidential election of 1856 the Republicans captured most Northern states, winning on a programme based on the Wilmot Proviso. The election was won, however, by James Buchanan, who was strongly supported in the South and had won some Northern states.

Buchanan's presidency was notable for two events that heightened the growing crisis, the Supreme Court's decision in the *Dred Scott* case and John Brown's raid on the Harpers Ferry federal arsenal. It was an added complexity in the political geometry of the United States that the Supreme Court could in effect alter the Constitution by due process of law, while the political leaning of the Court could be altered over time by appointment of justices, which was a power that lay in the hands of the president. Because there had been a long run of Southern presidents, the Court's composition in 1857 favoured the delivery of pro-Southern judgements. Southern fears over the alteration of the human character of the Court if an anti-slavery president were to be elected heightened the developing crisis. The *Dred Scott* case brought the judicial, and also the political, crisis towards a head. Scott was a Southern slave who had been taken by his owner into the North, where he had been kept for several years. He subsequently sued in court for his freedom. When the case reached the Supreme Court, six judges, five of them Southerners, ruled that he had no case and by extension that slavery was permissible in the territories. Jefferson Davis decided to press the point by introducing into the Senate a resolution requiring the federal government to afford slavery legal protection. He also announced that he would have the resolution written into the Democratic Party's policy statement for the 1860 presidential election.

The *Dred Scott* judgement infuriated anti-slavery opinion in the North. John Brown's raid on Harpers Ferry in October 1859 terrified the South. John Brown was a wild man, ferociously anti-slavery, who had contributed actively to the growing civil war in Kansas. His motive in attacking the federal arsenal was to foment slave rebellion, precisely the eventuality most feared in the South, where in some parts, notably Mississippi and South Carolina, blacks outnumbered whites. His raid was a forlorn hope. He led only eighteen men and, though they found the arsenal undefended, a government force, led by Colonel Robert E. Lee, assisted by Major J. E. B. Stuart, both of whom would later rise to eminence in the coming war, quickly rounded them up. John Brown was tried for treason and murder and hanged, with six of his followers. Though his disreputable life did not merit it, he was soon hailed in the North as an anti-slavery martyr, and the song composed to commemorate his death would become one of the marching rhythms of the Union army in the Civil War.

There had been other, less extreme outbreaks of violence before Harpers Ferry and many threats of violence. Massachusetts Senator Charles Sumner had been beaten into insensibility on the Senate floor by a South Carolina colleague. The bringing of weapons into Congress became commonplace, as did fistfights and the exchange of insults. During a prolonged dispute over the election of the Speaker of the House of Representatives in 1860, an exchange of pistol fire was widely expected, and the governor of South Carolina wrote to one of the state's congressmen offering to send troops to Washington if violence did indeed break out.

It did not come to that, but plenty of political sensation was shortly to follow. It was a presidential election year and so one of party conventions. The Democratic convention was the first to meet in Charleston, South Carolina, perhaps the place least likely to produce a peacekeeping result. Stephen Douglas expected the nomination and thought he had a right to it. However, he had lost his following in the South because of his opposition to the introduction of a slave code in Kansas, the so-called Lecompton Constitution. There were sufficient Northern delegates, however, to carry a call for the adoption of a platform of popular sovereignty in the territories, effectively guaranteeing anti-slavery laws, and the convention could not reach a conclusion and agreed only to reconvene in Baltimore. When it did so, the convention had already split. The Northern Democrats nominated Douglas; the Southerners, meeting separately, selected John Breckinridge, the vice president, a Kentuckian.

The Republican Party, fighting only its second national election, met in Chicago. On the third ballot it chose Abraham Lincoln, who, though a Kentuckian by birth, was an Illinois resident. He was also an ex-Whig, as were so many others in the party, and he had a glittering reputation as a speaker who had proved a match for Stephen Douglas in their widely reported debates during the campaign for the Senate in 1858. The choice, undoubtedly a true reflection of opinion in the party, caused deep alarm in the South, because Lincoln made no attempt to disguise his abhorrence of slavery or his belief that the institution must be extinguished if the union was to survive.

Today, Lincoln would be unable to deliver the speeches on which he won the nomination in 1860. Lincoln, as he expressly made clear, did not believe in the personal equality of black and white. He held the black man to be the white's inferior and irredeemably so. He also, however, held the black man to be the white's legal equal, with an equality recognised by the founding laws of the United States, a recognition requiring legal empowerment. Blacks must have the same access to the law as whites, and exercise the same political rights.

Most Southerners held an exactly contrary view and believed that unless the inequality of blacks was legally enforced, their own way of life would be overthrown. Some Southern ideologues argued fervently that slavery was a guarantee of freedom, not only the freedom of the whites to live as they did and to organise the Southern states as they were organised but the freedom of the blacks also, since slavery protected the blacks from the economic harshness suffered by the labouring poor in the Northern factory system. Books were written to argue and demonstrate the case, and Southern polemicists advocated it unashamedly with their Northern opponents. There is no doubt that it was believed also, since the spectacle of apparently happy blacks living under paternal care on well-run plantations did seem to support the idea of slavery as a sort of welfare system. Those who advanced the theme of "Slavery as freedom" no doubt knew that what they were really justifying was a method of controlling four million people of different race by restricting their freedom of action and movement and what today would be called their human and civil rights. Southerners, however, unless they were unashamed racists, as many were, were adept at disguising their real motives from themselves, all the more so if they had, as many did, a benevolent and humane disposition to the blacks they knew as servants and workpeople.

By the spring of 1861, differences between North and South had passed beyond prospect of settlement by the power of words. In the South, particularly the Lower South, politicians and crowds were bent on pressing the difference to the point of action. On February 4, representatives of the seven seceding states met in Montgomery, Alabama, to concert schemes for an organised breakaway polity, to be known as the Confederate States of America. Within a month, the representatives of secession had framed a constitution, closely modelled on that of the United States, though with crucial alterations to permit the legalisation of slavery, and had elected a president, a Mississippian, Jefferson Davis, a former United States senator and secretary of war, who had graduated from West Point and served with distinction in the Mexican War. In his inaugural address he affirmed the Confederacy's desire to live in peace with its neighbours, but in private he had uttered threats of using force if opposed.

Lincoln meanwhile was striving to form his own new government. He, too, promised peace despite the challenge of secession, expressing a mood that was widespread in the North. It was widely accepted there that the Upper South—Virginia, North Carolina, and Arkansas—and the border states of Missouri, Maryland, Delaware, Tennessee, and Kentucky, which had not yet seceded, might be persuaded to remain within the union if the new president's declared policy were sufficiently emollient. Given the large number of Unionists known to be found in the South, many Northerners hoped that by a deliberate policy of non-provocation moderate opinion in the South might be brought to deter the extremists from irreversible action. Admirable though their sentiments were, they partook of wishful thinking and exaggeration. Secession, where declared, was widely popular in the South, while the number of Southern Unionists, who were concentrated in areas where slave owners and slaves were few, or not present, such as western Virginia and eastern Tennessee, was smaller than claimed by some compromisers. Moreover, irreversible action had already occurred. In the seceding states, the new governments had already seized federal property, courthouses, mints, and military buildings and were appropriating federal revenues, such as customs duties. The ownership of federal fortifications was a particularly contentious matter since the coastal forts, which symbolised the reality of the Monroe Doctrine, also represented the federal government's largest single investment in public works. The coastal fortresses of the First and Third Systems as the three stages of the military programme were called, included Fortress Monroe, at the tip of the Virginia Peninsula; Fort Sumter, at Charleston, South Carolina; Forts St. Philip and Jackson, below New Orleans at the mouth of the Mississippi; and Alcatraz at San Francisco. The First and Third System forts remain today among the most magnificent examples of fortress architecture in the world, but they had been built to defend the United States against attack by the European powers, not to safeguard the Union. That task required armed men in numbers, numbers far larger than 16,000, the extant number of federal soldiers, and men equipped and able to carry war against the South. Of the huge forts of the First and Third Systems south of the Mason-Dixon line, all but five—Fortress Monroe, at the mouth of Chesapeake Bay; Fort Pickens, at Pensacola, Florida; two small forts in the Florida Keys; and Fort Sumter—had by early 1861 been occupied by Southern garrisons. Of those remaining to the North, Fort Sumter was the most contentious, since South Carolina was the heart of secession and the state's artillery commanded the fortress from the shore. Sumter, built on an artificial island, represented a new idea in fortification, seeking to dominate by massing large numbers of heavy guns inside thick brick walls instead of hiding itself behind low earthworks. It was still under construction in 1861 and had only a skeleton garrison, though its full complement of guns. Its commander, Major Robert Anderson, was a Kentuckian but a forthright Union loyalist. His opponent, a Louisianan, General Pierre Gustave Toutant Beauregard, had been Anderson's student in artillery science at West Point. Even as late as March 1861 there was no sign of federal retention of Sumter provoking a military crisis. Most federal buildings in what was now the Confederacy had passed into rebel control without conflict or friction. Southern representatives had visited Washington to request Sumter's transfer and the secretary of state, William Seward, advised Lincoln to let it go. Lincoln was reluctant, his reluctance fortified by outraged headlines in Northern newspapers where rumours of treason began to circulate. Lincoln's difficulty was that Sumter was short of men and short of rations. An attempt to strengthen the garrison in January had failed for practical reasons. He could not, however, abandon those federal soldiers stationed there. They had been smuggled into Sumter by Anderson in a bold act of deceit under cover of darkness. Lincoln knew he had to resupply them, if the honour of his government were to be maintained. He was unwilling, however, to use force in resupply, and thus bear the blame for what would certainly be the inception of war. He hit eventually on an ingenious compromise. Supplies would be sent to Sumter, but on the public understanding that if the supply boats were not fired upon, the fort would not fire back. If the Confederates fired, they would bear the blame for aggression. Lincoln would thus protect his credentials as defender of the Union but escape condemnation as a warmonger. On April 6, 1861, Anderson sent a note to the governor of South Carolina: "I am directed by the President of the United States to notify you to expect an attempt will be made to supply Fort Sumter with provisions only; and that, if such attempt be not resisted, no effort to throw in men, arms, or ammunition will be made without further notice, or in case of an attack upon the fort."[1]

The Confederate cabinet in Montgomery understood at once the dilemma in which Lincoln was placing the South but, urged on by firebrands, decided to be caught all the same. Beauregard was ordered by Jefferson Davis to fire on Sumter before the relief arrived. He did so, having issued a formal call to surrender, which Anderson dismissed. Beauregard gave orders for the bombardment to begin at 4:30 a.m. on April 12, 1861; there was competition to fire the first shot. Thirty-three hours later, after 3,340 further shots had landed, the garrison surrendered. They had fired a thousand shots in reply but were battered and worn out—though, miraculously, neither side had suffered any fatal casualty. A mule was the only fatality. Anderson and his garrison were allowed to withdraw by ship and make their way to the North. None was made prisoner. It was as if the South still did not wish to formalise the opening of a war.

Yet the fall of Sumter brought war all the same. In the North it prompted President Lincoln to issue a call for the loyal states' militia to be mobilised, to the strength of 75,000. Such was the enthusiasm in some states that their quotas were quickly exceeded. In the South the effect of Sumter was to propel more of the militants into secession and to polarise public opinion. By April, eight Southern states still remained in the Union. Virginia was electrified by the news of Fort Sumter's fall and Lincoln's mobilisation. On April 17 a convention assembled to consider Virginia's position and voted for secession, 88 to 55. The state government had already sent its militia to seize the federal arms factory at Harpers Ferry and the naval dockyard at Norfolk. Secession was ratified by popular vote on May 23 by a huge majority, two days after the state government's offer of Richmond as a capital city for the Confederacy had been accepted by the Confederate government in Montgomery, Alabama. Among the Virginians agreeing to take service under the new flag of stars and bars was Robert E. Lee, who had been offered but rejected appointment as commander of the Union army by General in Chief Winfield Scott. Lee affirmed that he had to go with his state.

The thinly populated state of Arkansas, which had a sizable anti-secession party drawn from the non-slave Ozark Mountains, voted for secession on May 6. North Carolina's convention, elected on May 13, unanimously voted for secession on May 20. Though one of the most northerly of the Upper South states, North Carolina was curiously detached from the rest of the Confederacy; its borders were difficult for Union troops to approach and its coastline was narrow and inaccessible. It would not suffer Northern invasion until right at the end of the war. Tennessee did not formally secede but passed a declaration of independence on June 8. Its eastern counties, where slave owners were few, voted heavily against secession. Lincoln was to make the liberation of Tennessee loyalists from the secessionists one of his principal war aims. Maryland and Delaware, geographically part of the North though heavily Southern by temperament, did not secede despite strong efforts by their pro-secession minorities. In Delaware they were restrained by the movement of federal troops, making their way to Washington. Maryland, also coerced by federal force, ultimately failed to find the nerve to secede, its legislature refusing to vote for secession or to call a convention to do so. Later, after the Confederate victory of First Bull Run, the secessionist legislators would summon up courage to threaten the Union again, but their bravado was quickly dissipated by arrest and imprisonment.

Kentucky, a border state whose population almost equally divided for North and South, also attempted to evade the issue by a declaration of neutrality. Lincoln cannily declined to force the point and did not attempt coercion. An out-of-term election held in June returned a large pro-Union majority to Congress, after which, as the strength of loyalist militias within the state grew, it came over to the Union, all the more readily after the Confederacy made the mistake of trying to seize the state by force. Nevertheless, many Kentuckians left home to join Confederate units, in a proportion of two to every three joining the Union army. Its neighbouring state of Missouri, also sharply divided, had a strongly Confederate governor who set out to take his state into the Confederacy with the active support of many of its citizens. He was frustrated by the initiative of the local Federal commander, Captain Nathaniel Lyon. Although the beginnings of a vicious internal guer- rilla war were already raging in Missouri, Lyon seized the stores of arms in St. Louis, took command of the local pro-Union militia, and overcame their pro-Southern opponents. That was not the end of the trouble. The state legislature left for the Arkansas border, where it set up as a government in exile and was eventually recognised as legitimate by the Confederates, which admitted Missouri as a Confederate state. Its functions at home were assumed by the convention assembled to decide for or against secession, which had a strong Unionist majority. Missouri was thus represented in both wartime governments during the war. The Unionists of Tennessee, who dominated the state's east- ern counties, also attempted to secede but, lacking the support of Union troops on the ground, failed in the attempt. Tennessee there- fore counted as a Confederate state, although 30,000 of its sons fought in the Union army.

Thus, by May 1861, a month of hiatus, the lines of division between North and South had been drawn. Would they become lines of battle? So far there had been little blood shed, none at Sumter, a sprinkling only in skirmishing and rioting. Young men were gathering, however, putting on uniforms, drilling, learning to march in formation, to stand in ranks, to handle muskets and rifles. North America was not yet a continent organised for war but its mood was increasingly warlike, and newspaper editors and politicians were demanding action. The two capitals, Washington and Richmond, lay only a hundred miles apart, little more than three days' march. "On to Richmond," which had begun as a newspaper slogan, was becoming a popular catchphrase in the North. Virginians, residents of the Confederacy's frontline state, were alert for the tramp of Northern feet. The outskirts of Washington were already being crisscrossed with defensive earthworks. The Potomac River had become an important military obstacle. If war came, where would it strike? Secession had not only divided one of the largest countries in the world, it had also created a gigantic theatre of war, confronting both combatants, if they fell to fighting, with one of the most complex military problems ever to face war-making governments. Leaders and soldiers on both sides were already puzzling not only how but where to take the armies that were forming in the search for victory.

CHAPTER THREE

Improvised Armies

A MERICA WAS NOT prepared for war, any war, let alone a great internal war. It had almost no soldiers. The Founding Fathers of the United States, in their rejection of all that was bad about the Old World, had hoped to dispense with a standing army altogether, just as the parliamentarians who restored Charles II to the throne after England's Civil War had hoped also. Domestic rebellion—trivial in both cases but alarming while it lasted—prompted them to reconsider. As a precaution against recurrence, the English Parliament kept in being a few of the existing regiments, Cromwellian or royal; the American Congress preserved some units of Washington's army. In 1802 it established a military academy at West Point to officer them. West Point's graduates, trained as engineers, were also expected to supervise the construction of the new nation's public works, building bridges, dams, and harbours, for many of which the U.S. Army Corps of Engineers remains responsible to this day.

Yet West Point classes were so tiny, yielding sometimes only a dozen trained officers a year to the army before 1861, and the other sources of officer recruitment were so haphazard—service in one of the nation's foreign or internal wars—the War of 1812, the Seminole War, the Creek War—that there was no reserve of experienced, professional military leaders on which to draw when the Civil War came in 1861. Things were quite different in Europe, where "military families" flourished, sending some of their sons into particular regiments for some of their youth as a matter of course, and where the national armies inducted young men for limited periods of service as reserve officers. It is true that America possessed several families with military traditions, such as the Lees of Virginia; but they were too small and isolated to found military dynasties, as existed elsewhere in the world.

As a substitute in the absence of an officer class, North and South in 1861 turned to the middle class, to lawyers, teachers, and businessmen, often those with political experience. Such men had standing in their communities. Standing in the community did not, however, necessarily translate into ability as a military leader, particularly not of military innocents. All too often the big man of a locality proved to lack the power of command, or even soldierly common sense.

The United States' tiny army had valiantly defended the republic against British invaders during the War of 1812; in 1846 it achieved a complete victory over the army of Mexico, harvesting as a consequence of the ensuing peace an enormous addition to the national territory in the southwest, which would become the states of Texas, Utah, New Mexico, Nevada, Arizona, and California. The Mexican War brought an expansion of army strength. Afterwards it dwindled again, so that in 1861 it numbered only 16,000, deployed for the most part in fortified posts in Indian territory, west of the Mississippi, or in the great federal fortresses that guarded the nation's coasts, from Boston harbour to the bay of San Francisco.

The military philosophy of the United States was that, if required, any large number of soldiers should be supplied by the militia, a body authorised by the Second Amendment to the Constitution. In his 1829 inaugural address, President Andrew Jackson had referred to "a million of armed freemen, possessed of the means of war," as the republic's chief means of defence. The militia was important in American history. A military system brought from England by the early colonists, it required the able-bodied to muster for service when called upon to do so by the local authority. At the outset that meant the individual colony, and it was upon the colonies' militias that the eighteenth-century rebellion against the Crown had been organised. In the aftermath of independence, however, the militias had withered away. In some of the states, successors to the colonies, they continued to turn out and to train; in the majority they subsided into paper organisations.

They might have disappeared altogether—as the militia did in England after the Napoleonic Wars, surviving at best as a source of recruits for the regular army—had not America become infected after 1859 by the fashion for "volunteering" that swept England in that year. An entirely unfounded fear of French invasion impelled the civilian British in 1859 to form units of "rifle volunteers," encouraged by publicists, who included Alfred, Lord Tennyson. His poem "Form, Riflemen, Form" was a major motivation of the rifle movement. The

volunteering impulse spread to the United States and took root particularly in the South, already infected by the urge to take arms against
the spectre of Northern aggression. By 1861 many volunteer rifle
corps, and also artillery units, had appeared in the South, adopting gal-
lant designations—the Palmetto Guard of South Carolina, the Lexington Rifles of Kentucky (which went south with its first commander,
General Simon Bolivar Buckner), the North Carolina Sharpshooters,
the Washington Artillery of New Orleans—and flamboyant uniforms
to match the regimental titles. "Cadet gray"—worn at West Point—
was the preferred Southern colour; but many Southern volunteers
wore Union blue or, particularly favoured, varieties of French uniform; in 1861 Napoleon III's army, recently victorious against the Austrians, was the leading military power in the world. The French style,
short jacket and baggy trousers, was the favoured outfit of most Southern units at the start of the war.

Some Southern units went further, to adopt Zouave costume, modelled on the dress which the French army had borrowed from their
tribal enemies during the conquest of Algeria after 1830. The Zouaves'
baggy red trousers and embroidered waistcoats made for a very dramatic appearance, which proved even more popular in the North than
the South. Among Northern Zouave units were numbered the New
York Fire Zouaves, formed from members of the New York Fire
Brigade and led by Elmer Ellsworth, a friend of Abraham Lincoln's. A
Southern equivalent was the Louisiana Zouaves, known after their
commanding officer as Wheat's Tigers. Other borrowings from contemporary European military fashion included the feathered hats of
various "Garibaldi" regiments and, surprisingly, the tailcoats and towering bearskins of such units as the 40th Massachusetts, which mimicked the uniform of the City of London's volunteer regiment, the
Honourable Artillery Company.

The well-dressed among the would-be soldiers of 1860–61 were
the minority. Surprisingly few volunteer units, on both sides, adopted
anything resembling the uniforms of their British rifle volunteer
equivalents, who turned themselves out in the tweed shooting-suits of
contemporary country gentlemen, with stylish results. The overwhelming effect achieved, North and South, once the first finery was
outworn, was one of drabness—dull colours, Northern blue, Southern
gray, but more often the "butternut" of homespun dyes, and uniformly
shapeless cut. The armies of the Civil War were the worst tailored of
any great conflict, and the effect was heightened by the almost univer-

sal abandonment of shaving. Beards were both military and modern, adopted in Britain in imitation of the returning veterans of the Crimean War, who had been excused from shaving during the bitter winters outside Sebastopol in 1855–56. The British fashion for beards spread to America, where it took such hold that by 1861 scarcely any mature man remained clean-shaven. All leading generals of the war—Ambrose Burnside, Nathan Bedford Forrest, U. S. Grant, A. P. Hill, John Bell Hood, Stonewall Jackson, E. Kirby Smith, Lee, Irvin McDowell, George Meade, John Pope, William Rosecrans, William Sherman, and Jeb Stuart—cultivated a full set of whiskers; Beauregard and McClellan wore luxuriant moustaches and small "Napoleons"; Burnside invented a style of "sideburns," or sideboards, that perpetuates his name to this day. However worn, and it was usually worn long enough to conceal both mouth and chin, facial hair gave almost all but the youngest Civil War soldiers a sombre, preacherish look, perhaps appropriate to men who were fighting for an idea.

The enthusiasm for volunteering, to supplement the legal requirement to maintain a militia, varied in intensity from state to state. On the eve of the war, only a handful of states maintained efficient militias. They included, in the North, Massachusetts, with 5,000 active militiamen, and New York, with 19,000, and in the South, Georgia, which had many volunteer and militia companies, and South Carolina, heartland of secession, with numbers of well-trained and well-equipped volunteer companies. Kentucky, a bitterly divided state, had 73 State Guard companies, of Southern sympathy, and 66 Home Guard companies sympathetic to the North. Ohio had 30 companies, Vermont 22, Wisconsin 1,993 militiamen, Maine 35 companies, all available to the Federal government. Virginia had 8 militia regiments, all ready to declare for the South, and Mississippi had 3,927 volunteers, belonging to 78 companies, all of which would go south. Many states, including several located in Northern and Southern heartland territory, were quite unorganised for war, including Alabama and North Carolina (South) and Connecticut, Illinois, Indiana, New Hampshire, and New Jersey (North). Kansas was full of armed men who had been fighting the Civil War before it began but were unorganised. Texas had its own eccentric military organisation, the Texas Rangers, largely dedicated to protecting isolated settlers.

Despite the lack of trained men, shortage of manpower was not to prove a problem to either side at the outset of the war. Such was the enthusiasm for cause—the Union or states' rights—that regiments could be formed as quickly as weapons could be found to arm them or officers to lead, indeed without either necessity in many cases. America in 1861 was a populous country, and growing, partly thanks to immigration, partly to the fertility of its well-fed population. Size of population, and population growth, favoured the North. The census of 1860 enumerated a total population of approximately thirty million: 20,275,000 whites in the North and 5,500,000 in the South; blacks in the North added 430,000, in the South 3,654,000. Almost all Southern blacks were enslaved; so were some Northern blacks, in the District of Columbia itself and in the border states of Tennessee, Delaware, Maryland, and Missouri. Blacks did not count in the military population (until 1863, when Lincoln's Emancipation Act officially authorised their enlistment, as unofficially they had been enlisted since the previous year). The white population of military age—men under thirty, though many older men joined—was about 2,500,000 in the North, 900,000 in the South.

The barely existent administrative machinery of the Confederacy could not in 1861 have mobilised an army to challenge the Union; fortunately for the cause of secession, the necessary men came forward unbidden. Many were members of militia units, whether long-established or recent; many were spontaneous volunteers. Not until April 1862 would the Confederacy have to legislate for conscription. The pattern of enlistment was similar in the North, initial and widespread volunteering in numbers, often centred on existing militia or volunteer units; in the headstrong days of 1860–61 the distinction between the two was easily blurred. Legislation attempted to regularise the popular response, if only to provide the money needed to pay and equip the patriot enthusiasts. On March 6, 1861, the Confederate Congress authorised the creation of an army of 100,000, much of which already existed. In May it increased the army's size to 400,000, the War Department soon having to turn away half those coming forward, for want of weapons. Confederate efforts to organise were hampered by the weakness of the central government and the persisting primacy of the states, whose governors frequently sought to retain both weapons and soldiers within state borders. The Confederacy never did form a regular army; its fighting strength was composed of states' forces, supervised by its War Department. The system that emerged in the North was similar. The regular army was scarcely expanded and its pre-war regiments were largely left in their pre-war stations, on the western frontier; the Civil War army was a federation of volunteers, organised on a state basis and bearing state

titles. Thus Ulysses S. Grant, before the war a retired U.S. regular officer, originally commissioned into the infantry from West Point, was
appointed in 1861 to command the 21st Illinois, a volunteer regiment, of
his home state, and returned to the regular army, as a major general, only
after his victory at Vicksburg in 1863.

The Civil War system, if anything so complex and confused can be
called a system, anticipated that adopted in Great Britain at the outbreak of the First World War. There the regular army was left almost
intact at the outset, while expansion was organised through the Territorial Army, which descended from the volunteering movement of
1859, supplemented by a renewed volunteering impulse, which produced the "New" or "Kitchener Armies" of Pals and Chums battalions
immortalised by their self-sacrifice in 1916 on the Somme, Britain's
Gettysburg. Both the American Civil War and the British Great War
responses to military crisis had a common Anglo-Saxon origin,
descending originally from Alfred the Great's *fyrd* and the Norman
posse comitatus of the English counties.

President Lincoln's initial response to Southern rebellion after the
firing on Fort Sumter was, on April 15, 1861, to call into Federal service 75,000 state militiamen for "ninety days." His federalisation of the
militia, an entirely constitutional act under a law of 1795, had the same
effect on the American North in 1861 as Field Marshal Lord Kitchener's appeal for 100,000 men to serve for three years had on the
British in 1914. Kitchener's "First Hundred Thousand" were soon followed by a Second and a Third. Lincoln's 75,000 were soon outnumbered by the offerings of the states. He had asked Indiana for six
regiments; its governor promised twelve. Ohio's governor, required to
organise thirteen regiments, reported that "without seriously repressing the ardour of the people, I can hardly stop short of twenty."[1] Confronted with both a deadly military threat to the Union and an
outpouring of Northern patriotic response to it, Lincoln on May 3
called for 42,000 volunteers for the army, to serve for three years, and
18,000 for the navy, at the same time authorising the enlargement of
the regular force by 23,000. Congress in July not only retroactively
legalised these executive decisions but actually sanctioned the enlistment of an additional million volunteers, to serve for three years.
Within a year of the firing on Fort Sumter, the Union had 700,000
men under arms; the South may have had 400,000. Circumstances,
however, make exact enumeration problematic. Some of the North's
original "ninety-day" men insisted on the letter of their enlistment and

returned to civilian life when their time was up; so did some whole regiments. Even a number of three-year men, and regiments, took their demobilisation while the war continued, much later on.

Steadfastness in service was also undermined by the temptation to desert. In the richer North, where bounties were paid to encourage joining up, many volunteers took advantage of the opportunity to take the bounty, decamp, and join up again, often several times over. As the bounty at its largest was as much as $1,000, calculated desertion could be a profitable practice. In the South, after the first heartfelt year, desertion was more often a matter of necessity. Small farmers and landless labourers, informed by the mail of family hardship, would leave the ranks, often with a sincere intention to rejoin, in order to get in the harvest or put in a spell of breadwinning. Small slaveholders might be impelled to return home for fear of leaving their womenfolk unprotected on isolated farms where male slaves remained the only men out of uniform. Whatever the reason, and whatever the difference of motivation, North or South, desertion at any time could rob the armies of as much as a third of their strength.

In 1861, however, desertion was a problem to trouble governments in the future, not the present. At the outset the embryo armies of both sides were most concerned to provide weapons and munitions for their soldiers, to find means of clothing and feeding them, and to furnish them with officers. Equipping its army was a particularly severe problem for the South. Although the Confederacy benefited in the first months after secession by the seizure of Federal arsenals, most of the weapons acquired were old-fashioned muskets, flintlock and unrifled. Such weapons could be adapted, by reboring the barrels and altering the firing mechanism to accept the percussion cap; the chief source of armament, however, lay in Europe. It was a principal purpose of Confederate blockade-running, and of its overseas procurement programme, to buy weapons abroad. The favoured arm was the British Enfield rifle, closely similar to the Federal Springfield.

The South, by its acquisition of the machinery at Harpers Ferry, supplemented by that of existing arsenals at Richmond and Fayetteville, North Carolina, was able to begin domestic weapon manufacture in 1861. The equipment of its artillery was more difficult. Capture of cannon at Fort Sumter and the federal naval base at Norfolk yielded some equipment, but fortress cannon were too heavy and immobile to fit out large numbers of field batteries. The deficiencies were made good from the inventories of pre-war volunteer units, foreign imports, and the output of the Tredegar Iron Works at Richmond, which was to become the arsenal of the Confederacy. The South also proved adept at improvising munition production. Two of the ingredients of gunpowder, charcoal and sulphur, were readily available. The third, saltpetre, or nitre (potassium nitrate), was not. Josiah Gorgas, appointed the chief of ordnance in April 1861, set out to fill the deficiency by finding sources of supply within the Confederacy. One of his subordinates identified such a source in limestone caves in the southern Appalachian Mountains; others were found in the contents of chamber pots and on the walls of stables and cow byres, scraped for the deposits yielded by the urine of horses and cattle. Against every probability, the South never risked defeat through shortage of powder, most of which was produced at a purpose-built mill located at Augusta, Georgia.

In the summer of 1861 the North faced a problem of equipment and supply quite as severe as the South's, with these differences: first, it possessed a manufacturing base not only vastly exceeding the South's in size but adequate, once mobilised, to supply all the Union's military needs; second, production could be supplemented by imports, since Northern harbours were not subject to blockade, almost the whole of the American merchant marine remained under Northern control, and, most important, Northern credit abroad remained strong; third, credit also remained strong at home, thanks to skilful financial management. The secretary of the Treasury, Salmon P. Chase, pioneered the practice of selling government bonds—in effect war debt, to be repaid in better times—directly to small investors. At the same time the Treasury persuaded Congress to legalise the issue of paper money; the Confederate Treasury almost simultaneously began to issue paper dollars, with disastrous results; by the end of the war, with inflation calculated to have risen to 9,000 percent, Confederate paper dollars were worthless. The Union paper dollar held its value because the Treasury instituted a rigorous system of war taxation, which imitated that imposed in Britain during the Napoleonic Wars. The American military system was a historical derivative of the British. American war taxation, consciously or not, mimicked the emergency measures introduced in Britain to finance Nelson's fleet and Wellington's army. It went further. Not only were luxuries and incomes taxed, so were services, business transactions, and inheritance. By 1865 the United States was the most comprehensively taxed polity in the world. The yield covered war expenditure—about three billion dollars—handsomely, and kept depreciation below 90 percent. The war taxes, including income tax, were all rapidly discontinued after 1865.

Wartime financial policy could not, however, at the outset equip the Union armies. The necessary material had not been manufactured and so was not available for purchase. There was much else that was lacking, including the tens of thousands of horses and mules necessary to work as draught animals for artillery batteries and transport wagons; the animals existed but had not yet been brought into government service. It was the inanimate necessities which in 1861 were more necessary of procurement—not only muskets and cannon, but uniforms, belts, pouches, packs, boots, tents, saddles, harness, and the hundred and one things a properly organised army needs in order to operate: medical stores, kitchen equipment, blankets, veterinary necessities, telegraph cable, an almost endless list. Mid-nineteenth-century armies hovered on the brink of true modernisation, half belonging to the military past, when martial vigour and numbers were alone thought to count, but already entering the military future, when technology would predominate. The underdeveloped South was linked to the past, the North was being transported by the industrial revolution into the future. The South would perform prodigies of improvisation to sustain its war effort and, despite shortages of almost everything, was not ultimately defeated by want of essentials; nevertheless, the Confederacy led at best a hand-to-mouth existence. The North, by contrast, was propelled into dominance of the world's economy by the war. An apparently open-ended boom, created by the demand for war goods and including agricultural products—wool for uniforms, leather for boots, and grain and meat for rations—as well as manufactured items would drive the United States economy to the first place in the world by 1880. Much of the expansion of output was in categories of product to be expected—track for the U.S. Military Rail Roads, armour plate for river gunboats—but much was not. As James McPherson emphasises, two of the most creative innovations stimulated by war demand were the adoption of standard sizes in men's clothing manufacture and of the Blake-McKay machine for sewing soles to uppers in boot factories.[2]

After the initial crisis, the equipment of regiments receded in urgency. By 1862 most, South as well as North, had acquired a musket per man and a set of uniforms. Finding officers to supervise and lead their soldiers remained a difficulty as America possessed no officer class, as existed in the historic kingdoms in Europe. The idea of an officer class was indeed at odds with the founding ethos of the great republic, which had outlawed ranks and titles of nobility in its defining documents. The idea of election, so strong in American life from the Revolution onwards, was widely thought by the militiamen and volunteers of 1861 to apply to military as well as political affairs. Election of officers was common practice in the new regiments, but many of the chosen, though big men in civil life, proved incompetent in war. What neither militiamen nor volunteers understood was that close-formation fighting—and the Civil War was to be one of the last in which superiority in close formation determined the outcome—was a highly technical business. Officers had to know how to form their soldiers in ranks, how to manoeuvre the ranks in the face of the opposing enemy ranks, and when exactly to give the order to fire. Too soon and fire was "thrown away"; too late and the enemy might get his volley in first. The Springfield rifle took half a minute to reload. Ranks which had fired too early, and failed to damage their opponents, could be devastated by better-commanded troops while they fumbled with cartridge and ramrod.

"Big men"—local worthies, political fixers, who knew how to talk men into volunteering—usually lacked any knowledge of how to manocuvre the regiments they had raised when the enemy was encountered. The predicament of their followers was actually worse than that of volunteers of 1914 who, armed with a magazine rifle, were capable of covering their front with a volume of fire sufficient to keep the enemy at a distance; by 1914, moreover, riflemen were taught to lie down on the battlefield, unless they were attacking. The riflemen of 1861, equipped with a single-shot weapon, were expected to stand up, shoulder to shoulder, concentrating their firepower in a carefully timed volley, since only thus could they hope to overcome their opponents.

Mastery of the tactics of close-formation fighting could only be learnt by repetition. To their credit, some of the new regiments of 1861 drilled themselves hour after hour at the outset; a few set up "schools" or "camps" of instruction, to which officers and sergeants went before recruits were inducted. Drilling, however, could not teach inexperienced troops mastery of battlefield craft. That skill required years, not weeks, of practice; or else battlefield experience, which in mid-1861 was not yet available. The only soldiers with the requisite understanding of manoeuvre and fire were the Northern regulars, who were too few to train the volunteer and militia units, and the graduates of America's military colleges.

The annual intake at West Point was small; classes were fewer than a hundred strong, often many fewer, and the output, after four years, fewer still. In 1861 there were 239 cadets at West Point, of whom 80 came from the South; 76 resigned or were dismissed for refusing to take the oath of allegiance to the Union. The South was overrepresented among officers of the army; 313 resigned their commissions to "go with their states," leaving 440 West Point graduates in Union service. Others rejoined one army or the other from civilian life after the outbreak, but the total of graduates of serviceable age was under 3,000, so the pool was too small to provide professional leadership on the scale required. West Pointers returning to duty from retirement were usually appointed commanding officers of volunteer or militia regiments, as was Ulysses S. Grant in Illinois. Many rose quickly to general rank, 300 in the Union army, 150 in the Confederate. The Civil War was, on the level of high command, to be a West Point war.

Numbers of trained officers in the South were amplified by the graduates of private military colleges, distinctively Southern institutions. The two best-known were the Virginia Military Institute (VMI), founded in 1839 at Lexington, and the South Carolina Military Academy, Charleston, to become celebrated as the Citadel. VMI graduates numbered 455 in 1861, but counting those who had attended without graduating there were 1,902 available altogether. Of these, 1,791 fought in the Civil War; VMI provided one-third of Virginia's field officers (majors and colonels) in 1861. The Citadel and VMI were not, however, the only sources of privately trained officers in the South. Others included the North Carolina Military Institute at Charlotte (1859), the Arkansas Military Institute (1850), and the West Florida Seminary (1851). Alabama had three small military colleges: the Southern Military Academy at Wetumpka (1860), the La Grange College and Military Academy (1860), and the Glenville Military Academy (1858). There were three in Mississippi: the Mississippi Military Institute at Pass Christian, Brandon State Military Institute, and Jefferson College, Natchez. The date of founding of the Alabama and Mississippi military colleges is significant. They probably represented the working of war fever in the Deep South during the last days of peace; they may have been little more than military boarding schools. The University of Alabama formed a cadet corps in 1860. Universities, however, were not characteristic Southern institutions, despite the existence of such ancient foundations as the University of Virginia and the College of William and Mary, at Williamsburg. Rich Southern boys went to Princeton; few went to Harvard or Yale.

The United States Naval Academy, located at Annapolis, Maryland, was judged to be in too exposed a position and was transferred to the Atlantic House Hotel at Newport, Rhode Island, on May 9, 1861, to be safe from the risk of Confederate attack. The Confederacy founded its own naval academy on March 23, 1863; it had its premises at first aboard the CSS *Patrick Henry* in the James River, below Richmond, later ashore nearby at Fort Darling; the outline of the earthworks, still to be seen, suggests dank accommodation.

The Confederacy started to establish a navy as soon as war broke out, seizing warships of the national navy wherever they lay in Southern waters, commandeering or chartering civilian vessels and starting the construction of its own. Creating an army to defend the seceding states was, however, the more vital task. It began even before the firing on Fort Sumter, though not in any logical way. As in the North, two powers, central and state, were at work, and often in conflict, and three principles of military organisation: the regular army, the state militia, and the emergency volunteers, exactly as in Britain during the Napoleonic Wars. On February 28, 1861, the Confederate Congress authorised President Jefferson Davis to accept state troops, or volunteers who had state governors' consent, for one year's service. This was the beginning of what Professor Peter Parish has called the "provisional" army of the Confederacy. On March 6 the Confederate Congress enacted the creation of a regular army, but its size was set at only 9,000 and little more was ever heard of it. On the same day the "provisional" army was considerably expanded, Congress authorising the president to appeal for 100,000 volunteers to serve for twelve months, and to accept the service of state militias for up to six months. On May 6 he was empowered, without waiting for the approval of the states, to take units into Confederate service for three years or the duration of the war, if less. In August, with 200,000 men under arms, he was authorised to call for another 400,000 volunteers.

The character of the "provisional" army was thenceforth fixed. Men in its higher ranks held Confederate commissions as general officers, though usually also in the militias of their states. The rank and file, and their regimental officers up to the rank of colonel, belonged to the state militia or wartime volunteer organisations, a situation almost exactly paralleled in the North. After April 16, 1862, however, when the Confederate Conscription Act was passed, all fit white males between the ages of eighteen and thirty-five were compulsorily enlisted; the age limits were extended to seventeen and fifty in February 1864, though the older and younger were liable only for state defence. Illogically, soldiers continued to be enlisted in state regiments, with state names and numbers, though collectively they formed a single Confederate army. Yet the power of state governors persisted. Conscription was unpopular in the South, with willing patriots because it devalued their voluntary commitment to serve, with the reluctant because it brought them into the ranks willy-nilly. The very reluctant could use state connections to secure exemption, by joining state militias retained for home service. The better-off could buy substitutes, not otherwise liable for conscription, to serve for them, or claim exemption for "essential service," such as school teaching. There was a sudden creation of new schools in the South immediately after the passage of the Conscription Act. Particularly unpopular with poor patriots was the "Twenty Negro" law, introduced in October 1862, which exempted one white male from the draft on every plantation with twenty or more slaves, to protect the women left by their menfolk's enlistment. Approximately 4,000 to 5,000 planters or overseers attained exemptions under the law, representing only 15 percent of plantations, but the class-dividing nature of the law caused much tension and resentment among ordinary whites.

Overall it remains difficult to judge whether conscription, "the drafts," as modern America knows it, served its purpose or not. About 900,000 Southerners enlisted, perhaps 500,000 joining as volunteers in 1861–62, a considerable number even afterwards, possibly impelled by the threat of compulsion. There is, again, an analogy with Britain in the First World War. There the volunteering impulse of 1914 brought nearly two million men into the ranks in 1914–15; as the impulse lost force, conscription had to be enacted in 1916 to keep up the army's numbers. The British Great War state's machinery was, however, far more efficient than the Confederacy's or the Union's of fifty years earlier. Exemptions were difficult to obtain, evasion or desertion almost impossible. Civil War desertion, by contrast, was frequent, widespread, and easy; inside a mobile and expanding population (though the war did depress immigration), with an open frontier to the west and, for Northerners, a neutral neighbour to the north, men could disappear without great risk.

Desertion may have been easier in the North than the South, with its smaller population, neighbours well-known to one another, and western frontier closed by wide water barriers. On the other hand, the backcountry was empty and armed defiance of authority by lawless bands of bushwhackers a temptation. Maintaining control of an army nearly a million strong, to say nothing of equipping and supplying it, put both central and state governments in the Confederacy under relentless strain, and it is evidence of how powerful a hold the cause of secession exerted over the Southern mind that a collapse was averted for as long as it was.

Lincoln's first task, as war began to overwhelm the Union, was to expand its military forces, the tiny regular army, the state militias, and the volunteers serving as state forces. The small marine corps, though one of its regiments fought at First Bull Run, was scarcely expanded either; over half its junior officers defected to the South. The numbers of general and staff officers of the regular army were increased, though only slowly; many brigadier and major generals were at first appointed into the volunteers, to receive regular commissions, if they did so at all, only later. Major general was the highest rank granted; the exception was Ulysses S. Grant, promoted lieutenant general in March 1864, on taking up the appointment of general in chief, under a new act of Congress.

Lincoln's first mobilisation measure of April and May 1861 was to call for 117,000 volunteers to be found by the state governors from their militias and to serve for three months, later extended to three years. The states responded immediately, directing organised regiments towards Washington, the frontier post of the North-South confrontation, and promising more to follow. On May 3 Pennsylvania, one of the most populous states, promised twenty-five regiments, Ohio, most important of the Midwest states, twenty-two. New York had 20,000 men under arms. The smaller New England states offered four regiments ready and four to follow (Massachusetts), Vermont, Connecticut, and Rhode Island one each, Maine one ready and three nearly so, New Hampshire one mustered, two or four to follow. From the Midwest, Wisconsin reported one regiment ready, one in camp, two more at a day's warning, Iowa two regiments drilling, Michigan six at various stages of preparation.

All these regiments were stronger on paper than in reality. They lacked training, and above all trained officers; they lacked arms and equipment; they even lacked coherent organisation. Plans of organisation were much debated in Washington at the outset, between the various officers of state Lincoln had inherited or appointed to run military offices. The ancient Winfield Scott, general in chief, was too old to undertake detailed administration; he confined himself to devising a war-winning national strategy, leaving the formation of a national army to colleagues. Simon Cameron, secretary of war, was not esteemed by Lincoln, who managed to entrust organisation of the volunteers to Salmon P. Chase, Treasury secretary. Chase was very good at solving complex problems and, though also abrasively ambitious, had thereby impressed both Lincoln and Scott. Chase enlisted two men to help him, William B. Franklin, the superintending architect of the Treasury but also a West Point graduate, and Brigadier General Irvin McDowell, the assistant adjutant general.

McDowell, later to hold high command, was an experienced staff officer of some cultivation who had travelled abroad. He knew about European military systems. The American system was English in origin, based on small, independent regiments not subject to superior organisation; the emergency of 1861 had produced a mass of willing men subject to no system at all. McDowell and Franklin therefore proposed the creation of a national army along European lines: the volunteers were to be enrolled in regiments numbered nationally, of two active battalions with a third to feed them, led by officers holding Federal commissions. The states were to be left a role, but it would be confined to providing men in proportion to their representation in Congress and to nominating officers for the president to appoint. Salmon Chase, a canny politician who had served as governor of Ohio, rejected their proposal as overbalanced in favour of the centre. Volunteers from the states, and voters at home, would expect regiments to have state titles and numbers and their officers to be appointed by state governors. He even insisted on sticking to the historic but familiar militia regimental system. As a result, though the regulation of May 1864 laid down that regiments of volunteers in Federal service should have two battalions, in practice most fielded only one, which almost always had difficulty in keeping up its numbers. Throughout the war the states found it easier to create new regiments than to make good the gaps in the ranks of existing regiments left by casualties, disease, or desertion. The weight of the old British royal master's hand lay heavy on the great republic's saving force: tiny regiments from the historic colonies and their later equivalents, commanded by successors of the old colonial governors, were to fight democracy's battles. Their opponents were to be of the same sort. The military world of federal troops and state National Guards lay half a century in the future.

Such officers as had travelled or visited armies abroad—Henry Halleck, McClellan, McDowell—were familiar, however, with organisations above the regimental level, with brigades, divisions, corps, even separate armies. The larger formations were unknown in American military history; even during the Mexican War of 1846 Generals Taylor and Scott had organised nothing larger than brigades and divisions. The crisis of 1861, however, presented a new challenge. Lincoln, Scott, Chase, and McDowell recognised at the outset that to meet it separate armies, and appropriate subordinate formations, would have to be created, under generals with consonant responsibilities and subject to orthodox hierarchy. Out of the disparate ranks of state militias and U.S. volunteers, an army of Napoleonic formality would have to be formed. In the North, its outlines began to appear almost as soon as rebellion became manifest; brigadiers were named to lead brigades, major generals to command divisions. By mid-June, however, well after the first exchange of shots at Fort Sumter and between troops elsewhere in the field, the North still had only the makings of five operational armies: one at the arsenal of Harpers Ferry, abandoned but destroyed by its pre-war garrison, under the aged General Robert Patterson; one under General Benjamin Butler at the great Virginian stronghold of Fortress Monroe; General McDowell's army at Washington; General George McClellan's small but recently victorious force in western Virginia; and General Nathaniel Lyon's in Missouri.

Lack of men was not the factor limiting the expansion of forces in the field. On the contrary: men abounded, as the case of New York, state and city, exemplified. In the first flush of enthusiasm, the state government announced that it would raise thirty-eight volunteer regiments, the men to serve for two years. The city simultaneously offered fourteen, provoking a dispute with Washington over whether the volunteers would serve for three years or two. The city's military committee, which was financing recruitment and equipment from the city's enormous wealth, but was anxious to transfer the cost to the national government, agreed to three, but then began to quarrel with the state government over whether the city's fourteen regiments should count as part of or in addition to its thirty-eight. The dispute was eventually settled by Lincoln's decision that they should be an addition. During the course of 1861 New York, state and city, raised 120,000 men, forming 125 regiments, battalions, or artillery batteries.

If lack of numbers was not, or rapidly ceased to be, a problem for the Union, lack of equipment, arms, and even provisions presented very serious problems indeed. The difficulty of feeding armies in the field was a historic check on war-making; only the most advanced states learnt how to buy provisions in bulk and distribute them to soldiers; war-making states too often were driven to outright requisition of supplies in the theatre of operations, a recourse which rapidly ate it out and forced retreat. The South, whose soldiers were raised on corn bread and pork belly, and which fought largely on its own soil, at the outset kept up an adequate supply of rations; as the war dragged out, it was forced to resort to the Impressment Act, which required farmers in operational areas or near railroads to sell their produce at prices fixed below those of the market. The foreseeable result was grain hoarding and the concealment of livestock. Confederate soldiers consequently often went hungry or lived on the scantiest fare, the scantier the longer the war lasted. In the North, by contrast, after an initial stage of disorganisation, supply was brought to a high level of efficiency. The mastermind was Montgomery Meigs, a graduate of both the University of Pennsylvania and West Point who, as an officer of the Corps of Engineers, erected the dome of the Capitol (under construction during the war) and built Washington's water supply. Meigs was supremely competent and incorruptible.

Although not directly responsible for providing rations, which was the business of the Subsistence Department and its subordinate commissary officers, Meigs purchased and organised the trains of horses, mules, and waggons that brought the food to the armies. His assumption of office coincided with the beginnings of the revolution in food production in America, when the exploitation of the Great Plains as a grain-growing region and the organisation of meatpacking, of both fresh meat and preserved, at Chicago, was to make the United States the world's leader. Meigs, as quartermaster general, working in cooperation with the Subsistence Department, was able to assure that every Union soldier received a daily supply of hardtack bread and canned or salted meat, supplemented by dried vegetables, coffee beans, pickles, and molasses. Union army rations rarely amounted to a feast; but they banished hunger altogether, making the Northern soldier the best-fed man in the history of warfare to that time.

Meigs also clothed the army, decently if unglamorously, and he moved it, by river, road, and rail. The North, with its extensive railroad network—expanded during the war—was never in danger of failing at the level of strategic communication. Meigs's most striking achievement was to guarantee the effectiveness of the Union army's tactical transport system, by wagon and draught animal. Both Confederacy and Union had vast reserves of horses and mules. Meigs purchased and fed horses on a huge scale. By 1863 the Union army had half as many horses as men, a proportion hitherto unknown in warfare; the proportion Meigs made standard was one horse or mule to every two to three men, one wagon for forty men, when operating in Confederate territory. A campaigning army of 100,000 men therefore required 2,500 supply waggons and at least 35,000 animals, and consumed 600 tons of supplies each day. Livestock wore out very quickly; overworked and badly fed, horses and mules had a life expectancy in service of only a few months.

Wagons were easily built, while the supply of draught animals, despite the attrition rate, never ran out. The most pressing shortage at the outset of the war was in small arms and artillery weapons. The Federal government manufactured arms at Springfield, Massachusetts, and Harpers Ferry and maintained arsenals at several provincial centres. State governments also kept stocks of weapons to outfit their militias, though many were of obsolete pattern. In April 1861 there were about 600,000 small arms in the country, some 240,000 in the South, the rest in the Northern states. The Springfield armoury had an annual output of 20,000. It was soon to be increased to 200,000, but in the meantime the North had to purchase abroad, as the South did also before blockade became effective. Lacking funds, the South by August 1862 had acquired only 50,000, but the North had bought 726,000. Though the South's manufacturing shortfalls forced it to continue purchasing in Europe, eventually to a total of 580,000 rifles, the output of Springfield and twenty private contractors supplied the North's needs. It was a great advantage that the British Enfield rifle, the most common import, had a bore of .58 inch, and so could accept the Springfield bullet, of .57 inch. Interchangeability suited the South as well as the North, since by capture in the field and the seizure of Federal arsenals it acquired 100,000 Springfields early on, besides purchasing many Enfields. Springfield and Enfield alike used the minié ball, a conical lead bullet grooved to expand into the rifling when fired. They were accurate to 500 yards and caused dreadful wounds.

It was to be at least a year, however, before the armies standardised on the Springfield and Enfield. Well into 1862 many soldiers, particularly in the South, were still equipped with smoothbore flintlock muskets, or with muskets bored out with rifle grooves and adapted to accept the percussion cap. Whatever the model—and the North during the war accepted 226,000 Austrian, 57,000 Belgian, and 59,000 Prussian rifles—all were muzzle-loading. Some Union cavalry and sharpshooter units received breech-loading rifles but they formed a tiny minority. The mass of the soldiery continued to force bullet and powder down the barrel by ramrod and to prepare to fire by placing a percussion cap under the hammer. Experienced soldiers might achieve a rate of fire of three shots a minute.

In even shorter supply than small arms were artillery cannon. In 1861 the Union army had only 5 Napoleon 12-pounders, a number that increased to over 1,100 as the war progressed. The South acquired about 600, a remarkable achievement given its lack of foundry and engineering capacity. The Napoleon was smoothbore, with a maximum range of 2,000 yards. Union field artillery also acquired during the war 587 Parrott 10-pounders, a rifled gun accurate to 2,000 yards, 925 three-inch ordnance rifled cannon, 388 12-pounder mountain howitzers, and some 24- and 32-pounder howitzers.

Battlefield artillery on both sides, however, comprised largely 12- and 10-pounders, in surprisingly small numbers. The war was to be a rifle rather than an artillery war, but artillery, when present in quantity, did terrible execution. Yet, although deployed at the forward edge of the battlefield, field artillery was rarely captured, perhaps because it was so valuable to both North and South that extreme care was taken to protect it. Siege artillery, the weapon that began the war with the firing at Fort Sumter, was surprisingly plentiful, probably because the federal government's First and Third System fortification-building programme had required it to found appropriate armament. It included Rodman guns of calibres between 8 and 20 inches and older 24- and 32-pounders. The Confederacy, which benefited from capturing large numbers of Federal heavy guns at Fort Sumter and the Norfolk naval base, deployed several 8-, 10-, and 15-inch Columbiads. Both sides deployed large numbers of short-range mortars.

All Civil War artillery was muzzle-loading. The heavier artillery was immobile or movable only by great and time-consuming effort. Field artillery—the Napoleon and Parrott guns—was organised into batteries of four or six guns, six horses to a gun and caisson. The essential ammunition column was also horse-drawn. Gun and caisson could manoeuvre across country at speed and, when brought into action, the crew of six or seven gunners could fire up to two rounds a minute. The rate delivered was usually slower, but because gun drill was a series of methodical steps, each performed by one man, even amateur crews could learn to cooperate quite quickly. Civil War batteries became effective sooner than rifle regiments, in which loading and firing by hundreds of individuals was more difficult to coordinate.

Engineers, signallers, and railroad troops were easily recruited by the North, which needed them more than the South, from the ranks of men engaged in building industrial America. The Corps of Engineers had been the elite of the pre-war army and consisted almost entirely of officers; wartime recruits into the rank and file were organised into labour units, sometimes called sappers, miners, pioneers, or pontoneers, according to European practice. They were occasionally required as combat engineers, to build bridges in the field, but more often worked on the construction of roads and earthwork defences. The South began by forming a corps of officer engineers, supervising a small company of sappers and miners but, as the war prolonged, created more regiments of rank-and-file engineers and pioneers. In 1862 it also formed a signal corps, whose tasks including intercepting Union signals and other intelligence work. The South did not, however, form a dedicated intelligence service, nor did the North, besides employing the Pinkerton detective agency, unsatisfactorily as it turned out. Because of the permeability of the North-South border, a great deal of intelligence circulated; neither side seemed impelled to undertake organised espionage against the other.

By 1865 the Union army, which had begun as a replica in miniature of the British army, and the Confederate army, which had not existed at all, had grown into the largest and most efficient armies in the world, divided and subdivided into elaborate operational formations and units and comprising every branch of military specialisation. Though dismissed by European military grandees as amateur and unprofessional, each, but particularly the United States Army, outmatched the French, the Prussian, and the Russian in up-to-date experience and, but for the interposing Atlantic, would have threatened any of them with defeat.

CHAPTER FOUR

Running the War

THE GOVERNMENT OF the United States never declared war on the Confederacy, an omission which had odd legal consequences. But it was legality which prevented it from doing so. In Northern eyes, the South was not independent but remained constitutionally part of the Union. The Union could not fight itself or even part of itself.

The North's dismissal of the South's claim to legal independence made it easy for the Confederacy to frame its constitution as a mirror image of that of the Union it claimed to have left. So the Confederacy drew up a constitution that followed, often word for word, that of the United States, except when it had to refer to, and endorse, as the Constitution of 1787 did not, the institution of slavery. Its form of government exactly imitated that sitting in Washington, with a president and vice president, but each appointed by the founding convention, not elected by the people. The convention nominated the members of its House of Representatives and Senate, chosen from the delegates the seceding states had sent to Montgomery, Alabama, while the Confederacy's states continued to act exactly as they had done before secession; the elected governors and state legislators remained in office and proceeded as they had done before. The president and vice president were initially provisional, until confirmed in office by congressional election in November. The new government also accepted en bloc all the laws, institutions, and procedures of the United States, with the exception of a Supreme Court.

There were several candidates for both president and vice president. The man eventually selected as president by the convention was a former United States senator and secretary of war, Jefferson Davis of Mississippi. Davis, like Lincoln, had been born in a log cabin in Kentucky, but his father, shifting to Missouri, had prospered as a farmer and sent his son first to a local university and then to West Point. Davis, unlike the gawky Lincoln, whose height, squeaky voice, and unkempt appearance were frequently mocked in the North, looked the part. He had an austere manner and persona and was always well-dressed. He lacked the personal qualities that Lincoln displayed in office. He was a fusspot who wasted time and energy on detail. He was incompetent in personal relations, standing on his dignity, which the genuinely humble Lincoln did not, and too often falling into quarrels with colleagues over disagreements which Lincoln would have avoided with a quip or one of his jokes, of which he had an inexhaustible store. Davis was also a valetudinarian, afflicted by psychosomatic ailments, indigestion, headaches, insomnia, and disabling aches and pains. These defects were balanced by his evident personal probity and Confederate patriotism. He was also hardworking and brought to office a reputation for efficiency he had won at the War Department. He also had a genuine military reputation, having fought with distinction in the Mexican War.

While Lincoln grew in stature during the war, however, Davis did not. He liked to be right, a quality which merely irritated his colleagues rather than reinforcing his authority, and he was excessively formal, addressing the slaves on his Mississippi plantation by their surnames since he disliked the familiarity of first names. In private life he was an affectionate husband and father and warm friend, but he lacked the ability to show his humanity in public affairs.

Partly as a result, the government in Richmond, which became the Confederate capital in July 1861, was from the outset much less efficient than the ongoing government in Washington. That was in a way surprising, since the provisional government had acted with great despatch and decision, perhaps because it was trying to impress the legislators of the Upper South before they took the decision to secede or not. There were some effective men in Davis's early cabinet, and some in his last, such as James Seddon, the long-serving secretary of war. Both his secretaries of the Treasury, Christopher Memminger and George Trenholm, made a remarkable job of supporting finances which in practice had no foundation at all. Some sort of economic life continued within the South even at the end, when inflation and money printing had robbed the Confederate dollar of all value and the government lacked the means to pay its bills. The legislative overshadowed the executive in Richmond. Southerners had long dominated the

United States Congress, because of their loquacity and appetite for argument, and they carried those characteristics into the Confederate House and Senate, making long speeches and relishing the pursuit of points of order. Howell Cobb, a Georgian who was a candidate for the presidency in 1861, put his finger on the disabling weakness of the Confederate government when he observed that there was a want of brains in Richmond, a lack of common sense that confined both law-makers and officers of government to matters of policy and deflected them from constructing a vigorous and coherent administration. The central government was also oppressed throughout, and more weight-ily as the war progressed, by the selfishness of the states. Since the war, in Southern eyes, was about states' rights, it was to be expected that state governors and legislators insisted on pursuing local interests and frustrating the objects of the Confederate presidency. But the conflict was allowed to develop too much energy, with deleterious effects on vital military policy, particularly in recruiting and the allocation of manpower. The armies at the front were deprived of men because state officials kept men at home, in state militias, and consumed resources that should have gone to the armies in Virginia and Tennessee.

Such difficulties did not afflict the North, where the peacetime machinery continued to work as normal. The War Department and the Treasury, the two key agencies of United States power, merely expanded without having to learn their business as they went along, as was the case in the South. Lincoln, though he had to teach himself to be a war president, as he did very effectively, enjoyed the support of able men in his cabinet. His task of leadership was greatly complicated by the need to play ambitious rivals, several anxious to replace him as president, off against one another. His success in doing so further com-pels admiration of his powers as war leader.

Lincoln also had to deal with the difficulty, which did not really arise in the South, of conducting party government and winning national and state elections while overseeing the conduct of the war. The election of 1860 had returned a Republican majority to Congress. As the party was of such recent origin, however, and divided between its former Whig members and its ex-Democrats, it needed handling with a great deal of tact. Fortunately Lincoln excelled at personal rela-tions with men of opinion, and although his own policies, particularly on slavery and reconstruction, were controversial and divisive, he avoided any final breaches with individuals or factions in the capital. Remarkably, he also contested three national elections during the war and was successful in all, if with some losses in 1862. His campaigns benefited from the departure south in 1861 of many of the congressional Democrats. Nevertheless, in the midterm elections to Congress in 1862, he secured a majority, even if bad results in the mid-Atlantic and midwestern states had to be offset by votes in California and New England. In local elections in 1863 he secured his position, while in the presidential election of 1864 he carried the popular vote five to one. What in retrospect is even more remarkable is that the bureaucratically complicated procedures of countrywide elections were successfully conducted in the midst of a war, in which few concessions were made to the absence of soldier-voters at the front. Either by granting leaves of absence or organising postal ballots, all the men in uniform were enabled to vote.

Both governments had to conduct complex diplomacy while prosecuting the war, with the difference that while the Union sought merely to sustain normal good relations with the outside world, the Confederacy hungered for recognition as a sovereign state conducting a war of self-defence. The matter was of central importance, since recognition would transform the Confederacy's prospects, and for that reason was opposed tenaciously by the Union. Fortunately for the Union, it could demonstrate consistency in its foreign policy, since the Monroe Doctrine had laid down, from the early days of the republic, that the federal government would resist any intervention by any Old World government in the office of the New. Originally conceived as a means of preserving New World freedoms against any extension or renewal of colonialism, the doctrine very neatly served Union purposes in the war with the South. The Confederacy, by contrast, was all too eager to abrogate the doctrine, since such a move would open the sea-lanes to aid from Europe. At the outset popular belief held that the South would be able to prise recognition by economic leverage. The European and, particularly, the British textile industries depended on cotton imports to work, and the imports came from the South, which shipped up to four million bales a year across the Atlantic. In the South it was widely believed that suppression of supply would cause such distress in the textile spinning and weaving towns of the north of England that protest, by mill owners and workers alike, would prevail upon the government to extend recognition forthwith. As a result, an embargo of cotton exports was organised in the South by managers of the cotton trade itself, not the Confederate government, to bring about that result. The embargo certainly had its effect. By 1862 a cotton famine had caused output in the mill towns to fall very sharply. However, opinion proved more fickle than expected. The mill people, who were abolitionist to a man and woman and almost all Baptist or Methodist, had principled objections to their government extending recognition to the slave power and held out against it. Historians have disputed the extent to which principle subordinated economic interest during this period. It did so by no means completely, but its effects were offset by the existence of stockpiles from a pre-war surplus of imports, by the provision of supply from new sources of production in India and Egypt, and by the rise of alternative forms of work stimulated by boom in the flourishing Northern economy; in effect, the cotton famine never really took hold to the extent that fervent believers in the primacy of King Cotton anticipated that it would. Moreover, support for the South was patchier in Britain than might have been expected. Though there was a residue of anti-Yankee feeling in Britain dating from the War of Independence, supporters of the North included such unlikely figures as the Duke of Argyll, one of Britain's largest landholders, together with most radical opinion, leadership of the Nonconformist churches, and the literary and intellectual classes. Support for the South also came from unexpected directions; inexplicably, Gladstone was a pro-Southerner while the prime minister Lord Henry Palmerston and his foreign secretary, Lord John Russell, opposed recognising the Confederacy throughout the war. In general Britain maintained its pro-Northern position from beginning to end, fundamentally because anti-slavery had become an almost universal tenet of British political belief since the days of Wilberforce earlier in the century.

Yet pro-Northern policy was put under severe strain at times, notably in November 1861 during what became known as the *Trent* affair, when an American naval officer, acting on his own behalf, stopped a British ship, the *Trent*, carrying representatives of the Confederacy on the high seas. The Confederate officials were removed to Union territory and the British government naturally protested in the strongest terms at Union interference with the free movement of foreign shipping. There were demands for military action in Britain and many demands for military resistance in the North of the United States. For a time the crisis threatened a breach of relations between Britain and the North until calmer counsels prevailed and the Confederate officials were allowed to continue their journey.

The *Trent* affair brought recognition of the Confederacy as close to the point of fulfilment as was ever reached. No subsequent event ever reached such a level of intensity, and while transatlantic relations were strained again, particularly over the building in British ports of Confederate blockade-runners and commerce raiders, not even these provocations deflected the British government from what became its settled intention to keep out of the North-South conflict. The South's only other potential supporter was France, which was also affected by the cotton famine. Its ruler, Napoleon III, was keen to overcome the embargo but also anxious to avoid crossing the North, because of his own interests in American affairs. In 1862 he had sent an expeditionary force to Mexico as a means of extracting repayment of loans made to the Mexican government, a familiar nineteenth-century pretext by colonial powers to intervene in the affairs of a potential conquest. Napoleon announced the supersession of the republican government of Benito Juárez and installed in his place a client ruler, Prince Maximilian, a Habsburg archduke, who assumed the title of emperor. The intervention was a flagrant violation of the Monroe Doctrine which also provoked a long and bitter internal war. Foolishly, the Confederate State Department conceived the idea of winning recognition from France by endorsing Maximilian's legitimacy. Since Napoleon III knew that recognition of the Confederacy was a step guaranteed to bring about a breach with Washington, the last outcome he wanted, he did not encourage the Confederacy's support for his Maximilian adventure, which ended in failure and tragedy. Confederate diplomacy was no more successful in forming creative relations with any other great power. It was in an insoluble predicament, incapable of winning without foreign assistance, but able to extract such support only if it were victorious.

It could win victories only by superior military leadership, since it had no hope of bettering the North in numbers, in the output of military goods, or in superiority of military technology. As many well-placed men in the North knew, since so many of them had been at West Point with their opponents, the South possessed a remarkable number of talented commanders. Robert E. Lee was almost universally recognised as a general of exceptional ability. Winfield Scott had offered him command of the Union army before he insisted on "going with his state." He was eventually, though too late, appointed Confederate general in chief in 1865. In the preceding four years, Jefferson Davis had acted as his own commander in chief, a post to which his office entitled him but which he lacked the qualities to fill. Davis was knowledgeable enough about military affairs to command the Confederate armies, administratively. What he lacked was the vision to frame a war-winning strategy and the will to put it into action. But then no one in the Confederacy and only a handful of latecomers in the Union had the intellectual power to conceive a war-winning strategy.

Lincoln was besieged by men who wanted military appointments or, if they were already officers, promotion. They were supported by politicians from their states or their communities, particularly Germans, and by wives. As General George C. Marshall, the U.S. Army chief of staff under Franklin D. Roosevelt, was to discover at the outbreak of the Second World War, old acquaintances would beg for favours on the flimsiest acquaintance. Marshall set his face against such petitioners, choking off old friends and the wives of old friends. Lincoln was a softer touch. Of a wife who wanted her husband to be made a brigadier general, he wrote, "She is a saucy woman and I am afraid she will keep tormenting me until I may have to do it."[1] He did not object to being lobbied: from the beginning he was anxious to identify men of talent, and he was prepared to try anyone in whom he glimpsed ability. The trouble was that such men were very rare, and revealed themselves only in the harsh circumstances of battle. Far more numerous were men who accepted promotion, often offered for political reasons, but then expected the president to tell them what to do.

Had the U.S. War Department been as inefficient as were most headquarters in the field, it is unlikely that the North could ever have got the war under way. Purely by good fortune, however, the key officials in 1861 were men of ability. The first secretary of war, Simon Cameron, was inefficient and Lincoln got rid of him by appointing him ambassador to Russia. His successor, Edwin Stanton, was almost excessively efficient. He had complete confidence in his own abilities, correctly so, but spared no feelings in pointing out to others their deficiencies. He almost made a point of being rude to military contractors, because he rightly suspected corruption on any level. He was completely honest himself and administered war contracts with great skill. In this he was ably assisted by the quartermaster general, Montgomery Meigs. Like Stanton, Meigs was completely honest himself and spent $1.5 billion on war equipment without the slightest imputation of dishonesty. As Josiah Gorgas was to Confederate armaments, so was Meigs to Union military supplies. He sponsored the adoption of standardised sizes in the manufacturing of clothing and of the mechanical sewing of soles to boots, both practices which spread to civilian businesses after the war and led to a revolution in the American tailoring and outfitting industry.

What Lincoln lacked was an equivalent to Stanton as adjutant general, the officer who runs personnel policy, organises careers, arranges promotions, and chooses commanders. He never found the man, and had to select generals himself on the haphazard evidence of their success in combat and on campaign. His first three choices proved wrong. Irvin McDowell, whom he sent to command at First Bull Run, had the right qualifications but proved to lack the force of character necessary to direct a large army in the field. George McClellan was also well qualified on paper. Events would reveal that, though a brilliant organiser and trainer, he lacked the killer instinct and could not, in a Lincolnian phrase, "put things through," in the sense of bringing an encounter with the enemy to a successful conclusion. Lincoln was impressed enough to make him general in chief after Winfield Scott had to retire from office, but he too had to be replaced, as he was by Henry Halleck, known to his fellow West Pointers as "Old Brains" because he had published a treatise on infantry tactics. His intellectual reputation was unjustified, since he had done little more than translate from the French. He was nonetheless a competent and hardheaded man, who performed useful work as Grant's chief of staff in the latter years of the war. By then Lincoln had, by trial and error, worked out his own method of running the War Department and supervising operations in the field. His need then was to find generals who could command armies. By 1862, McClellan had failed him, as had several subordinate commanders in secondary theatres, such as John Frémont in the West, Don Carlos Buell, also in the West, Ambrose Burnside, Nathaniel Banks, and John Pope.

Some successes were beginning to stand out, however, to Lincoln's great relief, Grant foremost, but also William T. Sherman and, with reservations, George Meade. With the appointment of Grant as general in chief in March 1864, Lincoln solved both the problem of assuring himself of absolutely sound strategic advice and that of having a better than average chance of winning battles. Grant was both an absolutely clear-sighted strategist and a ruthless battle-winner. His record was not to be completely trouble-free, as the cost of the campaign of 1864 would demonstrate, but he believed wholly in his own ability to win the war and, because he did, ultimately set all Lincoln's anxieties at rest.

Jefferson Davis's problems in running the war were the obverse of

Lincoln's. He had several outstanding battlefield commanders who showed their quality from the start, notably Thomas "Stonewall" Jackson, Robert E. Lee, and, in the leadership of cavalry, J. E. B. Stuart and Nathan Bedford Forrest. What the South lacked, both at the outset and throughout the war, was a strategic mastermind. The lack may have been due to the inherent weakness of the South's strategic position, cut off from the outside world and unable to match the North in mobilisable manpower. In the circumstances it was remarkable that the Confederacy did as much militarily as it did. Still, it might have prolonged the war even longer had it adopted and persisted in the strategy Joseph E. Johnston advocated and practised in 1864, avoiding battle, conducting an offensive-defensive campaign, and exchanging space in preference to fighting. But large though the South was, it had a finite amount of space to surrender. Grant applauded Johnston's strategy but did not concede that it was a war-winning one. Lee was not really a strategist, though he was a brilliant tactician and operational leader. His campaign of limited offensives into the North in 1862–63 is still a model of how a weaker power may bring pressure to bear on a stronger. It may be argued that Lee's failure was in lack of boldness. Had he been able and willing to organise a long-range drive across the North's waist, from Tennessee to Ohio, he might have triggered sufficient panic in Washington and the cities of the Atlantic seaboard to have transformed the conditions of the war and forced the North to fight defensively for a prolonged period. Lee never attempted such a campaign, probably because he lacked the base from which to launch it and the logistic resources with which to sustain it. The Confederacy was also at a major disadvantage throughout the war because of its inability to win diplomatic recognition from the European great powers. Given the economic importance of the United States, it was understandable that neither Britain nor France should have wished to offend Washington by accepting ambassadors from Richmond or appointing envoys in return. Still, in its virtual monopoly of cotton production, it enjoyed a considerable power of leverage in international affairs, and it is possible to believe that with more diplomatic skill the South might have won a higher degree of recognition than it did. As it was, it won none at all, an extraordinary failing in a government that was able to threaten to put that of the United States under siege.

CHAPTER FIVE

The Military Geography of the Civil War

G EOGRAPHY, the most important of all factors that impinge on war-making, has had a cardinal importance in war-making in North America, where the vast extent of territory and its varied and dramatic character oblige soldiers to conform to its demands more rigorously than in almost any other region of the world. By 1861 there had already been a great deal of European war-making in North America. European wars had acquired American names to denote the parts of the action fought there: Queen Anne's War for the War of the Spanish Succession, King George's War for the Austrian Succession, the French and Indian War for the Seven Years' War, 1756–1763. The Seven Years' War was by origin American, bleeding back across the Atlantic to provoke campaigns in Europe and as far away as the Indian Ocean, a tribute to the commercial importance colonial America had achieved by the mid–eighteenth century.

Geography had determined how the chief protagonists of colonial war-making, the British and the French, had fought each other on American soil. At first they had struggled to take control of key points on the Atlantic coastline. As they extended control inland, the conflict had shifted to control of lines of communication, mainly rivers. By 1754, when the French and Indian War broke out, France had defined a strategic policy for North America, based on securing possession of what it controlled, largely the Great Lakes and the eastern tributaries of the Mississippi, and of denying Britain any opportunity to penetrate the territory of New France. The policy, called the "policy of posts," had its origins as early as the 1680s, when Governor D'Iberville had begun to build forts blocking the ways leading from the coastal plains across the Appalachian Mountains into the Ohio country, watered by the great Mississippi tributaries, the Ohio, Tennessee, and Cumberland rivers. The French were also determined to control the smaller northern rivers, the Mohawk and Richelieu, which led from the New England coast to "the great highway of the continent," the St. Lawrence. The logic of French policy was simple. Since they lacked population, while the British colonists were numerous, possession of the continent required that the British be confined to the coast east of the Appalachians, held there by the operations of the French colonial militia, a small French regular army, and their Indian allies. For eighty years the policy of posts served very successfully. In the end, however, numbers told. In 1754, when there were only 55,000 French colonists, there were a million British, many of whom were on their own initiative seeking the gaps in the French defences to reach into the interior. The Cumberland Gap, the easiest crossing place through the Appalachians, had been discovered in 1750 and exploited by adventurers to take trade goods to the Indians on the other side, in return for furs, America's chief product of wealth. In 1759 the British broke into the St. Lawrence Valley and destroyed the bases of French power at Montreal and Quebec. Once the St. Lawrence was theirs, the British quickly secured control of the Great Lakes and got onto the Mississippi. That spelt the end of New France, since its "policy of posts" depended on keeping control of two cordons, the Appalachian chain and the line of the Mississippi, in order to deny to the British entry into the vast area in between, the Ohio country, the "Old Northwest," and the huge tracts which would become the central United States. The French policy was unsuccessful. Their tiny settler population, reinforced with the assistance of Indian allies, was overwhelmed by the sheer size of their empire, most of which was not settled at all. The French had done much to define the outline of what would become the United States. They had traversed the Mississippi along its whole length, from its confluence with the Missouri to the Gulf of Mexico; they had founded the cities of New Orleans and St. Louis; they had penetrated as far west as the Black Hills of Dakota. They had not, however, reached the Pacific or discovered the Rockies.

The British, in the brief period when they ruled North America unchallenged, added little to the French achievement. Their American empire remained a coastal one. They even perpetuated the French attempt to keep the settlers east of the Appalachians, though as a sop to the Indians of the Ohio country rather than as strategic policy. The war they fought to suppress their colonists' rebellion was fought in a narrowly confined area, down the Atlantic coast and along the border with Canada. Like the French they were prevented from attacking the thirteen colonies from the landward side by shortage of numbers. Unlike the French they could compensate for their inability to manoeuvre in the interior by their control of the sea, though they profited little by it. Their decisions to carry the war into the South in the latter years of the War of the Revolution did not hamper the colonists' war effort as it might have been expected to do. Throughout the war George Washington showed himself the superior of the British by the skill he displayed at using waterways to cover his lines of march and the coastal forests as hiding places. However, both the human and physical geography of northeastern America told against the British. There were no long-distance roads, while the rivers of the Atlantic coast, being short and running west–east, did not lend themselves to use as strategic avenues. The campaigns of 1776–82 anticipated in many respects those of 1861–62 during the Civil War, and for the same reasons: bad or nonexistent roads, misleading maps or none at all, and rivers that ran the wrong way.

Geography defeated the French attempt to conquer America and undermined the British. By the time the Civil War came to America in 1861, the political extension of what was by then the United States seriously compounded the problem. It was greatly to the North's disadvantage that a geostrategic overview of the territory of the United States scarcely existed. Generals could say, as Winfield Scott did right at the beginning, where the armies ought to go and what places ought to be secured. They could say it, however, without knowing what difficulties lay en route or whether the marches they predicated were even possible. There was the absence of maps, for one thing; for another, there was an absence throughout the United States of the sort of knowledge of the country soldiers in Europe, even in a country as vast as European Russia, could take for granted.

European armies had staff colleges and schools of military geography in which geographic lore was studied and collated. No such body existed in America, North or South. West Point was a school of military engineering in the narrow sense. There was no other or higher school of military science in the country. The South's military academies, state or private bodies such as VMI and the Citadel, were imitations of West Point and of lower academic status. Had the United States possessed a staff and war college and had it collected the available topographical knowledge, a graduate might have summarised the geostrategic problems facing the United States Army in 1861 something as follows:

The principal problem confronting the Federal government in its effort to restore the union is that of distance. From the northern border of Virginia to New Orleans is a thousand miles. From the mouth of Chesapeake Bay to the Mississippi at Memphis is nearly nine hundred miles. From Louisville, Kentucky, to Mobile, Alabama, is more than five hundred miles. The territory of the eleven seceding states thus forms a rough quadrilateral of nearly a million square miles' extent. No through roads penetrate this enormous area; within much of it, roads are of local significance only and do not connect with others in neighbouring states or even counties and often peter out without apparent reason. Railroads provide some long-distance communication, over a total distance of 8,783 miles, as compared to 22,000 miles of track inside Union territory. Southern railroads, however, are of flimsy construction, most having been hastily engineered as cheaply as possible. They also fail to conform to a standard gauge. Some lines are the normal 4'8½" but some were 5' and others 5'6"; where they met, transhipment has to take place. As a result, there are only two through routes in the South, one running from Richmond via Chattanooga to Corinth, Mississippi; the second, still under construction, from Montgomery, Alabama, to Petersburg, Virginia, via Atlanta, Augusta, and Wilmington. The two systems scarcely interconnect, the only links between them being from Chattanooga to Atlanta and, less usefully, the Corinth link with Mobile.

The separateness of the Southern rail systems is dictated by the large landforms, particularly the Appalachian chain, which diagonally divides the Upper from the Lower South; the Chattanooga–Atlanta rail link makes use of the Chattanooga gap as a way through the mountains. Although the Appalachians complicate the South's inland communications, they also offer a valuable defensive barrier against attack from Union territory in the Midwest, shielding northern Virginia and the Carolinas from invasion, though also providing Southern armies, should they adopt an offensive strategy, a covered approach corridor into the Union's mid-Atlantic states in the Shenandoah Valley.

The Appalachians are not the only major geographical feature to lend protection to the rebellion. Equally important are southern and borderland rivers.

On the other hand, the great topographical features offer advantages to the Union, as well as conferring disadvantages. The Miss-

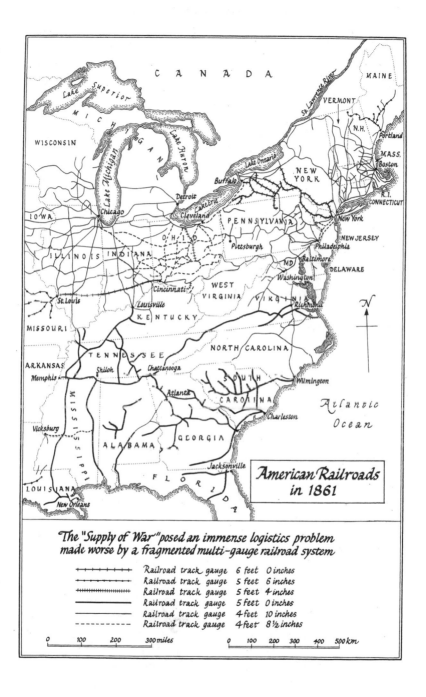

The "Supply of War" posed an immense logistics problem
made worse by a fragmented multi-gauge railroad system

American Railroads
in 1861

	Railroad track gauge	6 feet	0 inches
	Railroad track gauge	5 feet	6 inches
	Railroad track gauge	5 feet	4 inches
	Railroad track gauge	5 feet	0 inches
	Railroad track gauge	4 feet	10 inches
	Railroad track gauge	4 feet	8½ inches

0   100   200   300 miles   0   100   200   300   400   500 km

issippi and the Appalachians impose critical internal divisions, the Mississippi in particular. Can it be seized, Texas and Arkansas are thereby cut off from the rest of the Confederacy. The eastern Mississippi basin then becomes a theatre of war on its own, which it should be a Union object to dominate. Entry into the basin will be facilitated by using the river itself as an axis of advance and its tributaries, the Ohio, Tennessee, and Cumberland, as approach routes.

The eastern boundary of the Mississippi basin is the Appalachian chain. It cannot be captured and secured as the great river can be. Nevertheless, it too defines a theatre of war, that of Georgia and the Carolinas, bounded to the east by the Atlantic. Control of Georgia and the Carolinas is an essential war aim, because of the wealth of the region and size of its population, particularly its male population. The region, however, is difficult of access, its seacoast being low-lying and waterlogged, its mountain boundary forming a natural rampart, and its rivers running the wrong way to provide avenues of advance. The region can only be entered from the north, through Virginia, or the south, via Alabama, or by a flank march round the bottom of the Appalachians. All these routes present physical as well as military difficulties.

Any Northern war plan is also complicated by the absence of any obvious objective for a major offensive operation. Unlike the Union, which contains a number of large cities situated within easy striking distance of its borders—Baltimore, Philadelphia, even New York—the South lacks large cities and those that it has almost all lie deep within its territory—Charleston, New Orleans, Atlanta—and are difficult to approach. Only Richmond lies within easy reach and it is defended by complex water barriers. Its status as the Confederacy's capital makes it, moreover, an obvious target and will encourage the Confederate government to defend it with strong man-made defences, which will probably necessitate prolonged siege operations if a way in is to be forced. The rural character of the Southern interior and the absence of large centres of population imposes on the Union the need to make long cross-country marches with the object of bringing the enemy to battle where he can be found. If the enemy refuses battle and chooses to fight a campaign of evasion and delay, the war will be very prolonged. Even if the enemy does fight, his enormous extent of territory offers him the opportunity to disengage at will and retreat into his territory's empty spaces, which, while sparsely built up, are agriculturally productive enough to provide ample supplies to passing Confederate armies.

The Union therefore faces the prospect of fighting a long-distance, hard-marching war, characterised by the difficulty either of bringing the enemy to battle or, if he does fight, of having to fight fiercely and perhaps frequently on ground of the enemy's choosing. The only regions where the Union enjoys an uncontested advantage are coastal, where its naval superiority will allow it to land forces at advantageous points, threaten Southern cities, and shorten marching distances. The retention of some of the great federal sea fortresses further favours such amphibious strategy. An important and obvious line of coastwise advance is down Chesapeake Bay, from which there are riverine approaches towards Richmond, and a secure base at Fortress Monroe.

Had such a geostrategic appreciation been written at the outset of the war, events would have borne out its accuracy. Perhaps the most prescient of the observations would have been that touching on the ferocity and frequency of battle. During almost exactly four years of conflict, 237 named battles were fought, together with many minor actions and skirmishes, the largest characterised by their bitter intensity and high casualties on both sides. The American Civil War was to prove one of the most ferocious wars ever fought, a factor of its geography, since the enemy's personnel, in the absence of obvious geographic objectives apart from each side's capital, presented itself as the only target at which to strike.

CHAPTER SIX

The Life of the Soldier

MILITARY LIFE FOR the vast majority of the young men, North and South, who went off to war in 1861 began by joining friends, neighbours, and schoolfellows in the informal assembly that would make a company or a regiment. Those who joined included almost none who knew anything of the soldier's trade: no drill, no manual of arms, no habit of obedience to orders. There were few to instruct them, at best a militia officer or two, perhaps a veteran of the Mexican War or a recent immigrant who had served in a European army. Everything had to be learnt, from any available drill book. Learning began with forming ranks and marching in step, turning left and right, advancing, retiring. If there were weapons available, the recruits then progressed to handling whatever muskets or rifles were to hand, basic drill movements at first, followed by the steps necessary to load and fire a round, though live firing would come later.

In the early stages of forming the company came the appointment of officers, usually chosen either from anyone with military experience or from among the local worthies who had taken the lead in forming the unit. Election was a common means of appointment, though it could often lead to trouble if those who thought they had a claim to rank were not chosen. The trials of service could lead to the supersession of early appointees who proved unsuitable.

As the unit learnt the rudiments, other practical matters assumed importance: acquiring uniforms and shelter, making cooking arrangements. In the North the government soon began to supply standard blue coats, caps, and trousers, often to replace privately chosen outfits, which were sometimes a version of fashionable foreign dress, such as the French Zouave costume, the chasseur style, or the Garibaldi feathers and pantaloons. Southern units outfitted themselves or were clothed at state expense, at first where possible in cadet gray, later as supplies ran out in locally dyed homespun in a brownish colour that came to be called butternut.

At the outset soldiers lived in whatever buildings were available, public halls or schools, mills, taverns; some early arrivals in Washington in 1862 were accommodated in the capital's museums. As quickly as possible, however, the new regiments tried to acquire tents and set up orderly tented encampments. The standard dwelling was the so-called Sibley tent, a bell-shaped structure accommodating sixteen men. More common, because handier in the field, was the dog or pup tent, made by stretching the soldier's waterproof shelter half on a pole or rope. It could house four or, at a squeeze, six. Inside the soldier bedded down in the blanket which he carried folded in his haversack. Since the war began in early summer, skimpy bedding kept him warm enough. During the first winter the armies learnt to improvise portable stoves.

Supply is the first prerequisite in war and has always been at the forefront of a commander's preoccupations. Wellington, both in India and in the Iberian Peninsula, wrote constantly about the need for bullocks, which, driven forward with the army on the march, provided meat on the hoof and could also be used as beasts of burden. Even when he had animals to carry provisions, however, the perishability of foodstuffs was a constant concern. As a result, commanders have historically often succumbed to the temptation to live off the land, which means in practice pillaging the local population, an unsatisfactory expedient since it poisons relations with civilians yet is an undependable source. Armies rapidly eat out a campaigning area; cavalry armies eat it out at lightning speed. By the nineteenth century ministries of war were investing heavily in means to preserve food. Margarine was developed in response to a competition organised by the emperor Napoleon III to find a substitute for butter for his armies on campaign.

Fires were also necessary to cook, which from the outset soldiers did, very badly, for themselves. Because of the abundance of food in agricultural America, there was rarely a shortage at the beginning, though the diet was monotonous. The armies of the Civil War, and particularly the Union army, benefited from recent developments in food preservation, particularly canning. The Union army, in consequence, rarely went short. The Northern soldier, benefiting from remarkably efficient supply arrangements, could depend on a steady ration of staples. Indeed, it was calculated by comparison of his regulation rations with those of the British, French, and Russian armies that the Union soldier was the best fed on record. Regulations in the Union army prescribed a daily individual issue of twelve ounces of pork or bacon or twenty ounces of fresh or salt beef, together with six ounces of soft bread or flour or a pound of hard bread or twenty ounces of cornmeal. To every hundred rations was added fifteen pounds of beans or dried peas, and ten pounds of rice, ten pounds of coffee beans, fifteen pounds of sugar, four quarts of vinegar, about four pounds of salt, thirty pounds of potatoes, and one quart of molasses. Everything except meat and bread was known as "small rations." The Confederate soldier fared worse than the Northerner except at the start of the war. There was plenty of food in the South, but the Southern distribution system was poor and erratic. Northern soldiers could count on regular supply brought by railroad and wagon. Confederate supply was much more chancy and often arrived spoilt after waiting beside the railroad too long for onward movement. Staple diet was much the same as in the Union army, but corn bread substituted for wheat and rapidly palled, and while the Union soldier's ration was increased during the war, the Confederate's shrank.

In practice, the soldier lived on salt meat, hardtack, coffee, and hard biscuits, called by the men "crackers," which they pounded up and recooked. The most common supplements were dried vegetables, beans, split peas, or desiccated potatoes. Once food was procured, the next problem was to cook it. The soldiers cooked in messes of six or eight, each taking a turn. Flour was usually turned into flapjacks, dough paste baked in the flame wrapped round a bayonet or ramrod. Cooking utensils were in drastically short supply because they were the first stores to be discarded on the eve of battle and were the means by which soldiers dug entrenchments. As a result the cooking was even worse than the cook's lack of skill could make it. Meats, and many other foods, were fried. Indeed frying was often the only culinary technique soldiers had, though the result, soaked in grease, was unappetising. One of the reasons for the resort to frying seems to have been the shortage of cooking utensils; frying pans or skillets were the most frequently available, perhaps because they were easily carried on the march. Most soldier dishes were rough stews of crumbled hardtack and dried vegetables with scraps of issue meat thrown in, often known as "cush" or "hoosh."

Food parcels from home, on which Confederates depended to a surprising degree, often arrived spoilt or in broken containers. Northern soldiers got parcels from home also, as well as fresh produce which they bought from the sutlers' wagons that followed the line of march. Few soldiers starved though many, particularly Confederates, often went short. The memories of even the well fed, though, were of hard-tack and salt pork in unrelenting monotony. Coffee was the soldier's chief consolation. It seemed always to be plentiful on the Union side and was a means of barter for Southern tobacco, the South being unable to supply it in the quantities that were drunk by Northern armies.

Alcohol, though not part of the ration, was fairly freely dispensed, particularly for medical reasons, and was widely available. Officers, including some generals, were often accused of imbibing too freely, an accusation levelled at Grant. Grant undoubtedly succumbed to drink on occasion but usually when he was separated from his wife, who was a beneficent influence on him in every way. His fault was binge drinking when under strain; normally Grant was perfectly sober.

Bad cooking was a common cause of the intestinal disorders which afflicted all soldiers and were a major cause of death in the ranks. In the first months, diarrhoea or dysentery could afflict whole regiments, and though the incidence declined as the troops were hardened to the experience of campaigning, over a million cases were recorded by the Union War Department between 1861 and 1865, of which 57,000 resulted in death. Treatment was rough and ready, dosing with opium, strychnine, calomel, and whisky being the commonest resort. Many soldiers dosed themselves, often with remedies sent from home. Malaria, which caused many casualties among Northern soldiers campaigning in the Mississippi Valley in the summers of 1862–64, was also treated with whisky, together with quinine. Typhoid, common when clean water was not available, was also treated with quinine, and with turpentine, carbonate of ammonia, and a widely used pill called blue mass (mercury and chalk).

Despite improvement of treatment, both surgical and medical, the cost of the war in human life was very high, about 620,000 between 1861 and 1865, of which 360,000 were Union deaths, 260,000 Confederate. Among these, deaths from disease occurred in the proportion of two to one, against death from wounds—figures that contemporaries would have accepted as perfectly normal. Indeed, the incidence of fatal sickness was somewhat lower in Civil War armies than in those of the Crimean War and much lower than in the Napoleonic Wars.

Sickness consistently depressed the numbers available for duty, often by as much as half of a regiment. The prevailing below-strength state of regiments in both armies was largely the result of disease. Desertion and absence without leave were also causes, most noticeable during periods of demoralisation, increasingly common from 1863 onwards. Soldiers left the ranks if unsupervised or overstayed their leave or did not return from furlough at all. That had the effect of deterring commanders from granting furlough, though in principle it was a soldier's right, often generously conceded. Southern soldiers, who often served in their home districts, might get as much as forty days' leave. Some Union soldiers got no leave at all throughout the war. As the war situation worsened for the South, some deserters combined in armed bands, hiding in the woods, to resist return to the ranks. Desertion seems to have been less common in the Union army, which organised a system of severe punishment for those caught, including the death penalty. During 1865 desertion became endemic in the Confederate army, with as many as 100,000 absent without leave at any one time. The numbers rose as defeat approached.

There was little material inducement to remain obedient. Union pay was thirteen dollars a month, at a time when the war economy boomed. The Confederate soldier was paid less, eleven dollars, in paper currency which began to depreciate in value in 1862 and by the end of the war had lost its value altogether. Moreover, Confederate pay was usually in arrears, by as much as six months or a year.

Duty and devotion to comrades were therefore the motives that kept men in the ranks. Personal reputation counted in units where men came from the same locality and had known one another at home. A good name was particularly powerful in Southern regiments and was maintained by, among other means, letters home, which travelled with remarkable promptness.

Immaterial motives were also important. Many Northerners were outraged by rebellion and held it a high duty to put it down. Some Northerners were also principled abolitionists, though even abolitionists expressed different views when confronted with the spectacle of the black way of life in the South. Southerners, at least at the outset, were strong in their denunciations of Northern oppression, and most remained horrified right to the end at the prospect of black liberation, which for many supplied the strongest reason to fight.

Religion reinforced sentiment. Nineteenth-century America was a deeply religious nation. At the beginning of the century, a powerful revival, the Second Great Awakening, had swept the country and inspired church building, sectarian college founding, and evangelising everywhere. The North-South divide had split churches, particularly over the issue of whether blacks and whites might worship together. The Baptist and Methodist churches both splintered off Southern factions, which fell out of communion with their Northern brethren. Though denounced as unchristian, Southerners continued to insist on the authenticity of their Christian faith, which they often practised fervently in small-town and rustic churches. Both Yankee and Rebel soldiers took their religion to war with them. The fervently pious may have appeared to be odd men out, but the decently observant were commonplace and unbelievers probably the exception.

The coming of the war coarsened religious feeling. Pious young men were shocked at the profanity of army life, the bad language, the gambling, drunkenness, and abandonment of Sunday observance, and Christian worthies who visited the armies were outraged by the sexual licence all too visibly on view. The Civil War armies, as was the case with armies everywhere in all times, rapidly attracted a following of prostitutes and fell victim to the diseases of sexual promiscuity. Yet sin was not the distinctive mark of the Civil War armies, which remained religious in a way distinctive to the America of the period. Both armies, despite a great deal of profanity, drinking, and recourse to loose women, were also deeply affected by the contemporary practice of religion. Regiments both Northern and Southern had their regimental chaplains, some of whom exerted a powerful hold over their parishioners. The chaplaincy of the regiment, like the surgeon's post, was authorised by the War Department and usually filled by election by the officers. Chaplains were expected to conduct regimental services at which they preached, with prayers and hymn singing. In the aftermath of the Second Great Awakening, religious practice was enthusiastic and widespread both North and South, in exclusively Protestant form outside the cities, where Catholics were growing in numbers. Soldiers underwent conversion experiences in the ranks, held Bible classes, prayed, and sang hymns with an unaffectedness which would be found startling today. Letter and diary writers noted the devotion shown by comrades in arms. Some soldiers "got religion" in the ranks, perhaps responding to the revivalists who roamed the armies as they did all American communities of the period, and returned home far more observant than they had joined, though in general army service encouraged lack of observance rather than its opposite.

Hymn singing was popular in camp, as was singing generally. Favourites included "Jesus, Lover of My Soul," "Rock of Ages," and

"Just as I Am." Popular secular tunes, often taken up across the lines so that the armies seemed to be serenading each other, were "Lorena," "Just Before the Battle, Mother," and "Tenting on the Old Camp Ground."

A distinctive feature of service in the West was the regularity with which Union regiments were entertained by the singing of ex-slaves and displays of dancing. An Illinois soldier wrote from Virginia, "There were five negroes in our mess room last night, we got them to sing and dance! Great times. Negro concerts free of expense here . . . hope I shall not be obliged to leave."[1] The West proved to be not only one of the most hard-fought theatres of the war, but one in which fighting was most protracted. The final surrenders there did not take place until May 1865.

The Christian Commission, a church-based equivalent of the Sanitary Commission, was a potent force for observance and revivalism throughout the Union army and provided much material as well as spiritual comfort to the troops. Its representatives were held in regard, and not just for the coffee and writing paper they distributed on their visits to the regiments.

Their generals invoked the Almighty freely in exercising their powers. Several were notable for their religious practice, including Leonidas Polk, who was an Episcopalian bishop. Religious observance depended greatly on the example set by officers. McClellan and Burnside both issued orders for the holding of religious services while General Oliver O. Howard of the Army of the Tennessee led divine services, and Colonel the Reverend Granville Moody, who commanded the 74th Ohio, regularly preached to his own and other regiments. While Lincoln seems to have been no more than a deist, Robert E. Lee was a devout Episcopalian, and Stonewall Jackson was a Presbyterian of formidable piety. General Rosecrans was a devout Catholic and therefore an odd man out, since in both North and South the temper of the armies was overwhelmingly Protestant, though particularly in the North they included many Catholics. Rosecrans's co-religionists in the North were notable, however, for their lack of enthusiasm for the war. Most were German or Irish and had left their homelands to escape the power of government and therefore resisted conscription. Distinctively Protestant, in a revivalist manner, was the widely held belief that the war was God's punishment of America for its sins, the sin of slavery to many Northerners' way of thinking, the general sinfulness of the nation's habits to many puritan Southerners. To the idea of punishment was linked the belief that, in a millenarian fashion, one great event, a decisive battle on a monumental scale, would bring the war to an end.

Many soldiers, North and South, did not live to see the war's end but were already dead and buried before it was over. Both sides tried if possible to give their dead Christian burials, usually a matter of the time available and who inherited the battlefield. Even before the war was over the North was creating impressive national cemeteries for their dead heroes. Abraham Lincoln would of course speak at the inauguration of the Gettysburg cemetery in November 1863. The Federal government did not, however, confer the dignity of a decent burial on the rebels, who were held not to merit it. The Southern dead, outside the South, were either left in their hasty battlefield burial places, if interred by comrades, or bundled into mass graves, if disposed of by the Northerners. Hence the character of Civil War cemeteries to this day. This apartheid is evidence of how deep the division of secession bit. Even during the world wars, the British and French buried the German dead, and the Germans buried their enemies. It was left to Stalin to obliterate the German cemeteries on Soviet soil. The Union treated those who died in rebellion against it as non-people. Few Southern soldiers are buried at Arlington, and one searches in vain for Confederate gravestones at Gettysburg.

CHAPTER SEVEN

Plans

THE VAST ARMIES of 1865 lay four years in the future when the guns spoke at Fort Sumter in April 1861. The war had begun. People and politicians on both sides were eager to prosecute it. How, though, was force of arms to be applied? How was victory to be won?

Scarcely through the medium of such tiny armies as had been hurried into the field. They were too small to do disabling damage to each other. They were too small altogether to dominate the vast distances and space over which the war was to be fought. The theatre of war constituted by the United and Confederate States was the largest single landmass over which any conqueror had ever attempted to impose his will, larger than Napoleon's Europe, larger almost than Genghis Khan's Eurasia. In the opening month of the conflict, such armies as had been brought into being were pinpricks on the map: McDowell's 35,000 defending Washington, confronted by Beauregard's 20,000 at Manassas Junction, twenty-five miles to the west; the geriatric Robert Patterson's 15,000 at Harpers Ferry, opposing Joseph E. Johnston's 11,000 Confederates in the Shenandoah Valley; McClellan's 20,000 in western Virginia, easily outnumbering Confederates in a region that would shortly secede from the Confederacy as the new-fledged state of West Virginia; at Fortress Monroe, the great artillery fortification guarding the tip of the Virginia Peninsula, General Ben Butler commanded 15,000 men, watched by the Confederates Magruder and Huger at Yorktown and Norfolk, the Federal naval base which had fallen to Southern attack. Smaller Confederate forces, matched in places by Union handfuls, occupied positions in the West, particularly along the Mississippi and Missouri rivers: Memphis, Island No. 10, and New Madrid. Even in the barely inhabited regions of Arkansas and New Mexico tiny bands of supporters of one side or the other were taking to arms. A war which seemed at first to concern only the old thirteen colonies and the immediate trans-Appalachian region of post-independence settlement was developing into a war for the whole of non-British North America.

It was the sheer size of the fragmented union—three thousand miles from ocean to ocean, over a thousand miles from Washington to the Gulf of Mexico—that so complicated the task of devising war plans. For the South the task appeared straightforward; simply to stand on the defensive and repel attacks wherever mounted, counting on Southern space and the absence of critically important centres of wealth and production to defeat Northern efforts to land crippling blows. President Jefferson Davis advocated such a strategy at the outset. It might well have worked, and would probably have averted Southern defeat well beyond 1865. Davis was prevented from implementing it for two reasons: one was the objection of local politicians and magnates to allowing Northern armies to penetrate their territories, even against the promise of eventual victory; the second was popular sentiment. Southerners, in reality as well as romantic belief, really did believe in their ability to defeat superior numbers of Yankees, whom they held to be an inferior breed. "The idea of waiting for blows, instead of inflicting them, is altogether unsuited to the genius of our people," argued the *Richmond Examiner* in September 1861.[1] Southerners wanted to invade the unseceding states and win victories on their soil, not just oppose Northern advances into the Confederacy. In retrospect the South's strategy may be perceived as an amalgam of both strategies: opposing Union armies around the borders of the Confederacy and carrying war into the North when the chance offered. The South's mistake was not to exploit the advantages geography conferred upon it. The South's perimeter was very strong, penetrable only at a few widely separated points: down the Washington–Richmond corridor, up the Mississippi from New Orleans, down the Mississippi from the vicinity of Memphis. The South held the approaches to Richmond almost to the end, and opposed the descent of the Mississippi stoutly until 1863. Weakly, and fatally, however, it surrendered the mouth of the Mississippi far too easily, thus giving away one of the key entrance points to the Confederate heartland. Had the South, instead of sustaining the mass of its force in northern Virginia, conserved sufficient strength to create a mobile reserve in the lower states, ready to intervene against Union threats down or across the Mississippi, the integrity of its heartland might have been preserved for longer than it was.

In practice, Southern leaders articulated strategies more explicitly than is usually credited. Southern strategy is misunderstood or overlooked in part because it was given no underlying theme at the outset, as Union strategy was by Winfield Scott with the Anaconda Plan. Yet there was a Southern strategy, or several variants of a single strategy, particularly associated with Jefferson Davis, Robert E. Lee, and Joseph E. Johnston. Davis's strategy was essentially political, as befitted his role as president of the Confederacy. It was designed to take account of the popular choice to preserve the whole territory of the new polity, by denying access to Union invaders at every point around the South's enormous perimeter. Its execution required the stationing of military forces at the borders and the waging of major defensive battles wherever invasion threatened. The first act of the Davis strategy was the first battle of Bull Run. Yet though a victory, the aftermath of Bull Run, and of similar battles that followed, revealed the strategy's shortcomings. Though it solved an immediate problem, it did not deter a repetition, nor did it inflict disabling damage on the North, nor did it open up the prospect of any new strategic initiative. Indeed by 1862 it was made obvious that the North, despite Bull Run, was able to attack the South at any point it chose, a facility that would require the Confederacy to fight defensive battles in interminable sequence. Davis therefore refined his idea, proposing what would become known as the "offensive-defensive strategy." Places and areas of secondary importance at the outer edges were not to be defended. Scattered forces were to be regrouped to operate on the South's "interior lines," moving by railroad to confront Northern armies as they appeared. One effect of this revised strategy was the virtual abandonment of the South's West, in the trans-Mississippi region. Another effect, however, was to provide the South with larger striking forces that could be used to mount offensive operations as opportunity offered.

This conception of the "offensive-defensive" was embraced by Robert E. Lee once he became Davis's chief commander and led to his effort to carry the war into the North in 1863. His object was to win a great victory or series of victories that would dishearten his opponents and the North's urban population. Lee, though it was part of his genius that his demeanour and pronouncements disguised his inner anxieties, had decided after the defeats in the Mississippi River system in 1862 that the South was losing the war and lacked the human and material resources to reverse the trend, unless by sensational events. By 1864, after the South's defeats on Northern soil and the loss of more territory in the Mississippi Valley and around the coasts, it was obvious that Lee's aggressive strategy was not working either, and the commander of the South's only other large army, Joseph E. Johnston, operating in Georgia, had adopted another variant of the "offensive-defensive," though with the emphasis on the defensive. His scheme was to take up a strong position and wait to be attacked. If bypassed, he retreated and repeated the process. Johnston's strategy was self-defeating, since there was a finite limit to the amount of territory the South could surrender before it was completely overcome, almost the outcome he achieved as long as his command lasted.

Little of that could be seen at the outset; in any case, the spirit of the seceding South was aggressive, not defensive. The view from the opposite direction was equally obscured. Those Northerners who had abandoned hope of conciliation, and some had wanted a fight even before Sumter fell, were baffled by the sheer strength of the South as to where to begin—Richmond, state capital of Virginia, to which the Confederacy's capital had been transferred by vote on May 21, lay only 110 miles from Washington; but in July 1861 the Confederate outposts stood only 25 miles distant from the national capital. The waterways of northern Virginia were as much a deterrent as Confederate armed strength.

The Shenandoah Mountains form a section of the Appalachian chain, which runs diagonally southwest–northeast from Georgia to New England, at a distance varying between two hundred and one hundred miles from the Atlantic. The Appalachians had for nearly two centuries formed the dividing line between English, later British, America and the French interior, a major military frontier, never breached, only turned by the British capture of the Great Lakes region after the capture of Quebec in 1759. The Civil War revived the strategic significance of Appalachia, since the mountain barrier protected the Carolinas and Georgia from attack from the Midwest, not only because of the difficulty presented by its terrain but also because it was traversed neither by rivers nor railroads, the two principal means of movement for Civil War armies.

West of the Appalachians the military significance of the continent's great rivers became dominant. That of the Mississippi was self-evident. It provided the Confederacy, as long as it could be held, with an avenue of rapid north–south communication from Tennessee to Louisiana and a bulwark against any attack from the west that might be mounted. Its eastern tributaries, particularly those flowing through Kentucky and Tennessee, vast in width and carrying huge volumes of water, the Ohio, Tennessee, and Cumberland rivers, were of almost equal importance. They lent barrier protection; they both provided and denied means of communication. The area of confluence of the Mississippi, Tennessee, Cumberland, and Ohio rivers was a particularly vital sector, forming, if held by the Confederacy, an offensive salient into the Midwest; if it could be seized by the North, a major re-entrant threatening an attack down the Mississippi towards Memphis, Vicksburg, Natchez, and New Orleans.

The seizure of the line of the Mississippi from Memphis to New Orleans would bisect the Confederacy, separating its western states of Arkansas and Texas from the rest, thus depriving the Confederacy of its largest stock of meat on the hoof and of draught animals, horses and mules. The diminution of its territory would also be a severe blow to its international prestige and domestic self-confidence.

The final ingredient of strength in the South's strategic geography was the impermeability of its seaward frontiers. From Chesapeake Bay, in the north, along the coasts of the Carolinas and Georgia, round Florida, and across the shores of Alabama and Mississippi to the mouth of the great river itself below New Orleans, there were almost no points of entry that promised success to an amphibious attack. The only routes inland by railroad ran from Norfolk, Virginia; New Bern or Wilmington, North Carolina; Charleston, South Carolina; Savannah, Georgia; Jacksonville and Pensacola, Florida; Mobile, Alabama; and New Orleans. All were strongly defended and all lay far from centres of Northern naval power. Moreover, in many cases the railroad lines of which they were the termini soon petered out inland or did not connect to long-distance routes.

The inadequacy of the Confederacy's railroads, while further arguing for its adoption of a defensive strategy, also complicated the North's problems of framing an offensive plan. By 1861 the United States had become the land of the railroad par excellence; the railroad was replacing waterways as the medium which bound the country together. Of the 31,000 miles existing, however, only 9,000 ran in the South, and Southern lines followed infuriatingly unstrategic routes. The North possessed several long-distance east–west routes running parallel to the northern frontier of the Confederacy and so serving as *lignes de rocade* for the movement of armies between the Atlantic states and the Mississippi Valley. That from Philadelphia to Pittsburgh and its branch through Columbus, Ohio, and Indianapolis to St. Louis, Missouri, might, as were the German railroads, have been built by general staff diktat, so strategic was its function. The North's *lignes de rocade* were, moreover, served by north–south feeder lines, as that between Indianapolis and Louisville, Kentucky, which ran straight into the zone of operations. The pattern, laid out to serve expansion westward and to gather in and carry the agricultural produce of the Midwest to the cities of the Atlantic seaboard, had direct if unintended military utility.

The pattern of the South's railroads, by contrast, had been determined by the needs of its exporters, particularly cotton exporters, and so ran outwards to the sea. There was only one trans-Confederacy line, that from Richmond to Corinth, Mississippi. Otherwise the systems were largely internal to the states and scarcely interconnected. The railroads of the Carolinas and Georgia were an almost self-contained network, laid out to carry cotton to the Atlantic coast; they had only one link with Florida's two lines and barely any with Alabama's. The Mississippi lines likewise had been built to bring cotton down country to Mobile and New Orleans and had but the scantiest connections with Tennessee and only two spurs, served by ferry, with Arkansas. Most defectively of all, the Virginia, Tennessee, and Mississippi systems connected to those of the Carolinas and the Lower South by only a single link, from near Chattanooga in Tennessee to Atlanta, Georgia. Buried as it was deep inside the Confederacy, the Chattanooga–Atlanta link was secure as long as the perimeter of the South itself remained inviolate. It would prove a magnet to Northern armies as the war progressed, however, and, if cut, the break would divide the South in two. The strategic geography of the South was thus intrinsically fragile, in a way that that of the North was not. The North had a few vulnerable points, Washington itself the foremost; but no single offensive success by the South could disable it as a combatant power. The South, by contrast, and despite its enormous size and strong frontiers—the sea, the Mississippi, the mountains—had to be held together as a unit if it were not to be dismembered.

Yet in the summer of 1861 it was the South's strength rather than its vulnerability that weighed on those Northerners seeking to devise a war plan. They could not see how to begin. Lincoln, who started by expecting, wrongly, that his generals would form his mind, tentatively suggested on April 25 that the first steps were to safeguard Fortress Monroe, at the mouth of the Chesapeake Bay, to assure the safety of Washington, to blockade the Southern ports, and then attack Charleston, South Carolina. The strategic sketch revealed that at the outset he was thinking exclusively of a war to be fought in the east and of a victory to be gained by military means alone. His postmaster general, Montgomery Blair, soon afterwards suggested a military-political approach. Like some others in the Federal government, he suspected that the South was not solid for secession and that the Confederacy might be undone by undermining rebellion. In a letter to the governor of Massachusetts on May 11, he proposed the organisation of a Union Army of the South, with its own commander, staff, and troops, to be concentrated at Hampton Roads—the tip of the Virginia Peninsula—to "menace Newport and Richmond." Its appearance, he argued, would provoke a popular revolt against the standard-bearers of Southern revolt and return Virginia to the Union—presumably, in his imagination, bringing the rest of the Confederacy with it. There were others in the North, including the president himself, who recognised the significance of pro-Union sentiment in the South; none of importance, however, shared Blair's belief in the possibility of using it to collapse the Confederacy from within and his plan remained private to himself.

George McClellan, a West Pointer who had returned to Federal service after a spell as a railroad executive and who early distinguished himself in the opening skirmishes for control of the borders, proposed an alternative strategy in late April 1861. His plan, like Blair's, took account of Southern pro-Union sentiment but in more realistic fashion. Since western Virginia was solidly loyal, he suggested transporting an army of 80,000 troops, to be raised in the Midwest, across the Ohio River and marching it up the Great Kanawha Valley to capture Richmond. Alternatively, such an army was to be transported across the Ohio at Cincinnati or Louisville to capture Nashville in Tennessee. McClellan's plan showed geopolitical understanding. The Kanawha is a major waterway of the Ohio River complex and the backbone of the region which, by popular sentiment, seceded from the Confederacy to become the state of West Virginia, a process begun in August 1861. Nevertheless, his idea was both too complex and took too little account of loyalties in the Upper South. It is most unlikely that a march from the region of the Great Kanawha Valley by an invading army could have overcome the resistance of solidly secessionist populations, supported by field armies, in either Tennessee or Virginia proper. Successful operations inside the Confederate heartland would have to await victories on its perimeter that were not achieved until later in the war.

Lincoln's difficulty was that he had no strong, unmuddled mind to advise him and that, while he himself was wholly unmuddled, he lacked the military experience necessary to put his ideas for winning the war into action. Lincoln arrived, indeed, at the presidency almost without a personal entourage or following. He was completely an outsider in Washington, despite having sat as a congressman for Illinois, his state of residence, from 1847 to 1849. Mid-century Illinois, though by then a settled state with a growing metropolis at Chicago, was entirely agricultural, with many farms but few towns. He had been raised on a farm, in poverty, and lacked formal education. Although he passed the bar exam and practised successfully as a lawyer, his law was almost entirely self-taught and his knowledge of public affairs was acquired as a state assemblyman (1834–42) and as a captain of militia in the Black Hawk Indian War. He possessed nevertheless strong political ideas, grounded in his belief in the importance of popular self-government and developed in the speeches he made against the talented Stephen Douglas in the contest for the Senate in 1858. Lincoln, though without a good speaking voice, had remarkable powers of oratory, and his side of the Douglas-Lincoln debates, which he largely devoted to an attack on slavery as an institution, was widely reported and won him a national reputation. In the American party system, he began as a Whig; but when that historic party split over the issue of slavery, he joined, in 1854, the new Republican Party, in which, largely thanks to his reputation as a speaker, he secured in 1860 the nomination to stand as its presidential candidate. When elected, exclusively on Northern votes, he arrived in Washington without any direct knowledge of how government was administered; of the prosecution of war he had no knowledge whatsoever. Nevertheless, common sense and his powerful mind provided him with a foundation of well-judged fundamental ideas, which, soon after First Bull Run, he summarised when he wrote to Halleck to say, "I state my general idea of this war to be that we have the *greater* numbers and the enemy has the *greater* facility of concentrating forces upon points of collision (because of his interior lines); that we must fail, unless we can find some way of making *our* advantage an over-match for *his*; and that this can only be done by menacing him with superior forces at *different* points, at the *same* time; so that we can safely attack, one, or both, if he makes no change; and if he *weakens* one to *strengthen* the other, forbear to attack the strengthened one, but seize, and hold the weakened one, gaining so much."[2]

To turn this general idea into a practical plan of action required much thought and planning and the carrying of support in the cabinet and the higher ranks of the army. The difficulty there was that the army's higher ranks contained few officers who had any grasp of the necessities of war, let alone experience. Winfield Scott, the general in chief, was enfeebled by age and infirmity. Among the cabinet officers, some were competent and energetic men, particularly Edwin Stanton, secretary of war from January 1862, who was extremely efficient and a great prop and support to Lincoln, though he, if anything, was hyperactive. Salmon Chase, the Treasury secretary, a public financier of exceptional ability who raised the money to fight the war without debasing the currency, was highly capable and incorruptible but running the Treasury was a full-time job, though Lincoln loaded him with many others. Blair, the postmaster general, who belonged to a leading Washington political family, was notably efficient and fulfilled many functions beyond that of supervising the Federal postal system. Gideon Welles, secretary of the navy, was excellent at his job; but naval strategy, though vitally important to the Union's war effort, was not going to win the war on land. William Seward, secretary of state, who also acted as the cabinet's man of reason, was the nearest thing Lincoln possessed to a chief executive. He was sensible and highly capable and had the gift of talking Lincoln out of ill-judged schemes. Yet on none of these men could the president really rely for guidance. Many of them were possessed by rivalry and several could not prevent themselves from calculating their chances in the 1864 presidential campaign. They quarrelled and intrigued and manoeuvred for political position. Lincoln had to placate and cajole to keep them sweet and effective, meanwhile having to come to his own decision about what best could be done if the Union was to be restored.

Without dependable assistance from colleagues or soldiers, Lincoln sought guidance where it could be found. At the outset he set himself to reading books on military science, in which predictably he found little help. As it happens, however, the higher direction of war and the higher calculations in politics, at which Lincoln already excelled, ran through the same channels. It was along those lines that he proceeded. He quite quickly shed his belief, then very widely held, that the war could be ended by a single great victorious battle. Instead he came to see that the Union would have to achieve victory at many widely scattered points. He had the inspiration, however, to perceive that victories, if widely scattered in space, ought to be concentrated in time, since simultaneous defeats were very disheartening to an enemy. McClellan, who anyhow shrank from the test of the battlefield, was dilatory in his methods and allowed long intervals to elapse between inflicting blows on the enemy. Grant, by contrast, believed in "winning and moving on" to further victories. From exposure to the methods of McClellan and Grant, Lincoln learnt the vital importance of choosing the right subordinates, not simply those who could draft inspiring plans but those who also deliver results. He never learnt the importance of visiting armies in the field, from which he might have discovered a great deal. He never visited the armies in the West, as even Jefferson Davis managed to do. He did learn, and perhaps knew instinctively, the importance of war oratory. He may thus have influenced another war leader, Winston Churchill, who was undoubtedly inspired by Lincoln and who achieved much of his notoriety by his mobilization of the English language and sending it into battle, as the great American broadcaster Edward R. Murrow recognised in 1940. Churchill, like Lincoln, had great difficulty in identifying and appreciating good military subordinates. He was hampered, however, by his preconceptions about war, of which Lincoln had none, and he enjoyed war, while Lincoln and, so surprisingly, Grant detested it. Churchill, a hardened warrior who had himself shed blood, declined in his powers as leader as his war progressed. Lincoln, the military innocent, grew in stature and competence until eventually he came to dominate the war as no other individual did. At the same time, he had to deal with his generals, which in practice meant, for the first three years of the war, to tell them what to do, meanwhile having to come to his own decision about what best needed to be done if the Union was to be restored. Beyond his immediate political circle, moreover, he had to manage the wider politics of the war. Local, state, and presidential elections were all held in 1862–64 and the preservation of the Republican position in the contests required Lincoln's constant and close supervision.

McClellan's plan was given attention but failed to win support. It was effectively quashed by the opposition of Winfield Scott, who objected to it on both political and practical grounds. He thought it likely to provoke anti-Union sentiment in Kentucky and western Virginia; he believed the likely costs prohibitive.

Scott had already proposed his own scheme for the suppression of Southern rebellion, eventually to become known, at first disparagingly, as the Anaconda Plan. Called "Anaconda" after the great constrictor snake, its informing idea was to defeat the Confederacy by asphyxiation, with as little violence as possible, revealing the remarkable depth of the old warrior's understanding of war and of his country. Scott was not a doughface, a Northerner of Southern sympathies; he was an old-fashioned patriot, personally devoted to the new president, Lincoln, anxious to avoid a breach with the South if at all possible but, if it came about, determined to mend it by the threat or use of force if that was all that sufficed. Scott's plan advocated organising a close and efficient naval blockade of the Confederacy's seacoasts and major ports, so as to deny Southern exporters and importers the opportunity to pursue trade and to starve the rebellious government of the imported means of making war, should the crisis come to war. The Anaconda would also cripple the South's internal trade because, by taking the Mississippi as the principal military theatre and by closing it at its top and bottom, Cairo and New Orleans, it would interrupt the movement of goods north–south and also their distribution east–west along the great rivers' tributaries. He had correctly identified that the Southern heartland—Virginia, the Carolinas, Louisiana, Tennessee, Georgia, Mississippi, Alabama, and the appendage of Florida—formed a territorial bloc that could be surrounded by Union forces, land-based, naval, and riverine, denied access to the outer world, and then subjected to penetrative attack—he suggested by a striking force operating along the Ohio River—into the Southern heartland.

An element of Scott's Anaconda Plan would eventually provide one of the means by which the North overcame the South. The plan was never, however, formally adopted as the Union's principal strategy, and rightly not. It was too passive and *attentiste* in character. Scott cherished the belief, as did many other moderate Unionists, that, if given time to reflect, sufficient Southerners would repent of secession to collapse the Confederacy from within, perhaps as early as 1862. Time would tell, very little time in practice, that the Confederate idea was a great deal more robust than Northern optimists credited and that constriction alone would not bring the South to submit; only hard blows and victory in the field would restore the United States.

Between those who hoped to bring an end to the war by giving Southerners time and those who realised that the imperative was for action there could be the making of no agreed plan. Among the activists, by contrast, there was some common ground. McClellan agreed with Scott that the Southern rivers were vital strategic avenues.

Scott agreed with Lincoln that blockade would prove a vital means of weakening the South's ability to make war. It would take time, however, to construct a cohesive and comprehensive war plan from such slender common elements. Eventually, the achievement of effective blockade, combined with offensives along the rivers into the Southern heartland, would lay the foundation for Northern victory. Its consolidation, however, would also eventually entail a railroad war, contrived to deconstruct the Southern network, and the organisation of long-distance overland campaigns inside Southern territory.

At the outset, the need was to initiate the naval blockade, beginning at the places where the North could utilise an advantage, and to choose entry points into the South's great interconnected waterways, the Mississippi and its tributaries, the Ohio, Cumberland, and Tennessee rivers.

Advantage was given to the North in initiating a blockade by its undisturbed possession of several of the great fortresses built in the early years of the republic around the Atlantic and Gulf of Mexico coasts. The Founding Fathers and their successors had sought to make the United States not only separate from the Old World but impregnable to it. That required the building of fortifications around America's coasts to deny Europeans, particularly the British, whose navy commanded the ocean's surface. The young republic could not afford the cost of a navy to match Britain's. Forts were reckoned to be an alternative means of defence. It was probably an unwise decision financially. Forts are expensive. At the outset of the war the balance of coastal control was about equally divided between Union and Confederacy, though the latter, of course, had no foothold in Northern territory. The South held the coasts and harbours of Virginia, the Carolinas, Georgia, Florida, and the Gulf states, with strong points at Charleston, Savannah, and the mouth of the Mississippi, and enjoyed the use of the intracoastal waterway inside the Sea Islands of the Carolinas and Georgia, which provided a protected route for coastwise shipping and bases for blockade-running. The North, through its possession of Fortress Monroe, controlled Chesapeake Bay and dominated Norfolk; it also had important naval outposts off Florida and, at Fort Pickens, in the Gulf. Once the plan to impose a tight blockade became a campaign, in 1862–63, the dots on the map would be joined up and further important points seized. The geography of the coastal war was simple and the steps to be followed self-evident. Entry into the great Southern river system, by contrast, was by no means dictated by the geography, which was highly complex. The first steps would be tentative and the essential way forward identified only by trial and error.

A particular problem for Northern soldiers seeking to operate inside Southern territory was their ignorance of its terrain and the lack of accurate maps, often of any maps at all. North America, even by the mid–nineteenth century, was poorly surveyed and had not been surveyed systematically as, say, Britain and its Indian empire had been. The federal government maintained a coast survey, the navy a Hydrographic Office, and the army a Corps of Topographical Engineers to map areas of importance inside the United States. The U.S. Post Office also prepared route maps, showing post office towns and distances between them, while the Department of the Interior ran a Pacific Wagon Road Office, which recorded rail routes, as did, very accurately, the railroad companies themselves.[3] The results of their work, however, were piecemeal, as was that of state and county land surveyors, who delineated public and private landholdings and claims for settlement. Their maps were accurate, as far as they went. What lacked was an overarching survey, reconciling all observation and measurement inside a single system. That would have required a continent-wide triangulation, based on accurate measurement from an agreed set of intervisible points of prominence. The British had completed such a triangulation of India, the Great Survey of India, between 1800 and 1830, but it had been an enormous labour made possible only because the whole of India was settled and centrally administered. Such conditions did not apply in the United States, much of whose territory was still unexplored in 1861.

The need for comprehensive survey had been recognised as early as 1785 with the passage of the Land Ordinance, which required public land offered for private sale to be divided into square-mile lots laid out along an east–west baseline and a north–south meridian. Two factors militated against this leading to the production of accurate maps. The first was that squatters staked out claims first and awaited survey later. The second was that, while the delineation of latitude could be easily fixed by astronomical observation, that of longitude, which required triangulation, could not. As a result, comprehensive maps of the United States, of which several existed by 1861, were patchworks of survey which did not coincide.

Moreover, worthless land—swamp, mountain, upland, and areas of aridity, of which there was a great deal in the United States—did not merit survey; nor did worked-out areas of early settlement, abandoned by cultivators, of which there was already a surprising amount by 1861, notably the Wilderness of northern Virginia, scene of one of Grant's most difficult campaigns in 1864. The inadequacy of available maps infuriated and tantalised Civil War generals. Even Confederate generals, operating inside their own territory, could express frustration at the lack of maps showing ways through. Northern generals, usually campaigning inside Confederate territory, found fault with everything. Often they had no maps at all or had to make do with outdated maps bought in bookstores which did not show heights or gradients—contouring was a concept few American mapmakers had yet adopted—or stopped at county boundaries, so failing to depict the continuation of essential roads onto the next sheet. Other faults were lack of differentiation between strong and weak bridges, deep and shallow fords, and paved and unpaved roads, in each case information essential to the movement of armies. Inexplicable variation of place-names also misled. "Cold Harbor, Virginia, was sometimes called Coal Harbor and there was also a New Cold Harbor and a 'burned' Cold Harbor. Burned Cold Harbor was known by the locals as Old Cold Harbor. Many roads were known by one of two names: the Market or River Road; the Williamsburg or Seven Mile Road; the Quaker or Willis Church Road. To add to the confusion, there were sometimes other nearby roads with the same or similar names that ran in completely different directions." It would have been little consolation to Union generals, blundering about inside Confederate territory, to know that their opponents were often equally blind. Brigadier General Richard Taylor, son of former president Zachary Taylor, complained that "the Confederate commanders knew no more about the topography of the country than they did about Central Africa." Recalling the campaign in northern Virginia, he went on, "Here was a limited district, the whole of it within a day's march of the city of Richmond, capital of Virginia, and the Confederacy . . . and yet we were profoundly ignorant of the country, were without maps, sketches, or proper guides, and nearly as helpless as if we had been transferred to the banks of the Lualaba."[4]

Yet the course, flow, depth, and interconnection of rivers would become, during the western campaign of 1862–63, the most essential of all information sought by Union commanders. President Jefferson, who sponsored the Lewis and Clark transcontinental expedition to plot a route to the Pacific in 1804, had been keenly aware of the need to understand the riverine system of the United States. In 1809 he had speculated if "a river called Oregon interlocked with the Missouri." He probably meant what is today called the Columbia and Snake rivers, which do not "interlock" with the Missouri, but flow into the Pacific. The Missouri, however, does "interlock" with a whole network of waterways, the Mississippi, Ohio, Cumberland, and Tennessee, and their numerous tributaries, which even today dominate the human and economic geography of the entire United States, and in 1861, because of the primacy of steamboat transport and the termination of the railroads on the Mississippi's eastern bank, provided the most important arteries of strategic movement within the American theatre of war.

The difficulties of prosecuting the war west of the Mississippi did not derive principally from lack of cartographic information but from the disproportion of space to force. In Arkansas, New Mexico, and adjacent territories neither side had troops enough to form garrisons at key points, let alone stage decisive battles. Yet both had ambitions to control the Far West. To the Union it was national territory not to be surrendered to rebel hands. To the Confederacy it was a potential addition to their new country's extent which would bring prestige and open the promise of a way to the Pacific coast.

Supply was the crux of campaigning west of the Mississippi. The Union solved its problems, the Confederates did not, hence the Union's ability to hold on to the distant states and the Confederacy's failure. The whole of the campaign in the West, however, from the capture of Forts Henry and Donelson to the Chattanooga campaign of 1863, was a strategic anomaly, since the theatre of operations was so far from the main centre of power, Union and Confederate alike, that either side might have lost altogether the ability to sustain its war effort there. What the commanders on both sides had been taught at West Point should have deterred any one of them from the inclination to wage so awkward a campaign.

West Point orthodoxy was acquired from the teachings of the Swiss Napoleonic theorist Henri de Jomini. Jomini taught, among other things, the necessity of obedience to geometric rules, notably that a line of operations should lie at right angles to the base from which it was sustained. In that respect the war in northern Virginia was strictly Jominian. Both sides were squared-up to each other across the plain of the Chesapeake waterway and both concentrated their efforts at driving down it. There was, except for the recurrent effort to seize the Shenandoah Valley, no divergence from that narrow battleground. In the West, by contrast, it was difficult to define where, if at all, the base of operations lay. The axis of offensive ran, for the North, down the Mississippi, thereby determining that the South's defensive efforts must run up and along it. Neither side, however, had a firm base, as defined by major cities or economic centres, running at right angles across the line of operations. Indeed, any attempt to delineate the geometry of the war in the West on a map would produce a cat's cradle of deviations and crisscrossing lines and arrows. For the South, state boundaries, particularly those of Tennessee, imposed a certain symmetry. For the North, however, the whole theatre of the western war defied Jomini in any form. It lay in detachment from the main mass of Northern territory, and communication could be maintained only by following wide loops of river or rail lines. Indeed once the North's campaign left the Mississippi Valley, as it did in 1863, and began to burrow eastward, and then northward, into the Southern heartland, all Jominian principle was lost and the picture of the campaign could be kept in focus only within a general's mental perception, as it was so tenaciously first by Grant and then by Sherman. In a sense the North's ability to wage the war in the West was as much a triumph of the imagination as it was of logistics.

During 1863, in particular, Grant would teach himself, by laborious trial and error, exactly which waterways in the Mississippi Valley it was profitable to follow and which were not useful for military purposes. In 1861, however, learning the secrets of distant geography was a less pressing problem than organising the armies for war. It was not only the troops that had to be trained. So had the officers, staff officers as well as regimental officers; without efficient staff officers plans could not be given operational form. Yet staff officers were in 1861 the scarcest category of military personnel. A few veterans of the Mexican War, fifteen years earlier, remained in or had rejoined the ranks; otherwise only those officers who had served in the quartermaster general's or adjutant general's branches knew military procedure.

The American staff system, such as it was, derived from the British. The adjutant general's and quartermaster general's branches concerned themselves with personnel and supply matters, respectively; what would today be called operational matters were the responsibility of commanding generals and their attached officers. In European armies there were procedures and forms regulating communication between all staff branches and downwards to formations—corps, divisions, brigades—and units, the regiments. Corps and divisions did not exist in the pre-war American army; brigades were only just coming into being. No staff college existed to teach students routines or formalities. Mexican War veterans, and regulars who had seen service on the western frontier, were familiar with the paperwork of minor campaigning. No one, except McClellan and McDowell, who had been sent to see European armies, knew how large forces conducted themselves. The war, as a result, would be fought by commanders and staff officers who were learning on the job. The advantage would lie with the natural warriors, such as the Confederate Nathan Bedford Forrest, or those who learnt fastest, such as Ulysses Simpson Grant. Grant had the gift of fluent and rapid composition on paper, enabling him to write dozens of clear orders in an evening's work in his tent, as well as the ability to visualise terrain in his mind's eye. He also understood evolving technologies, particularly that of the telegraph, which he used with apparently effortless facility.

In July 1861 improvised armies and tentative plans would combine to usher in the war's first effort at decisive battle, at Bull Run in northern Virginia, to be called Manassas by the Confederates, after the railway junction nearest the field. It was not the first engagement of the war. There had been skirmishes at Fairfax Court House and Vienna, just across the Potomac from Washington, in June, and between June 3 and July 13, McClellan won small but striking victories in western Virginia at Philippi, Rich Mountain, and Carrick's Ford.

All three places lay on the western edge of the Allegheny Mountains, in territory farmed by Virginians quite different in outlook from those of the Tidewater on Chesapeake Bay. Few were rich and almost none were slave owners. They had long resented the domination of the state's politics by the plantation aristocrats and remained strongly pro-Union during the secession crisis. When in May McClellan's troops began to arrive from Ohio they received a warm welcome, not least from two Unionist Virginia regiments. The advance guard quickly captured the town of Grafton, on the Baltimore and Ohio Railroad, from which they advanced to Philippi on the Monongahela, lower down which lay the scene of General Edward Braddock's disastrous defeat in the Pennsylvania wilderness on the eve of the Seven Years' War a century earlier. Philippi was a trivial affair, in which few Confederates and no Northerners were killed, but it had the effect of prompting the leaders of the Unionist majority in western Virginia to repudiate secession and set up at Wheeling a "restored" government of Virginia on June 11. The Federal government shortly afterwards admitted two western Virginia senators and three representatives to

Congress. The legalities were doubtful, since constitutionally only by vote of a state legislature could a new state be formed from the territory of an existing one, a vote seceded Virginia certainly would not pass. In August, however, the Unionist convention which had set up the "restored" government met to agree to such a formation, subject to plebiscite. On October 24, the plebiscite took place and, despite a small turnout and widespread abstentions in pro-Confederate districts, convincingly endorsed "secession from secession." The creation of the new state of West Virginia—it might have been called Kanawha, after its principal river—was agreed to by the U.S. Senate in July and by the House of Representatives in December, and it was admitted to the Union in June 1863.

The Confederacy struggled hard to retain western Virginia within the undivided state. Immediately after the rout of Confederate forces at Philippi, Robert E. Lee, acting as Virginia's commander in chief, sent a small army under Robert S. Garnett to occupy the passes through the Alleghenies near Philippi. McClellan, who had ample numbers of Ohio volunteers, organised a counter-offensive, with a West Point near-contemporary, William S. Rosecrans, as his chief subordinate. His plan was to take Garnett in a pincer movement at Rich Mountain, which the Northerners, outnumbering their opponents nearly three to one, were well placed to do. In an event which would be replicated frequently in his subsequent career, McClellan failed on July 11 to reinforce Rosecrans's initial success, mistaking the sounds of victory for those of defeat. "There was," wrote Jacob Cox later, "the same overestimate of the enemy, the same tendency to interpret unfavourably the sights and sounds in front, the same hesitancy to throw in his whole force when he knew that his subordinate was engaged."[5] Garnett was able to disengage and withdraw. Such was his disarray, however, that on July 13 McClellan's pursuit force caught his rearguard at Carrick's Ford on the Cheat River and defeated it. Garnett was killed in the action, the first general of either side to lose his life in the war. An indirect casualty of the western Virginia campaign was Robert E. Lee. The setback, which led to the loss of the South's main lead deposits, brought him scorn in the newspapers and his transfer to superintend coast defence in the Carolinas.

Meanwhile, there had occurred another military episode, in the borderlands. St. Louis, Missouri, was the location of a Federal arsenal, dangerously situated in a state which contained a large secessionist minority. The arsenal's 60,000 firearms were coveted by the Confederate volunteers who had assembled and were drilling at Camp Jackson, so called after the secessionist governor, Claiborne Jackson. The regular officer commanding the small Union force guarding the arsenal, Captain Nathaniel Lyon, managed to smuggle 21,000 muskets across the Mississippi into Illinois but then set out to disband the secessionist militia. Surrounded at Camp Jackson, they surrendered without resistance. Civilian secessionists in the city, however, rioted when Lyon marched his prisoners through the streets, shooting began, and soon there were dozens of dead and wounded. The state legislature in Jefferson City voted to prepare Missouri for war, and it seemed likely that an internal civil war would break out. To avert it, Lyon met Jackson to negotiate a settlement, but the terms Jackson demanded incensed Lyon: Jackson would keep Confederate troops out of the state in return for Lyon excluding Union troops. Lyon threatened war on his own account and on June 16 occupied Jefferson City, at which the legislature fled to the southwest corner of the state, Lyon in pursuit. This sequence of events left Missouri effectively without government. The lack was supplied by the reconvening of the convention which had earlier voted to stay within the Union during the secession crisis. It appointed state officers who assumed power. The rumps of the legislature, under Jackson, responded by declaring secession after all, on November 3, leading to the recognition of Missouri as the twelfth Confederate state by the Richmond government on November 28. But secession never became effective. The remnants of the legislature were soon driven out of the state, which continued to be represented in the U.S. Congress by its pre-war senators and congressmen, while three out of four white Missourians who fought in the Civil War did so in Union blue. The Lyon-Jackson quarrel left a bitter domestic aftermath. Missouri was worse afflicted by neighbourly strife than any other state, and guerrilla warfare persisted between partisans of one side and the other even after 1865. Among the most notorious Confederate bushwhackers were Jesse James and his brother Frank, later to become celebrated as gunfighters in the sparsely settled West.

Lyon's Unionist victory in Missouri made him a national hero in the North, at least briefly; he was to be killed, as a brigadier general, in a final fight with the Confederate Missouri militia at Wilson's Creek, near Springfield (one of the twenty-four places called Springfield in the United States), on August 10. McClellan's small victories in western Virginia had also made him a national figure; they identified him in the eyes of both politicians and people as a coming man. It was on another general, however, that Northern eyes were fixed in early July 1861: Irvin McDowell, commanding the troops around Washington. Some were committed to the capital's defence, but a sufficient surplus existed to form a field army, to be marched against the enemy. McDowell could find about 35,000 troops for an offensive, to confront 20,000 under General Pierre Gustave Toutant Beauregard at Manassas. Beauregard came from the old French Acadian community in Louisiana, had served with distinction in the Mexican War, and in early 1861 had been superintendent of West Point, until removed because of his Southern sympathies. McDowell, an exact West Point contemporary of Beauregard, class of 1838, had also served in the Mexican War and been a West Point instructor. A large man, devoted to the table although a teetotaller, his experience had been exclusively as a staff officer. He had never commanded troops in the field and was soon to attract the reputation of a man for whom things never went right. In July 1861, however, he was as yet untested and he approached the challenge of action with confidence.

His base, at least, was secure. In the weeks since the firing on Fort Sumter a dense girdle of earthwork fortifications had been dug around Washington, on both banks of the Potomac River and on the Maryland shore of its eastern reach, enclosing Georgetown and Alexandria as well as the Federal capital, most of these earthworks stood on ground now occupied by the city's modern suburbs, reaching as far away as Falls Church. McDowell set up his headquarters in Robert E. Lee's pillared mansion above Arlington. The forts were garrisoned and were supplied with artillery. The surplus troops were encamped, ready to march forth to give battle with the enemy across the Potomac in northern Virginia.

McDowell submitted his plan of battle to Lincoln and the cabinet in the White House on June 29. Three days earlier the *New York Tribune* had published what would be remembered as one of the most influential editorials of the war, "On to Richmond." Many in the North believed that a single heavy blow would indeed open the way to Richmond and bring the end of the war. McDowell was less sanguine. He proposed only the mounting of an attack across the little river of Bull Run, a tributary of the Occoquan twenty-five miles west of Washington, designed to force an entrance into northern Virginia.

Beauregard's army was centred on Manassas Junction, where the Manassas Gap Railroad joined the Orange and Alexandria. To the north ran Bull Run, crossed by the Warrenton Turnpike, which led to

Alexandria over the Stone Bridge but was also fordable at six points: from left to right, Sudley Springs, Poplar Ford, Farm Ford, Lewis Ford, Ball's Ford, and Mitchell's Ford. The ground was higher on the southern side of the run, thus giving Beauregard an advantage. He had, however, the disadvantage of fewer numbers and fewer guns.

McDowell began his advance, with 34,000 men, organised in twelve brigades, on July 16. The inexperience of his troops and the lack of organisation in his supply column slowed his advance. Not until the early morning of July 21 was the head of his column at Centreville, a clapboard village three miles short of Bull Run. Beauregard's Confederates were drawn up, on the south bank of the run, on a front of about eight miles, from Sudley Springs to Mitchell's Ford, where there had been a preliminary skirmish on July 18.

McDowell's plan was to fix the centre of Beauregard's line by staging a strong demonstration at the Stone Bridge, where the Warrenton Turnpike crossed Bull Run, while sending the bulk of his army on a long looping march across country towards the ford at Sudley Springs, with the intention of crossing the river and enveloping Beauregard's left flank. Beauregard had now been joined by Joseph E. Johnston, bringing troops from Winchester in the Shenandoah Valley; here Johnston came under Beauregard's command, but control remained with Johnston for the time being. Most of his strength was on his right, near Mitchell's Ford, where there had been a preliminary skirmish on July 18, and his plan, insofar as it was arranged, was to attack McDowell's left, at the moment, though he did not know it, when McDowell would be attacking his right. There was, therefore, a mismatch of intentions. Moreover, though Beauregard stood on the defensive, he was outnumbered. The only difference in quality between the two sides was that, on the Confederate, such regular officers as were present were divided between all the volunteer regiments; whereas, on the Union side, they were, because of Winfield Scott's irrational prejudice against dispersing regulars, concentrated in McDowell's four regular units, an infantry battalion, a battalion of U.S. Marines, and two artillery batteries, commanded by Captains Ricketts and Griffin.

The first major battle of the Civil War began about nine o'clock in the morning of July 21 when Beauregard's blocking force at the Stone Bridge, a small collection of infantry, cavalry, and artillery units, was fired on by troops under the command of General Daniel Tyler. General Nathan Evans, the West Pointer in command at the bridge, correctly estimated that the firing was intended to detain rather than

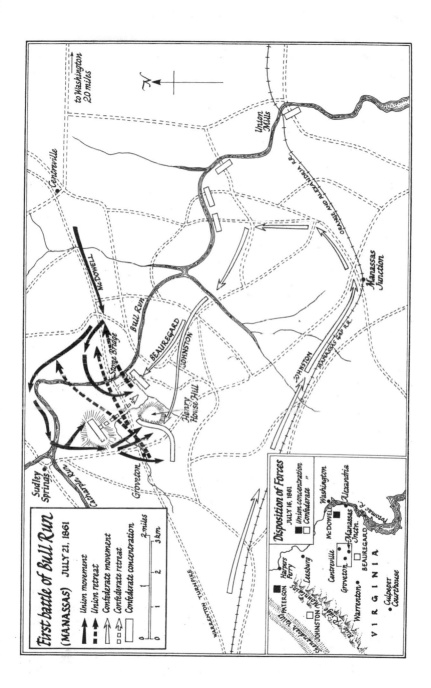

First battle of Bull Run
(MANASSAS) JULY 21, 1861

Union movement
Union retreat
Confederate movement
Confederate retreat
Confederate concentration

0 1 2 2 miles
0 1 2 3 km

to Washington
20 miles

Centreville

McDOWELL

Bull Run

Stone Bridge

Sudley Springs

Cub Run

BEAUREGARD

JOHNSTON

Henry House Hill

Groveton

WARRENTON TURNPIKE

MANASSAS GAP R.R.

JOHNSTON

ORANGE AND ALEXANDRIA R.R.

Union Mills

Manassas Junction

Disposition of Forces
JULY 16, 1861
■ Union, concentration
□ Union, concentration "
□ Confederate

Washington
Alexandria
McDOWELL
Manassas Junction
Centreville
Groveton
BEAUREGARD
Warrenton
Culpeper Courthouse

VIRGINIA

PATERSON
Harpers Ferry
Leesburg
JOHNSTON

Potomac

destroy him and, prompted by a signal from one of Beauregard's staff officers, Captain Edward Porter Alexander, who was observing the scene of action, decided to divide his force. Leaving four companies to watch the Stone Bridge, he took the rest northwards to oppose the Union advance across Sudley Springs. His two most substantial units were battalions from South Carolina and Louisiana.

Shortly after the Confederate units came into position, McDowell's advance guard appeared. It consisted of regiments from New Hampshire and New York and two from Rhode Island, supported by his two regular batteries, Ricketts's and Griffin's, and was commanded by General Ambrose Burnside. Burnside had difficulty manoeuvring his inexperienced troops into a line of battle; but eventually the correct formation was achieved and the regiments, supported by the regular batteries, began to knock the Confederates about. General Evans sent an urgent request for reinforcements. A brigade brought by Joseph E. Johnston from Harpers Ferry, consisting of the 6th North Carolina, the 4th Alabama, and the 2nd Mississippi, appeared, under the command of General Barnard Bee, was hurried forward and stemmed the tide, at least for a while.

Sensing stiffening Confederate resistance, McDowell sent orders to Tyler, commanding at the Stone Bridge, to increase the pressure. Tyler judged that pressure would be better applied elsewhere and, when a brigade under General William Tecumseh Sherman appeared, directed it to Farm Ford, just above the Stone Bridge. Sherman, West Point class of 1840, was destined to become one of the Civil War's most illustrious commanders. In token of his future eminence he now led his brigade forward across Bull Run, at a fordable point, and sent it up onto the high ground there dominating the battlefield, a slight rise crowned by a house owned by the Henry family.

The Henry House Hill was to be the focus of the battle of Bull Run's climax. Johnston was the first to recognise its importance. Impatient at Beauregard's fixation with enveloping McDowell's right, in mid-afternoon he suddenly announced, "The battle is there—I am going," and, jumping into the saddle, galloped his horse off to the scene of action. On arrival, he found that his subordinate General Thomas J. Jackson, commanding a brigade of Virginia troops which had previously served in the Shenandoah Valley, was drawn up on the summit. Jackson, West Point class of 1846, was a consummate tactician. He had so positioned his brigade that it stood on the hill's "military crest" and thus was visible to the Federal troops only when they had breasted the "false crest." Jackson's five Virginia regiments were supported by Hampton's Legion, a composite unit of South Carolina infantry and cavalry, under the higher command of General Bernard Bee. Not a man otherwise to be remembered, Bee spurred his horse forward as the Union troops appeared on the Henry House frontier, shouting to the South Carolinians, and other less resolute remnants of Beauregard's army who temporarily found comrades on the Henry House Hill, "Look! There is Jackson standing like a stone wall. Rally behind the Virginians!"[6]

Some did, enough to drive off Sherman's and other Federal formations and so to create a legend, that of "Stonewall Jackson." Stonewall, as he would forever afterwards be known, insisted that the sobriquet belonged to his brigade, which, indeed, was afterwards deemed the Stonewall Brigade by the Confederate government. Fighting raged around the Henry House all afternoon. McDowell himself appeared, to ascend the upper floor of the Henry House, in which the eighty-four-year-old Mrs. Henry had been killed by a Federal artillery round just before. Shortly after McDowell's appearance, the Federal forces, though still outnumbering their Confederate opponents, began to fall back. By late afternoon the retreat had become a full-scale rout.

There was no rational reason why McDowell's army should have collapsed as it did. Beauregard had been reinforced during the course of the afternoon's fighting, in part by a brigade brought by rail from the Shenandoah Valley, which had detrained directly onto the battle-field, an unprecedented event in warfare. The reinforcements had delivered counter-attacks into McDowell's columns deploying from beyond the Bull Run. The two regular batteries had been severely shaken by the close-range musketry of a blue-clad Confederate regiment, mistaken by the gunners as belonging to their own side. Jeb Stuart had delivered an effective cavalry charge, which had driven off the New York Fire Zouaves and completely disorganised the marine battalion, unsurprisingly as its men were raw recruits.

Nevertheless, none of these episodes amounted to a decisive act; nor indeed did anyone take a decision. When the firing broke out around the Henry House, Johnston had ridden there, but on arrival he had not taken effective control. Nor had McDowell, when, rather later, he arrived at the same place. Beauregard led a counter-attack up Henry House Hill, turning back a Federal column, after which the Union retreat became general. Exactly why, no one could tell. Thousands of soldiers were in motion, milling about this way and that. As many as 12,000 Federals, it was estimated, had lost their regiments. Fewer Confederates had fallen into disarray. That was probably the reason for the Confederate success, unorganised as it was.

By late afternoon the Warrenton Turnpike, leading back towards Alexandria and Washington, was jammed with soldiers, horses, and military transport, struggling to leave the field; many of the fugitives were possessed by the belief that Stuart's cavalry, any sort of cavalry, was at their heels. Intermingled with the soldiers were many civilians, who had come out by carriage that morning, with picnic lunches, to watch the battle, expecting a sort of pageant to unfold. They included at least ten congressmen and six United States senators. By evening they were anxious for supper, in safety. Civilian carriages found themselves wheel to wheel with artillery limbers and ammunition caissons in the press to get out of danger.

The Confederates were in scarcely better state. Many of their regiments had lost cohesion and individual soldiers were wandering about the rear of the battlefield in crowds, bereft of officers and not knowing what to do. Jefferson Davis, who had come up by train from Richmond, believed at first that he had arrived at the scene of a Southern defeat, and began trying to rally stragglers. The first man on his own side he met who believed a victory had been won was Stonewall Jackson, getting a minor wound dressed at a field hospital. "We have whipped them," he shouted. "They ran like sheep. Give me five thousand fresh men and I will be in Washington City tomorrow!"[7]

Jackson, uncharacteristically ebullient, exaggerated. Beauregard's army had not won a notable victory. It had merely avoided defeat, and by a comparatively narrow margin. It retained no capacity to pursue McDowell's shaken forces and none at all to take Washington. The line of the Potomac and the bridges over it were as secure in the aftermath of the battle of Bull Run as they had been on its eve. The line of metropolitan defence, indeed, lay farther forward. Centreville, a grandiose place-name for a collection of clapboard shacks, was garrisoned by several intact brigades under Colonel Theodore Runyon and were soon reinforced by unbroken elements of the Bull Run army, Blenker's brigade and Major George Sykes's battalion of regulars. Beauregard was anxious to get past Centreville. He never would.

Bull Run had substantially damaged both armies. Although a quarter of McDowell's army had escaped action during the day, and about a third of Beauregard's, 460 Northerners had been killed, 1,100 wounded, and more than 1,300 taken prisoner; the Confederates had lost 400 dead and 1,500 wounded, though almost no prisoners, the real token of their success. Bull Run was not only the first major battle of the war. It was also the first episode in an entirely new way of warfare, a struggle between beliefs fought by populations quite untrained to fight. Its result, so ambiguous militarily, served to strengthen passions on both sides. In Richmond and throughout the South, the news of Manassas, as it would be called there, was taken as that of a major victory, and so as encouragement to persist. Ordinary Southerners believed that their own inferior numbers had defeated a greatly superior force, a portent for the future and of eventual victory. In the North, the news dashed hopes but also stiffened resolve. An opening setback would, patriots thought, soon be succeeded by triumph. The justice of the Union's cause was a guarantee in itself that rebellion must be defeated.

Meanwhile, in Washington, Lincoln spent the aftermath of the battle contemplating means by which strategic ideals could be made into reality. He sketched out some bland desiderata—improving the training of troops at Fortress Monroe, strengthening the Federal occupation of Baltimore—and he outlined plans for offensive action against the South, by firmly securing the railroad at Bull Run and opening a front on the upper Mississippi. More significantly, he reemphasised the importance of strengthening the blockade; and he turned his mind towards change of command at the top. Although he had neither reproached nor quarrelled with McDowell, he had formed doubt about him—too cautious, insufficiently decisive. As a replacement his thoughts now focused on the only Union general to have as yet achieved any sort of success against the Confederate army, George McClellan, the victor of the little battles in West Virginia in early July. On July 22 he telegraphed McClellan to report to Washington.

It was no arbitrary matter that the first clash of arms in the Civil War took place on the seaward frontier of South Carolina, a spot where the armed force of a wholly secessionist state was confronted by the military power of the Union at Fort Sumter. Elsewhere, the confrontation was by no means so clear-cut nor division of opinion and people so pronounced. The battle lines were least clearly drawn in the border states, where slaves were least numerous if the state counted as a slave state, and votes for secession least concentrated and numerous. Some border states such as Kansas, Missouri's western neighbour, were not secessionist at all, though Southern immigrants had brought slaves into the state during the troubled 1850s. Virginia, almost a northern state geographically, was secessionist by majority, but the northwestern counties were only thinly slaveholding and could not be relied upon to support the state government in a vote to remain within or leave the Union. Kentucky, Tennessee, and Missouri were obviously divided, containing fair-sized slave populations but few large slave owners among their electorates. Maryland was thought to be Southern in sentiment but was not wholly a slave state. Tiny Delaware, though containing slaves, was too overshadowed by its Northern neighbours to risk secession.

The crux of the border state dilemma—whether to hold firm to the Union or to follow its slave-owning factions South—lay in Tennessee, Kentucky, and Missouri. Tennessee, whose eastern half was solidly pro-Union, was led into secession by its governor on June 8; it nevertheless provided the Union with large numbers of volunteers and was one of the states which had named regiments in both armies. Lincoln was particularly tender towards Tennessee, and his strategy in the western theatre was to be heavily influenced by his desire to restore the state to the Union. Kentucky was perhaps the most divided of all the states, so much so that the governor, Beriah Magoffin, declared neutrality, as if the state were a sovereign entity beyond the United States (as, of course, extreme secessionists held to be the case throughout the country), and negotiated with Washington and Richmond as long as he could. In the end Richmond overplayed its hand and invaded Kentucky, which prompted the legislators to ask for the Union's protection. It thereby remained within the Union, though a Richmond-sponsored state government maintained a precarious existence throughout the war, allowing secessionists to count the state as part of the Confederacy. Kentuckians volunteered for both armies, though in the war's aftermath citizens of the state began to display a curious sympathy for the Southern cause, prompting the judgement that Kentucky "seceded after the war was over."

The secessionist crisis took its worst form in Missouri, since there it broke into open warfare of a costly and vicious sort. The low-level pre-war bickering in Kansas, which had resulted in so many killings between neighbours, had bled over into Missouri before 1861, leaving a legacy of local hatreds, which became entangled with pro- and anti-slavery sentiment, since Missouri was a cotton state with a sizable slave population. Kansas-style raiding and killing began again in Missouri on news of Fort Sumter. (Lincoln had appointed the fort's commander, Robert Anderson, to command the Union militia in Kentucky after his return from Charleston.)

After Nathaniel Lyon saved the St. Louis arsenal, there was an attempt to avert civil war in Missouri, one of many being made at several points on the borders, and indeed within the South, at the time. The Union commander, the Southern-born brigadier general William S. Harney, negotiated an agreement by which General Sterling Price agreed not to use his troops in any way that would exacerbate tensions. Price, an officer of volunteers, had volunteered his services to Governor Jackson. Lyon and Congressman Francis Blair at once decided to view the Price-Harney agreement as likely to accelerate secession and not deter it, and, with presidential authorisation, Lyon quickly removed Price from command, which he assumed himself. He and Blair then met Governor Jackson and General Price in St. Louis to agree on terms for the government of the state. Lyon demanded the right of free movement for Union troops throughout Missouri. The governor refused and the conference dissolved into quarrelling. In the aftermath Jackson sent for Confederate troops from Arkansas, Louisiana, and Texas. Their arrival stimulated the clashes between pro- and anti-secessionists which had already broken out across the state. In early July, the Unionists of two counties in the north of the state had been driven from their homes; Jayhawkers, anti-slavery activists, from Kansas appeared in western Missouri to attack secessionists. Lyon now sponsored a state convention which declared the governorship and other state offices vacant and installed a firmly Unionist governor in power, and moved the state capital from Jefferson City to St. Louis.

This brought the simmering civil war in Missouri to a head. Both sides began to concentrate troops. Lyon marched out to challenge Price at Wilson's Creek, near Springfield, Missouri, in early August. What followed, though trivial as a military engagement and contributing very little to the outcome of the war as a whole, was nevertheless highly significant, since it displayed features which were to mark battles in the Civil War wherever and whenever they were fought. It was bitterly fought, leaving high casualties on both sides, and wounding many who escaped death; yet despite its cost in human life, it was militarily inconclusive, leaving the issue of whether North or South dominated the state of Missouri to be decided in the future. Wilson's Creek was both a typical Civil War battle and the precursor of many to come.

Lyon, who commanded the concentration of Union troops, had been campaigning about Missouri, fighting skirmishes here and there when he encountered the enemy. He had now identified the main rebel body near Springfield, and determined to attack it in its encampment near Wilson's Creek. His troops numbered 6,200, 500 of which were Home Guards with almost no training and deficient in equipment. Better trained and better armed were the rest, organised into three brigades. The first was composed of regular soldiers of the 1st Infantry and a battalion of the 2nd Missouri Infantry, and the second of regular soldiers of the 2nd U.S. Infantry and some local recruits. The third, commanded by Colonel Franz Sigel, a political appointee but one with experience of European warfare, consisted of Missouri volunteers. The little army also contained several companies of regular U.S. cavalry and several batteries of artillery, including the regular Battery F of the 2nd U.S. Artillery. When deployed for action in the first day of battle at Wilson's Creek, August 10, 1861, Sigel counted his men to number 1,118 with six pieces of artillery.

The enemy considerably outnumbered the Union forces, numbering about 10,175 with fifteen pieces of artillery, organised as two divisions, including regiments from Missouri, Arkansas, Texas, and Louisiana, mainly infantry but some cavalry. The whole was commanded by Brigadier General Ben McCulloch, assisted by Major General Sterling Price. The countryside was rolling hills, broken in places by ravines, with Wilson's Creek running between high banks. There was a sprinkling of trees, which in places grew thick.

Lyon advanced his troops to within sight of the enemy encampment during the evening of August 9, while Sigel led his men on a circuitous flank march to arrive in the enemy's rear by daylight on August 10. The weather was mild but drizzly. Lyon's plan was to mount a pincer attack on the Confederates. He would attack against their camp from the north, Sigel from the south. Though the Confederates greatly outnumbered the Unionists, they were almost wholly untrained and very poorly equipped. Most carried only fowling pieces or old flintlock muskets, while most of the Union men had percussion rifles.

Lyon waited until the sound of firing from the south and the flash of rifle and artillery fire signalled that Sigel had opened his attack. Lyon then advanced down the west side of Wilson's Creek, driving off a Confederate cavalry force, which retreated to a ridge that would become known as Bloody Hill. When Lyon's men reached the crest of the ridge, however, they were taken under fire by the Pulaski artillery, located on a ridge across the creek. This intervention allowed Price to organise a firing line on Bloody Hill.

Sigel, hearing the sound of action, had meanwhile turned his

Abraham Lincoln, president of
the United States, 1861–65

Jefferson Davis, president of
the Confederate States, 1861–65

General Thomas "Stonewall" Jackson, "The Sword of the Lord"

General George McClellan, commander of the Union armies, 1861–62

Former slaves, ca. 1862

Company E, 4th U.S. Colored Infantry, 1863

Zouave Company, 14th Pennsylvania Infantry

A Springfield percussion rifle-musket, ca. 1857

A cavalry repeating carbine, ca. 1855

Flag Officer (Admiral) David Farragut, the captor of New Orleans, 1862

Officers of the USS *Monitor*, posed before revolving turret

The Confederate ram *Stonewall*, 1865. A typical warship of the inland waterways.

Above: Improvised Union hospital, Savage's Station, near Richmond, during the Seven Days' Battles. *Below:* Basic amputation set of the type that would have been used in the field by the North.

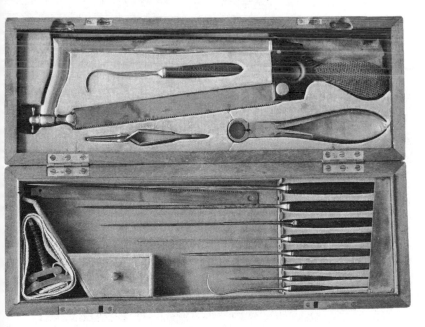

Confederate dead in ditch at Antietam, right wing

Dead Confederate infantrymen in the Devil's Den, aftermath of Gettysburg,
July 1863. The photograph was probably posed.

artillery against the Confederate encampment and driven its occupants into panic-stricken rout. He then advanced northward to join in the battle for Bloody Hill. By 6:30 a.m. the fighting on Bloody Hill was bitter and intensifying. Nathaniel Lyon, mounted and in the heat of the action, ordered infantry under Captain Joseph Plummer to the east of Wilson's Creek to protect the Union left flank. Plummer saw the effect the fire of the Pulaski battery was having on Plummer's comrades and advanced to take it under fire themselves. McCulloch responded by sending two infantry regiments to reinforce the rebels in the centre of the battlefield. They engaged the enemy in a cornfield to the north of Bloody Hill. The Union troops retreated from the cornfield and retired across Wilson's Creek, a move which allowed the Confederates to concentrate all their strength against the Union line on Bloody Hill. Sigel then suffered a calamitous setback when he mistook an advancing regiment of Louisiana troops for the Union 1st Iowa Infantry, which, as was common in this early stage of the war, was still wearing gray militia uniforms. Confused by the attack of what they took to be friendly forces, the Union party broke and ran. The Confederates now massed all their efforts against Lyon and his men on Bloody Hill. There were three Confederate attacks during the next two hours. Lyon, who displayed reckless courage throughout the battle, was slightly wounded early on and unhorsed, but remounted and continued to encourage his men, waving his hat and shouting orders. Then he was hit in the chest by a minié ball and killed. Soon after, Price, in overall Confederate command, organised his units, about 6,000 strong, into a single line a thousand yards long and advanced to engage the surviving Union troops. They were supported by artillery and came as close to the enemy as twenty feet, deluging them with continuous fire.

The battle line by this stage was enveloped in a dense cloud of smoke, a common result of heavy musketry on Civil War battlefields, which explains why infantry continued to fire while under heavy fire themselves: they simply could not see the enemy and so were sheltered from the psychological effect of close-range musketry. The Union resisted so stoutly that despite the death of their heroic leader and the hail of musketry they pushed the Confederates back. Shaken and badly depleted in numbers, however, they were unable to consolidate their line and, as the Confederates disengaged to regroup, began to retreat to the north. They did not stop until they had reached Springfield.

By keeping possession of the ground, the Confederates could claim

Wilson's Creek as a victory. The intrepid Lyon and Sigel had, however, unhinged their position in Missouri, and the Union was able to retain possession of the state and its state government even though the Confederacy appointed a puppet regime and admitted a rump of representatives to the Confederate Congress.

The Union lost 223 killed, 721 wounded, and 291 missing, totalling 1,235, at Wilson's Creek, out of 5,400 engaged, about 20 percent of those present. The Confederates lost 265 killed, 800 wounded, and 30 missing, a total of 1,095 out of 10,175 present, about 10 percent of those present. Compared to the bloodbaths of the east, such as Fredericksburg and Chancellorsville, Wilson's Creek was not a costly battle. As a human experience, however, it was horrifying, and it exhibited features which were to be repeated on many battlefields throughout the Civil War, including a high proportion of casualties among senior officers. Besides Lyon, the first Union general (he had just been promoted) to be killed in the war, the Union also had two colonels wounded; the equivalent Confederate figures were one colonel killed, one mortally wounded, one brigadier general and three colonels wounded.

CHAPTER EIGHT

McClellan Takes Command

I T IS NOT ENTIRELY FANCIFUL to characterise George Brinton McClellan as the Patton of the Civil War Union army. Like Patton, he was a handsome man, soldierly in appearance and insistent on the military dignity he thought his due. Like Patton, he enjoyed the social assurance brought by superior upbringing; the McClellans were not rich as the Pattons were, but McClellans's father was a distinguished Philadelphia physician and the family was respected in the city. The younger McClellan had been educated at a Philadelphia prep school and had been for two years at the University of Pennsylvania, a future bastion of the Ivy League, where he had excelled at the classics and foreign languages. He had, however, always wanted to be a soldier, an ambition which brought him to West Point in 1842, to join what would, before the class of 1915, become the most renowned in the academy's history, the class of 1846. Among his classmates were George Pickett, of Pickett's charge, Ambrose Hill, and Stonewall Jackson. None of these stood out, however, as McClellan did. Ranked by merit second in his class, he was regarded from the start by his contemporaries as the coming man. "The ablest man in the class," a classmate judged; "we expected him to make a great record in the army, and if opportunity presented, we predicted real military fame for him."[1] His early military career bore out his promise. In the Mexican War of 1846 he was twice awarded brevet rank, promise of future promotion, and in the aftermath he was selected to travel to the "seat of war" in Europe, the Crimea, where France and Britain were fighting Russia to prevent it destroying the Turkish Ottoman Empire, to report on developments in conflict between the great military powers. The appointment was a real distinction for McClellan, since the United States armed forces were certainly not in the forefront of modernity; American citizens, moreover, as yet rarely found the opportunity to travel abroad. McClellan proved a keen observer of the Crimean fighting and delivered a report which impressed his superiors. Then the promising young officer announced a divergence from what seemed a certain if laborious career of military advancement. He resigned his commission and became chief engineer and vice president of the Illinois Central Railroad Company. To friends and family it should not have been an unexpected move. In the 1850s, railroads were the most dynamic sector of America's explosively expanding economy. Railroads promised, as they shortly would, to unify physically the United States. Any young man who could offer competence in the skills necessary to make railroads work could command his own terms. McClellan was such a young man.

He was an engineer, trained in the West Point school of engineering, then the foremost centre of technical learning in the United States and one of the few of its kind in the world. Those that did exist—the Royal Military Academy at Woolwich in England, the École Polytechnique in Paris—were military establishments, since technology was only just beginning to escape from its identity as a tool of war-making. Fortunately for McClellan, the West Point engineering professors, like their European counterparts—the Woolwich professor was Michael Faraday—drew the boundaries of their subject widely beyond the traditional limits of the attack and defence of fortresses. McClellan, thanks to such West Point professors as William Bartlett, who stood in the forefront of his discipline, had imbibed a full scientific and technical education, fitting him to occupy any of the executive positions in engineering that America's mid-century industrial revolution had brought into being. By 1861 the Illinois Central was not the only railroad to which McClellan had contributed his services. He was, at the outbreak of the Civil War, a formidable contender for advancement to high command in the conflict embracing his country, a trained military engineer, an experienced combatant, and a corporate executive of proven experience. Little wonder that within weeks of the war's outbreak McClellan should have been promoted major general of U.S. volunteers and appointed to command in West Virginia.

McClellan was one of the first West Pointers to attain general officer rank. Though by 1860 the U.S. officer corps was eight-tenths filled by West Pointers, none had yet been promoted above colonel. The old guard—the seniors of the Mexican War, the Seminole Indian Wars, even the War of 1812—still dominated the high command and were reluctant to admit the book-learning boys of the academy to equality.

Only the coming of war, and the sudden need for commanders of brigades and divisions and for staff officers, unfroze the block. Few were promoted to such command as quickly as McClellan. He owed the acceleration to the fact that no other Union commander had yet achieved success in the field, though it should be noted that he was not present at any of the three battles for which he was so rapidly celebrated. William Howard Russell, the London *Times* correspondent who arrived fresh from the Crimea and had formed close acquaintance with experienced field commanders, dismissed McClellan in an early despatch as "a little corporal of unfought fields."[2] The gibe was unfair but stated a valuable warning to American enthusiasts for quick victories. Winfield Scott, the only American soldier with personal knowledge of how victory was achieved, was particularly concerned to quash hopes of early triumph. In a note added to his endorsement of McClellan's first plan of action, he warned against the "great danger now pressing upon us—the impatience of our patriotic and loyal Union friends. They will urge instant and vigorous action, regardless, I fear, of consequences."[3]

It was the demand for instant action, "On to Richmond," which had led to the debacle of Bull Run. The Union defeat had reversed the moral climate of the war. Before Bull Run, it was the South which had, by its own estimation, lain under threat, though bravado prevented it from admitting so. After Bull Run it was Washington, not Richmond, that was threatened. A strategic rationalist, surveying the scene, would have thought otherwise. Despite the proximity of the Confederate line, advanced from Bull Run to Centreville and overlooking the Potomac, the South lacked the force on the ground to capitalise on the advantage it had gained. On the evening of Bull Run itself, Winfield Scott dismissed all panic rumours that the Confederates were at the gates. To a staff officer who brought in a report that Arlington, Washington's southern suburb, had been occupied and that the Confederate vanguard would soon be in the capital itself, he burst out, "We are now testing the first fruits of a war and learning what a panic is. We must be prepared for all kinds of rumours. Why, Sir, we shall soon hear that Jefferson Davis has crossed the Long Bridge at the head of a brigade of elephants."[4] Scott, hyperbole apart, was making a valid and considered point. The Confederacy did not have the force necessary to invade the North—not yet at least—and the Union's proper business was to set unfounded anxiety aside and search for means to carry the war to the enemy.

McClellan, bursting with the enthusiasm of the newly appointed favourite, arrived in Washington with a plan for winning the war without delay. Lack of delay was a concept very popular in the North at the outset of the rebellion. Nobody, including the president, though he harboured realistic fears, wanted to contemplate a long war. Few in the North liked the idea of serious fighting either. General Scott had convinced himself at the outset and sought to persuade others that, if subjected to the discomforting pressures of blockade and threat, the pro-Unionists in the South, whose numbers he maximised, would yield so that the Union could be restored without grievous bloodshed. McClellan, a veteran of war on two continents, was sufficiently realistic to accept that Scott's vision of reconciliation without conflict could not be assured. He accepted that battle was a necessary means to suppressing rebellion. The plan he brought to Washington envisaged, therefore, operations on a huge scale. It was a bad plan—that is universally admitted in retrospect—too diffuse, insufficiently ruthless. Nevertheless, as Sherlock Holmes might have said, it had points of interest. The first of these was that it included a maritime dimension. The second was that it cast a very wide strategic net, revealing an appreciation of the geographic factor in war-making on the North American continent that did McClellan considerable intellectual credit. McClellan proposed a seaborne advance towards Charleston, South Carolina, and into Georgia. The amphibious operation should be combined with a drive from the Midwest, based on securing firm possession of the Ohio and upper Mississippi rivers down the Great Kanawha Valley into Virginia. The Great Kanawha River is one of the few which crosses the Appalachian chain; it rises in North Carolina and feeds the Ohio River. On it stands Charleston, capital of what today is West Virginia. Physically the Great Kanawha is a major waterway, but in the nineteenth century the terrain it flowed through was undeveloped, with few towns or roads and no railroads. McClellan's choice of the Great Kanawha as an axis is difficult to understand. McClellan wished to combine the Great Kanawha offensive with another from Kansas and Nebraska down the line of the Missouri and Mississippi rivers, directed at the South's interior and eventually at Texas. Strategically none of this was to be faulted. What McClellan did not explain to Scott, or to Lincoln, was where he would establish his base of operations or, more critically, how he would stock it with troops, munitions, and supplies.

Lincoln and Scott, though at first apparently approving of McClellan's plan, did not actually adopt it, or make available the resources that would have set it in train. This left the Anaconda Plan, which Scott had proposed in early May, to confine the Confederacy by blockading the seacoasts and controlling the Mississippi River. Economically, the Anaconda Plan was correctly conceived and practically feasible. The North, because it controlled most of the U.S. Navy's ships and men, and almost all American shipbuilding yards, was in a position to close the South's exits to the sea quite quickly; because river craft were largely Northern-owned, the Union was also well placed to take control of traffic on the great waterways. Once it did so, the South's great exporting capacity, in which it took such understandable pride, would be rendered irrelevant. Four million bales of cotton, an enormous store of wealth, would lose all value if they could not be shifted from the warehouses. At the outset of the war, some in the South persuaded themselves that it was to the Confederacy's advantage that the supply of cotton to the world market should be interrupted. The resulting slump in the manufacturing industry of the north of England and of France would, so they believed, oblige Unionist moderates to urge acceptance of secession on the Federal government and the South's powerful foreign trading partners to recognise her independence. These beliefs were to be proved wrong. Cotton starvation did cause a slump in the European mills, but so strongly did the millworkers support the anti-slavery cause that economic distress did not translate into political protest. Mill owners, and the propertied generally, were more sympathetic to the South; there was still sufficient resentment at the rebellion of the thirteen colonies for the old-fashioned to take pleasure at seeing republicans in difficulty. Nevertheless, the power of the anti-slavery cause, which Britain had virtually made its own in the first half of the century, national pride in the success of the Royal Navy in suppressing the slave trade, and simple common sense about the conduct of foreign policy proved the decisive factors. The Foreign Office, though much lobbied by Southern representatives, held out against granting recognition of Confederate independence.

Diplomatically, therefore, the Anaconda Plan, when instituted, did its work. The Mississippi campaign, to which it gave rise, by the successive capture of Cairo, Memphis, and, at the river's mouth, New Orleans, bisected the South and isolated its western half from the Dixie heartland. Explaining the object of his scheme to Lincoln on May 3, Scott wrote that his intention was to "clear out and keep open this great line of communication . . . so as to envelop the insurgent states and bring them to terms with less bloodshed than by any other plan."[5] This observation was highly characteristic of Scott. A man who had won a war, he had no need to look for means to prove his own martial virtue. In his eyes McClellan's plan was defective because it required great offensives to be launched into the South, which he rightly doubted would work, but which he also correctly anticipated would kill many whom he preferred should be kept alive. Alas, Scott's plan, for all its virtues, was defective also. It was as if Adam Smith had set out to practise strategy rather than economics. An unseen hand was to achieve the outcome desired by the commander, without the intervention of any of the unkind apparatus of war. Notable in Scott's Anaconda Plan was the omission of any mention of battle. Key points were to be captured, waterways controlled without apparently provoking any reaction from the enemy. The territory of the South was to be bisected without Confederate protest. Scott's estimable desire to avoid bloodshed between fellow citizens would apparently be shared by the enemy. Such was certainly not the case. The South was bursting with enthusiasm for a fight, partly to get the war over and won, partly because it longed to trounce the inept and effete Yankees. Nevertheless, the Anaconda Plan did have the merit of presenting to Lincoln an alternative to McClellan's schemes for operations in Virginia and of alerting him to the strategic importance of the Mississippi.

The West and the Midwest troubled Lincoln. As theatres of Confederate offensive operations they posed no great danger to the Northern heartland, but the risk that their divided populations might be swung into the Southern camp, with the loss of prestige and Northern morale that would follow, certainly nagged at him. He correctly believed, moreover, that the Kentucky-Missouri-Tennessee bloc offered a base from which successful invasions of Virginia and its neighbours might be launched. The first appointee to command in the West, John Frémont, Republican candidate for president in 1856, soon had to be replaced. Though famous in the United States as "the Pathfinder" because of his pre-war exploits as an explorer of western territories, and though a regular officer, he lacked both experience of and talent for war. He was also a fervent abolitionist and as commander of the Western Department made it one of his first acts, in August 1861, to free all slaves belonging to rebels in Missouri. But immediate emancipation was not Union policy, since many, including Lincoln, believed that it would alienate pro-Union sympathy in the border states. After Frémont's removal, McClellan—who had been named general in chief in succession to Scott, whom illness and McClellan's disregard had brought low—divided the Western Department into two, appointing Don Carlos Buell to command eastern Kentucky and Tennessee, Henry Halleck to command the rest. Buell had a high reputation in the pre-war army for efficiency. Halleck had been McClellan's chief rival for command of the Army of the Potomac. Neither was to display great practical talent, either in the coming campaign in the West or later.

Unfortunately for both, it was at this point in December 1861 that Lincoln and McClellan began to press them into activity. McClellan was himself under pressure to institute a long-delayed advance into Virginia across the old Manassas battlefield, while Lincoln, who also wanted action by McClellan, was anxious that Buell and Halleck should coordinate their movements with a view to liberating eastern Tennessee and its anti-Confederate population. Lincoln hoped that both Knoxville and Nashville could be taken. He was downcast when Buell and Halleck alike confessed to lacking sufficient strength to undertake or cooperate in either operation. The western generals' incapacity did not dishearten only Lincoln. McClellan had looked to Buell to make a move in Kentucky that would ease his own advance into Virginia, the operation he had been promising to Lincoln for the past several months. McClellan's Virginia action was so long considered and consequently so much postponed that eventually doubt grew, in the cabinet and the newspapers (since the secret, never well concealed, leaked out) whether McClellan was serious in his intentions. Uncertainty meanwhile grew also within McClellan over the likely success of his offensive. This was the first manifestation of what would be revealed as his disabling defect as a commander: readiness to take counsel of his fears. It is probable that had McClellan mobilised his resources in August or September, even as late as October, he could have brushed aside the Confederates defending the route south to Richmond and achieved a respectable advance. By November, however, he had begun to invest the enemy at Manassas with force they did not possess. He had a bad chief of intelligence, the head of the Pinkerton Detective Agency, and he compounded the errors of intelligence by those of his imagination. Soon he was estimating Confederate strength at over 100,000, and as he did so, he began to plead for reinforcements, disclaiming the possibility of taking action against such superior numbers.

Since McClellan never did mount a Manassas operation, it seems probable that he never would have. Yet the Virginia offensive did not merely fizzle out. Instead it was replaced by another, far more ambitious, which came into being in a strangely indirect way. In late November, when alone with the Army of the Potomac's chief of engineers, General John Barnard, McClellan mentioned that he had an idea for capturing Richmond. He would embark the Army of the Potomac at Washington and take it down Chesapeake Bay to the mouth of the Rappahannock River and then march it overland to Richmond, which he calculated he could seize before the Confederates at Manassas had time to reach the capital. It was a typically McClellanesque scheme for achieving a large result without taking a large risk, such as a major battle fought at a distance from a secure Union base. The idea grew and was eventually adopted, with strange results. What was strangest, however, about the "Urbana Plan," as it was initially called, after the place at which McClellan proposed to debark, was how he had hit upon it in the first place. Neither Scott, Lincoln, nor any other Union commander had proposed any amphibious element in operations designed to defeat the South. There was no amphibious tradition in the American way of warfare. British seapower had been little used in the deployment of the king's armies against the rebels during the War of Independence. The United States had scarcely employed its navy in the campaign against Mexico in 1846, which had been fought exclusively on land. Wherever, then, did McClellan derive his scheme for a large-scale waterborne descent onto the approaches to the Confederate capital? Given his cautious and highly conventional military outlook it was a most improbable adventure for him to advocate.

The answer may lie in his European experience. When McClellan observed the conduct of the Crimean War, fought by Britain and France to deter Russia from destroying the Turkish empire, he saw that the main difficulty facing the Anglo-French war effort was the inaccessibility of the tsar's empire. Though Russia could be invaded through eastern Europe, France and Britain had no bases or allies there. That forced them to look elsewhere, which meant by seeking points of entry around Russia's coastline. Here the similarity with the Confederates, which perhaps struck McClellan, may be perceived. Russia's enormous size equates to that of the South; indeed, the comparison is often made. But just as the South was protected by wide oceanic barriers backed by extensive mountain chains with areas of arid land and huge internal waterways, Russia was almost entirely cut off from the outside world by frozen seas. Climatically Russia was landlocked. The Anglo-French strategists puzzling as to how to get at their enemy fixed eventually on only three points at which it could be attacked. One was in the Baltic, itself very difficult of access. The second was on its Pacific coast, north of Japan, where Russia had naval bases in the Kamchatka Peninsula. The difficulty with both the Baltic and Pacific theatres as scenes of action was that their hinterlands were unsuitable for conventional ground operations and, in the case of the Pacific region, far from any possessions of value to the Russian government. Those considerations caused the allies eventually to choose the remaining point of entry, the Crimean Peninsula in the Black Sea. As a target area, it too had disadvantages, since the Crimean Peninsula connected badly with the Russian mainland and contained only one place of value, the port city of Sebastopol. Nevertheless, it could be attacked and so, there being little other choice, was selected by the allies for their debarkment. Having established a base on the west shore of the Black Sea, they concentrated their fleets and expeditionary forces and began the invasion. Its outcome, which resulted in the British and the French becoming drawn into an unsuccessful siege of Sebastopol, ought, had the Crimea indeed been McClellan's inspiration and had he reflected more deeply on its implications, to have warned him against initiating the Urbana Plan.

Yet the attractions of resort to an amphibious solution of his problem look obvious, given what we know of McClellan's exposure to the Crimean expedition. McClellan felt himself blocked on the land route to Richmond, perhaps through his own overestimation of the enemy's strength, perhaps because of the aura of defeat that hung about the Manassas region. Positively, Chesapeake Bay, which would be the axis of the Army of the Potomac's advance, was a body of water offering copious possibilities to an imaginative commander. On a dull coastline, which America's Atlantic shore is, being low-lying, generally unindented, and much choked with barrier islands and swamps, the Chesapeake is a fascinating complex of subordinate bays, peninsulas, and estuaries. Its proximity to the Appalachian chain, which collects the rainfall from the Atlantic, means that a very large number of rivers and lesser waterways flow across the levels of northern Virginia and Maryland to empty into the Chesapeake at dozens of outlets. Most flow parallel to one another, infuriatingly from a military point of view, since south of Washington the overland route to Richmond is crossed every twenty miles or so by a water barrier, such as the wide Potomac itself, running down from Harpers Ferry, at the head of the Shenandoah Valley, but also the Rappahannock, the Mattapony, the Chickahominy, the

Appomattox, the James, and the York, many fed by smaller streams which, when confronting an army on the march, prove formidable obstacles. In combination, the feeder streams of Chesapeake Bay make it one of the most easily defensible and therefore militarily difficult regions for offensives anywhere in the Northern Hemisphere; little wonder that McClellan, inexperienced and overpromoted, isolated in Washington as general in chief, at the beck and call of a president whom he did not understand and without friends and supporters of his own, leapt at the opening presented to him by his perception—if one may guess that this was what came to him—that the inaccessibility of the Confederacy might be cracked by disregarding the obvious over-land route and, instead, seeking to appear on the South's back doorstep by amphibious means.

Whatever the origins of the Urbana Plan, it came to be accepted perhaps even more swiftly than McClellan anticipated. During his long period of inactivity in October and November, while he procrastinated with Lincoln over the restaging of the advance on Richmond through Manassas, he added to his own difficulties by falling ill of typhoid fever. Lincoln was exasperated. On January 10, 1862, several weeks after the renewed advance on Richmond should have begun, he received a despatch from General Halleck in the western theatre, re-emphasising his inability to do the president's will in Kentucky. Lincoln seems to have been seized by despair, an understandable but not characteristic mood. He went to see Montgomery Meigs, the quarter-master general, a powerful man in the Washington wartime scene. Lincoln poured out his troubles. Halleck and Buell were not winning the war in the West. There was financial trouble in Washington. The electorate was demanding victories. The Union's principal soldier had taken to his sickbed. Meigs agreed that something had to be done since, if the Confederacy attacked out of its Manassas positions at the present moment, Washington itself might be threatened. Meigs suggested a council of war, always a dubious resort in time of danger. Lincoln nevertheless called the most senior and available soldiers—including McDowell, who had lost at Manassas—and politicians to advise him. At its first meeting the generals gave Lincoln mixed advice, though William B. Franklin recommended a waterborne advance on Richmond; he knew what was in McClellan's mind. McDowell again pressed the Manassas case. Inevitably word of this meeting reached McClellan on his sickbed and inevitably he was outraged. With reason he felt that his political chief was going behind his back. Suddenly recovering, he appeared at the White House on the evening of January 13; the mood of the meeting was bad-tempered and the outcome inconclusive, though Lincoln did eventually declare himself satisfied that McClellan was about to undertake action.

The action promised was in the West, not Virginia, but Lincoln was so desperate for activity of any sort and still so committed to his "Young Napoleon," as McClellan was known to the newspapers, from a supposed resemblance, that he did not demur. Action he shortly got, though in a curiously indirect way. Halleck, the eternal prevaricator, suddenly launched his subordinate Ulysses S. Grant in an advance up the Cumberland River in Tennessee towards a Confederate earthwork, Fort Henry, blocking the river. The pattern of waterways in this section of Tennessee is as complex as that west of Chesapeake Bay, with this difference: the rivers, which are tributaries of the Ohio and fed by the waters running off the western slopes of the Appalachians, particularly the Cumberland Mountains, are far wider than their Virginia equivalents and carry much larger volumes of water. Topography, moreover, exhibits the same curious effect of disposing waterways with widely separated sources into channels that run in close proximity and parallel to each other. So it is with the Tennessee and the Cumberland rivers. The Cumberland rises on the Virginia border, the Tennessee in Tennessee, west of Knoxville; however, just before they flow into the Ohio, they run almost parallel for a short distance. Because the Union held the Ohio at the points where the Cumberland and Tennessee discharge into it and so were well placed to use the two tributaries as avenues of entry into the important borderlands of Kentucky and Tennessee, from which there were easy avenues of advance into Missouri and Alabama also, the Confederacy had taken the sensible precaution of fortifying the Tennessee-Cumberland river system at its confluent point. The earthwork forts of Henry and Donelson supported each other and blocked upstream movement into the Tennessee interior. The forts, moreover, were strongly garrisoned, by 21,000 men under the command of Gideon Pillow and Simon Bolivar Buckner.

THE EMERGENCE OF ULYSSES S. GRANT

Pillow and Buckner's Union opponent, Ulysses S. Grant, had known both men previously; he had command of an equal number of men, based at Cairo, on the Mississippi just below the confluence with the Ohio. He also had the support of a gunboat fleet commanded by Andrew Foote, who was to emerge as one of the most talented officers of the U.S. Navy's freshwater fleet. Grant, the beginning of whose meteoric career the Henry-Donelson campaign was, would become the towering military genius of the Civil War, displaying all the qualities that Lincoln hoped to find in McClellan but failed to do. The Grants were old colonial stock who when U. S. Grant was born, were settled in Point Pleasant, Ohio. Like most early settlers they had made their way by honest labour, eked out by paid public service. Ulysses' father set up a tannery business, and the son had a modestly comfortable upbringing and decent schooling. In 1839, however, to his surprise and distaste, he was nominated for a vacancy at West Point and, through family influence, found himself appointed. He went off resentfully and never changed his attitude; he did not want to be a soldier, did not like the army, and hated war. In his wonderful autobiography he describes both the Civil War and the Mexican War of 1846 as "unholy." Had the West Point system worked with its full vigour, Grant would have not survived to graduate. He was ill-disciplined and he did not take his academic work seriously, strangely, for he was a serious, if wilful and headstrong, young man in an age when the U.S. Military Academy was one of the few places in the Western world to offer a training in mathematics, science, and technology. Grant boasted that he never revised, a failing that could easily have resulted in his being relegated and eventually dismissed. Grant was, however, exceptionally clever. He found no difficulty with the academy's mathematical syllabus, the core of the course, so little indeed that on graduation he applied for and was accepted for an instructor's post. By then, however, the army had taken him over and he was on his way to the Mexican War. Despite his disapproval of the conflict, Grant did well in the war, was rewarded for his distinguished service, and ought to have been assured of a successful if slow-moving career. It was not to be. Temperament was against it. Posted to a peacetime station in California, with little to do and without the company of his beloved wife, Julia Dent, he took to drink and discord. After falling out with his commanding officer, he resigned his commission and tried his luck in civilian life, only to find himself on a continuation of the downward slope. He tried small-scale commerce; he tried farming, at a place discouragingly known as Hardscrabble, and by 1861 was reduced to working as a clerk in his father's tannery. At the moment when terminal obscurity might have overtaken him, his fortunes were changed by the outbreak of the Civil War. Suddenly any man with military credentials could find employment, income, and, with luck, social standing and the chance to recover self-respect. At the outbreak Grant was in Galena, Illinois, and, through a chapter of accidents, found himself engaged by the state government to assist in the organisation of the state's first volunteer regiments. Not long after he was in command of one of them, the 21st Illinois. Soon after taking command Grant was ordered to find and engage a rebel regiment at Florida, Missouri. He undertook the advance through deserted countryside, with growing trepidation until, finding the Confederate colonel Harris's campsite abandoned, he realised that Harris "had been as much afraid of me as I of him."

This exceedingly valuable lesson he was to retain all his military life. Boldness was in consequence to be a distinguishing mark of his generalship, sometimes too much so. As James McPherson has remarked, "Grant's determination sometimes led him to see only that which was in his own mind, not what the enemy might be intending, with unfortunate results. Still boldness never brought Grant to disaster."[6] Soon after the Harris episode, boldness led him to attack a superior enemy force at Belmont, opposite Columbus, on the Mississippi. His force was surrounded; lightheartedly he announced that having cut their way in, they would cut their way out. He possessed another characteristic which was a function of his powerful self-confidence: a refusal to retrace his steps. "I will take no backward step" was one of his best-known sayings, usually interpreted to denote his reluctance to retreat. Grant indeed disliked retreat as a measure of war, but those words meant exactly what they said. When finding his way across country, he preferred to press forward in the hope of arriving at his destination than to begin again. He had a keen topographical sense. He collected maps and guidebooks (Wellington had a similar enthusiasm) and at the outbreak of the Mexican War proved to have a better cartographic library than the army itself. Grant's feel for ground was to stand him in good stead during the war, fought as it often was over unmapped, overgrown, or abandoned countryside, as in the dense woodlands of Shiloh in 1862 or the Wilderness in 1864, cleared land which had gone back to secondary forest.

His situation on the Tennessee River in January 1862 was not topographically disfavoured. The countryside was open and only sparsely wooded. The outline of the defences was clear to the eye. The problem was military: how to take possession of the forts in the teeth of their powerful artillery defences and substantial garrisons? In any event, the Confederates muffed their chances. The gunners at Fort Henry, which Grant chose as his first point of attack, could not match the firepower of the Union gunboats. When Grant's infantry, which the riverboats had landed behind the fort, appeared on February 6, the Confederate commander sent the bulk of his garrison away to Fort Donelson and surrendered. The gunboats proceeded upstream, destroying a vital railroad bridge and capturing important riverside towns. By mid-February, Grant and Foote between them had secured the line of the Tennessee as far south as Muscle Shoals, near Florence, Alabama, thus opening a direct riverine route from the North's Ohio stronghold into the heart of the South.

Grant was left with the unsubdued and now reinforced Fort Donelson, eleven miles across the floodplain from Fort Henry, which had to be captured because it controlled the approaches to Nashville, Tennessee, state capital and one of the South's few manufacturing centres. Grant's declared intention to capture Donelson put the Confederates in a spot. The senior Confederate was Albert Sidney Johnston (always so known to distinguish him from Joseph E. Johnston), supreme commander in the West. His difficulty was that his force was divided between Donelson and Bowling Green, near Nashville. The Union forces were also divided, with Grant's 21,000 near Donelson and Buell's 50,000 near Louisville. These dispositions gave the Unionists more options than the Confederates: the options included concentric attack by Grant and Buell at Bowling Green or waterborne attacks on Columbus and Nashville. Johnston, by contrast, could not coordinate the actions of his two forces because of the loss of Fort Henry and the cutting of the Louisville–Memphis railroad. When he and his Southern generals considered the situation at Bowling Green on February 7, a newcomer, Pierre Beauregard, the victor of Manassas, self-confidently proposed attacking Grant and Buell in turn, believing both could be defeated. Johnston did not. Unfortunately, while wondering what to do, he got into a muddle; he decided to take most of his troops to Nashville but leave enough at Fort Donelson to give Grant a real fight. On February 14, however, Grant was strongly reinforced, both with troops and gunboats. He mounted an attack with the gunboats, to intimidate the garrison, while deploying his fresh troops to encircle the fort securely. The gunboats came off the worse in the artillery duel, while driving snow all night reduced many of the Northern soldiers to shivering inactivity. On February 15 the Confederates, commanded by John Floyd—a wanted man in the North, which he had served as secretary of war under the previous president and so was held to be in violation of his official oath of loyalty to the Constitution, staged their breakout for Nashville. The thrust carried the Union back a mile and seemed about to bring on a collapse when Grant, who had been absent elsewhere, suddenly appeared at the gallop and began to set matters to rights.

What saved the situation, however, was not his intervention, but a sudden collapse of will in the Confederate fortress commander, General Pillow. Disheartened by the sight of the losses his men had suffered in the early-morning fighting, Pillow decided that the survivors, who were in fact the victors, could not safely be risked in a cross-country retreat to Nashville and ordered them to return to their trenches. It was at this point that Grant made his appreciation. Reckoning that the enemy were giving up the ground they had taken, he remarked to his staff officers that they were unlikely to resist if counter-attacked, which, under covering fire from some of the gunboats, his hastily reorganised brigades did, with success.

In the night that followed, Floyd, Pillow, and another divisional commander, the darkly handsome Simon Bolivar Buckner, debated their predicament. Floyd and Pillow had reason to fear capture. Both escaped by water before daybreak, Pillow with 1,500 soldiers. Buckner stayed to negotiate terms, but gave permission to a subordinate, Nathan Bedford Forrest, to make his best way out with his cavalry brigade. Forrest found an unguarded but negotiable stream and led his men through it. Had Grant been aware of the prize that lay within his grasp, he would have reproached himself, for Forrest, a self-made, self-taught man from nowhere, turned himself into the outstanding cavalry commander of the war on either side. It may have been the combination of his headstrong character with his total ignorance of the rules and practices of warfare which made him so effective.

Buckner, who had been at West Point with Grant and served with him in the army, now opened, as he believed, negotiations for surrender, suggesting the recognition of an armistice as a preliminary step. That was perfectly proper, according to the conventions of regular warfare. Grant, however, did not regard what he was fighting as a regular war but as an illegal rebellion, and so his enemies were not entitled to treatment under the conventions of lawful warfare. To Buckner's civil request, therefore, he returned one of the most peremptory refusals in the records of the conduct of war. It read, "Sir, Yours of this date, proposing armistice and appointment of commissioners to settle terms of capitulation, is just received. No terms except an unconditional and immediate surrender can be accepted. I propose to move immediately upon your works. I am, Sir, very respectfully, your obedient servant, U. S. Grant. Brigadier."[7]

In reply, Buckner declared himself forced to accept "the ungenerous and unchivalrous terms" proposed. Later that day he surrendered 11,500 men, 40 cannon, and much equipment. He also effectively surrendered Confederate control of one of the most strategic avenues in the Confederacy. Possession of the Tennessee River, if it were used correctly by the North, would give access to southern Tennessee, northern Alabama, and the upper Mississippi, and lend support to operations down the Mississippi River itself. The capture of Forts Henry and Donelson effectively marked the end of the opening stage of the Civil War in the West. That war, unlike the conflict in the Washington–Richmond corridor, was always to have a local and slightly irregular character to it. Important though it was to both sides, it was always a distraction to the central struggle, which dominated public attention. Neither government in 1861 had set out to fight in the West; both hoped at best to avoid losing territory there and to avoid defeat, should it come to fighting. At the outset, however, shortage of troops made fighting difficult to organise, as did ignorance of the terrain. Since leading Northern generals were confined by the geography of northern Virginia, which lay on the capital's doorstep, it is not surprising that the distant, sparsely inhabited, and largely unmapped lands bordering the Mississippi and the Gulf should have failed to focus clearly or quickly in the military minds of either side. Lack of information put regular troops at a disadvantage. The most effective fighters were locals who knew the ground at first hand and could exploit their intimacy with it. Unfortunately for the Confederacy, which needed to defend the northern rim of the Mississippi-Alabama-Georgia tier of states if it were not to collapse and also had the strongest interest in supporting pro-Southern groups in the next tier up—Tennessee, Kentucky, and Missouri—there were insufficient organised irregular forces to dispute the issue with the Union, as opposed to making the lives of pro-Union residents a misery, while its positioning of regular troops, understandably oriented towards defeating the Union in northern Virginia, left the states of the West in an unsatisfactory disposition. The loss of Forts Henry and Donelson made that worryingly apparent. Grant's victory left Albert Sidney Johnston's forces scattered as much as 175 miles apart between Murfreesboro and Memphis. Johnston had the ear of the supreme command, which recognised the danger of Southern dispersal in his area of command. During March, forces were collected and sent from the coast to Tennessee. Braxton Bragg's 10,000 men were moved at speed from Mobile, on Alabama's seacoast, to Corinth, east of Memphis, but close to the upper reaches of the Tennessee River, which Grant was currently using to concentrate a large force near a riverside stopping point known as Pittsburg Landing, near a Sunday meeting place called Shiloh Church.

Why there should have been a major battle at Pittsburg Landing is difficult to explain. Grant wanted a fight, to follow up his success at Forts Henry and Donelson; so did Halleck, his immediate superior, whose longer-term objective was the railroad town of Corinth nearby. Union control of the local strategic communications, the Tennessee River itself and the railroad reaching Corinth from the north, suggest that both Grant and Halleck envisaged transforming the Memphis-Corinth area into a major base for offensive operations both eastward towards Chattanooga and southward down the Mississippi. In late March and early April, Halleck concerned himself principally with reinforcing the area, chiefly by bringing Buell's large force down from Nashville. He meanwhile urged Grant not to engage with the Confederates until he was strong enough to be certain of success. Grant, however, was spoiling for a fight. He would have been encouraged to know that the enemy was equally keen. On April 5, General A. S. Johnston gave orders for an attack on April 6, the preliminary objective to be the Union encampment which had grown up in the last few days around Pittsburg Landing.

The target was tempting. The Northern divisions, commanded by John McClernand, Lew Wallace (the future author of *Ben-Hur*), Stephen Hurlbut, Benjamin M. Prentiss, and William T. Sherman, had pitched camp on the low ground between the Tennessee River and its small tributary, Owl Creek. The encampment, however, was not entrenched or otherwise defended and was ripe to be taken by surprise. The environment of the battlefield, as the area was to become, favoured surprise. The ground was covered by scrubby woodland and broken forest and cut up by small streams and rivulets. This terrain readily disguised the Confederate approach when it began at about six o'clock in the morning. The initial onset might have ended the battle, had Johnston not mismanaged the Confederate deployment and Grant not appeared on the scene at a critical moment. Johnston's intention had been to attack in columns, retaining a reserve to reinforce success. Instead he attacked in lines, which soon became intermixed and disori-

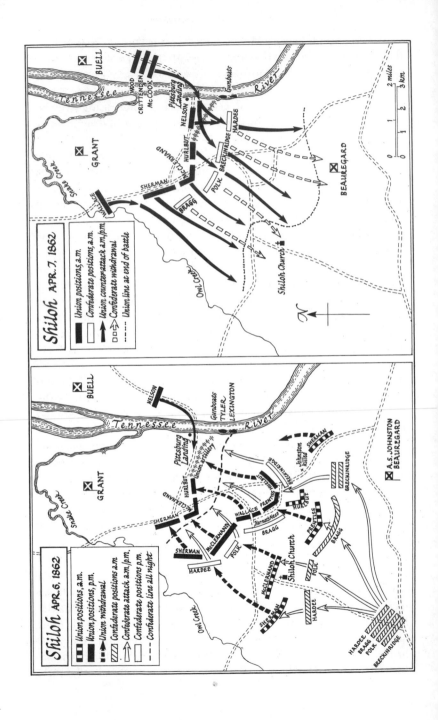

Shiloh APR. 6, 1862

Union positions, a.m.
Union positions, p.m.
Union withdrawal
Confederate positions a.m.
Confederate attack a.m./p.m.
Confederate positions p.m.
Confederate line all night

Snake Creek

GRANT

BUELL

Tennessee River

NELSON

Pittsburg Landing

Gunboats
TYLER
LEXINGTON

HURLBUT

Union artillery

McCLERNAND

SHERMAN

WALLACE

PRENTISS

Hornets Nest

A. S. JOHNSTON
BEAUREGARD

Johnston killed

BRECKINRIDGE

HILL CITY

BRAGG

PRENTISS

POLK

SHERMAN

McCLERNAND

POLK

Shiloh Church

HARDEE

Owl Creek

SHERMAN

HARDEE

BRAGG

HARDEE
BRAGG
POLK
BRECKINRIDGE

Shiloh APR. 7, 1862

Union positions, a.m.
Confederate positions, a.m.
Union counter-attack a.m./p.m.
Confederate withdrawal
Union line at end of battle

Seale Creek

GRANT

BUELL

WOOD
CRITTENDEN
McCOOK

Pittsburg Landing
NELSON

Gunboats

Tennessee River

HURLBUT

HARDEE

BRECKINRIDGE

McCLERNAND

SHERMAN

POLK

BEAUREGARD

WALLACE

BRAGG

Owl Creek

Shiloh Church

N

entated. Without a reserve to reenergise the advance, the Confederate battle formation lost direction and cohesion and succumbed to confusion, imposed by the oppressive woodland. The worst confusion and heaviest fighting occurred on the edge of the encampment along a feature which became known to the Union as the Sunken Road and to the Confederates as the Hornet's Nest. The Confederates made the mistake of attacking it repeatedly, at ever-growing cost. Eventually, late in the afternoon, the Union commander accepted defeat and surrendered his survivors, 2,500 in all, to the Confederates, who surrounded his position on three sides.

The battle so far had taken the form of a "soldier's battle," its shape formed by the reactions of the soldiers as they stumbled across each other in the prevailing woodland, rather than by their commanders seeking to impose order and purpose on their stumbling movements. Yet commanders were involved. Johnston, who had ridden about the battlefield trying to organise a flanking movement that would drive the Union troops away from the Tennessee River towards Owl Creek, got so involved in the fighting that he suffered a bullet wound that severed an artery in his leg and caused him to bleed to death. Sherman, who had discounted the possibility of a Confederate attack, was also wounded twice, but slightly; though he lost three horses, he kept his composure, and by riding constantly about his line, giving encouragement and bringing reinforcements, he preserved its integrity.

On April 5, whilst convalescing after a fall from his horse had rendered him unable to walk without crutches, Grant had written to Halleck: "I have scarcely the faintest idea of an attack being made upon us, but will be prepared should such a thing take place." He was, however, eight miles distant when the sound of battle reached him early the next day. He immediately returned to Pittsburg Landing by riverboat, finding the shore crowded with early fugitives of the battle. In open country they would have fled to the rear, but in the dense Tennessee woodland rear and front were almost indistinguishable, the river providing the only point of reference. Grant began to round up the runaways. Fortunately for him Confederates were also running away in thousands from what had developed in three hours into the fiercest battle yet seen in the Civil War, indeed one of the fiercest to be fought until the coming of mass warfare on the Western Front fifty years later. The conditions were not dissimilar. Large numbers of soldiers were involved: six Confederate divisions, five Union, about 30,000 men on each side. The shape and character of the battlefield—dense woods, confined by a large water barrier and crossed by other, smaller water-ways which constricted movement—had the effect of throwing men together into sudden and unexpected confrontations, from which escape seemed possible only by the use of firepower. At its most intense the battle pitted about 60,000 men against one another in a space only eight miles square, conditions that imposed a terrible logic of "kill or be killed" on those present. It would be similar conditions that caused the appalling level of casualties at Antietam, still the costliest single-day battle in American history.

By the end of the day Beauregard, now in command on the Confederate side, was urged by his subordinates to mount a final attack which, they believed, would finish Union resistance. Beauregard demurred; he sensed that his men were near the end of their energy. Grant, on the other side, had come to the same conclusion. Some of his subordinates urged retreat, given the level of losses the Union had suffered. Grant refused. Reinforcements were arriving, including Lew Wallace's division, which had taken a wrong turning on its march to the battle and lost its way, and the vanguard of Buell's 50,000 from Nashville. Asked to agree that April 6 had been a defeat, Grant made a noncommittal reply, then articulated, "Whip 'em tomorrow."

April 7 would indeed go better for the Northerners—if such terms can be applied to any battle as horrible as Shiloh. Early that morning Buell's Army of the Ohio, as his command was officially designated, together with Grant's Army of the Tennessee, resumed the fight. For several hours the Northerners had things their own way and recovered ground lost the day before. Then the Confederates rediscovered their spirit and began to resist. For both sides, however, the battle had lost momentum. The Southerners could not regain ground lost, while both sides were sickened by the spectacle of suffering that lay all around them, as the trench warriors of 1916 would be. Rain was falling in torrents; the casualties of the previous day, uncollected and unprotected during a bitter night, lay on sodden ground, calling out for help, which the army could not supply. Many of those left to lie were already dead, their wounds a warning to soldiers of both sides of what persistence in this dreadful combat would entail. By early afternoon the front line of battle had returned to that which marked the Union position before the Confederate attack had opened. It was suggested to Beauregard that he should consider quitting the field. He agreed and ordered a retreat. The Union troops were too exhausted to pursue the

Southerners towards Corinth. Beauregard's men left behind a ghastly spectacle and an objective tragedy. Out of 100,000 men engaged, more than 24,000 had been killed or wounded. Many of the wounded had died during the bitter night of April 6–7, of shock and exposure to chilling rain. So fiercely had the battle raged that little attempt had been made to bring them help. Their pitiful condition was an awful reminder of what was worst about the big Napoleonic battles (there had been 40,000 wounded left on the field of Waterloo) and an anticipation of the medical disasters of the First World War (casualties on the first day of the Somme were so numerous that, even if they could be brought to help, the British medical service was forced to sort the less hopeful cases from the more, and simply leave them to die in some sort of comfort). Shiloh was in many respects an unexpected battle—in time and place but particularly in character. It was a terrible demonstration of what a determined man with a rifled firearm could do to his enemy. Veterans of 1846, accustomed to the low velocities of the musket's spherical ball, were quite unprepared for those of the conical minié bullet. In the absence of facilities for blood transfusion or trauma surgery, it was a lucky victim of a minié strike who was not killed outright or left with a permanently disabling wound. Shiloh was the first battle of the war that exhibited these effects on a large scale. As a result, it profoundly influenced the outlook of those who took part and survived. Grant, a military realist of markedly delicate moral sensitivity, concluded in the aftermath that all hope of a swift termination of hostilities by a single victory was chimerical. No exchange of fire could be so unequal as to leave one side the unchallengeable victor, the other cowed and quiescent. Shiloh showed to Grant, and to other soldiers as intelligent as he, that they were engaged in a war of attrition, in which casualties would be equally distributed and the decision would be won by the army best able to bear the agony.

It was in a way appropriate that this important lesson was taught in a landscape so characteristically American as that presented at Shiloh. Forest and water were far more representative of the war's mid-century environment than the cleared and settled land of northern Virginia, Maryland, and Pennsylvania. There would be more Shiloh than Manassas in the encounters that lay ahead, and Grant's exposure to forest fighting was an essential introduction to his years of high command, now opening before him. The end of the battle reopened old complaints against Grant—that he was a drunk at worst and at best inefficient. Lincoln paid no attention. In the aftermath, he uttered one of his most memorable apothegms of the war, in answer to a critic of Grant, with the words "I can't spare this man, he fights."

Grant had done more than fight. Though still relatively junior and not involved in Washington's plans for the conduct of the war, he had inadvertently helped to shape its future course. Northern military leaders had yet to take advantage of the fact that the water lines in the Mississippi Valley formed an avenue of military advance into the Deep South, culminating eventually at New Orleans, exactly contrary to the way that those of northern Tennessee, counting the upper Mississippi and the Ohio rivers as a single military obstacle centred on St. Louis and Louisville together, contributed an almost impenetrable barrier to invasion of Indiana and Illinois from the South. It did not take Grant long to twig. The South had made the mistake in February of evacuating the river town of Columbus, where ill health prevailed, and on April 8 it lost the strategic Island No. 10, below Columbus. Watermen and boatbuilders came forward to assist the South's river defences, and on June 6 they steamed out to confront a similar fleet of Union rams and gunboats, which had arrived to challenge them for control. This encounter quickly developed into the most bitter inland waterway battle yet fought in the war. Ramming proved to be a particularly effective technique in the confined riverine waters and several Confederate vessels were sunk or disabled by collision. Six Confederate warships were put out of action; only one survived. By the time the encounter was over, Memphis, the fifth largest city in the Confederacy, had given up resistance and the Union river fleet was ready to press southward towards Vicksburg, the last Confederate bastion on the Mississippi. It was the last because, in April 1862, the senior Union sailor, Flag Officer (equivalent to Admiral) David Farragut, had completed his triumphant reduction of the defences of New Orleans, at the mouth of the Mississippi River.

New Orleans was important for a number of reasons. It was the South's largest city. It had also in the days of peace been one of its principal gateways to the outside world and the highways of world trade. Its loss would prove a severe blow to Southern prestige, besides opening a direct route from the Gulf of Mexico into the Mississippi Valley.

THE OPENING OF NAVAL WARFARE

On April 19, 1861, President Lincoln had issued the Proclamation of Blockade Against Southern Ports:

Whereas an insurrection against the Government of the United States has broken out in the States of South Carolina, Georgia, Alabama, Florida, Mississippi, Louisiana, and Texas, and the laws of the United States for the collection of the revenue cannot be effectually executed therein conformably to that provision of the Constitution which requires duties to be uniform throughout the United States: And whereas a combination of persons engaged in such insurrection, have threatened to grant pretended letters of marque to authorize the bearers thereof to commit assaults on the lives, vessels, and property of good citizens of the country lawfully engaged in commerce on the high seas, and in waters of the United States: And whereas an Executive Proclamation has been already issued, requiring the persons engaged in these disorderly proceedings to desist therefrom, calling out a militia force for the purpose of repressing the same, and convening Congress in extraordinary session, to deliberate and determine thereon: Now, therefore, I, Abraham Lincoln, President of the United States, with a view to the same purposes before mentioned, and to the protection of the public peace, and the lives and property of quiet and orderly citizens pursuing their lawful occupations, until Congress shall have assembled and deliberated on the said unlawful proceedings, or until the same shall have ceased, have further deemed it advisable to set on foot a blockade of the ports within the States aforesaid, in pursuance of the laws of the United States, and of the law of Nations, in such case provided. For this purpose a competent force will be posted so as to prevent entrance and exit of vessels from the ports aforesaid. If, therefore, with a view to violate such blockade, a vessel shall approach, or shall attempt to leave either of the said ports, she will be duly warned by the Commander of one of the blockading vessels, who will endorse on her register the fact and date of such warning, and if the same vessel shall again attempt to enter or leave the blockaded port, she will be captured and sent to the nearest convenient port, for such proceedings against her and her cargo as prize, as may be deemed advisable. And I hereby proclaim and declare that if any person, under the pretended authority of the said States, or under any other pretense, shall molest a vessel of the United States, or the persons or cargo on board of her, such person will be held amenable to the laws of the United States for the prevention and punishment of piracy. In witness whereof, I have hereunto set my hand, and caused the *seal of the United States* to be affixed. Done at the City of

Washington, this nineteenth day of April, in the year of our Lord
one thousand eight hundred and sixty-one, and of the *Independence
of the United States* the *eighty-fifth*.[8]

The triumph in the Mississippi Valley was the indirect outcome of a
distant and much larger campaign down the Confederacy's Atlantic
coast and the first of what was perhaps Lincoln's earliest and most
important effort to make grand strategy. In his memorandum for a plan
of campaign of October 1, 1861, he had recommended that the navy
should seize Port Royal, off the coast of South Carolina. It was to be
one element in his scheme for a general blockade, a programme which
he raised more and more often in the first year of the war. It was obvious
enough as a plan. The South's was an exporting economy and the South
an importing society. It lacked the means to manufacture many of its
necessities, particularly the necessities of war, and without the freedom
to export it lacked the means to pay for what it bought. The South,
moreover, was particularly susceptible to blockade. Though its coastline was nearly 5,000 miles long, it had few major ports or easily penetrable river estuaries. Moreover, on the Atlantic side its shoreline was
cut off from the ocean by long chains of low-lying banks and islands
which, if taken into Union hands, would become barriers of the blockade, besides providing sheltered anchorages for a blockading fleet. Lincoln was more interested in the value to be derived from blockade than
were his generals, who thought exclusively in Napoleonic terms of
defeating the South by winning great land battles. The U.S. Navy was,
of course, interested in blockade, but unlike the Royal Navy, it was not
the senior service and had comparatively little influence over the making of strategy. Nevertheless, it had influence enough to persuade Lincoln and the secretary of war to allow it to finance and organise an
expeditionary force in November 1861 to seize the most important of
the anchorages behind the protective banks at Port Royal.

The Southern defenders, shortly to be put under the command of
Robert E. Lee, thought Port Royal safe because its entrance was
strongly fortified. The Union naval commander, Flag Officer Samuel
du Pont, was not deterred. He may have been aware of the British success in overcoming fortifications in the Baltic during the Crimean
War; the overwhelming of the great fortress of Bomarsund was a case
in point. At any rate his bombarding ships quickly suppressed the fire
of the Port Royal forts, causing the flight of the defenders and of the
Confederate population of the nearby Sea Islands, the richest centre of

production of high-quality cotton in the South. The Port Royal anchorage quickly established itself as a blockade centre, from which several successful expeditions were soon launched against the North Carolina ports in the Albemarle and Pamlico sounds. During 1862 the Northern naval offensive moved south along the Atlantic coast, taking one place after another: Roanoke Island, Cape Hatteras, New Bern, Elizabeth City, Fort Macon, and then, below Port Royal, Fort Pulaski—one of the massive forts of the Third System, protecting Savannah, Brunswick, Fernandina, and Jacksonville—and, on March 11, 1862, St. Augustine, the oldest inhabited place in North America. The offensive also reached round the corner into the Gulf, to take, before mid-summer 1862, Apalachicola, Pensacola, Biloxi, and the strongpoints on the approach to New Orleans: Fort St. Philip, Fort Jackson, Head of Passes, and Pass Christian. General Burnside was much involved in the maritime offensive in North Carolina; the seaward defences of New Orleans were the target of David Farragut during his 1862 offensive.

Of all these seizures of coastal strongholds, Fort Pulaski, at the mouth of the Savannah River, was the most remarkable. The fortress, built from 1829 onwards, was one of the monsters of the Third System, specially reinforced in the rear with giant timber baulks to help absorb the shock of shot striking the outer face of its immensely thick walls. This enormously expensive method of construction proved no use at all against the North's newly developed rifled artillery. In two days, ten batteries set up on an adjoining island—they were named for such leading Union generals as Grant, Sherman, Burnside, Halleck, and McClellan—and firing at ranges of up to 3,000 yards, broke the carapace open, while shells from heavy mortars devastated the interior. Local Confederate forces lacked both the artillery to counter-bombard and landing craft to launch troops against the Union gunners. The operation was a perfect demonstration of the North's amphibious freedom of action which, by this offensive, completed its acquisition of a chain of coastal footholds and protected anchorages running from Fortress Monroe, at the mouth of Chesapeake Bay, to Mobile, in the estuary of the Alabama River. At the outset of the amphibious campaign, the United States Navy had retained only two Southern bases from which to conduct a blockade, Fortress Monroe and the offshore island of Key West. By its end, it was the South which was left with only two Atlantic ports, Wilmington, North Carolina, and Charleston, South Carolina, the pivots of Cornwallis's campaign before Yorktown eighty years earlier. The situation was a terrible setback for the Southern cause, all the more so because it had come about almost inadvertently. Keen though Lincoln was on the concept of blockade, he had had no idea that it could be realized as completely and cheaply as it was. For its part, the South had given away its coastal security, making almost no effort to protect its most valuable harbours and points of seaward entry from its enemy.

The South's one serious attempt to achieve maritime superiority failed through bad luck. Both navies, Union and Confederate, were aware in 1861 that the ships they possessed belonged to the past and that if either could build or acquire examples of the new ships that were taking to the seas in Europe, it would triumph. The French and the British had each built such a ship, *La Gloire* and HMS *Warrior*, which were steam-propelled ironclads. Disraeli said of *Warrior*, seeing her in the naval anchorage at Portsmouth in 1861 among the old wooden walls of the Channel Fleet, that she looked like a "snake among the rabbits." The only ships the U.S. Navy possessed in 1861 were rabbits. The Confederate Navy had no ships at all, except those trapped in Southern ports when war broke out; they were rabbits also. Both sides knew that they would have to acquire some snakes rapidly if they were to keep the sea. The South just won the race. Their hope of achieving naval supremacy was invested in a U.S. Navy steam frigate, *Merrimack*, which had been scuttled on secession but raised and repaired. To transform her, the Confederate Navy Department commandeered the output of the Tredegar Iron Works in Richmond so as to cover her in iron plate, enough to protect her 172 feet, but that, of course, robbed her of freeboard. She lay so low in the water that she resembled a raft. On her first outing, March 8, 1862, the raft, whose pre-war engines generated too little power to move her at any speed, came out of the Norfolk Navy Yard, which the Union had lost to the South, to attack the Union's fleet of wooden warships in Hampton Roads just across the water. Union shot bounced off the *Merrimack*'s carapace, damaging its fixtures and fittings. The *Merrimack*'s rifled guns did terrible damage in return. Two large wooden warships were sunk outright, either by gunfire or ramming, and the survivors fled into shallow water for safety, where the *Merrimack* could not follow. The enormous weight of *Merrimack*'s plating caused her to draw twice her pre-conversion draught.

Next day should have spelt the end for the survivors of March 8. By the strangest of coincidences, however, the Brooklyn Navy Yard, which had been racing to design and build an ironclad, had got one launched and on its way south the day before. The *Monitor* really was a raft, with a revolving turret mounting 11-inch guns perched on top. Highly unseaworthy, it just survived the Atlantic seas between Sandy Hook and Norfolk to arrive on March 9 and take station next to one of the survivors of the previous day's massacre. The *Merrimack*'s crew mistook the *Monitor* for a dockyard repair vessel. Only when it opened fire did battle commence, and then very haphazardly, since neither vessel, try as it might with ram and cannon, could land a disabling blow. After two hours of ineffectual circling and lunging, the crews called it a day and withdrew.

Naval experts all over the world recognised, however, the significance of March 9, 1862. The building of wooden warships stopped almost immediately, to be replaced by ironclads, though of better design than the ungainly *Monitor* and *Merrimack*. Neither long survived their revolutionary encounter. *Monitor* foundered in the open sea while being taken south to strengthen the blockade; *Merrimack* had to be abandoned when Norfolk fell to McClellan's troops later in 1862. *Merrimack*'s failure was a decisive event. It deflated for good the South's hopes of defeating blockade by technical means. Its few subsequent essays in ironclad building were inland craft. It never again attempted to challenge the Union navy for command of the sea, and by failing to do so, it conceded the power of Northern blockade. The South built and bought abroad numbers of swift blockade-runners; they were better adapted, however, to making fortunes for their owners than to denting the barrier the North erected around the South's coasts. Blockade reduced the South's export trade by two-thirds. It was not only that the North's active blockade was as effective as it was, but also that by 1863 one blockade-runner in three was taken by the Union cordon. Even if a blockade-runner slipped through, it had, after 1863, few ports into which it could make its way. In 1864 the only port cities which had not been taken by the Union were Wilmington, North Carolina; Savannah, Georgia; and Charleston, South Carolina. As a result the blockade-running trade was transferred to offshore, foreign ports, Nassau in the Bahamas, Bermuda, and Havana, from which goods had to be transshipped, which did not ease the problem of delivery. Goods got through, with as many as nine out of ten ships successfully running the blockade in 1861, and still one out of two in 1865. Nevertheless, blockade crippled the South's ability to earn foreign exchange and so slowed its consumption of foreign goods, not luxuries alone but also necessities, including munitions and firearms. Shortage, of course, stimulated a substitution economy in the South, but of a limited sort since it lacked essential natural resources and the industrial means to process them, while its neighbour, Mexico, was too underdeveloped and too poor to organise a market. Blockade was a killer to Confederate ambitions. It was only because the South was a backward region, whose population was accustomed to life at the margin, that it was able to survive privation as long as it did.

It still needed, of course, to distribute essentials within its landmass, but essentials meant little more than corn and pork, which its agricultural districts produced in abundance. The movement of such produce was usually short-range. Most Southerners ate what they or their close neighbours grew. Still, there was also a need for strategic transport, to move war material and troops. Such movement was provided by railroads and rivers, particularly in the Mississippi Valley. Following Grant's success in interrupting rail communication across the Tennessee River, and so separating Memphis from Chattanooga, the South's need to keep open movement down the Mississippi River became urgent. Were the line of the Mississippi, so much of which had fallen under Union control following the capture of New Orleans Island No. 10, and nearby Fort Pillow, to pass out of Confederate hands altogether, the Confederacy would be cut in two and the agricultural riches of Arkansas, Missouri, and Texas, repository of much of the South's livestock, lost to the Southern war effort altogether. It was therefore essential to hold the surviving Confederate strongpoints along the river's course.

Essentially that meant Vicksburg, a gracious city where one of the river's many wide undulations follows a bluff two hundred feet above its surface. It was a formidable defensive position, presenting the fire of more than two hundred guns to any Union river gunboat that attempted to run past. Farragut, who had subdued New Orleans and its defending forts with a force of nearly thirty warships, and believed he could do it again at Vicksburg, came upriver twice, on the way taking the city of Natchez, a place of summer retreat for local planters, and Baton Rouge, Louisiana's state capital. The inland fleet that had captured Memphis came downstream to meet him. What had been easy in the delta now proved in June 1862 to be very difficult in the broad central reaches. When called upon to surrender, the military governor of Vicksburg returned Farragut a defiant refusal. More menacingly, the forces set to protect Vicksburg, under the command of

Earl Van Dorn, who had led at the hard-fought battle of Pea Ridge on the Arkansas-Missouri border in March 1862, proved intractable. Pea Ridge was one of the many bitter but almost unknown battles of the war, causing heavy casualties on both sides but remembered by few but the shocked survivors. Whatever their past experience, Van Dorn's veterans proved too stout a party for Farragut's crews. Farragut brought infantry up from New Orleans but Van Dorn outnumbered them. The Union had got itself into a classic pickle on the river. To take Vicksburg it needed to bring to the scene a large ground force to attack it from the landward side. The only means, however, of deploying such a force was by water, which the Union river fleet was unable to achieve because of the Confederate batteries on the bluff above the great bend. For much of 1862–63 Grant puzzled over how to solve the problem. In a thoroughly American way, he sought solutions in engineering, trying to get behind Vicksburg by digging channels across the neck of loops, at Lake Providence, Pass Yazoo, and Milliken's Bend. A great deal of earth was shifted to no profit.

Part of Grant's trouble at getting forward in the Mississippi Valley lay in the theatre's distance from Washington, which denied it the close attention of the high command. The West was the second front in a two-front war, in which the first front of northern Virginia willy-nilly monopolised attention. That is not to say that Grant lacked for troops or resources. He did not. The pro-Union western states raised large numbers of troops, who were available to serve in their home areas, and Washington did not stint money or supplies. The revolutionary river rams and gunboats, built by the shipbuilders Eads and Ellet, were financed uncomplainingly from central funds. It was not material that lacked but vision. Lincoln knew what he wanted in the western theatre: the frustration of any further inroads by the Confederacy into the divided populations of the border states and the outright consolidation within the Union of their pro-Northern populations, particularly in eastern Tennessee. What he could not formulate was an overarching strategy to bring his wishes about. Had he been able to visit the theatre himself, he might have been able to impose his will; but he could not leave Washington. The men on the ground did not seem able to formulate the necessary plan. Grant, if promoted to supreme command, no doubt would have been able to do so, but he as yet lacked the reputation to dominate. The men Lincoln had been obliged to entrust with authority, Frémont, Halleck, and Buell, were lesser beings. None would defer to Grant, understandably since he was their junior, but none could rise above the day-to-day difficulties of operating in the tangled and confused geography of the Mississippi and its associated waterways and design a clear-cut campaign-winning strategy. They were not wholly deserving of blame. Militarily, the theatre is one of the most complex in which large armies have ever fought, not because geography blocks the correct way forward—indeed rather the opposite, since the great rivers all lead straight south—but because meanders, swamps, and undulations made cross-country communication between separate armies difficult, and usually achievable only by recourse to water transport. As so often in the war, difficulties were compounded by the shortage or absence of maps. Lincoln and his cabinet officers in Washington can have been able to form but the vaguest picture of what the Union armies were attempting during the manoeuvres around Vicksburg in 1862–63.

The campaign of 1862 in the East, in which Lincoln took all too close and well-informed an interest, unrolled over completely different terrain. Northern Virginia was cleared farmland, which had been under cultivation since the seventeenth century. It was as well mapped as any area of the United States was at the time and as well provided with roads, and though few of these roads were all-weather, soldiers could not complain about it as a campaigning theatre. With this caveat: whereas in the Mississippi Valley the waterways all led towards objectives of importance—Cairo, Corinth, Vicksburg—the rivers in northern Virginia, running off the Blue Ridge Mountains of the Appalachian chain into Chesapeake Bay, ran directly athwart the North's desired line of advance towards Richmond, though also across the South's towards Washington. These short rivers were nature's obstacles to movement but also lines of defence; indeed, First Bull Run had been fought where it was because Bull Run provided the Confederates defending Richmond with an obvious line on which to stand and formed the front line between the two armies for most of the winter of 1861–62. The Chesapeake rivers presented armies marching southward across country with the necessity for frequent bridging and probably also with the likelihood of having to force a crossing in the teeth of opposition.

Opposed river crossings are greatly disliked by soldiers. No wonder that in November McClellan had conceived the idea of bypassing the short Virginia rivers by crossing their point of outfall, Chesapeake Bay, as a means to arrive peremptorily by ship on Richmond's back doorstep. There were practical and political objections to the scheme. Practically it required the assembly of a large quantity of shipping.

Politically, it alarmed Lincoln because it took the Washington defence force far away without any guarantee that it would be returned quickly if the Confederates resumed their offensive against the capital. The practical difficulty proved quite easy of solution. Politically, it was to take nearly seven months for the Urbana Plan to become "the Peninsula Campaign" with troops actually on the ground, months largely wasted in debate and doubt. Urbana had to be abandoned as an objective because in early March the Confederates shifted their point of concentration behind the Rappahannock, onto ground on which McClellan had planned to stage his departure for Richmond. He therefore advanced to the abandoned Manassas position, which the Washington press detected had not been occupied by as large an army as McClellan alleged. The observation fuelled a suspicion, which was to grow, that McClellan exaggerated his difficulties. His obsession with being outnumbered really began to possess him, however, after he eventually landed the Army of the Potomac at the tip of the Virginia Peninsula, between the York and James rivers, under the guard of Fortress Monroe, at the beginning of April. The road to Richmond lay open and undefended, except by a force of about 11,000 Confederates under General John Magruder, which occupied the old earthworks dug by the British to defend Yorktown during the War of Independence, eighty years earlier. Magruder could have been brushed aside. Instead McClellan laid formal siege and began to pester Lincoln for reinforcements. His besetting obsession now jarred with Lincoln's, which was the security of the capital.

Both men were troubled by attempting to alter the balance of forces in the northern Virginia theatre. Beside McClellan's large concentration in the peninsula, part of his army, McDowell's corps, had been held back by Lincoln to guard Washington. The other sizable Union forces within striking distance were the army of Nathaniel Banks in the Shenandoah Valley and that of Frémont beyond it in the west Virginia mountains. The Shenandoah Valley, like the Chesapeake, was a strategic corridor of the greatest importance, an easy avenue of advance up the Appalachian chain leading into the plains above Washington and near Baltimore. Control of the Shenandoah conferred great strategic advantage. In early 1862 it was on paper controlled by the Union, because of Banks's occupation of its northern end near Harpers Ferry. Also in the valley, however, was a small Confederate army, 15,000 strong, commanded by a former professor of the Virginia Military Institute, Thomas Jackson, known since First Bull Run as Stonewall.

Jackson was a member of the West Point class of 1846 and so a class-mate of McClellan's. Like most West Pointers of his generation, he also knew many other leading figures in the two Civil War armies. What distinguished Jackson was his deeply religious temperament, his very difficult character, and the fact that he was a military genius, the only truly original soldier, besides Grant, to emerge from the conflict. Jackson's genius was of a sort, however, that was not transferable to others. His short, famous epigram of his operational method, "Always mystify, mislead, and surprise the enemy," though incontestable, required his gifts of command to be put into practice. Thus, although he rightly remains one of the most admired soldiers who ever fought, very few—perhaps only Erwin Rommel—have been able to replicate his tech-nique, which works best with a small army in an environment suitable for rapid movement and unexpected manoeuvre.

The Shenandoah Valley is exactly such an environment. Its eastern edge is formed by the Blue Ridge Mountains, its western by the Shenandoah Mountains, behind which lies the great mass of the Appalachian chain. It is thus an isolated and self-contained pocket, its geography further complicated by its internal highlands and water-ways. Dividing the Shenandoah Valley runs the central ridge of Mas-sanutten Mountain, flanked on each side by the two forks of the Shenandoah River. The mountains are cut by numerous gaps, which provide quick ways through; the rivers in 1862 were frequently crossed by wooden bridges that burnt easily. There was one good all-weather road, the Valley Turnpike, while three railroads threw spurs into the valley which connected with bigger systems.

Had Lincoln had an inkling of how creatively Jackson would use the complex Shenandoah geography, he would have had serious cause to worry, if not about the safety of Washington, then certainly about Jackson's ability to play upon McClellan's anxieties.

At the outset, McClellan was too busily engaged in the peninsula and Lincoln too concerned with the general's conduct of his expedition for either to feel serious concern about the events in the valley. Jackson quickly obliged them to pay attention. His strategy had a clear pur-pose: to prevent the Union forces in and near the valley from concen-trating against him, while appearing to threaten to transfer his army rapidly to Richmond so as to reinforce Joseph E. Johnston opposite McClellan. Jackson began the campaign at the head of the valley, where he had spent the winter. His opponent was Nathaniel Banks, who slightly outnumbered him. Jackson accordingly withdrew to

Strasburg, north of Massanutten Mountain. In the weeks to come he sought, by manoeuvre and rapid marching, to maintain contact with Banks but to avoid a battle he might lose, while feinting westward to keep Frémont at a distance, yet at the same time maintaining the deception that he could withdraw swiftly to reinforce Johnston opposite McClellan outside Richmond. Jackson achieved all his objects, though not without fighting. He chose, or was forced, to fight at Front Royal and Winchester in late May and Cross Keys and Port Republic in early June. In between these engagements his columns covered great distances at high speed on foot up and down the valley, keeping ahead of Banks or enticing him forward. The valley army was severely tried by the demands Jackson made of it. Often short of food and suitable clothing, in bitter weather and without footwear, many of the soldiers regularly marched dozens of miles a day barefoot. Those who survived acquired a toughness that made them formidable opponents in battle. They were proud to call themselves "foot cavalry." The valley army's final march of seventy miles in three days brought Jackson to Front Royal, where he won an untidy little victory over Banks, whose retreat he followed towards Harpers Ferry. These actions so alarmed Lincoln that he ordered both Frémont and McDowell to leave their current positions in the Alleghenies and outside Washington, respectively, and to march to Banks's assistance. The orders were given on May 24 and unwittingly contributed to the success of Jackson's campaign of diversion and distraction in the valley, since they negated any effort to reinforce McClellan outside Richmond. All objects of the valley campaign had now been achieved. Jackson, however, knew what he was about and drew his campaign of march and counter-march to a brilliantly successful conclusion. One of his few setbacks was the loss of his cavalry leader, Turner Ashby, a buccaneer in the mould of Nathan Bedford Forrest, who was killed in action at Port Republic on June 6.

Moving partly by rail and partly on foot, the valley army arrived at Richmond in time to take part in the final battles opposing McClellan's effort to capture the Confederate capital, and also to escape from the ponderous trap Lincoln had set to capture Jackson by coordinating the movements of Frémont, Banks, and McDowell. Jackson's arrival outside Richmond coincided with an important change of Confederate command. During the battle of Seven Pines, one of the defensive battles fought outside Richmond during McClellan's offensive, Johnston was wounded by shell splinters and had to be replaced as chief of the Army of Northern Virginia by Robert E. Lee, who had thitherto been acting as Jefferson Davis's chief of staff. Lee had unfairly acquired a poor reputation during the early fighting in the West. Yet he had been the outstanding cadet of his year at West Point and distinguished himself in the Mexican War. He came from one of the oldest and most distinguished families of Virginia, and his decision to "go with his state" in 1861 was reckoned a serious blow in the North, where he had been offered command of the Union army. He was to prove a master of war and now, assuming control in the midst of McClellan's efforts to break into Richmond, he began at once to demonstrate his powers.

McClellan had started his offensive against Richmond on April 7 by laying siege to Magruder's defences outside Yorktown, seventy miles to the southwest. A siege was quite unnecessary. McClellan had enough troops under his command to walk over the position, but his neurosis about being outnumbered was intensifying and he was to take nearly a month, and the deployment of a great deal of artillery, before he could force Magruder to leave. Then he followed the Confederate retreat achingly slowly, finally catching up outside Williamsburg, the first English town in Virginia and the original state capital. The battle which followed was a Union success, but not complete enough to prevent the Confederate army's withdrawal into Richmond, which was now heavily garrisoned and disappearing behind a sturdy line of earthworks. As McClellan edged forward in its aftermath, Johnston decided to inflict a spoiling attack on McClellan's advance guard, which had got on the wrong side of the Chickahominy River. McClellan had allowed this mistake to happen because the Confederates had succeeded in blocking the most obvious approach to Richmond from the southeast by barricading the James River with tangled trees and ship hulks. However, McClellan was spared the consequence of the mishap because James Longstreet, Johnston's subordinate, also mishandled the spoiling attack. At Seven Pines, as the battle became known, he succeeded in committing his troops piecemeal instead of concentrated, and so in getting himself defeated in detail.

McClellan, though now convinced that he was outnumbered 200,000 to his own 105,000 (the real Confederate strength was 90,000) and that Jackson was about to arrive from the valley (when he was still heavily engaged within it), uncharacteristically decided to persist in the offensive. What followed became known as the Seven Days' Battles, a series of engagements fought around the perimeter of Richmond, the Union troops pivoting on the right, the Confederates wheeling backwards on their left, until the outskirts of the city were left behind and

McClellan found himself once again out in open country, Richmond to his north and the estuary of the James River at his back. The battlefields, which lie very close together, are known as Oak Grove (June 25); Mechanicsville (June 26); Gaines's Mill (June 27); Savage's Station— White Oak Swamp (June 28–29); Glendale (also known as White Oak Swamp or Frayser's Farm, June 30); and Malvern Hill (July 1).

All today are beautifully preserved by the National Park Service, and few give any sense of having been places of bloodshed. With one exception: the fighting at Mechanicsville drifted away from the original scene of encounter and came to focus at Beaver Dam Creek, where the Chickahominy flows invisibly through an open space in the surrounding trees. The creek bottom is fordable at this point, but the place is waterlogged and overgrown with sedge and weed. It was completely unsuitable for a military action. Yet Northerners and Southerners fought across it with a will on June 26, 1862, the Southerners attacking the Northerners, who had hastily constructed timber stockades on their side of the creek. They had also brought up artillery to fire from the higher east bank. A Confederate gunner thought the Union position "absolutely impregnable to front attack." By any rational judgement he was right. Even today Beaver Dam Creek retains a sinister atmosphere. In 1862, when the surrounding trees were thick with riflemen determined to defend their positions, it must have been a terrifying place. It is the closest of the Seven Days' battlefields to the city, which perhaps lent a particular force to the Confederates' determination to drive the Union troops away. In the process 1,475 Southerners were killed or wounded. The 1st North Carolina lost its colonel, lieutenant colonel, major, and six captains. The 44th Georgia lost 335 men, 65 percent of its strength. Mechanicsville should have counted as a Northern victory, had McClellan been willing to profit from it. As was becoming increasingly usual, he was not. When Stonewall Jackson had appeared at Mechanicsville but, uncharacteristically, declined to act, McClellan decided that the battle had been a reverse, that Jackson posed a grave danger, and he ordered the local corps commander, Fitz-John Porter, to fall back to the Gaines's Mill position.

When the Confederates began their attack, on the morning of June 27, 1862, at Gaines's Mill, they found Porter's corps emplaced on top of a steep plateau with forested slopes. It numbered about 27,000, but was stronger in artillery, with about a hundred guns to the South's fifty. Tactically, however, the Confederates were in the stronger posi-

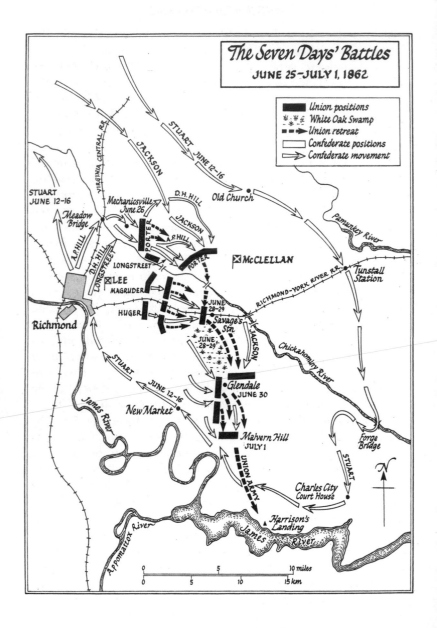

The Seven Days' Battles
JUNE 25–JULY 1, 1862

Union positions
White Oak Swamp
Union retreat
Confederate positions
Confederate movement

STUART
JUNE 12–16

VIRGINIA CENTRAL R.R.

JACKSON

STUART
JUNE 12–16

Old Church

D.H. HILL

Mechanicsville
June 26

JACKSON

STUART
JUNE 12–16

Meadow
Bridge

A.P. HILL

D.H. HILL

PORTER

A.P. HILL

Pamunkey River

☒ McCLELLAN

Tunstall
Station

LONGSTREET

PORTER

LONGSTREET

☒ LEE

MAGRUDER

RICHMOND–YORK RIVER R.R.

Richmond

HUGER

JUNE
28–29

Savage's
Stn.

JACKSON

Chickahominy River

JUNE
28–29

STUART

JUNE 12–16

Glendale
June 30

New Market

James River

Mahvern Hill
JULY 1

Forge
Bridge

STUART

UNION ARMY

Charles City
Court House

N

Appomattox River

Harrison's
Landing

James River

| 0 | | 5 | | 10 miles |
| 0 | 5 | | 10 | 15 km |

tion, fielding six divisions to the Union's two. The only advantage the Union enjoyed was the higher ground.

Fitz-John Porter felt that his corps was vulnerable to a Confederate offensive, and begged McClellan for reinforcements; ironically, it was McClellan who was always begging reinforcements from Washington. He also asked for axes, to fell timber to barricade his front. The axes proved useless, but with others borrowed from the artillery he managed to cover part of his front with rails, stuffed with knapsacks. During the afternoon, Porter's men were able to repel a succession of attacks mounted by the troops of Longstreet, A. P. Hill, D. H. Hill, and Stonewall Jackson. As his defence succeeded, Porter considered shifting forces to his right to take the enemy in flank, but recognition that he was too heavily outnumbered to move from his defended position dissuaded him.

As the afternoon drew on, Confederate attacks on Porter's left grew in intensity and panicked the horses of the artillery deployed there. Twenty-two guns were lost in the confusion. After nightfall Porter was asked to McClellan's headquarters, where he was ordered to retreat across the Chickahominy River, which ran along his rear, and then to retreat to the James River, on which McClellan had decided to concentrate his army. In the concluding stages of the battle, Porter was much concerned for the safety of some volunteer aides-de-camp, the comte de Paris and the duc de Chartres, members of the French royal family who had offered themselves to his staff. As the comte de Paris was pretender to the French throne, it was put to Porter that he should order them to safety. This wholly irrelevant distraction troubled him when he should have been giving his full attention to fighting the battle.

During the retreat from Gaines's Mill, Jackson left his corps to make a reconnaissance of the Union lines. He did so without asking permission of his superior or explaining his intentions to his subordinates. The man he left in charge while he was away was not a soldier, but a professor from a theological seminary, the Reverend R. L. Dabney. Such was the respect in which Jackson was held that none of his subordinates questioned the theologian's authority. Another incident of the retreat was the "charge" of a Union commissary who, driving his wagon loaded with such delicacies as canned pineapple, ran into a Confederate column on the road and, hoping to save his stock-in-trade, drove into the Confederate ranks. After causing some disruption he and his delicacies were captured, to the ordinary Confederate soldiers' delight.

Prisoners were taken in the concluding stages of the Gaines's Mill battle. Among those captured by the Confederates were some of D. H. Hill's West Point contemporaries. One was General John Reynolds, who on being brought before his captor put his face in his hands. They had been messmates in the old army and for six months had shared a tent. Reynolds said, "Hill, we ought not to be enemies." He had gone to sleep during a pause in the battle and been captured when found separated from his troops. Hill assured him that there was no hard feeling and that his downfall was just the fortune of war, notoriously fickle. Reynolds, who had then been exchanged, was killed at Gettysburg.

The retreat from Gaines's Mill brought the fighting on June 29 to Savage's Station, where a large hospital had been set up by the Union. The struggle at Savage's Station was altogether less severe than at Gaines's Mill, since the point of it was not offensive, to attack Richmond, but to secure a line of retreat to Malvern Hill, on which McClellan had fixed as a point of departure and disengagement from the theatre of the Seven Days' Battles. Most of the fighting was between artillery batteries. It led on to the battle of Glendale's or Frayser's Farm, again a Union thrust to get away from Richmond down to the James River at Malvern Hill. Glendale was counted a Union success because the Confederates were repulsed at all points, the army's artillery and supply train was evacuated safely to Malvern Hill, and the infantry were enabled to concentrate at Malvern Hill, fresh for the battle of July 1.

The Union had positioned thirty-six guns, of six batteries, together with a Connecticut siege battery, on the high ground, able to fire over the heads of their own infantry at the attacking enemy lines. During the fighting of June 30, the Union artillery caused heavy loss and destruction among the Confederate batteries deployed opposite. It was not until late afternoon of July 1 that the Confederates began to press infantry attacks against the Union line, where the Northern infantry lay interspersed between the gun positions. The Confederates suffered very heavily and were everywhere driven back. As darkness fell, the Union began its withdrawal to the banks of the James River at Harrison's Landing. Union losses in the seven days totalled 15,855, those of the Army of Northern Virginia 20,204.

Lincoln despatched Halleck, newly appointed as general in chief, to see McClellan, view his army, and advise on its next moves. In conversation in Washington, Lincoln stated that he was certain McClellan would not fight again during the campaign. He said that if he was able to send McClellan 100,000 men, he would be in ecstasy and would announce that he was about to capture Richmond. The next day, however, he would report that the Confederates numbered 400,000 and that he could not advance unless he was sent yet more men. Halleck arrived at Harrison's Landing, where an entrenched camp had been dug, and asked McClellan his intentions. McClellan insisted that he would advance on Richmond, along the line of the James River, taking Petersburg on the way. Halleck asked him to consult his officers, which he did. They voted to advance on Richmond if reinforced by 20,000. McClellan also continued to estimate the size of the opposed armies as 90,000 to 200,000, making his plans for the attack nonsense. On Halleck's return to Washington, moreover, he telegraphed to Lincoln to say that on reflection, he would need not 20,000 but 40,000 more troops. No such numbers were available, and Lincoln therefore instructed Halleck to order McClellan to withdraw. Ships were sent, and in the last days of August the Army of the Potomac was embarked and taken back to Washington.

So ended the best chance the Union was to enjoy throughout the conflict of ending the war quickly. Lee had conducted the Seven Days' Battles with great skill. McClellan had muffed every chance. His position at Mechanicsville–Beaver Dam Creek was unfavourable. He might, however, have gained an advantage at any of the intermediate engagements, of which only Glendale–Frayser's Farm and Gaines's Mill were really hard-fought. At Malvern Hill he enjoyed every advantage, a strong and dominating position, superiority of artillery strength, and enough infantry numbers. Malvern Hill was a Union victory, but McClellan did not squeeze its results to yield an outcome which could have been transformed into a turning point on a subsequent day. The whole campaign confirms his critics' view that McClellan was psychologically deterred from pushing action to the point of result. Fearing failure, he did not try to win.

Both political leaderships, North and South, reposed high hope in the power of superior generalship to achieve their ends. George McClellan expressed his philosophy of Civil War–making most fully, if not persuasively, in a letter written to President Lincoln on July 7, 1862, actually after the Seven Days' Battles, which it might be thought to have called into question the belief that the Confederacy was wholly committed to dividing the Union. The war, he wrote, "should be conducted upon the highest principles known to Christian Civilisations. It should not be a War looking to the subjugation of the people of any State, in any event. It should not be, at all, a War upon population, but against armed forces and political organisations. Neither confiscation of property, political executions of persons, territorial organisation of states, or forcible abolition of slavery should be contemplated for a moment."[9] Needless to say, almost every one of the principles advanced by McClellan were to be broken, including his stricture against the "territorial organisation of states," which was violated by the separation of western Virginia from Virginia proper, not only practically undesirable in McClellan's judgement but also constitutionally dubious. Northern moderation was not reciprocated by the South, where there was a thirst for victory from the outset; but the South believed itself to be the aggrieved party, subjected to attack by an overweening North.

CHAPTER NINE

The War in Middle America

S HILOH WAS AN unexpected battle in an unforeseen place, to which Grant's army was drawn down the Tennessee River by his victories at Forts Henry and Donelson. Its effect was to open up a new front in the centre of nineteenth-century America, in Tennessee, a crucial state for both Union and Confederacy, since it borders Alabama, Mississippi, and Georgia, and, across the Mississippi, Arkansas and Missouri. To the north it gives on to Kentucky, leading to Illinois, Indiana, and Ohio, all solid and important Union territory, which was to be raided by Morgan's cavalry in July 1862; eastward it also offered a route into South Carolina. Eastern Tennessee itself, covered by the tail of the Appalachians, was solidly pro-Union, the largest pocket of Unionist loyalty inside the Confederacy; being mountainous and relatively infertile, it was a region of subsistence farming almost without slaves.

At the beginning of the war, Tennessee was spared an outbreak of fighting because the state government, while not seceding, concluded an alliance with the Confederacy. This transparently evasive measure did not stick. Washington continued to regard Tennessee as a state of the Union and its elected representatives continued to sit in both houses of Congress. While the Confederacy also deemed Tennessee a member state, its political leaders formed at best a government in exile. The eastern counties had voted strongly against secession when a convention was held. Richmond was determined to fight to keep Tennessee out of the Union camp, but at first there were almost no opposing forces inside the state until Grant and Halleck appeared to organise the Army of the Tennessee, which was eventually confronted by Bragg's Army of Tennessee. Thus a new front was opened, or a "line" as fronts were called in the Civil War. The term "front" did not come into use until the First World War, when it was borrowed from the vocabulary of meteorology, on the analogy with weather fronts of low and high pressure. There was an obvious front in Virginia in the region of high pressure between Washington and Richmond. Not so in the West, where troop density was low and there were few cities of importance. Yet gradually central Tennessee would become what a later generation would recognise as a distinctive front, whose crucial features were rivers and railroads. The key to organising the war in the region was to concentrate the scattered forces of the two sides and form campaigning armies. The main components were with Halleck at St. Louis and Beauregard's Confederate survivors of Shiloh. Other Confederate troops were reaching Tennessee from the Atlantic coast and also from Arkansas. During April 1862, Halleck succeeded, by summoning Pope from the Mississippi front at New Madrid and Island No. 10 and Grant from near Shiloh, in forming an army of 100,000 men. Its generals included many of the Union's future leaders, including not only Grant, but also Sherman and Sheridan, Don Carlos Buell, Rosecrans, and George Thomas, the "Rock of Chickamauga." The Union army in the West was organised by Halleck; its three armies were named after the region's major rivers, the Army of the Tennessee under Grant, the Army of the Ohio under Buell, and the Army of the Mississippi under Pope. Laymen may misunderstand the use of the term "Army." It was entirely organisational and hierarchic. Battalions made regiments (two), regiments made brigades (three), brigades made divisions (three or more), divisions made corps (two or more), corps made armies (two or more). On the Union side armies were called after the river near which they operated (for example, the Potomac). In the Confederacy, armies were called after the region in which they operated (e.g., Northern Virginia). Armies also tended to be regional in composition, so that the Armies of the Tennessee and the Ohio, having been raised in the Midwest, were largely recruited from midwesterners.

Halleck opened his campaign against Beauregard by advancing on Corinth, a small railroad town in northern Mississippi which the Confederates had fortified. Intimidated by news of Halleck's approach, Beauregard abandoned Corinth in late May and retreated southward. His army was much depleted by sickness and desertion. He nevertheless initiated a threat to middle Tennessee and Kentucky, and Halleck, rather than engage him, devoted his energies to fortifying Corinth further, thereby converting it into one of the strongest places anywhere in the zone of war. Halleck apparently expected the Southern troops to offer him an advantage by attacking his fortifications, but they did no such thing, instead attacking the Union railroads and threatening advances towards the lower Southern states. Halleck distributed his forces widely in an attempt to safeguard his new area of responsibility, choosing only an advance on Chattanooga as an active measure. In Washington, Lincoln was tiring of Halleck's lethargy. He respected, however, his powers as an organiser and on July 11 summoned him to the capital to assume the post of general in chief, in McClellan's place. As Lincoln would soon find, however, and Grant had already painfully learnt, Halleck was as temperamentally averse to offensive action as the young Napoleon. He was also equally dedicated to detail and to faultfinding with subordinates. Command in Tennessee passed to Grant, but the opportunity to strike during the interregnum was lost by the Confederates, since Beauregard, displeasing Jefferson Davis by taking sick leave at that inconvenient time, was also relieved of command, to be replaced by Braxton Bragg. Bragg, though a fighter, was also bad-tempered and alienated most of his subordinates by insulting them. Unlike both Halleck and McClellan, he had an offensive outlook and did not adhere to the Jominian idea that the purpose of a campaign was to manoeuvre an opponent out of position without actually fighting him. As soon as he succeeded Beauregard, Bragg set about confronting Grant in his headquarters at Corinth. His first plan was to march directly against him. He then reconsidered and decided on a roundabout approach through central Mississippi from the west. Grant, conscious of his threat, responded by getting up the forces, but Halleck, with his obsession about defending everywhere, had second thoughts about Tennessee and Kentucky.

While he was absent deploying his troops, Bragg left large detachments in northern Mississippi under Generals Price and Van Dorn, while he transferred to Kentucky, from which he appeared to threaten Louisville and Cincinnati. In early September 1862, he summoned Price and his 16,000 men. Grant, feeling understandable alarm, concluded correctly that the most likely place Price would strike was Iuka, a railroad village near Corinth which was a depot for a large supply of food and warlike stores. He selected a Wisconsin brigade, known after its mascot as the Eagle Brigade, to defend Iuka. Rosecrans led the advance while Grant, with General Edward Ord under command, waited in reserve. Rosecrans advanced to combat behind a cloud of skirmishers, with an accompanying battery. A tremendous firefight ensued. The ground was covered with dense thickets of scrub between which Blue and Gray dodged as the fight raged. By the end of the afternoon two Northern and two Southern brigades had suffered 790 and 525 casualties, respectively, out of strengths of 3,100 and 2,800. Despite the disparity, the Union got the better of the battle, forcing the Confederates to withdraw.

Grant was waiting in reserve only a few miles from the battlefield, but because of the direction of the wind and other factors was prevented by "acoustic shadow" from hearing any sound of the firing at all. He learnt that the battle had taken place from a despatch from Rosecrans only when it was over. He at once joined Rosecrans in a pursuit of Price and the defeated Confederates, but to Grant's intense displeasure, Rosecrans abandoned the pursuit after Grant left him and Price made good his escape. He and Van Dorn then joined forces. Together they numbered about 22,000 men, whom Price led into southern Tennessee to threaten Corinth, Grant's railroad base and centre of supply, the linchpin for his outposts at Jackson, Memphis, and Bolivar. By early October Grant detected that the rebel army, now commanded by Van Dorn, had repositioned itself to attack Corinth from the north. By October 3 the rebels were ready to attack. The Union troops, under the command of Rosecrans, were less well prepared, Rosecrans having been dilatory in concentrating his men. They were stationed in the old Confederate earthworks defending Corinth, behind which was a second and better position on College Hill. All day during October 3, the Confederates pressed hard against Rosecrans's line, losing heavily but refusing to disengage. Instead they pressed onward, mounting one attack after another, pushing the Union troops back into the streets of Corinth. One formation that withdrew was the so-called Union Brigade, composed of regiments disorganised at Shiloh. Once among the houses of the town, however, they rallied and after meeting other units, resumed resistance and held the attackers at bay. General Rosecrans rode about what was left of his lines at this stage of the battle, shouting at his men to hold fast. Aided by Union artillery fire they did so, repelling one attack after another. Eventually the fighting concentrated round a Union earthwork, Battery Robinet, where the Union inflicted heavy casualties. Fifty-four Confederate dead were later found in the battery ditch, among them the colonel of the 2nd Texas, who had been hit thirteen times. At the culmination of the struggle for the battery, the Confederates turned in retreat. They had suffered 4,000 casualties, the Union 2,500. Moreover, the Confederates' line of retreat was blocked by the Hatchie River, across which Van Dorn sought a crossing. Bridges were hard to find but Rosecrans did not press his pursuit. He was another example of a Union general who lacked the will and insight to exploit a victory when won. Rosecrans halted his army's advance to the Hatchie for two successive nights, making its pace snail-like. His soldiers were frustrated and many pushed ahead without orders. When the flat bottom land of the Hatchie was reached, the Union troops found several Confederate batteries in place to defend the crossing places, and a murderous fight broke out, reinforced from both sides. Eventually it relapsed into stalemate, as Grant was able to recognise even from a distance. He sent orders to Rosecrans to back off, but as Van Dorn made good his escape, Rosecrans all too typically insisted that he was on the brink of a great victory and that Grant was cheating him of a golden opportunity. Van Dorn found sanctuary behind strong defences at Holly Springs in northern Mississippi, a position too strong to attack without lengthy preparation, as Grant also recognised. Rosecrans was to continue to complain of missed opportunity, but Grant knew better. He was already determined to close down the campaign in central Tennessee and to transfer his effort to a direct thrust on Vicksburg.

The campaign in central Tennessee had not, however, been without benefit to the Union. At its end, western Tennessee was largely swept clear of regular Confederate troops, though not of guerrillas, and northern Mississippi was in Union hands; loyal eastern Tennessee had not been liberated but was under threat of Union invasion. The great Union advantage in the region was that it lay adjacent to the Middle West, where troops could be raised in larger numbers.

The summer of 1862 was otherwise a time of troubles for the Union. The abandonment of the Peninsula Campaign and the humiliation of the withdrawal from Richmond was followed by the South's assumption of the offensive in the East and its advances into northern Virginia again and then into Maryland. Defeat in the second battle of Bull Run was swiftly succeeded by the costly stalemate of Antietam. And it was not only in the eastern theatre that the war seemed to be going badly for the Union. In the West, Grant was failing to make progress in his campaign around Vicksburg to open up the valley of the Mississippi to Union traffic. There had been large-scale cavalry raids into the dubiously secure Union territories of Tennessee and the liberation of Arkansas underwent setbacks. Worst of all, in July, Braxton Bragg, the Confederate commander in Mississippi, embarked on a full-scale invasion of Kentucky. Kentucky was probably the most borderline of all the border states, counted by both sides as part of their governed territory and with regiments and large numbers of young men in both their orders of battle. The real danger for the Union in Kentucky, however, was not political but geographical. Its northern border was formed by the Ohio River, just across which lay the great city of Cincinnati, still more important than Chicago as an industrial and railroad centre, with a strong Union population acutely sensitive to the danger of military advances by the Confederacy. The way to Cincinnati, moreover, lay across easily marchable territory. If the Confederacy could drive a corridor across its central section, the territory of the Union would be bisected, in exactly the same way as the developing Union campaign in the valley of the Mississippi threatened to bisect the South. It was vital, therefore, that Bragg's invasion should be defeated.

The difficulty was to organise a counter-offensive. The two Confederate cavalry leaders who had ridden so cavalierly through the region, Nathan Bedford Forrest and John H. Morgan, were still active, while a subsidiary army to Bragg's, commanded by Edmund Kirby Smith, was advancing from Knoxville towards the Cumberland Gap, historic gateway into trans-Appalachia, from which he rapidly arrived at Richmond, Kentucky, only seventy-five miles south of Cincinnati. There he was confronted by a Union division, but all its troops were newly enlisted and it was swiftly dispersed at heavy loss of killed, wounded, and captured. Braxton Bragg had little enthusiasm for offensive war-making, but he was, at this stage and this place, a better bet than his opponent, Don Carlos Buell.

From Washington, however, Halleck so harassed Buell with directions to advance, to put pressure on Bragg, and to fight that eventually Buell had no alternative. He could not plead lack of strength, since he had by mid-September received the reinforcement of two divisions from Grant, while in Louisville and Cincinnati 60,000 recruits, raised locally, were being put through their training. During September, while Buell prudently retired towards Louisville, Bragg attempted to set the stage for a major battle to settle the balance of power in Kentucky. From his position near Louisville, he sent a request to Kirby Smith, who was then in the area of Lexington and Frankfort, the state capital, to meet him with his 20,000 men at Bardstown, south of Louisville. With their combined strength, Bragg believed he could defeat Buell and so settle matters in the borderlands. He also felt that fighting a major battle would pull the Kentuckians off the fence and bring them conclusively to the Confederacy.

Buell was at last conforming to Washington's wishes and during early October appeared in the vicinity of Bragg's army at Bardstown. He concentrated 60,000 men, to the Confederates' 40,000. They were now, in Bragg's temporary absence, under the orders of Bishop Leonidas Polk, who led his men to the small town of Perryville, south of Louisville. What drew him there was a need for water, the Southern summer having dried up the streams. A prolonged drought had left the Chaplin River a string of stagnant pools. As that was the only water available, both sides wanted it. Polk got to it first but was soon attacked by the advance guard of Buell's army, commanded by the up-and-coming Philip Sheridan. Sheridan was aggressive and directed his division's efforts to such effect that it defeated Polk's army and advanced into the streets of Perryville, driving its remnants before them. At this stage, Buell should have completed what was turning into the victory of Perryville and destroyed, with reinforcements, what remained of Bragg's army. By the meteorological accident of acoustic shadow, however, no sound of the battle raging in Perryville reached the ears of anyone else under Buell's command. He therefore failed to march to Sheridan's assistance, though as darkness fell the Confederate line was defended by only a single brigade which would have dispersed if attacked aggressively. Next morning, when Buell positioned his army for a general advance, the ground was empty. Bragg had during the night decided he was beaten and had led his army away.

Perryville was an all-too-typical Civil War battle in its lack of decision, despite high casualties on both sides. The indecisiveness of battles is one of the great mysteries of the war. In the East, particularly from 1864 onwards, it was largely explained by the recourse to digging, which produced earthworks from which it was almost impossible to expel the enemy. In the West, by contrast, particularly in the earlier years, earthworks were less commonly constructed. The explanation therefore seems to lie in two unconnected factors: the lack of a military means, such as large cavalry forces or mobile horse artillery, that could deliver a pulverising blow, and the remarkable ability of infantry on both sides to accept casualties. Casualties at Perryville—4,200 Union and 3,400 Confederate—were certainly high, but neither side seemed shaken. An eyewitness, Major J. Montgomery Wright of Buell's army, describes the strange phenomenon of the acoustic shadow. Riding as a staff officer on a detached mission, he "suddenly turned into a road and therefore before me, within a few hundred yards, the battle of Perryville burst into view, and the roar of the artillery and the continuous

rattle of the musketry first broke upon my ear. . . . It was wholly unexpected, and it fixed me with astonishment. It was like tearing away a
curtain from the front of a great picture. . . . At one bound my horse
carried me from stillness into the uproar of battle. One turn from a
lonely bridlepath through the woods brought me face to face with the
bloody struggle of thousands of men." Major Wright witnessed the
effect of the struggle on one group, which suggests that the battle was
having a decisive effect upon them: "I saw young Forman with the
remnant of his company of the 15th Kentucky regiment, withdrawn to
make way for the reinforcements, and as they silently passed me they
seemed to stagger and reel like men who had been battling against a
great storm. Forman had the colours in his hand, and he and several of
his little group of men had their hands upon their chests and their lips
apart as though they had difficulty in breathing. They filed into a field
and without thought of shot or shell they lay down on the ground
apparently in a state of exhaustion."[1] Yet despite such efforts the Union
line did not break, nor did the equally punished Confederate. Bragg,
who rightly recognised he was outnumbered, swiftly decided to withdraw during the night of October 8 and fell back to Knoxville and
Chattanooga, abandoning his invasion of Kentucky altogether. The
Southern press, and several of his generals, seethed with dissatisfaction; Bragg was called to Richmond to account for his failure, but he
had a friend in Jefferson Davis, who accepted his explanations and
allowed him to continue in command.

Bragg's abandonment of the attempt on Kentucky completed a general Confederate failure on the central front in the West. Just before
Perryville, Generals Price and Van Dorn had been defeated by the
Union general Rosecrans at Corinth in Mississippi. It followed
another Confederate defeat at nearby Iuka. Grant, who was engaged in
the campaign at a distance, had hoped to trap the Confederates either
at Corinth or Iuka and was disappointed not to do so. He blamed
Rosecrans, for a movement of his troops he thought dilatory, though
the recurrence of acoustic shadow may have played a part. For whatever reason, however, the Confederates had failed in their efforts to
reverse the balance of power both in Kentucky and Tennessee, in what
proved to be the last unforced Confederate offensive west of the
Appalachians. As the fighting died down, Grant gathered his forces to
renew his campaign against Vicksburg. The citizens of Cincinnati and
Louisville relapsed into calm, after what had been some disturbing
weeks. Though it was not realised in Richmond, the failure in the West

was a grave blow to the Confederacy, reducing their range of strategic options to the well-worn pattern of keeping alive Union fears of an advance against Washington or feints at Pennsylvania and Maryland, theatres where the North enjoyed permanent advantages. The drive into Kentucky and threats against Tennessee were the only imaginative moves made by the Confederacy throughout the war; their failure and the failure to repeat them confirmed to objective observers that the South could now only await defeat. It might be long in coming, but after the end of 1862 it was foreordained and inevitable.

There were objective observers. Two were Karl Marx and Frederick Engels, then in exile in England, where in March 1862 they composed an analysis of the progress of the Civil War of quite remarkable prescience. Marx and Engels's interest in the Civil War was not political. As revolutionaries they hoped for nothing from the United States. It was simply that as men with a professional interest in warfare and the management of armies they could not prevent themselves from studying military events, and prognosticating based on their lessons. Marx concluded that, following the capture of Fort Donelson, Grant, for whom he had formed an admiration, had achieved a major success against Secessia, as he called the Confederacy. His reason for so thinking was that he identified Tennessee and Kentucky as vital ground for the Confederacy. If they were lost, the cohesion of the rebel states would be destroyed. To demonstrate his point, he asked, "Does there exist a military centre of gravity whose capture would break the backbone of the Confederacy resistance, or are they, as Russia still was in 1812 [at the time of Napoleon's invasion], unconquerable without, in a word, occupying every village and every patch of ground along the whole periphery."

His answer was that Georgia was the centre of gravity. "*Georgia,*" he wrote, "*is the key to Secessia.*" "With the loss of Georgia, the Confederacy would be cut into two sections which would have lost all connection with each other." It would not be necessary to conquer the whole of Georgia to achieve that result, but only the railroads through the state.

Marx had foreseen, with uncanny insight, exactly how the decisive stage of the Civil War would be fought. He was scathingly dismissive of the Anaconda Plan, and he also minimised the importance of capturing Richmond. To that extent, his foresight was defective. The blockade, a major element of the Anaconda strategy, was crucial to the defeat of the Confederacy, and it was indeed the capture of Richmond that brought the war to an end. In almost all other respects, however, Marx's analysis was eerily accurate, testimony to his grisly interest in the use of violence for political ends. The analysis was published in German, in Vienna, in the review *Die Presse*. It may not have been noticed in the United States.[2]

Marx, who had the keenest eye for strategic geography, did not discuss the importance of Tennessee and Kentucky as a weak spot in the defences of the Union. Materialist as he was, he had already assured himself that the vastly preponderant industrial and financial power of the North guaranteed its victory. He made insufficient allowances, however, for the necessity of fighting for that outcome and for how relentless the struggle would be.

CHAPTER TEN

Lee's War in the East, Grant's War in the West

T HE SECOND HALF of 1862 inaugurated a transformation of the war, which suddenly became much more serious, bitter, and hard-fought than that of the first year. The change had something to do with a shift in personnel. McClellan, whose career was about to peter out, not only lacked the killer instinct, a failing which unfitted him for both of the posts Lincoln had given him, chief of the Army of the Potomac and general in chief. Worse than that, McClellan actually had a philosophy of war, at least of the Civil War, which deprecated hard knocks. Like many other Northerners, he found the effects of division almost as painful as division itself. He regretted the hatreds the war had fostered and sought to fight in a way that would not intensify them—so no confiscation of enemy property, no living off the land, certainly no emancipation of the slaves. Though reemployed by Lincoln after the retreat from Richmond at the end of the Seven Days' Battles, for want of anyone else, he had by now lost the president's confidence and it was certain that one more failure in command would lead to his supersession for good. Lincoln was so uncertain of his reliability that, following the withdrawal to Harrison's Landing, he divided the Union forces in northern Virginia to form two armies, leaving, however reluctantly, McClellan in charge of the Army of the Potomac, but combining the forces from West Virginia together with McDowell's corps from the Army of the Potomac to form the Army of Virginia under John Pope. Pope, quite unlike McClellan, was extreme in his views and believed the war could be won quicker if the Southern people were made to suffer. He was not given a chance to see whether his harsher methods might have worked, for while Halleck, appointed general in chief to succeed McClellan in July 1862, was bringing back McClellan's army from the Virginia Peninsula, Lee glimpsed the opportunity to invade the North and perhaps inflict a defeat, while the two big Union armies, those of Virginia and the Potomac, were out of touch with each other. Lee's line of departure was the Rappahannock. Close at hand he had Jackson's tried and tested troops. Jackson struck the first blow, inflicting a sharp reverse on Pope at Cedar Mountain. It was a significant battle because, although comparatively small in scale, it required Jackson to show his battle-winning talents rather than, as during the valley campaign, his strategic guile. Such talents were not displayed. His old valley opponent, Nathaniel Banks, commanded the Union army, which Jackson's outnumbered, but by refusal to concede defeat and by the hard fighting of his soldiers, Banks denied Jackson a victory at Cedar Mountain and left him only the consolation of occupying the field at the battle's end, which cost both sides about three hundred killed, though the Union missing exceeded the Confederate.

In a campaign which, if properly conducted by the Union, should have resulted in Lee's army being caught between the two big Union forces, Lee now glimpsed an opportunity to crush Pope. In practice Pope, by skilful manoeuvre, evaded Lee's efforts to pin him between the Rapidan and the Rappahannock and decided that he could now take Jackson at a disadvantage. His decision was based on the supposition that Jackson, who was manoeuvring to cooperate with Lee, was in retreat to the Shenandoah. He was not. Instead, by resuming his foot cavalry technique, he was marching—at a speed of thirty-six miles in fifty-four hours—to place himself in Pope's rear. The spot he chose to occupy could not have been more dangerous to Pope. It was at Manassas Junction, where Pope had set up his supply base. The lightning march provided Jackson's soldiers with an abundance of food and necessities, while the position threatened Pope, as Lee intended, with being cut off from his line of retreat towards Washington. Indeed, the result of Jackson's occupation of Manassas Junction obliged Pope to fight a repetition of the first battle of the war. Second Manassas, or Second Bull Run, was a much fiercer encounter than the first, evidence of how much both sides had learned in thirteen months of fighting. Jackson, hoping to take Pope at a disadvantage, launched his men out of the woods against Pope's when he received word from Lee that Longstreet was approaching, with strong numbers, from the valley. The disposition of forces should have ensured a crushing Confederate victory by envelopment, had it not been for the combat qualities of the Union troops. They included four midwestern regiments, one of which, the 2nd Wisconsin, had fought at First Bull Run. These regiments, forming the so-called Black Hat Brigade because they were dressed in pre-war regular army uniforms, fought with such determination that they held off all efforts by the Stonewall Brigade to break the Union line and so ensured that at the end of the day Lee's hope of inflicting a crushing defeat had been nullified. Once again Jackson displayed his less-than-complete powers of leadership in the heat of action. The culmination of his effort was an attempt to envelop Pope's right by a march around his flank to Chantilly, east of Manassas, which led to a small, confused battle, also known as Ox Hill. Jackson failed to envelop Pope, who kept open his line of communication with Washington. The Confederates foundered largely because there were by now overwhelming numbers of Union troops in and around the old battlefield, including most of McClellan's Army of the Potomac. Their numbers were so large that Second Bull Run should have been a clear-cut Union victory. That it was not was McClellan's fault. He had a dislike of Pope and in a fit of pettiness, which did the Union cause serious disservice, refused to go to Pope's assistance.

Second Bull Run therefore became a Union defeat, though with closely equal and very heavy losses by both sides, 1,724 Union soldiers killed to 1,481 Confederates. In the aftermath, Lincoln relieved Pope of command and recombined his Army of Virginia with the Army of the Potomac, which he brought to Washington to assure its defence—always the president's first consideration. The Union failure at Second Bull Run encouraged Lee to adopt a new strategy. Instead of using all his force to defend the territory of Virginia, he would alter the tempo of the war altogether and take it to the enemy by invading his territory, a strategy to which he would adhere for the next ten months of the war. Lee had thus far given no indication that he possessed any offensive impulse or the ability to bring attacking moves to a successful conclusion. Indeed, he had won an unwelcome reputation for defensiveness and dislike of risk-taking. The reason for his change of tempo was simple. The offensive raised the pressure of war from Virginia, his home state, and it made directly available the natural resources of the North to an invading army. Strategically, it altered the balance of the war, wresting the initiative from the North and threatening it with the spectre of defeat within its own territory. Such a change of strategy would also bring encouragement to the civilian South and to the Confederacy's supporters in Europe. The goal of diplomatic recognition always floated somewhere behind the South's war plans.

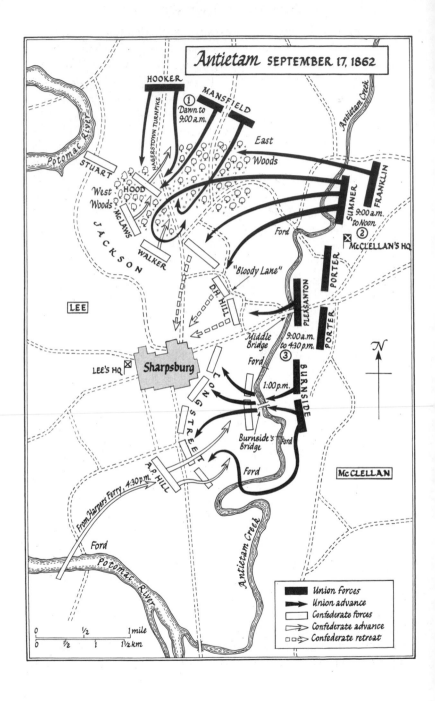

Antietam SEPTEMBER 17, 1862

HOOKER

MANSFIELD

① Dawn to 9:00 a.m.

HAGERSTOWN TURNPIKE

East Woods

STUART

Potomac River

West Woods

HOOD

JACKSON

McLAWS

WALKER

FRANKLIN

SUMNER

② 9:00 a.m. to Noon

⊠ McCLELLAN'S HQ

Ford

"Bloody Lane"

D. H. HILL

PORTER

PORTER

PLEASANTON

9:00 a.m. to 4:30 p.m.

LEE

Middle Bridge

Ford

③

LONGSTREET

LEE'S HQ ⊠

Sharpsburg

1:00 p.m.

BURNSIDE

Burnside's Bridge Ford

A. P. HILL

From Harpers Ferry, 4:30 p.m.

Ford

Ford

McCLELLAN

Antietam Creek

Potomac River

Ford

N

0   ½   1 mile
0   ½   1   1½ km

■ Union forces
⬛▶ Union advance
▭ Confederate forces
▷ Confederate advance
▢▢▷ Confederate retreat

Lee crossed the Potomac northwest of Washington on September 4–6, 1862, and advanced into Maryland as far as Frederick, where Barbara Fritchie defied the invaders—in John Greenleaf Whittier's famous poem: " 'Shoot, if you must, this old gray head, / But spare your country's flag,' she said." There he unilaterally divided his army into three, sending Jackson to Harpers Ferry; Longstreet to Hagerstown, on the upper Potomac; and keeping only the formations of D. H. Hill and J. E. B. Stuart with him. A strange episode then compromised his strategy. Lee's plans, set out in a special order, No. 191, detailing the separate movements of his army, were found by a Union soldier wrapped around three cigars in an abandoned Confederate camp. The paper was taken to McClellan's assistant adjutant general, who knew the man who had written it and so could authenticate the handwriting. Even the ever-timorous McClellan was persuaded that he had been granted the most extraordinary stroke of good fortune. The news reached him by September 13 and persuaded him to position his army behind South Mountain, near the little town of Sharpsburg. Characteristically, McClellan delayed issuing orders to march overnight and continued to proclaim, as usual, that he was outnumbered, even though the captured orders revealed precisely the opposite. Lee, though threatened by McClellan's deployment, rallied; informed by a breach of security at Union headquarters that Special Order No. 191 had fallen into enemy hands, he kept his nerve and positioned his 25,000 men, to the Union's 80,000, along a tributary of the Potomac known as Antietam Creek, which would give its name to the coming battle in Northern accounts; to the South it would be known as Sharpsburg. Both names would cast a chill for years to come; indeed, they still do. For September 17, 1862, was to become not only the bloodiest day of the Civil War, but the bloodiest of any day in any of America's previous wars and of wars to come, bloodier than June 6, 1944, during the landing on Omaha Beach on D-Day, or February 19, 1945, the landing on Iwo Jima. The reason for the costliness of Antietam was the nature of the battlefield, a constricted space only two miles square between two waterlines, that of the Potomac and its tributary Antietam Creek. The interior of the tiny battlefield was further cramped by the existence of a number of killing grounds, such as the one that became known as the Cornfield, and a sunken road to be known as Bloody Lane. Into this maze both Lee and McClellan thrust their forces as they became available. Lee's were arriving from Harpers Ferry, and the whole mass, 120,000 strong, was thereby compelled to do its worst. At the Dunker Church, a rustic prayer house, and at the Rohrbach Bridge over Antietam Creek, later to be known as Burnside's Bridge because of that general's repeated efforts to take it, Union troops struggled with Confederates, time and again nearly breaking Lee's line but always failing to do so because McClellan shrank from committing all the strength he had. As the dreadful day drew out, the number of dead and wounded mounted. The eventual total was 12,400 casualties on the Union side, 10,300 on the Confederate. Particular unit losses were staggering. The 1st Texas lost 80 percent of its strength killed or wounded. Of the 250 men of the 6th Georgia, only 24 survived unhurt. Colonel David Thompson of the 9th New York recorded a peculiar phenomenon of the battle: he saw at a particular moment "the singular effect mentioned I think, in the Life of Goethe, on a similar occasion—the whole landscape for an instant turned slightly red."[1] Lee's son, serving in the Army of Northern Virginia during the battle of Antietam, recalled the following incident:

> As one of the Army of Northern Virginia, I occasionally saw the commander-in-chief, on the march, or passed the headquarters close enough to recognise him and members of his staff, but as a private soldier in Jackson's corps did not have much time, during that campaign, for visiting, and until the battle of Sharpsburg I had no opportunity of speaking to him. On that occasion our battery had been severely handled, losing many men and horses. Having three guns disabled, we were ordered to withdraw, and while moving back we passed General Lee and several of his staff, grouped on a little knoll near the road. Having no definite orders where to go, our captain, seeing the commanding general, halted us and rode over to get some instructions. Some others and myself went along to see and hear. General Lee was dismounted with some of his staff around him, a courier holding his horse. Captain Poague, commanding our battery, the Rockbridge Artillery, saluted, reported our condition, and asked for instructions. The General, listening patiently looked at us—his eyes passing over me without any sign of recognition—and then ordered Captain Poague to take the most serviceable horses and men, man the uninjured gun, send the disabled part of his command back to refit, and report to the front for duty. As Poague turned to go, I went up to speak to my father. When he found out who I was, he congratulated me on being well and unhurt. I then said: "General, are you going to send us in again?" "Yes, my

son," he replied, with a smile; "you all must do what you can to help drive these people back."[2]

On the night following the battle, Lee withdrew his survivors across the Potomac. It was the beginning of his retreat from Maryland. McClellan could therefore claim, and did, that he had won a victory. Lincoln was not persuaded. As McClellan waited longer and longer to follow Lee's retreat, Lincoln grew ever more impatient with his failure and on November 7 removed him from command. That was not the end of McClellan. He was to run, unsuccessfully, against Lincoln as the Democratic candidate in the 1864 presidential election. It was, however, the end of his military career. His departure did not in any way dent his self-esteem, merely hardened his conviction that he was surrounded by dunderheads. Lincoln's hints of impatience at his inactivity grew broader and broader. He pointed out that McClellan could slip troops between Lee and Richmond. Hints were ignored. The general argued that his army could not march without boots or food, even though, as Lincoln told him, Lee's men did both. Lincoln eventually lost the patience he had preserved for so long. It was McClellan's intransigence that led to his replacement by Burnside as much as his incompetence. Burnside was a fighting general and a brave man, but he lacked McClellan's talents, which, though offset by much failure, were considerable. McClellan had also inspired the Union soldier, who believed fervently in the general's leadership no matter what setbacks he was led into. McClellan's departure was clearly and genuinely regretted in the ranks. No other general would find a comparable place in the army's respect and affection until the coming of Grant from the West in 1864.

Antietam left one other profound change beyond the removal of McClellan. The battle also altered for good the moral atmosphere of the war, by providing Lincoln with the opportunity to proclaim large-scale emancipation of the South's slave population, a measure long desired by the president himself and millions of his fellow countrymen. Lincoln had already written a draft emancipation act and had urged emancipation on the border states, though without success. Border state whites feared that emancipated blacks would misbehave; they also feared that the grant of freedom across state lines would attract masses of plantation slaves to take liberty on their soil. The fear of a northward migration of slaves seeking liberty was what also caused many high-minded Northerners to oppose emancipation while supporting the war. Lincoln had had to overrule Frémont's premature proclamation of liberation in the Western Department because of the danger that it might tip opinion in the border states. Now Antietam gave him a chance to initiate the reforms his great speeches of 1858—"this government cannot endure permanently half slave and half free"—had promised but that his first years in office had left unfulfilled. In the draft emancipation proclamation which he read to the cabinet on July 22, 1862, he had implored the slave states to liberate their bondsmen against the threat that they would be freed by presidential decree in states still in rebellion on January 1, 1863. William Seward, secretary of state, had prevailed on Lincoln to postpone issuing the draft until a change in the Union's military fortunes, at that moment at a low ebb following the debacle of the Seven Days' Battles, should make it more propitious. On September 22, five days after Antietam, Lincoln decided the moment had come. For political if not military reasons, he decided to accept McClellan's judgement that the battle had been a victory, if only because it had led to Lee's withdrawal from Maryland, and so he announced that on January 1, 1863, all slaves on the territory of states still in rebellion on that date would be legally free. The Emancipation Proclamation transformed the moral atmosphere of the war. Thenceforward the war was about slavery, an issue that crystallised attitudes. Abolitionists had got their way. Northern moderates at last knew where the Union stood. Southerners could now believe that the Union opposed states' rights as a means of abolishing slavery and thus impoverishing Southern property owners and undermining the basis of civil order inside the Confederacy.

Antietam had a further effect. Because Lincoln had decided that it was a victory, the European powers accepted it as such and their consideration of extending diplomatic recognition to the South faded. The South's best hope of winning recognition had come during the cotton famine of 1861–62, when an embargo on sales to Europe by producers and brokers had stopped production of cloth in many mill areas in Britain and France. The embargo ultimately failed because of the adoption of alternative supply and the existence in Europe of large stocks accepted during a period of overproduction in 1859–60. Isolated disputes and excitements apart, such as the *Trent* affair, the danger to the North of European diplomatic recognition of the Confederacy disappeared after Antietam. British recognition of Southern belligerency in May 1861, which brought the right to conduct operations at sea but fell short of diplomatic recognition, palliated the South's sense of injustice to some extent, without damaging Northern interests, though it did inflame tempers in the U.S. Congress.

The replacement of McClellan did not immediately improve the fortunes of the Army of the Potomac. Burnside at once compromised his new role. His plan of employment of the army was to shift it southward from the vicinity of Sharpsburg to that of Fredericksburg, on the Rappahannock River, from which he planned to initiate an advance on Richmond. To have any chance of success he needed to move quickly, which in turn required a surprise bridging of the Rappahannock. Bridging required pontoons, which had to be brought from depots in Washington· under the control of General Halleck. Either because Burnside did not make himself clear or because Halleck failed to understand, time was wasted in securing the pontoons and in making the crossing. Lee's army was given ample time to prepare to defeat the manoeuvre. The bridging at Fredericksburg itself was opposed, and the Union engineers emplacing the pontoons suffered heavy casualties. By December 13, nevertheless, the Army of the Potomac had crossed and was in position on the south bank, facing a line of heights occupied by the Army of Northern Virginia. Burnside's plan was for Joseph Hooker's and Edwin Sumner's men to fix the Confederate defenders, while William Franklin's made a feint at Stonewall Jackson's position on the high ground south of the town. If successful, the advance was to be transformed into a major attack, rolling up the Southern front from left to right. The difficulty with the plan was that there was too much high ground on the south bank of the Rappahannock and that the Confederate troops controlled all of it. They also dominated, with artillery, the low ground the Union troops would have to cross to come to grips with the defenders, who were protected by natural and man-made barriers.

As soon as the Union infantry appeared, the Confederates opened rapid and accurate fire from a sunken road, fronted by a stone wall that ran along the front of the high ground, Marye's Heights, behind Fredericksburg. The battle commenced on the morning of December 13, and, as the thick fog began to lift, the casualties, which the Confederate artillery commander had boasted would be high, started to mount rapidly. The Confederates enjoyed every advantage—a commanding position, protection from return fire—and so were able to shoot down the advancing attackers with ease and at little risk to themselves. During that short December afternoon, a bitterly cold one intensified by showers of snow, fourteen Union brigades were committed and by the end of the day 12,700 men had been killed or wounded. If comparisons are to be drawn, Fredericksburg resembled in its horror almost no other battle of the Civil War but anticipated some of the worst of the First World War. There were the same appalling climatic conditions, the same lack of cover, the same difficulty and delay in collecting and evacuating the wounded. For several hours the Union attackers lay pinned to the frozen ground by enemy fire; many of those who shifted cramped limbs suffered fresh wounds as they did so. Fredericksburg was, for the Union forces, a one-sided Antietam, in which they suffered comparable casualties without any chance of fighting back.

During 1862 the character of the First World War was also anticipated in the frequency of and shortening of interval between the battles fought in the eastern theatre. Second Bull Run, Antietam, and Fredericksburg were all fought in the period between August 29 and December 13. All were big battles, producing heavy casualties—Antietam and Fredericksburg exceptionally heavy casualties—and consuming very large quantities of munitions and other supplies. Battles such as these could not be waged without large reserves of men and equipment, any more than could successive stages of the battles of the Somme or Verdun. And like the Somme and Verdun, Second Bull Run, Antietam, and Fredericksburg wore armies out. By Christmas 1862, the Army of the Potomac was battered and exhausted by the strains of combat, of harsh existence in the field and on the line of march, and by appalling losses. The Army of Northern Virginia was even more so, because of the South's comparative shortage of manpower. Lincoln, though determined to sustain pressure on the Confederacy, was alarmed when he heard that Burnside intended to turn the army and cross the Rappahannock again in the face of Lee's force; the president rightly feared another disaster. Burnside admitted to Lincoln his full responsibility for the defeat and announced his intention publicly to confess it. Nevertheless, he still harboured the ambition to make another attempt. Two of his subordinates, General John Newton and Brigader General John Cochrane, were so concerned at his frame of mind that they went to see Lincoln. Denying that they sought Burnside's removal, they said nonetheless that his plan should be forbidden.

This was a command crisis with which Lincoln had to deal personally, much as he preferred to let his generals make their own decisions. On January 1, 1863, he called a conference at the White House. It took a deeply unsatisfactory form. Burnside called for the resignations of

Halleck and Stanton, but also declared that the army had lost confidence in him and asked to be relieved. Two days of inconclusive discussion ended in Burnside returning to the Rappahannock determined to cross, but asking Halleck's approval, which Halleck unequivocally refused to give. Burnside crossed all the same and attempted an advance which had to be terminated because of the glutinous state of the roads. It became known as the "Mud March," deeply disheartened the army, and prompted heavy criticism from Burnside's subordinates. Outraged by their disloyalty, as he saw it, he threatened to dismiss several of them. He even spoke wildly of hanging Joseph Hooker, one of his corps commanders. He had no legal power to do any of these things. Word of Burnside's discomposure swiftly reached Lincoln, who, over the course of the following days, decided that he would have to relieve him of command and replace him with Hooker, who had a fighting reputation. On January 25, the change was made, though Lincoln, who admired Burnside's personal qualities, refused to allow him to resign his commission. Lincoln probably recognised that Burnside was on the point of breakdown. The general was deeply affected by the Fredericksburg losses, as several generals of the First World War would be by the holocaust of the trench offensives on the Western Front. This was a new development. Commanders during the warfare of the absolute monarchs, though they presided over terrible slaughter, seemed untouched by it, perhaps because of long apprenticeship and the social distance separating leaders and led. Empathy with the common soldier was a function of American democracy and the populist character of the Civil War. It was by no means a universal emotion. Lee, a man of great humanity, never came near cracking, even as the destruction of his armies approached. Grant, who directed some of the bloodiest battles of the war, accepted casualties, perhaps because he had conceived for himself a philosophy of war in which the celebration of its glories played no part. Burnside, a modest, even humble man, did not seek a reputation at the expense of his soldiers' lives, despite his awful management of Fredericksburg. The spectacle of large-scale killing, which he had been spared before 1861 because he went late to the Mexican War, seemed to have been too much for him.

The opening of 1863 still found the Confederacy holding the initiative in the East. Though Lee was no longer on Union territory, and despite the reinforcement of the Army of the Potomac to a strength of 133,000, its highest so far, the debacle of Fredericksburg and the uncertainties aroused by the turmoil in the high command had robbed the Union of moral dominance. Lee had shown that he had the capacity to invade and to fight successfully on Union soil. His occupation of advanced positions in northern Virginia suggested that he would attempt invasion again, and many in the North rightly suspected that the Confederates might win. It was an uncertain New Year in Washington and the cities of the East.

News from Mississippi and the West brought little comfort. The hope of 1862, that the whole length of the Mississippi between New Orleans and Memphis might be opened to Union traffic, had not been fulfilled. Grant's army was still picking ineffectively at the backdoor of Vicksburg, while in Tennessee there had been a revival of Confederate fortunes. The passion for discord that took possession of the United States in 1861 did not confine itself to the densely settled and populated lands of the old thirteen colonies. It also took hold in the new territories of westward expansion, in regions where slavery was scarcely known, demonstrating that secession was a state of mind as much as of economic interest. During the summer and fall of 1861 there were outbreaks of fighting, often intense and bloody, in Kentucky and Missouri and as far west as Arkansas. Kentucky's population was heavily Virginian in origin, so it was not surprising that it should be tinged by loyalty to the new government in Richmond. Chronologically, the first action by the Confederate western armies was at Wilson's Creek, in Missouri in August 1861, where Nathaniel Lyon, who had saved the state for the Union, was killed in battle by a small army commanded by Sterling Price. The next area to spring into military life was eastern Tennessee, the main object of Lincoln's western strategy, since he hoped so earnestly to liberate the Tennessee Unionists, most numerous in the eastern half of the state, from Confederate control. The local Union commander proved unequal to the task of dislodging the Confederates and was dismissed, taking with him his subordinate, William Tecumseh Sherman, whose career would be only temporarily set back. The successor was Don Carlos Buell, who had under command George Thomas, the future Rock of Chickamauga. In January 1862, at Mill Springs in Kentucky on the Cumberland River, Thomas engaged General George Crittenden's 4,000 men at the battle, which is also known as Logan's Crossroads. Crittenden attempted an attack but was checked by Thomas, who then succeeded in counter-attacking and routing the Confederates, who were pursued from the field of battle. Though casualties were few, Mill Springs was a genuine Union victory. Lincoln was delighted, since the victory seemed to presage bringing assistance to his cherished Unionist enclave in east Tennessee.

The sequel to Mill Springs unwound, however, not in Tennessee but in Missouri, where following the Unionist setback at Wilson's Creek the Confederate general Sterling Price led his army of 11,000 southward into the northwest corner of Arkansas, to take position at a place called Pea Ridge. He there came under the command of General Earl Van Dorn, later to win renown as a Confederate cavalry leader, who had brought reinforcements. His opponent was General Samuel Curtis, whose Army of the Missouri was outnumbered. Curtis began his campaign on the offensive but was forced to retreat onto the Ozark Plateau, astride the Arkansas-Missouri border. There on March 7–8, 1862, he fought a bitter and costly battle, known both as Pea Ridge and Elkhorn Tavern, after the two places at which action was concentrated during the two days the battle lasted. The Union forces were better handled, at one point re-forming their lines through 180 degrees; their artillery made better practice, so that Pea Ridge was that rare Civil War encounter, a battle in which artillery achieved decisive effect. Van Dorn decamped eastward towards the theatre of operations that was opening on the middle Mississippi, south of Forts Henry and Donelson. In doing so, he abandoned Missouri and Arkansas to Federal forces. Curtis, a West Point graduate, appointed by Halleck to command the military district of southwest Missouri, had about 11,000 men, whom he grandiloquently titled the Army of the Southwest. In February 1862, he led the army against Price at Springfield, Missouri, along a road over the Ozark highlands, known as the Wire or Telegraph Road. His victory at Pea Ridge led to the unlocking of the whole campaign in the western theatre, setting in motion the army of Ulysses S. Grant that would lead to the battle of Shiloh. Curtis largely owed his success in this distant theatre, where the going was difficult and the surroundings rugged, to the exertions of his supply officer, Captain Philip Sheridan, a master of logistics, who managed to get food and munitions to him throughout the campaign. Sheridan would, during its course, come to the attention of Grant and through that connection begin his ascent to high command, which would culminate in his appointment as chief of Union cavalry in the Overland Campaign, the siege of Petersburg, and the surrender at Appomattox.

Union victory at Pea Ridge also precipitated operations even farther west, in New Mexico, which involved Union troops from California. Jefferson Davis was keen to carry the flag of the Confederacy to the Pacific coast. Union faintheartedness had allowed the Texas Confederates to advance into New Mexico. Canby, the Union commander, then found new resolution and defeated Sibley, his Confederate opponent and inventor of the ubiquitous Sibley tent, first at Johnson's Ranch (also known as Apache Canyon) on March 26, 1862. Action was resumed on March 28 at La Glorieta Pass, from which Sibley retreated all the way back to his starting place at San Antonio, Texas. Union troops consisted of the 1st California Infantry and a contingent of Colorado gold miners. The contribution of the far westerners stamped an all-American character on the Civil War, though they also terminated the Confederate effort to create a Southern outpost on the Pacific coast.

On balance, however, it was the Confederates who enjoyed the greater success in the borderlands in the summer of 1862, success which prompted the supreme commander in the theatre, Braxton Bragg, to decide on mounting an invasion of Kentucky. There he played on Lincoln's deepest fears, for not only was the president tenderly sympathetic to the fortunes of the pro-Unionists in the border states, he also harboured a keen geostrategic anxiety about the security of the Union "waist" between the Ohio River and the Great Lakes. This "waist" may have been a geographic figment. It was real enough in the president's mind, however, and he feared a Confederate drive northward through Kentucky and Ohio towards the southern shore of Lake Erie quite as much as the South feared, with better reason, a bisection of the Confederacy along the Mississippi Valley. Union success in the area of confluence of the Mississippi, Cumberland, and Ohio rivers earlier in the year appeared to have repelled the danger to the Union "waist." In September and October, however, the Confederates drove back into the region, reaching Corinth, Mississippi, the capture of which earlier in the year had seemed to crown the Shiloh campaign.

The campaign in the West in 1862 culminated in the opening of Grant's direct offensive against Vicksburg, frustrated though it was to be for months by appalling terrain. While Grant struggled to find a way forward, harassed by troopers of Van Dorn's and Forrest's cavalry, Rosecrans—who had succeeded Buell in command of the Army of the Cumberland—attempted to assist him by increasing the area of Union control within Tennessee. Rosecrans's advance was threatened by

Bragg, who at Murfreesboro—also known as Stones River—began a battle which, in terms of casualties as a percentage of numbers engaged, was to prove the costliest of the war to both sides. Fought over three days, from December 31, 1862, to January 2, 1863, it began with Confederate attacks on the Union positions, from which they were successively driven back. Eventually, however, the Union lines re-formed, leaving the Confederates exposed to the fire of massed Union artillery, which as Bragg's subordinate, General John C. Breckinridge, had correctly foreseen, massacred his infantry as they attempted to mount a battle-winning charge. Both armies claimed a victory, but both withdrew, each having lost about a third of their respective strengths. Murfreesboro, or Stones River, terminated the campaign in Tennessee for the winter.

The West was an enormous theatre, dwarfing that in the East, where only a hundred miles separated the two capitals and the road and rail networks, together with the tidewater channels, facilitated communica tion both east–west and north–south. From Memphis to New Orleans was 400 miles along the Mississippi; from Chattanooga to Memphis nearly 300 miles overland. The cross-country communications were poor, railroads differing in gauge or petering out in dead ends. For the Union there was no long-distance rail connection between the East and the Mississippi Valley except by the roundabout route through Cincinnati to St. Louis. Nor were the rivers helpful, as they were in the Ohio country. The tributaries of the Mississippi led westward into the South's backcountry. Its neighbours, like the Alabama and the Chattahoochee, were internal to the states they watered, not interstate axes of communication. Both the human and physical geography of the western theatre defied the effort to make organised war, condemning the armies that operated there to piecemeal campaigning or to raiding. Nor did the theatre, outside the Mississippi Valley, offer objectives the capture of which promised decisive results. To fight in the West was to act at a level little superior to that of exploration and pioneering, in a struggle to find the enemy and routes between potential battlefields.

Winfield Scott had therefore correctly identified at the very start of the war that the key to any success in the vast territory south of the Ohio River was the seizure of the Mississippi Valley, which by early 1863 had become Grant's chief purpose. The geography of the valley, however, frustrated his efforts. His seizure of Forts Henry and Donelson and domination of the confluence of the Cumberland, Ohio, and

Tennessee had quite fortuitously furnished him control of the Mississippi's upper reaches. Farragut's bold seizure of New Orleans had given the Union control of the river's exit into the Gulf of Mexico. But complete control of the river was still lacking in early 1863 because of the South's continuing hold on Vicksburg and, farther south along the river, Port Hudson. Vicksburg was the biggest obstacle.

CHAPTER ELEVEN

Chancellorsville and Gettysburg

UNION VICTORIES IN the Mississippi Valley in the first half of 1863 presaged the collapse of the Confederacy's whole western position, yet left the Union still under threat in what both governments and peoples regarded as the principal theatre of operations, the borderlands of Virginia, Maryland, and Pennsylvania. There were threats elsewhere, of course, and failings: in April a Union ironclad fleet failed to overcome the first of the forts defending Charleston harbour and suffered severe damage in the attempt. The war in Tennessee, whose Union constituency was so close to Lincoln's heart, might go the wrong way, for Rosecrans's army was nearly outnumbered by those of Bragg and Buckner. It was even possible that the surviving Southern armies at liberty in Louisiana might succeed in regaining New Orleans.

The real menace to Union fortunes, however, lay in the continuing presence of the Army of Northern Virginia in Fredericksburg, from which position it was poised to strike into Maryland or Pennsylvania, a move that would have panicked the residents of the great Northern cities and would certainly deeply alarm Lincoln and his government. Lee, supremely self-confident himself, also reposed strong confidence in the capacities of his soldiers, who, he believed, if properly supplied and led, could defeat any Northern army they encountered. Ironically, in view of the outcome of the approaching campaign, the recently appointed commander of the Army of the Potomac, General Joseph Hooker, also believed that he could beat Lee and displayed signs of sublime certainty in his superiority and that of his army. Known as "Fighting Joe" Hooker, from an injudiciously drafted newspaper headline, he had been chosen to succeed Burnside because of the appalling casualties that had occurred at Fredericksburg under that general's command. Hooker was actually a brave and normally competent officer. Unfortunately, he had decided to challenge Lee to a contest in manoeuvre warfare, an art of which Lee was already a master and perhaps the leading expert in the Western world. On April 12 there began those suggestive preliminaries to all great battles: clearing out the hospitals, inspecting arms, looking after ammunition, shoeing animals, issuing provisions, and making every preparation necessary to an advance.

First to move was the army's cavalry division, which Hooker intended to send against the railroad bringing Lee supplies. That move, however, required the crossing of the Rappahannock, but because heavy rain had swollen it, George Stoneman, the cavalry commander, was unable to proceed, forcing Hooker to postpone the army's advance. This was the first in a subsequent chapter of setbacks. Hooker hoped by cutting the railroad to starve Lee out of Fredericksburg and force him to fight a battle in the open. As a preliminary to the campaign, he divided his army, sending three corps across the Rappahannock eastward and the remaining four corps westward towards Chancellorsville, a spot on the landscape marked by a large mansion, the Chancellor House. Hooker's total strength, including cavalry, numbered about 125,000, Lee's under 60,000 plus cavalry. Hooker, however, was in a weakened position, since to dominate the river crossings he had divided his army and in such a way that Lee's army lay between the two halves. Initially Hooker retained the initiative, since his position dominated several roads which led to Lee's rear, thus allowing the possibility of cutting Lee's communications with Richmond should the Army of the Potomac advance in that direction. In mid-afternoon on May 1, however, orders came from Hooker to his corps commanders to fall back on Chancellorsville. His subordinates protested, agreeing among themselves that the open ground they occupied and the high ground to their rear formed a position highly favourable to a successful attack. Firing had by now broken out and Darius Couch hastened to the Chancellor House intending to persuade Hooker that the advancing Confederates should be attacked. Inexplicably, something had happened to Hooker. All drive to exploit his thus far successful manoeuvre had evaporated. "It is all right, Couch," he replied, "I have got Lee just where I want him. He must fight me on my own ground." Couch's inner thought was that "fighting a defensive battle in that nest of thickets was too much." He made his exit with the private notion that "my commanding general was a whipped man."[1]

Events would swiftly reveal the correctness of that conclusion. Hooker had succumbed to self-doubt, not a quality he had previously displayed, though his behaviour did not surprise his West Point contemporaries. It was about to be exploited by Lee and Jackson, neither of whom was afflicted by lack of confidence in any way. Indeed, during the next two days, May 2–3, Lee was to violate two inflexible rules of war—not to divide an army in the face of the enemy and not to march an army across the face of the enemy army deployed for battle—and to avoid the consequences, largely thanks to Jackson's iron grip on his nerves. The two generals met on the evening of May 1 in woodland a mile southeast of the Chancellor House. Jackson sat on a tree stump, Lee on an empty hardtack box, a small fire glowing between them, to discuss the situation and their prospects. Lee had been bewildered by Hooker's retreat, thinking at first it had come about because of the enemy's recognition of a weakness in their position. A personal reconnaissance revealed, however, that the Federal forces were deployed in "a position of great natural strength, surrounded on all sides by a dense forest filled with tangled undergrowth, in the midst of which breastworks of logs had been constructed." The description was of the locality known as the Wilderness, abandoned farmland which had gone back to secondary forest, forming one of the least passable regions in the whole Virginia theatre, though it had counterparts elsewhere. Ill fortune decreed that the armies would have to fight not once but twice in these fatal groves.

The two generals were at first dubious of the possibility of successfully engaging the enemy in such conditions. Then they received a report from J. E. B. Stuart, commanding the cavalry, which told them that Hooker's right flank lay outside the Wilderness, unprotected by natural obstacles, and was vulnerable to surprise attack. Lee ordered Jackson, who enthusiastically consented, to take his corps and march it along a woodland track twelve miles through the thickets and brush to take the Federals in the rear. It was a dangerous thing practically as well as doctrinally to undertake, since the advance would be protected from view only by screens of vegetation. Jackson nevertheless set out confidently next morning at 7:30 a.m. His rearguard was found and attacked by two Union divisions commanded by General Daniel Sickles, but Sickles failed to understand the reason for Jackson's presence in the area. At five o'clock, as dusk fell, Jackson's men had reached the encampment of the regiments of Howard's Eleventh Corps. Most of its soldiers were Germans, recent immigrants who had stacked their rifles and were preparing supper. In the years before the great Prussian victories in Europe of 1864–71, the Germans were not thought of as a military people, certainly not in the United States, where they enjoyed a poor reputation as soldiers. These unfortunates were about to fulfil it. Their ranks were first disturbed by the flight of a herd of deer, running ahead of Jackson's men, followed by a flock of rabbits and squirrels. Before they could divine the reason for the wildlife *sauve qui peut*, they heard the nerve-shattering rebel yell and were set upon by Jackson's ranks. The rebels' blood was up and they tossed the Union regiments into frenzied disorder, driving them out onto the nearby Plank Road, where other Union units were caught up in the frenzy. General Oliver Howard, whose corps suffered most, described with remarkable frankness the effect of the rebel attack: "More quickly than it can be told, with all the fury of the wildest hailstorm, everything, every sort of organisation that lay in the path of the mad current of panic-stricken men, had to give way and be broken into fragments."[2]

Riding just behind the advancing Confederate front line was Stonewall Jackson. One of his subordinates called out as the broken Union troops dispersed into the woods, "They are running too fast for us. We cannot keep up with them." Jackson shouted back, "They never run too fast for me. Press them. Press them." The Union troops opposite began to make a stand and, as their line solidified, Jackson rode forward of his own troops to make a reconnaissance. Returning in the gathering dusk he and his party were seen by men of A. P. Hill's division, who mistook them for the enemy. At a distance of about four hundred yards, fire was opened. A sergeant and a captain riding with Stonewall were killed. Then a regiment of North Carolina troops fired another volley and hit General Jackson three times. One ball lodged in his right hand, a second went through his left wrist. Then a third hit his left arm between elbow and shoulder and shattered the bone. He fell from his horse and when reached was bleeding heavily. Captain James Power Smith, a staff officer, helped General Hill with first aid. Stonewall's sleeve was cut open and a handkerchief tightened around the wound to staunch the blood. A carrying party of nearby troops was brought, with a litter, on which the wounded man was placed and carried off shoulder-high. Union artillery fire wounded one of the litter bearers and Stonewall almost fell but was steadied at the last moment. The carrying party was forced to take cover and the general was laid on the road. When the fire lifted, Captain Smith put his arms round Stonewall and helped him to walk into the woods, where the litter bearers got him onto their shoulders once more. Another bearer was hit and Jackson fell to the ground with a cry of pain but was helped to his feet and returned to a litter, on which he was eventually brought to a field hospital established near the Wilderness Tavern. There about midnight surgeons amputated his left arm near the shoulder and extracted a rifle bullet from his right hand.

His doctors and comrades were optimistic. No vital organ had been touched and he had been spared a serious loss of blood. He received a stream of messages from elsewhere in the army, expressing the belief that he would recover. He survived for a week, attended by his wife with her newborn daughter, but pneumonia and perhaps pleurisy as well set in and on the afternoon of Sunday, May 10, 1863, he died. His last words were "Let us cross over the river and rest under the shade of the trees," later adapted by Ernest Hemingway as the title of one of his novels of war, *Across the River and into the Trees*. Lee regretted the loss of Jackson ever afterwards, while the leadership of the Army of Northern Virginia never recovered; in Lee's words, "the daring, skill and energy of this great and good man" were now lost to the Confederacy and could not be replaced.

During May 3, while Jackson was gradually succumbing to his wounds, Lee renewed the attack on Hooker. Both armies were now divided, Hooker having sent a corps under General John Sedgwick to capture Fredericksburg. Lee ordered J. E. B. Stuart, who had assumed command of Jackson's corps, to unite the two halves of the Army of Northern Virginia. As Hooker's army outnumbered Lee's, he should have retained the advantage; however, his nerve had been affected by Lee's dashing attack and his own misreading of the battle. His only purpose now was to hold his position, to which end he ordered the abandonment of an important position at Hazel Grove, as a means of shortening his line. After occupying Hazel Grove, the Confederates pressed on to another hilltop called Fair View. The Union troops opposed their advance and a bitter fight broke out in the thickets of the Wilderness, described by General Howard as comprising "scraggy oaks, bushy firs, cedars and junipers, all entangled with a thick, almost impenetrable undergrowth and criss-crossed with an abundance of wild vines." It appeared impassable, and the skirmishers could only work their way through with extreme difficulty. Nevertheless, fighting reached a level of murderous intensity, lasting half an hour and forcing

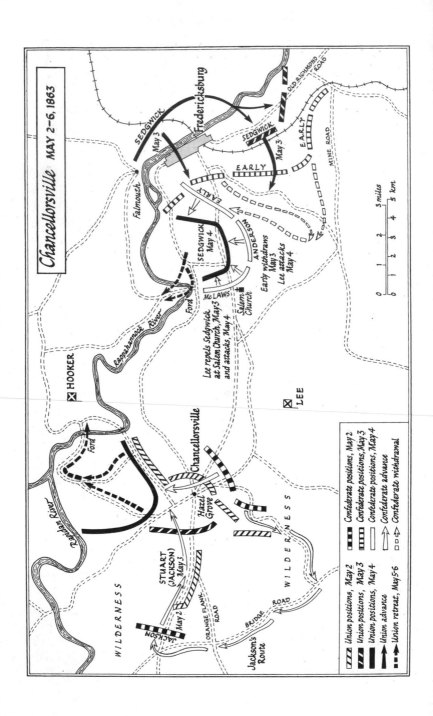

Chancellorsville MAY 2–6, 1863

Fredericksburg

SEDGWICK May 3

SEDGWICK May 3

EARLY

EARLY

EARLY

OLD RICHMOND ROAD

MINE ROAD

Falmouth

SEDGWICK May 4

ANDERSON

Early withdraws
May 3
Lee attacks
May 4

Rappahannock River

Ford

McLAWS

Salem Church

Lee repels Sedgwick
at Salem Church, May 3
and attacks, May 4

⊠ HOOKER

⊠ LEE

Rapidan River

Ford

Chancellorsville

Hazel Grove

STUART
(JACKSON)
May 3

WILDERNESS

WILDERNESS

ORANGE PLANK ROAD

May 2

BRIDGE ROAD

Jackson's Route

JACKSON

Jackson's Route

0   1   2   3 miles
0 1 2 3 4 5 km.

▨ Union positions, May 2
◼ Union positions, May 3
▨ Union positions, May 4
⟹ Union advance
▪▪▶ Union retreat, May 5–6

◼ Confederate positions, May 2
▨ Confederate positions, May 3
◻ Confederate positions, May 4
⟹ Confederate advance
◻◻⟿ Confederate withdrawal

the Union to abandon their position at Fair View. The Confederate artillery was now drenching the battlefield with fire, some of which fell on the Chancellor House, where Hooker had set up his headquarters. A shot hit one of the pillars of the house, against which Hooker was leaning, split it and threw Hooker unconscious to the ground. He remained in a dazed condition. On May 5 he gave orders for his army to cross to the north side of the Rappahannock. It was an admission of defeat, and Hooker had indeed been defeated comprehensively.

Everything from the start had promised a different outcome. Hooker had outnumbered Lee two to one; Lee had several times weakened himself by dividing his army in the face of the enemy. Hooker, though, simply by loss of nerve and failure to understand Lee's movements, had thrown away any advantage. Even at the very end, when he had announced his failure by withdrawing his army across the Rappahannock, he enabled Lee to achieve one more victory, by allowing Sedgwick, whom he had sent to Fredericksburg, to fight unsupported at Salem Church on May 3–4. Sedgwick then followed the rest of the army in retreat across the Rappahannock. Hooker's judgement on his lamentable performance proclaimed the self-justification of a weak incompetent. "My army was not beaten. Only a part of it had been engaged. My First Corps . . . was fresh and ready and eager to be brought into action, as was my whole army. But I had been fully convinced of the futility of attacking fortified positions and I was determined not to sacrifice my men needlessly, though it should be at the expense of my reputation as a fighting officer."[3] This was disingenuous. The Chancellorsville position was not fortified, except by the difficulty of the Wilderness itself and by hasty entrenchments and obstacles. In any case, Hooker sacrificed what reputation he enjoyed by declining to fight at times and places where he might have succeeded. Like McClellan, he had thrown away all his advantages for no good reason other than his own timidity.

Hooker's loss of nerve at Chancellorsville disturbed Lincoln, who spent the first two weeks of May 1863 trying to put backbone into him, when he was not simply trying to establish what the general was doing and intended to do. By May 6 Lincoln had at last learned that a major battle had taken place, resulting in "no success to us" and that the Army of the Potomac had withdrawn to the north bank of the Rappahannock. Holding this telegram communicating the news and showing a face gray with anxiety, he paced about the White House, repeating the words, "My God, my God. What will the country say? What will the country say?" That afternoon, in his distraction, he decided that he must meet and question Hooker, and left at once. When he arrived at the headquarters of the Army of the Potomac, he held a conference of senior officers, whom he disappointed by referring not at all to the battle of Chancellorsville. Nor did he give them an opportunity to recommend Hooker's removal, though several of the corps commanders wished it. Nevertheless, some of Hooker's critics discussed making a visit to Washington to put the matter directly to Lincoln, out of sight of their superior, and to suggest his replacement by George Meade, one of the corps commanders. In the event, they desisted, since Meade declined to be nominated.

Lincoln also interviewed Hooker alone, at which time, following his established habit, he gave the general a letter, in which he set out his views and asked the questions to which he needed answers. What he really wanted to know was what Hooker intended next, since the Confederates were clearly still in a dominant position in the theatre of campaign. Hooker wrote to Lincoln at Washington in reply, strangely evasively. He said that he had formed a plan, which he would reveal if Lincoln desired. A week later, May 13, he wrote again, announcing that he intended to attack across the Rappahannock immediately, even though he was now outnumbered, a familiar cry from the McClellan days. Also McClellan-like, he requested reinforcements. Lincoln asked to see him in Washington. Dropping his plan to attack Lee, Hooker left at once. On arrival he was given another letter by the president and told that it would be quite satisfactory for Hooker to hold his positions in Virginia and merely to keep Lee under observation. He was also told that Lincoln was receiving expressions of dissatisfaction at his conduct of operations from Hooker's immediate subordinates, which was perfectly true. Some generals had written to the president or been to visit him in Washington. Boldly, Hooker demanded names, which were refused, and then challenged the president to question every general who came to Washington.

Hooker must have sensed that the shades were drawing in. He had been involved in a whispering campaign against his predecessor, Burnside, and knew how confidence was undermined. The crisis of command, moreover, was quickening, for Lee had now begun on his plan to carry the war into the North. This was the opening of what would become the Gettysburg campaign. Lee had been to Richmond to persuade Davis that only a dramatic initiative could rescue the Confederacy from the military drift, which left the interior of the rebel state under deadly threat from Grant's army in the Mississippi Valley, where Vicksburg was now threatened with capture, and which also, despite a succession of limited victories in northern Virginia, failed to deliver decisive results against the Union's principal army. Lee argued, and persuaded Davis and the cabinet, and Secretary of War Seddon, that the correct strategy was to strike into the North, through Pennsylvania, strengthening the Army of Northern Virginia if necessary by withdrawals from the defensive forces in the Carolinas. He outlined a cluster of desirable outcomes from such a departure: relieving Virginia of the burdens of supporting its own troops and curtailing its exposure to Northern depredations; forcing the Army of the Potomac out of its strong positions along the Rappahannock onto more open ground to the north, where it might be brought to battle in favourable circumstances; spreading alarm into the North by menacing the great Atlantic cities, Baltimore, Philadelphia, perhaps even New York, as well, of course, as Washington; and, given a propitious outcome, reawakening the prospect of diplomatic recognition by the European monarchies.

The response was favourable, and on June 3 the Second Corps of the Army of Northern Virginia broke camp near Fredericksburg and began its march into Pennsylvania. It remained unclear to the Union forces whither Lee was headed, partly because through a recent reorganisation, the dispositions of the Army of Northern Virginia were unfamiliar to their opponents. Following the death of Jackson, his Second Corps had been given to Richard Ewell and the rest of the army had been reorganised into a First and Third Corps under Generals James Longstreet and Ambrose P. Hill, each with three divisions. The cavalry, under J. E. B. Stuart, consisted of seven brigades. It was this formation which was first into action. Lee's scheme of advance was not directly to his front, northward from Fredericksburg, but entailed a flank march into the Shenandoah Valley and then a change of direction northward towards Winchester, Harpers Ferry, and Harrisburg. The Blue Ridge Mountains at first masked his movements, but by June 8 it was clear to the Union that the Confederates were using the valley as their axis of advance and Union cavalry moved westward to intercept. On June 9, the Union troopers met Stuart's men at Brandy Station, on the Rappahannock, and fighting broke out which was to swell into the largest cavalry engagement of the Civil War. The Union took the initiative and generally outfought the Confederates, to Stuart's disgust. He was accustomed to getting the better of the opposing cavalry. Unusually, for the Civil War, the cavalry indeed fought as cavalry, from the saddle and with drawn sabres, rather than as dismounted infantry. Alfred Pleasanton, the Union commander, called off the action after he was satisfied that he had established superiority, though Union casualties were 866 and Confederate 523.

In the early stage of Lee's invasion of Pennsylvania, Lincoln was more agitated by the failure of Hooker to take adequate and confident steps to oppose the Confederate advance than by the actions of the enemy. Hooker, during mid-June 1863, gave a very lifelike representation of McClellan at his most indecisive. He was now north of the Rappahannock. His first proposal to Lincoln was that he should recross the Rappahannock and attack the rear of Lee's army at Fredericksburg. The president forbade him to do so, though he denied that he was giving orders, and said he wanted to be guided by Hooker and by Halleck, as general in chief. That was an ill-chosen thought. Hooker had conceived an animus against Halleck, whom he believed to be his enemy. Their differences could have been sorted out had Hooker visited Washington in a conciliatory frame of mind. He did not. Soon after proposing to fight at Fredericksburg, he made things worse by proposing to abandon the northern Virginia theatre altogether and march on Richmond, leaving Lee to be opposed by a force collected from the garrison of Washington. Had Hooker deliberately tried to arouse all Lincoln's worst fears simultaneously, he could not have succeeded better. The scheme awoke visions of McClellan's futile gesturing at the Confederate capital, while demanding reinforcements that could be found only by stripping the Union capital of its defenders. Lincoln answered Hooker's proposal on June 10, within ninety minutes of its receipt. His reply was succinct and exact, one of his very best pieces of strategic judgement written during the war. "I think Lee's army, and not Richmond, is your true objective point. If he comes toward the upper Potomac, follow on his flank, and on the inside track, shortening your lines whilst he lengthens his . . . If he stays where he is, fret him, and fret him."[4]

Lee did not stay where he was. His army was now in violent motion, tearing up the Shenandoah Valley and threatening the Federal garrisons at Winchester and Martinsburg, northwest of Washington, though not close enough to threaten the capital—yet. Lincoln was now urging Hooker to attack, which he was at last in a position to do, as he had eventually put his army into motion on the "inside track" that Lincoln had identified. His path took him closer to Washington and shortened the transmission time for messages, which now flew back and forth. Incautiously, Hooker telegraphed Lincoln to complain that he did not enjoy Halleck's confidence. He was preparing the ground for transferring the blame for any failure onto his superiors. Lincoln outsmarted him by writing instructions that placed him explicitly under Halleck's command while in the field and not simply for administrative purposes. "To remove all misunderstanding," he wrote, "I now place you in the strict military relation to General Halleck, of a commander of one of the armies, to the General-in-Chief of all the armies. I have not intended differently; but as it seems differently understood, I shall direct him to give you orders, and you to obey them."[5]

This letter did not improve the situation. Halleck was not operating as chief Union strategist; Lincoln was. On the other hand, acute though his military judgement had become, Lincoln could not directly conduct operations in the face of the enemy. Only Hooker was in a position to do so, though he was manifesting less and less capacity to carry that duty out. In the hope of easing his mind, which was now clearly oppressed by every sort of fear, Lincoln wrote Hooker a personal letter, urging him to make his peace with Halleck and to strike at Lee's extended line of communications, which he was now in a position to dominate. The situation did not improve. Hooker came to Washington, saw Lincoln and Halleck, and obeyed Lincoln as far as moving troops to protect Harpers Ferry, now under imminent threat. He persisted in his failure, however, to bring Lee to action, simply following the Confederates on a parallel track at some distance to their east. Lincoln was nevertheless encouraged by his meeting with Hooker and remarked to Gideon Welles, secretary of the navy, that "we cannot help beating them, if we have the man. How much depends in military matters on one master mind. Hooker may make the same mistake as McClellan and lose his chance. We shall soon see, but it seems to me he can't help but win."[6] This was a last gasp of Lincoln's wishful thinking about Hooker, who almost immediately repeated McClellan's display of timidity during the Peninsula Campaign. He had now convinced himself that he was outnumbered and could do nothing unless he received reinforcements. He repeated his demand for troops from the Washington garrison, Lincoln's weakest spot. When he was refused, he asked permission to abandon Harpers Ferry, a place of real strategic importance, so as to transfer its defenders to his field army. When he was refused—by Halleck—he asked to be relieved of his command. His reply to Halleck alleged that he had been given too many missions, to defend both Washington and Harpers Ferry and to fight a stronger enemy army. His nerve had finally and completely gone. That became clear in telegrams written on June 26 and 27. On June 27 Lincoln told the cabinet that he was relieving Hooker of command. In his place he appointed George Meade, commanding the Army of the Potomac's Fifth Corps.

Meade was a respected senior officer with considerable experience in command—subordinate command. He had never directed an army on campaign. His selection was by elimination. None of the other corps commanders equalled him in experience or ability, though General John Reynolds, commanding the First Corps, was considered as a replacement and was favoured by Meade himself. The circumstances of Meade's appointment were inappropriately jocose. Major James Hardie, of the adjutant general's office, who hurried from Washington to bring the news, found Meade asleep in a camp bed, and began by informing him that he brought bad news: Meade was to be relieved of command of his corps. Meade replied defensively that he had expected it. Hardie then answered that he was to assume command of the whole army, which Meade protested he was unfitted to exercise. Hardie said that the government would not accept refusal. Meade therefore submitted, though claiming he did not know where the different formations of the army were located. His attitude was entirely genuine. Though temperamentally peppery and given to outbursts of bad temper with subordinates, he was a man of personal modesty and, as events would show, of admirable firmness of character.

The date of his appointment was June 28. Both Union and Confederates had been manoeuvring about Pennsylvania for the better part of a month. The Union's best information placed Longstreet, commanding the Confederate First Corps, at Chambersburg; A. P. Hill, commanding the Second Corps, between Chambersburg and Cashtown; and Ewell, with the Third Corps, at Carlisle, threatening Harrisburg, the state capital. Stuart, with the cavalry, was moving round the Union positions past Centreville into Maryland. The Union army was disposed between the Potomac and Frederick and east of South Mountain. Meade at once decided to position the army so as to prevent Lee crossing the Susquehanna River, which divides Pennsylvania east–west. Hardie had brought orders, written by Halleck but decided by Lincoln, which reminded him that he had to cover both Washington and Baltimore, but was to bring the enemy to battle, though they laid down nothing limiting his freedom of action. Meade, who had considerable strategic acuteness, came to the following conclusions about his and Lee's respective instructions. Lee had to attack since he was an invader on enemy territory. Were he to withdraw without staging a fight, it would be a serious loss of face. Lee was dispersed, Meade relatively concentrated. If Meade concentrated further, Lee would be obliged to attack him. Meade decided his best plan was to assume a strong defensive position and await Lee's attack. Examination of the map suggested that Pipe Creek, just south of the Pennsylvania state line, was a suitable place to give battle.

News of the advance of Meade's forces alarmed Lee, who began hastily to gather his scattered troops. He concentrated them first at Cashtown, between Chambersburg and Gettysburg, but when it was reported that some Union troops were at Gettysburg, he then switched his point of concentration there. The added reason for so doing was that his scouts reported that a supply of shoes, of which the Confederates were always short, was to be found at Gettysburg. On June 30 a foraging party was sent and found Union cavalry filling the town and outskirts. A second reconnaissance, on July 1, would swell into the opening of a major battle.

Gettysburg was the centre of terrain well suited for defensive operations. The town, standing at the north of a tract of open, rolling countryside, only sparsely wooded, was a comfortable, prosperous place, containing a number of brick houses as well as the large, solid buildings of Gettysburg College and a Lutheran seminary, both with cupolas which officers of the North and South were to use as points of observation in succession. South of the town the terrain formed two ridges, known as Seminary Ridge to the west and Cemetery Ridge to the east. The north end of Cemetery Ridge swelled into the two low hills of Cemetery Hill and Culp's Hill. To the south the ridge culminated in the prominences of Little Round Top and Round Top. In front of the Round Tops the ground was broken and boulder-strewn, with fields and fences forming what would become the killing grounds of the Devil's Den, the Wheatfield, and the Peach Orchard.

At eight on the morning of July 1, the Union cavalry, two brigades in all, was met by advancing Confederate infantry. The Union cavalrymen made a spirited defence of the town, having the advantage of being armed with breech-loading carbines. At about ten o'clock, Union infantry started to come to their support, under the command of General John Reynolds. Soon after arriving he sent a report to Meade which warned that the enemy was advancing in strength and that he feared they would occupy the high ground before he could: "I will fight him inch by inch," he promised, "and if driven into the town I will barricade the streets and hold him back as long as possible." Soon after he handed his message to a courier, he was struck by a bullet in the head and fell dead.

About that moment General Lee arrived on the battlefield. His first remark on surveying the scene, which showed that there was fighting in front of Gettysburg, with Confederate units swirling about McPherson's Ridge, fronting Seminary Ridge, was that he did not want to bring on a general engagement that day. The situation was fluid in the extreme, however, and almost as he spoke, the Union line which was stretched across the Carlisle and Harrisburg roads leading into the town from the north gave way, the fugitives streaming south towards Cemetery Hill. The Union force on McPherson's Ridge and Seminary Ridge was shortly driven off and Lee now changed his attitude, deciding to fight as hard as necessary to hold as much critical ground as he could while the day lasted. Prisoners taken revealed that Meade's arrival, with the bulk of the Union army, was imminent. Lee therefore gave orders "to press" the Union units southward with the object of seizing Cemetery Hill before it could be entrenched. He ordered General Ewell, commanding the Confederate Second Corps, to take Cemetery Hill. Ewell's men, of whom 8,000 had become casualties since morning, were too disorganised to carry out the action and Ewell, riding forward to set his corps in motion, was hit as he did so. The bullet struck the leg he had lost at the second battle of Manassas, causing him to remark to the horseman next to him, "It don't hurt at all to be shot in a wooden leg."

General Meade was back at Taneytown when Reynolds's message reached him. He sent his best corps commander, Winfield S. Hancock, to the spot. Hancock opened a meeting with Howard, Reynolds's successor, by saying that he had been sent to take command of the three corps then deploying at Gettysburg. Howard objected that he was senior. Hancock said he had written orders in his pocket and would endorse any orders Howard gave but pointed out that he had also been charged by Meade to confirm. Casting his eye over the terrain from Gettysburg town to the Round Tops to its south, he concluded, "I think this the strongest position by nature upon which to fight a battle that I ever saw, and if it meets your approbation I select this as the battle field."

Ewell was supposed, by Lee's intention, to take Cemetery Ridge. He did not, instead riding about to gather his scattered units. The

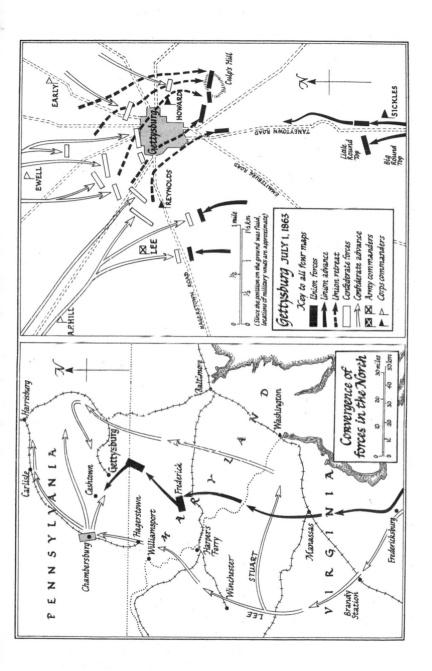

EWELL

A.P. HILL

⊠ LEE

REYNOLDS

EARLY

EWELL

HOWARD

Gettysburg

HAGERSTOWN ROAD

EMMITSBURG ROAD

TANEYTOWN ROAD

SICKLES

Little Round Top

Big Round Top

Gettysburg JULY 1, 1863

Key to all four maps

Union forces
Union advance
Union retreat
Confederate forces
Confederate advance
Army commanders
Corps commanders

(Since the position on the ground was fluid, locations of military units are approximate.)

0   ½   1   1½ km
0   ½   1 mile

N

PENNSYLVANIA

Carlisle
Harrisburg

Cashtown
Gettysburg

Chambersburg

Hagerstown
Williamsport

Winchester

Harpers Ferry

Frederick

MARYLAND

Baltimore

Washington

STUART

Manassas

VIRGINIA

Fredericksburg

Brandy Station

LEE

Convergence of forces in the North

0   10   20   30 miles
0   20   40   50 km

N

Union men meanwhile were digging to improve their positions, which they did during the night. On the morning of July 2, the second day of the battle, the two sides occupied parallel positions on Seminary and Cemetery ridges, separated by a shallow valley about two-thirds of a mile wide. All forces were well in place, the Confederates numbering about 64,000, the Union about 99,000, though both diminished by several thousand casualties suffered on the preceding day. Lee's intention for July 2 was to attack the Union left and then drive the rest of the army off the high ground. General James Longstreet, Lee's most experienced subordinate, to whom he entrusted the mission, was not enthusiastic. He preferred, as he had told Lee on the afternoon of July 1, to disengage, march the army south, and fight a defensive battle elsewhere in the Pennsylvania countryside. He now repeated his proposal. Lee would not hear of it, despite Longstreet's reasonable objection that if the Union was awaiting attack, it was because that was so wished; he was alluding to that convention of military wisdom, that a general should not do what the enemy wanted.

Lee insisted, "They are there in position, and I am going to whip them or they are going to whip me."[7] Longstreet held his tongue but showed no urgency in carrying out Lee's orders. It was not until 4 p.m. on July 2 that his units were in motion. When they moved, moreover, it was not northeast, as Lee wanted, up the Emmitsburg Road, so as to roll up the Union line from the south, but due east towards the Round Tops and the Devil's Den. The Confederates were soon in frenzied action among the giant glacial boulders of the Devil's Den and among the standing grain in the Wheatfield. John Bell Hood, one of the division commanders of Longstreet's corps, quickly became a casualty, wounded in the arm, but his disablement did not diminish the ferocity of the Confederate attack.

As the fighting in the Devil's Den reached its climax, the combatants were passed to the south by the 15th Alabama Regiment, which was heading for Little Round Top, via the higher Round Top. Meade's chief engineer, General Gouverneur K. Warren, had spotted the danger just in time. Little Round Top, if taken, would have allowed the Confederates to position artillery in enfilade and drench the whole length of the Union line with fire. With minutes to spare, he sent the 20th Maine to join the Union signal party on the summit to oppose the Confederate advance. The 20th Maine was commanded by one of the outstanding regimental officers of the Union army, Colonel Joshua

Chamberlain, who in peacetime taught rhetoric and foreign languages at Bowdoin College. Refused permission by the college authorities to join the army, he had taken study leave and joined up anyhow. At Little Round Top, with 386 men, he took steps, under withering enemy fire, which saved the Union left flank and probably Meade's entire army from defeat. His two brothers were officers in the regiment. Sending one ahead to seek out a place to collect the wounded and the other to the rear to keep the ranks closed up, he arrived on the summit of Little Round Top as the 15th Alabama was appearing. He deployed his B Company at an angle to the regimental line, to protect the flank, and then ordered sustained fire. His regiment also received heavy fire from the Alabamans. Very rapidly the 20th suffered 125 casualties out of its strength of 386 and was running out of ammunition. Chamberlain then ordered those still standing to fix bayonets and led a charge which swept the enemy off the hill and took 300 prisoners.

The success at Little Round Top and the preceding success in the Devil's Den and the Wheatfield achieved the effect of blunting the whole Confederate offensive that was intended to collapse the Union line. Much of the credit belongs to General Daniel Sickles, who, in disobedience to orders, had brought his Third Corps down from Cemetery Ridge to occupy the Peach Orchard–Wheatfield salient, thus deepening the Union line precisely at the point where Lee planned to breach it—creative disobedience, since it frustrated a most dangerous stroke by the enemy. Another small regiment, the 1st Minnesota, only 262 strong, turned the tide here, losing 216 of its soldiers killed or wounded in its counter charge to the Confederate attack. The 1st Minnesota had taken part in every major battle fought thus far in the east, which perhaps explains the effect of its action. By 7:30 p.m. the Union units had just succeeded in holding the northern end of its line on Cemetery Hill, but its line had been so weakened by the need to move units about that Meade began to fear that it could not be held the following day, July 3, when he expected Lee to attack again. As the Confederates had made their first effort at the northern end of the Union front and the second at the southern end, he expected the danger area on the morrow to be in the centre. He told General John Gibbon, commanding the division which held the ground exactly in the middle, "Gibbon, if Lee attacks tomorrow, it will be in your front." Lee had no option but to attack; if he broke off action now, he would have conceded defeat and risked severe loss in retreating from the field. Meade nevertheless had his own anxieties about carrying on the action and during the evening held a council of war to seek the opinion of his corps and some of his divisional commanders.

Eighteen years after the battle, a minute of the discussion was found among General Meade's papers. Three questions had been asked: 1. Whether to stay and fight or to retreat to a position nearer the army's base of supplies? 2. If to stay, whether to attack or await attack? 3. If to wait, for how long? Nine replies were noted. There was general agreement to stay, though some of the generals wanted to "correct" or "rectify" the army's deployment. Gibbon, who knew that his position was likely to be the focus of the Confederate attack, wanted to "correct the position of the army but not retreat," and thought the Union "in no condition to attack" but that it should wait "until [Lee] moves." Slocum, commanding Twelfth Corps, was the most succinct and resolute. He is recorded simply as answering "stay and fight it out." Meade announced "such then is the decision." The minute also records the remaining strength of the Army of the Potomac, after two days' fighting. The corps had 9,000, 12,500, 9,000, 6,000, 8,500, 6,000, and 7,000 respectively, totalling 58,000. The Confederates had also suffered seriously but retained their cohesion and offensive spirit.

The morning of July 3 was hot and humid. Firing at the northern end of the line began early. The Union troops were attacking to regain the trenches lost to the enemy on the first day. Elsewhere on the battlefield there was only sporadic fire, though much movement as commanders on both sides realigned their forces. Lee spent the morning riding along the crest of Seminary Ridge, keeping the Union line opposite under observation. He had decided that Pickett's division of Longstreet's First Corps should lead the attack, beginning in the shelter of the Seminary Ridge woods and then moving across the open and unprotected fields of the valley up the slope of Cemetery Ridge facing. Most of Pickett's men were Virginians; the brigades assigned to support his division included Alabamans and Texans. Pickett's men were entirely fresh, having come from guarding the army's wagon train during the days preceding the battle. Longstreet persisted in his reluctance to attack. Riding with Lee in the last hour before the battle, he again suggested changing the front of attack to the Federal left. "No," Lee answered, "I am going to take them where they are on Cemetery Hill. I want you to take Pickett's division and make the attack." He would reinforce him with six brigades from Heth's and Pender's divisions (under Pettigrew and Trimble, respectively) of the Third Corps. Longstreet, to what must by then have been Lee's irritation, sustained his objection. "That will give me fifteen thousand men. I have been a soldier, I may say, from the ranks up to the position I now hold. I have been in pretty much all kinds of skirmishes, from those of two or three soldiers up to those of an army corps, and I think I can safely say there was never a body of fifteen thousand men who could make that attack successfully." "The general," Longstreet observed, "seemed a little impatient at my remarks, so I said nothing more. As he showed no indication of changing his plan, I went to work at once to arrange my troops for the attack."

Longstreet positioned the army's artillery batteries so as to silence those of the Union—there were about forty batteries or 160 guns on each side to cover the march of the infantry as they advanced. He also ordered that there was to be no firing or movement until a double signal shot was fired. He remained tense with nerves throughout the period of waiting. The signal was fired at seven minutes past one and the bombardment that began lasted for two hours. The Confederates fired at the Union battery positions. The Union artillery commander, General Henry Hunt, ordered his batteries to slacken their fire towards the end of the bombardment, in order to give the impression that they were running out of ammunition. The din and smoke were shattering during the artillery exchange, which did less harm than appeared, much of the Confederate fire going too high. The Union salvoes did little harm either, as long as the Confederate infantry remained under cover of the tree line along the crest of Seminary Ridge. Eventually, as the Union fire slackened, Pickett rode up to Longstreet to ask permission to advance. Longstreet, by his own later account, could not speak, "for fear of betraying my want of confidence." He merely nodded.

The nod translated into an order to set out across the 1,400 yards of shallow valley that separated the two ridges. Lieutenant Colonel Edmund Rice of the 19th Massachusetts was standing near the clump of trees on Cemetery Ridge which Pickett had chosen as the objective of his attack. As the long lines of Confederate infantry appeared, one behind another, a third body of troops in battalion column in the third rank, Rice heard the Union men call out, "Here they come! Here they come! Here comes the infantry!"

They came forward with an "easy, swinging step," a line of skir-

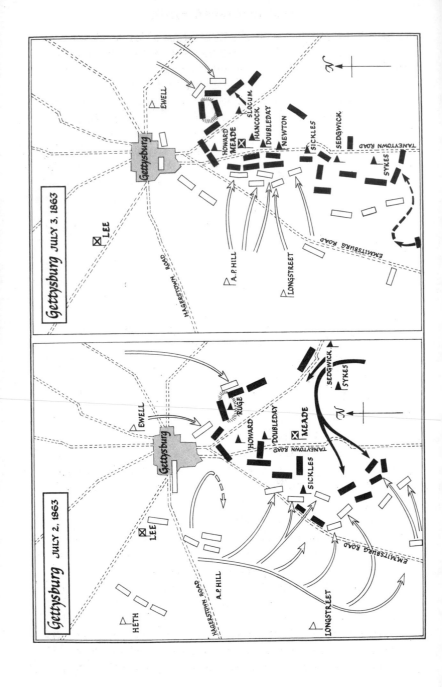

Gettysburg JULY 2, 1863

HETH

LEE

A.P. HILL

HAGERSTOWN ROAD

LONGSTREET

EWELL

Gettysburg

RUGE

HOWARD

DOUBLEDAY

MEADE

TANEYTOWN ROAD

SICKLES

EMMITSBURG ROAD

N

SEDGWICK

SYKES

Gettysburg JULY 3, 1863

LEE

HAGERSTOWN ROAD

A.P. HILL

LONGSTREET

EWELL

Gettysburg

HOWARD
MEADE

SLOCUM
HANCOCK
DOUBLEDAY
NEWTON

SICKLES

SEDGWICK

SYKES

EMMITSBURG ROAD

TANEYTOWN ROAD

N

mishers in front. They exchanged fire with the Union skirmishers, who quickly reached the fence of the Emmitsburg Road running along the foot of Cemetery Ridge. Colonel Rice had

> an excellent view . . . and could see the entire formation of the attacking column, Pickett's separate brigade lines [his division was composed of three brigades] lost their formation as they swept across the Emmitsburg Road, carrying with them their chain of skirmishers. They pushed on toward the crest and merged into one crowding, rushing line, many ranks deep. As they crossed the road, Webb's infantry, on the right of the trees, commenced an irregular, hesitating fire, gradually increasing . . . while the shrapnel and canister from the batteries tore gaps through those splendid Virginia battalions.
>
> The men of our brigade, with their muskets at the ready, lay in waiting. One could plainly hear the orders of the officers as they commanded, "Steady, men, steady! Don't fire!" and not a shot was fired at the advancing hostile line, now getting closer every moment. The dense line of Confederates was for a moment lost to view in a dip of the ground. An instant after they seemed to rise out of the earth, and so near that the expression on their faces was distinctly seen. Now our men knew that the time had come, and could wait no longer. Aiming low, they opened a deadly concentrated discharge upon the moving mass in their front. Nothing human could stand it. Staggered by the storm of lead, the charging line hesitated . . . and then all that portion of Pickett's division which came within the zone of this terrible close musketry fire appeared to melt and drift away in the powder smoke of both sides. At this juncture, some one behind me gave the quick, impatient order, "Forward, men! Forward! Now is your chance."
>
> I turned and saw that it was General Hancock, who was passing the left of the regiment. He checked his horse and pointed toward the clump of trees to our right and front. I construed this into an order for both regiments to run for the trees, to prevent the enemy from breaking through . . . With a cheer the two regiments left their position . . . and made an impetuous dash, racing diagonally forward for the clump of trees . . . Many of Webb's men were still lying down in their places in ranks, and firing at those who followed Pickett's advance which, in the meantime, had passed over them.
>
> One battle flag after another, supported by Pickett's infantry,

appeared along the edge of the trees, until the whole copse seemed literally crammed with men.

Rice's description became one of a long confused fight, with Blue and Gray intermingled at close quarters, men falling at close intervals, and no one in charge.

> This was one of those periods in action which are measurable by seconds. The men near seemed to fire very slowly. Those in rear, though coming up at a run, seemed to drag their feet. Many were firing through the intervals of those in front in their eagerness to injure the enemy. This manner of firing . . . sometimes tells on friend instead of foe. A sergeant at my side received a ball in the back of his neck by this fire . . . The grove was fairly jammed with Pickett's men, in all positions, lying and kneeling. Back from the edge were many standing and firing over those in front. By the side of several who were firing, lying down or kneeling, were others with their hands up, in token of surrender. In particular I noticed two men . . . one aiming so that I could look into his musket barrel, the other, lying on his back, coolly ramming home a cartridge. A little farther on was one on his knees waving something white in both hands.
>
> A Confederate battery, near the Peach Orchard, commenced firing . . . A cannon shot tore a horrible passage through the dense crowd of men in blue, who were gathering outside the trees.

Rice recognised that if he could get his soldiers' attention he could lead them quickly to a position where they would be out of the line of fire of both Confederate artillery and rifles, but, as he was stepping backward with his face to the men, he "felt a sharp blow as a shot struck me, then another; I whirled round, my sword torn from my hand . . . As I went down our men rushed forward past me, capturing battle flags and making prisoners.

"Pickett's division lost nearly six-sevenths of its officers and men. Gibbon's [Union] division, with its leader wounded, and with a loss of half its strength, still held the crest."[8]

Lewis Armistead's brigade of Pickett's division had reached the crest, with Armistead in the front rank, waving his cap on the point of his sword, to encourage his men forward. He reached the stone wall running along the crest, stepped over, and put his hand on the muzzle of a Union gun, as if to claim its capture. Then he was hit and fell mortally wounded. Armistead had last been with Union troops at the Presidio of San Francisco in 1861, when, at secession, he had bade farewell to some fellow West Pointers, then left to go with his state. Three hundred men followed him onto Cemetery Ridge, many falling in the final confusion of the charge. Their bravery came to be remembered as the "high water mark of the Confederacy." The Confederate army was never to penetrate farther into Union territory.

As the survivors of Pickett's charge were making their way back across the valley to Seminary Ridge, Robert E. Lee appeared on horseback. As he met the returning survivors, he called out, "All this will come right in the end. We'll talk it over afterwards. But in the meantime, all good men must rally. We want all good and true men just now!" He was joined by Pickett, who, riding up with tears streaming down his face, stumbled out, "General Lee, I have no division now." "Come, General Pickett," Lee answered. "Your men have done all that men can do. The fault is certainly my own."

Later, after night fell, Lee was met by General John Imboden, who commanded an independent brigade of cavalry. He helped Lee to dismount and then said, "General, this has been a hard day on you." Lee answered, "Yes, it has been a sad, sad day to us. I never saw troops behave more magnificently than Pickett's division of Virginians did today . . . And if they had been supported . . . we would have held the position and the day would have been ours." Then, after a pause, he cried out in a voice of agony: "Too bad! Too bad! OH! TOO BAD!"

How bad would be revealed as the armies took stock of their losses on the days following the battle. The Army of Northern Virginia had lost about 22,600 men, killed, wounded, and missing, the Army of the Potomac about 22,800. The worst loss in Hancock's Second Corps was in Gibbon's division, which had held Cemetery Ridge. Its First Brigade lost 768 altogether, of whom 147 were killed and 47 missing. One of its regiments was the 1st Minnesota, which began the battle only two hundred or so strong and was then almost extinguished by the energy of its own counter-attack. Another to lose heavily was General Reynolds's First Corps, which suffered 6,000 total casualties, 2,000 of them captured or missing, mostly during the first day of the battle. Figures for the missing were large in most Civil War battles, partly because soldiers did not wear identity tags, making the identification of bodies haphazard. Others missing no doubt included those lost in the hospital system or lack of system and the opportunity provided by wounding to the war-weary to slip back into civilian life. General John Sedgwick's Sixth Corps, by contrast, lost very few men, only eleven men wounded in one brigade, one killed and four wounded in another, only two wounded in a third.

Yet despite the sparing of some formations from heavy loss, Gettysburg had been a landmark, if not exactly a decisive, battle. It restored belief in the certainty of final victory to the Union, and dispirited the Confederacy, perhaps terminally. It was the largest battle of the war so far and would not be surpassed in scale. Those who had taken part, either as victors or losers, knew that they had participated in a historic event, the recollection of which they would carry within their memory for the rest of their lives.

On November 19, 1863, President Lincoln came to Gettysburg to take part in the dedication of the new national cemetery already created by extending the existing municipal cemetery. The principal speaker was to be Edward Everett, a former governor of Massachusetts and a noted orator. Lincoln had been asked merely to add a few words to the main oration.

Everett spoke for two hours, from a carefully prepared script, flowery and verbose in style. He evoked the funeral ovations of ancient Athens, subjecting his listeners to a display of laborious classical learning. When he eventually came to an end, Lincoln rose and spoke for two minutes. His words have become as remembered and as celebrated as the opening of the Declaration of Independence and the Constitution. He began,

> Four score and seven years ago our fathers brought forth on this continent a new nation, conceived in liberty and dedicated to the proposition that all men are created equal.
>
> Now we are engaged in a great civil war, testing whether that nation or any nation so conceived and so dedicated can long endure. We are met on a great battlefield of that war. We have come to dedicate a portion of that field as a final resting-place for those who here gave their lives that that nation might live. It is altogether fitting and proper that we should do this. But in a larger sense, we cannot dedicate, we cannot consecrate, we cannot hallow this ground. The brave men, living and dead, who struggled here have consecrated it far above our poor power to add or detract. The world will little note, nor long remember, what we say here, but it can never forget what they did here.

It is for us the living rather to be dedicated here to the unfinished work which they who fought here have thus far so nobly advanced. It is rather for us to be here dedicated to the great task remaining before us—that from these honoured dead we take increased devotion to that cause for which they gave the last full measure of devotion—that we here highly resolve that these dead shall not have died in vain, that this nation under God shall have a new birth of freedom, and that government of the people, by the people, for the people shall not perish from the earth.

Lincoln was dissatisfied with his two hundred and seventy words. "It's a flat failure," he said. The London *Times* correspondent agreed. "The ceremony," he wrote, "was rendered ludicrous by the sallies of that poor President Lincoln." Edward Everett, however, later wrote to Lincoln to say, "I shall be glad if I could flatter myself that I came as near to the central idea of the occasion in two hours as you did in two minutes."

CHAPTER TWELVE

Vicksburg

T HE NEWS OF defeat at Gettysburg was succeeded the following day, July 4, 1863, by news of the surrender of Vicksburg,
which had been a key to the Confederacy's ability to close
traffic along the Mississippi River between the Midwest and the exit to
the high seas below New Orleans. The opening was more symbolic
than substantial since the movement of goods in bulk from the interior
to the ocean by rail had already overtaken the traditional river traffic.
Nevertheless, securing the line of the Mississippi had been at the heart
of Winfield Scott's Anaconda Plan and was central as an aim both to
Union strategy and to Union hopes for the prosecution of the war.

The victory also simplified the way forward in the West, for which
no coherent Union strategy had been laid down. Indeed, the war in the
West (which is known today as the south-central United States) had
not followed any organised scheme but had developed as a result of
opportunities presented by sequential successes. The first of these,
from which all the rest followed, was the capture of Forts Henry and
Donelson, both in Tennessee, in February 1862. Grant had decided to
attack these two places because they stood on the Confederate frontier
in the West but also because they controlled movement along the
Cumberland and Tennessee rivers and led into territories Lincoln
eagerly sought to occupy, particularly loyal eastern Tennessee. Militarily, rivers in the West played a quite different role from those in the
East. The eastern rivers in Virginia, particularly, were chiefly valuable
as water obstacles, most useful to a defender. In the West, the rivers
were avenues of movement—the Mississippi foremost, but the Ohio,
Tennessee, and Cumberland also, since they offered points of penetration to the Union into Confederate territory, for the mass movement
of troops, artillery, and supplies. The Mississippi-Ohio-Tennessee-

Cumberland complex was of particular strategic importance since, in a Jeffersonian phrase, they interlocked, their interconnecting points or confluences, if held, conferring great advantages to the occupier. How keenly Grant perceived the importance of the riverlands is difficult to judge. Grant was as hindered by lack of good maps as any other general campaigning at the time inside the South, but it may be supposed that he glimpsed opportunities. Moreover, as soon as Henry and Donelson were taken he was off down the Tennessee, to strike deep into Confederate territory and to fight the bloody battle of Shiloh on the riverbank at Pittsburg Landing. Victory there allowed the Union's superior commander in the West, Henry Halleck, to open an advance on the railroad centre of Corinth, which the newly arrived General Beauregard evacuated before it could be captured. A newly formed army under General John Pope had already captured the fortified positions at New Madrid and Island No. 10 for the Union. The battle at Shiloh on the Tennessee River had thus indirectly opened the lower Mississippi to a Union advance. After the fall of Island No. 10, only Fort Pillow and Memphis stood between the Union force in Tennessee and Vicksburg on the lower reaches. Memphis fell quickly after the evacuation of Corinth, thanks to the intervention of a fleet of naval ironclad rams, constructed by a Pennsylvania designer, Charles Ellet. In a hard-fought battle on June 6, Ellet, several of whose close relatives served aboard his ships, engaged the Confederate flotilla at Memphis and defeated it, by gunfire and ramming. The attack was quite unexpected and shocked both the Union and the Confederacy by its surprise and swift conclusion. Before the end of the day, the Union flag flew over the Memphis post office. In a little over four months, vital stretches of the South's largest waterways had fallen under Union control; all of them were under threat.

This dire situation had been brought about by the nature of Confederate strategy, such as it was, in the western theatre. The reconsideration of Confederate strategy in the West was the work of George Randolph, the Confederate secretary of war. He believed in the coordination of operations by all the armies deployed from the Appalachians to Arkansas, of which there were several. He began by ordering General Theophilus Hunter Holmes of the Trans-Mississippi Department to bring his army across the river to assist in the defence of Vicksburg. When informed, Jefferson Davis at once vetoed the order. He emphasised that commanders of departments were expected to stay within their own departments and that any movement of troops must be authorised by the president. Randolph correctly recognised that this statement of policy deprived the secretary of war of any function and promptly resigned. Davis replaced him with James Seddon, a semi-invalid but an experienced Virginia politician. Seddon was less likely to take offence than Randolph; he also had the gift of planting ideas in Davis's mind in such a way that the president thought they were his own. Seddon's principal idea on taking office was that the Confederacy must rescue its western provinces from capture by the Union and that required the reconstitution, under a single commander, of a Department of the West. Davis was persuaded not only that he had thought of the plan for himself but also that he had chosen the commander, Joseph E. Johnston. That was a remarkable achievement since Davis and Johnston had a long history of quarrelling. Johnston was, however, a general of undeniable talent, if of quite different views from any other Confederate leader.

At an early stage, Albert Sidney Johnston and Jefferson Davis had together decided on a cordon defence of the lower Confederacy, along a line close to the western flanks of the Appalachians and reaching out via Bowling Green, Kentucky, and Forts Henry and Donelson, Tennessee, to Columbus on the Mississippi, a distance of 300 miles. Because the bulk of Confederate troops, and the best troops at that, had to be kept in Virginia on the Richmond–Washington axis, there were insufficient forces left to guard the long western frontier, and they were not of the first quality, either in leadership, equipment, or human fighting power. Nor did they benefit from the configurations of geography, since there was little high ground on which to form defensive lines, while the waterways flowed in precisely the wrong direction, as was not the case in Virginia. The South had to resort to the expedient of holding key points, on railways or rivers, as a principal means of impeding Union advances. It was in that context that the giving up of important places such as Island No. 10 cost them so dear. Even worse, because it inaugurated the fallback, was the surrender of the so-called Gibraltar of the Mississippi Valley, Columbus, Kentucky, in February 1862. By summer 1863 the whole run of the Mississippi, southward from Columbus, with the exception of Vicksburg and Port Hudson, was under Union control. The most spectacular Union success on the river had been the capture of New Orleans, the largest city of the Confederacy, in April 1862. The capture of New Orleans was the first noted achievement of the United States Navy in the war so far. The victor was Flag Officer (Admiral) David Glasgow Farragut, a Southern-born regular naval officer who had served the Union for thirty years and was unflinchingly loyal to it. When at secession time he heard other Southern-born naval officers discussing the military situation, and whether to go with their states, he warned that they would "catch the devil before they were through with this business." He had fought in the War of 1812 but retained a keen and original mind and the courage of a fire-eating midshipman.

Farragut opened the campaign on the Mississippi in February 1862 when he led a fleet of eight steam sloops and fourteen gunboats over the shallows of the river's mouth and 15,000 soldiers under General Benjamin Butler. The first obstacles to further advance were the two Third System forts, St. Philip and Jackson, which had fallen into Confederate hands at secession. Farragut bombarded both heavily for six days; when both declined to surrender, he decided to force his way through the chain barrier they defended, which, by April 25, he had done with his fleet, largely intact. He then proceeded immediately to New Orleans, exchanging fire with the riverside defenders as he went. When he got to the city, he met Butler's troops who were on hand. By April 27, New Orleans was in Union hands; its capture, the largest city in the South, was a tremendous fillip to the North's prestige and consonantly depressing to the Confederacy. Butler proved a harsh occupier, running a stringent military administration, though the city had never been a stronghold of secession. By June the Farragut fleet had got as far upstream as Vicksburg, taking en route Baton Rouge, the Louisiana state capital, and Natchez, and had made contact with the upstream Federal river navy. Both, however, had been fired on so heavily by the guns of Vicksburg and those on the adjoining riverbanks that they had not been able to linger in the city's vicinity nor to make any impression on its fortifications or garrison, which had been reinforced by the arrival of troops under Van Dorn. It had become clear that Vicksburg could only be taken, and so the river opened, by the effort of a large army operating on the eastern bank of the Mississippi. How to position such an army was to tantalise the thoughts of Union commanders for the ensuing year.

Quarrels over authority compounded the difficulties of the Union army on the Mississippi at the outset. Because of his successes at Henry and Donelson and at Shiloh, Grant was appointed commander of the Army of the Tennessee on October 25, 1862. Unfortunately a potential rival, John McClernand, who engaged considerable support in Washington, embarked on a personal scheme to capture Vicksburg at precisely the moment that Grant began on his own campaign. McClernand, a former congressman, was a protégé of Stephen Douglas's, and though his mentor was now dead, McClernand retained considerable political stature as the leading Democrat in Illinois. His gifts of oratory brought in significant numbers of recruits in the Midwest for service on the Mississippi, to which he was sending formed regiments, and this success brought him a commission as brigadier general from a grateful Lincoln. McClernand had his own ambitions. He recognised the political advantage to be won by pursuing a successful military career and, though his military experience was limited to a few weeks' service in the Black Hawk War, he unfortunately believed that he was a field commander of great talent, at least equal to Grant, and set out to get an independent command in the army and lead it to victory. Moreover, McClernand had his own line of communication to Halleck, the general in chief, and enjoyed the favour of Lincoln. He began by persuading Halleck in Washington to issue him an order that appeared to give him an independent mission in the West and then to take charge of Illinois regiments as they were raised and sent south. The regiments joined Grant's army, but McClernand exploited ambiguities in Halleck's communications to make it appear that they were forming for an independent operation against Vicksburg.

Grant puzzled over the McClernand problem throughout October and November 1862, discussing it with Sherman in a series of cases but coming to no conclusion. McClernand was cunning, never openly challenging Grant's authority but appealing in turn to Halleck and to political supporters in Illinois and other western states in a persistent attempt to enlarge his freedom of action. On paper he had scraps of authorisation to justify his insubordination, all of which he exploited shamelessly, but ultimately he was clutching at straws. He won none of the freedoms to which he aspired, and he lacked altogether the gifts of generalship he proclaimed to possess. Grant arranged to trammel him by reorganising the Army of the Tennessee into four corps and giving command of a fifth, the Thirteenth, to McClernand, thus exactly defining his powers. McClernand nevertheless continued to behave as if he were a fully fledged army commander and to correspond with Halleck and Lincoln. Fortunately Halleck, though no friend of Grant, was a stickler for military propriety and eventually tired of McClernand's machinations. Finally, in June 1863, McClernand went too far. In defiance of an army order forbidding subordinates from writing to the newspapers without permission, he published a self-congratulatory despatch about his actions at Champion's Hill in an Illinois newspaper. Grant at once relieved him of command, bringing his extraordinary career as a self-appointed leader of men to an end. He had certainly done nothing to advance the capture of Vicksburg, which throughout the early summer of 1863 remained beyond Grant's clutches.

The Vicksburg problem, though exacerbated by the quarrels over command, was fundamentally a geographical one. By the summer of 1863, Vicksburg was a mighty fortress, made so by the terrain that surrounded it and by the earthworks its Confederate garrison had built. The Walnut Hills, on which Vicksburg stands, are steep and in 1863 they were cut by many deep, wooded ravines. Their bottoms were choked with dense brush and cane, their sides, sometimes forty or fifty feet high, overgrown by standing timber, from which fell dead trees which frequently formed natural abatis—tangled obstacles with sharp projections to injure and impair the progress of attackers as they passed through. The defenders had also formed many artificial abatis, tree trunks pierced to take sharpened stakes, all lying about the approaches to Vicksburg's defences.

A European fortress or an American fortress in the East would have had its surroundings altered to make "dead ground" and provide fields of fire across a smooth glacis which could be swept by artillery fire and musketry. The nature of the ground and the abundance of vegetation at Vicksburg made the construction of such a glacis impossible. Both, however, contributed greatly to the strength of the earthworks. Around the enceinte, or enclosing wall, stood a number of strongpoints, artillery platforms, redoubts, strengthening features, redans, and lunettes, all terms derived from the international vocabulary of fortification science, largely French in origin, which was taught meticulously at West Point. These terms were to feature particularly in Grant's 1863 siege with the 2nd Texas Lunette, the 3rd Louisiana Redan, the Stockade Redan, the Railroad Redoubt, all named after the unit that had built or garrisoned them or after a nearby feature. The theory of the attack of fortresses prescribed an advance by infantry on the outer defences and walls, in an attempt to enter by storm, and, if that failed, a deliberate siege, by digging and bombardment.

The fortified city of Vicksburg, under the command of General John C. Pemberton, commander of the Department of the Mississippi, was therefore very strong, but even more important than the strongpoints and batteries in protecting it against Union attack was the nature of its surroundings. In December Sherman attempted an assault

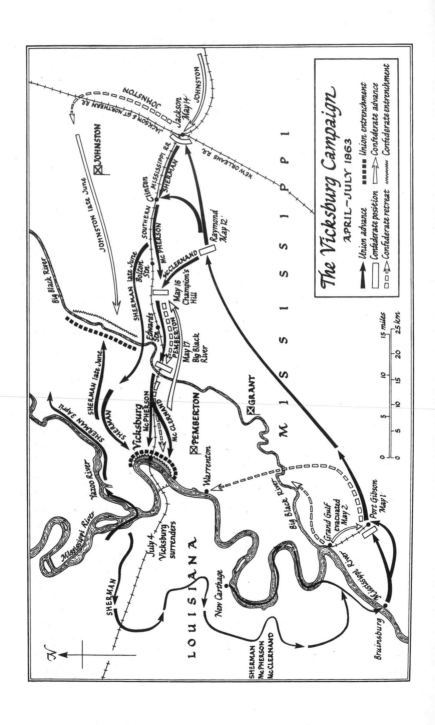

The Vicksburg Campaign
APRIL–JULY 1863

against Vicksburg from the rear, at Chickasaw Bluff. The piece of ground chosen to mount the assault, the only one available, lay across the Chickasaw Bayou. It was a narrow triangle which Sherman's men had to enter from the apex, and little dry ground could be found. Several assaults were made between December 27, 1862, and January 3, 1863, but the defenders outnumbered the Union attackers and were supported by artillery. Union losses eventually totalled 208 killed and 1,005 wounded against Confederate losses of 63 killed and 134 wounded. Sherman was obliged to withdraw his force. It had been defeated by geography, despite all the engineers' efforts at bridging and pontooning.

The land around Chickasaw Bayou was typical of the whole lower Mississippi Valley, which Grant described as "a low alluvial bottom many miles in width . . . very tortuous in its course, running to all points of the compass, sometimes within a few miles." There is high ground, the Vicksburg bluffs on the east bank, but the banks are generally low-lying and marshy, cut in many places by the bayous which are the distinctive feature of the river, shallow backwaters, drying out in summer but flooding in spring. Navigation was very difficult since the river and its tributaries and seasonal waterways were overhung by dense vegetation which had often to be cut if a vessel was to make headway. The meanders of the great river and of its subsidiaries were as convoluted as those of any river elsewhere in the world, often of hairpin form and forcing navigators to voyage long, wasted distances to advance in the desired direction. Adding to Union difficulties during the Vicksburg campaign was the summer climate—hot, humid, and disease-bearing, because of the dense insect life.

Grant had tried to march south on Vicksburg down the east bank of the Mississippi in November–December 1862, using as his line of supply the Mississippi Central Railroad, which led into Kentucky. Confederate cavalry raids, however, conducted by Forrest and Van Dorn, wrecked his forward base at Holly Springs, northwest of Vicksburg, and forced him to abandon the effort. He then reverted to the riverborne scheme, from several directions, including efforts by Sherman and McClernand. He called the components of his scheme "experiments," which indeed they were since he had no assurance that any would succeed and in all he was working in the dark in the highly uncertain circumstances of uncharted swamps, river loops, and muddy, inundated backwaters. His idea was to get forward by cutting canals that would allow his gunboat fleet, with its transports, to pass from above

Vicksburg to the Mississippi's main stream below the city without coming under fire of its batteries. He had tried re-engineering the Mississippi Valley first in the summer of 1862 but despite several months' digging had eventually had to abandon the attempt, because no end to the work came into view. In the winter he made four more attempts.

The first was an effort to complete the canal begun the previous summer, which cut across the neck of ground surrounded by the meander below Milliken's Bend, one of the major navigable reaches of the great river above Vicksburg. Rising waters of the spring floods eventually threatened to drown the diggers, who belonged to Sherman's corps, and the effort had to be abandoned again. The second was an attempt at Lake Providence, fifty miles above Vicksburg, from which diggings were to allow gunboats to reach the Mississippi's main course 400 miles below the city and thence, by a roundabout route through swamps and backwaters, to get to the vital dry ground in its rear. The troops were supplied by the corps led by General James McPherson. He was an engineer officer whom Grant had identified as a highly effective combat commander. Lake Providence defeated his engineering talents, however. The route was impeded by huge trees rooted on the waterway's bottom, which had to be sawn through. Months of that sort of labour, together with digging and dredging, dispirited both McPherson and his soldiers, to a point where the project had to be abandoned, as the Milliken's Bend had been. The third and fourth attempts were to dig and clear navigable channels through what was called the delta of the Yazoo, in fact a bewildering complex of waterways joining the Yazoo River to the Mississippi above Vicksburg, from which by altering water levels by blocking holes in the Mississippi banks it was hoped to reach the Tallahatchie River and then the lower reaches of the Yazoo, which gave on to the northern approaches of Vicksburg. The staff officer in charge was so afflicted by the mental ordeal of the engineering prospect that he began to show evidence of a breakdown. His troubles were heightened by Confederate felling of trees across the Yazoo, which made the waterways impenetrable to gunboats. At this stage the campaign resembled less a river war than an expedition through subtropical forest, so dense and intertwined were the branches of the trees lining the route. The attempt was defeated by the density of bankside vegetation and the complexity of the waterway's course, and was eventually driven off by the guns of the hastily built Confederate Fort Pemberton.

Three months were spent on these fruitless and laborious engineering efforts. Grant's critics in the East complained that he was wasting time and gaining nothing. Grant was resistant to criticism, having remarkable confidence in his own judgement; he claimed that his "experiments" kept John Pemberton, the Confederate commander of Vicksburg, off balance. He must, however, have been concerned about the effect of these operations on his troops, who were living in depressing, waterlogged conditions and forced to perform a great deal of heavy labour for no detectible outcome.

By early April 1863 Grant was in despair. Every effort he had made to get the Army of the Tennessee onto dry ground on the east bank of the Mississippi, from which he could mount an attack to capture Vicksburg, had been frustrated. Then a new idea came to him. If unsuccessful it would have dire consequences. If successful, however, it might well abolish all his difficulties and offer the prospect of complete success. Grant was not deterred by risk, and all his experience in the war thus far had fed his appetite for boldness. Unlike McClellan and Halleck, he was not encumbered by theory or by high military knowledge. He was thus not hampered by fears of cutting himself off from his base, which was precisely what he now intended to do. His base and his army were above Vicksburg. He proposed to transport his force to a decisive point below Vicksburg. What prevented him making a junction of ships and troops was the fourteen miles of guns lining the banks of the Mississippi on either side of Vicksburg, to which the soldiers could not be exposed without fearful loss. The ships might run the risk, however, if sailed by surprise, at speed and under cover of darkness. That was the essence of Grant's plan. He would march his army farther down the west bank, to a point where, if the fleet arrived, a crossing could be made by steamer to dry ground on the east bank near Vicksburg itself. David Dixon Porter's fleet would meanwhile be protected and prepared to withstand heavy gunfire. Then, under cover of the night, it would run the batteries from north to south, to meet the troops at the chosen crossing place below Vicksburg. He would thus be placing himself behind enemy lines twice over, once by crossing to enemy territory, secondly by leaving the enemy's main force in fortified positions athwart his line of communication and supply. Grant was determined not to be intimidated by the risks or the unorthodoxy of his intentions. Once on the Mississippi's east bank, he would live off the country, carrying only ammunition and taking food and fodder where he found it.

He was blessed with luck: on the night of April 29, with his troops encamped below Vicksburg at Grand Gulf, a local black man came in with the news that a crossing might be made a little lower down at Bru-insburg, near Grand Gulf. The information proved accurate. In a five-hour engagement, on the night of April 16–17, Flag Officer David Porter had already run the batteries of Vicksburg to a point thirty miles below the city, his gunboats protected by bales of cotton piled on their decks and manned by watermen who volunteered from the ranks of the army. One gunboat was sunk but three got through, and by April 22 sixteen transports and barges were sailed down. On April 30 the fleet began to transport the army across the river at Bruinsburg. To distract Pemberton, the Confederate defender of Vicksburg, Grant simulta-neously despatched Colonel Benjamin Grierson on a long-distance cavalry raid with 1,700 horse soldiers. Starting from La Grange, Ten-nessee, near Memphis, on April 17, he had ridden south between the Mobile and Ohio and Mississippi Central railroads destroying track and burning rolling stock. He also severely damaged the Southern Railroad before he joined forces with Banks at Baton Rouge on May 2. Grierson, by profession a music teacher, proved to have exceptional talent as a mounted marauder. In a sixteen-day march of 600 miles he devastated central Mississippi, tearing up fifty miles of railroad track and living off the country.

Pemberton had now taken his army out of Vicksburg to challenge Grant in the open field, much to the anxiety of Jefferson Davis and General Johnston. They ordered him back into Vicksburg, warning that he would lose both his army and Vicksburg if he fought beyond the protection of its defences. Pemberton disagreed. He had 30,000 troops to Grant's 10,000 and was confident he could hold his own and perhaps drive Grant back into Tennessee. He therefore arrived in central Mis-sissippi, manoeuvring between the river and the city of Jackson, the state capital. Grant was unperturbed. As he wrote in his memoirs, "I was now in the enemy's country, with a vast river and the stronghold of Vicksburg between me and my base of supplies. But I was on dry ground on the same side of the river with the enemy. All the campaigns, labors, hardships and exposures from the month of December previous to this time that had been made and endured, were for the accomplish-ment of this one object."

Grant's reference to his "base of supplies" is highly significant. He opened his own account of Vicksburg with the observation: "It is gen-erally regarded as an axiom in war that all great armies moving in an enemy's country should start from a base of supplies, which should be fortified and guarded." Now Grant was caught up in a vast, wide-ranging campaign in the interior of the Confederacy whose nature had forced him to diverge from geometry. Today technical experts would say that he was "operating on exterior lines," circling around the Confederacy's heartland, seeking where he might penetrate. A less imaginative man than Grant would probably have sought to define a geometrical base and line of operations. What Grant did, after bypassing Vicksburg, defied all contemporary rules of strategy. After effecting the rendezvous between Porter's fleet and his Army of the Tennessee, he had used the gunboats and transports to ferry his army across the river to the east bank.

From Grand Gulf he had sent two of his corps, those of McPherson and the tiresome McClernand, to march inland eastward towards Jackson, where Joseph E. Johnston was struggling to organise a new army. Johnston had been put in overall command of Confederate Mississippi on May 9. He fielded about 20,000 troops to the Union's 29,000 and might have made a fair fight of it, had Grant advanced and deployed in an orthodox fashion. Grant did not. Having abandoned the rules of Jominian warfare, he now also abandoned the rules of organised campaigning. Instead of bringing supplies with him, or organising a line of supply from the rear, he decided not to bother with supplies but to live off the land, as Sherman had done in the Arkansas campaign of 1862. He thus surprised Johnston at Raymond, outside Jackson, on May 12. Two days later the victorious Union troops defeated Johnston at Jackson, driving Pemberton to take his small army to a place on the railroad to the west of Jackson called Champion Hill, so named after a local plantation-owning family whose son was an officer in the 15th Mississippi. The town was highly defensible, standing as it did on a ridge seventy feet above the surrounding plain. On May 16, the Champion Hill position was attacked with success by the Union. McPherson's corps caused the Confederate line to cave in. McClernand's corps attacked less aggressively. This increased Grant's lack of trust in him, which was to result in his dismissal on June 19.

From Champion Hill, Grant pressed on to the Big Black River, which ran between him and Vicksburg. The rebel position was attacked on May 17 and at once gave way, after which Pemberton's ragged and half-starved army fell back within the lines of Vicksburg. Grant at once took the city under siege, and during May 19–22 he launched a series of assaults on the defences, all of which cost the Union heavily, so heavily that a soldier of the 93rd Regiment described the attack as like "marching men to their deaths in line of battle." After the last and most determined assault of May 23, Grant reverted to the tactics of deliberate siege. During that night, Union soldiers, whose attacks had carried them to the very lip of the Confederate entrenchments, stealthily withdrew to safer positions. The besiegers had suffered over 3,000 casualties during the great assault of May 22, at least 1,000 of which were caused by McClernand grotesquely demanding reinforcements for a success he had not achieved.

Johnston did not appear nor would he throughout the weeks of siege that followed, though the Vicksburg newspaper, in an effort to sustain morale, constantly reported his approach. The newspaper was now printed on the back of squares of wallpaper. Newsprint was not the only commodity in short supply; so were bread, flour, meat, and vegetables. The garrison and the citizens, who had dug themselves shelters against shellfire in the sides of the city's sunken roads, subsisted on mule meat, and peanuts, "goober peas," supplemented by skinned rats. Grant essayed his first assault on May 19, which was repulsed with heavy loss but renewed on May 22, again without success, despite a supporting bombardment by 300 guns firing from positions on land and on gunboats. On May 25, Pemberton, from within the fortress, declared a truce to enable the burial of the dead and the collection of the wounded. The stench of decomposing bodies hung around the defences. The same day, however, Grant ordered the renewal of deliberate siege, to be mounted against the sector dominated by the 3rd Louisiana Redoubt, or Fort Hill, as the Union soldiers called it. There were several more assaults in the ensuing weeks; in the intervals, Johnny Reb and Billy Yank fraternised across the earthworks, gossiping, exchanging taunts, threats, and boasts but also necessities including Union coffee and Confederate tobacco, as long as such supplies lasted.

Confederate defences at Vicksburg were so strong that, as would happen at Petersburg in 1864, the Union set about undermining them in an effort to secure a breach. Once a breach was established across the river on dry land, a crossing to the outworks of Vicksburg was effected with surprising ease. The difficulty in investing the fortification remained. It was carried out by classic European siege technique, sapping a way forward by digging entrenchments and parallels, but with an American variant. Ahead of the sap diggers, the sappers, the besiegers pushed a shot-proof shield, the sap-roller, which protected the sappers as they entrenched their earthworks. At intervals the sappers dug a battery position, in which artillery was installed to keep the

Confederates under fire at decreasing range. By June 7 the most advanced battery was 75 yards from the parapet of Fort Hill. The besiegers kept up a relentless rifle fire. The sappers also refined their task of sap-rolling by bringing up a railroad car loaded with cotton bales to absorb the enemy's fire, but the rebels reversed the advantage so gained by firing incendiary bullets into the railroad car, setting it alight and burning it to the ground. Nevertheless, the saps were pressed forward and by June 22 the sappers were at the foot of the Fort Hill breastwork. Colonel Andrew Hickenlooper, commanding the approach, then conceived a new technique. Calling for volunteers with experience of coal mining, he paid them to drive a shaft under the Confederate position. By June 25, it was completed, 45 yards long and ending in a chamber packed with 2,200 pounds of gunpowder. At 3:30 p.m. on June 25 the vast charge was exploded and most of Fort Hill rose into the sky as dust and ashes. When the cloud cleared, the attackers saw to their dismay that the defenders, anticipating the explosion, against which they had counter-mined, had dug a new parapet across the interior of the fort, from which they could shoot down at the Union soldiers as they stormed into the crater. Grant pressed attacks all evening and night until the floor of the crater was slippery with blood, but still the defences held. Eventually, after the loss of 34 men killed and 209 wounded, the assault was called off.

Almost immediately, however, the Union resumed tunnelling and by July 1 had driven a new shaft under the left wing of the fort, which was packed with powder. The Confederates counter-mined, using six slaves to do the digging. On July 1, 1,800 pounds of gunpowder was detonated by the Union miners, which destroyed the Confederate counter-mines and killed the counter-miners, all save one slave who was blown clean through the air, to land in Union lines. No assault, however, followed the explosion, which largely destroyed the 3rd Louisiana Redoubt. Instead, the attackers came up rapidly and opened a drenching fire on the entrance to the redoubt, which the Confederates tried to close with a new breastwork, eventually with success. Siege warfare was resumed all along the Vicksburg perimeter, where in some places the two sides were separated only by the thickness of a single parapet. New mines were begun in several places and trenches widened to prepare for a further ground assault, which Grant proposed to make on July 6. Unknown to the Union, though it was with reason suspected, the defenders were at their last gasp. At Milliken's Bend, 15 miles northwest of Vicksburg, on June 7, two regiments of black troops, eligible to bear arms since the Emancipation Proclamation, bravely repelled a Confederate attack, though at heavy cost to themselves.

Pemberton, meanwhile, was having boats built from the timbers of dismantled houses and so planning to force an escape to the eastern shore. Many of the garrison were on the point of mutiny, since they were starving. It was obvious that Pemberton would be forced to surrender very shortly. Word of the garrison's demoralisation had reached Grant, and he was reluctant to mount further costly attacks. Johnston was approaching from the east, but, outnumbered as he was, it was most improbable that he could raise the siege. On July 1, Pemberton questioned his subordinate commanders to test their opinion as to the likely success of an effort to break out. Two replied advocating surrender, the other two in almost the same terms. The condition of the garrison was desperate. The soldiers, together with the 3,000 remaining civilian residents, were starving, the men in too weakened a condition to maintain a steadfast defence. In the days after July 1 the spirit of the garrison collapsed. On July 3 white flags appeared at several places on the parapets, and at the 3rd Louisiana Redoubt voices were heard calling for a cease-fire. A Union party went forward to investigate and returned with two Confederate officers, blindfolded as the protocol of siege warfare required. One of them was Pemberton's aide-de-camp, carrying a letter for Grant. Pemberton had written to spare any further "effusion of blood," the words Lee was to use at the surrender at Appomattox two years hence. He was also requesting the appointment of commissioners to arrange terms of surrender, a normal and conventional procedure at the termination of a siege. Grant's view of terms was established and well-known. It was the same as he had offered at Fort Donelson in February 1862: "No terms except unconditional and immediate surrender can be accepted."

Grant, who had served with Pemberton in Mexico, was on this occasion less peremptory, though he made his meaning equally clear. Pemberton attempted to prolong discussions by meeting Grant outside the line, but the Union commander would not yield an inch. Pemberton quibbled and it seemed that the fighting might resume, until Pemberton's subordinate suggested that some chosen junior officers should discuss the matter. Grant agreed, on condition that he was not bound by what they might agree to. His emissary, General Bowen, returned to Grant with Pemberton's suggestion that the garrison be accorded the "honours of war," which meant that it should be allowed to march out but under arms, subsequently to be retained. Grant refused the suggestion outright but said that he would make a final offer before midnight. He held strictly to his view that the enemy were in rebellion and could not enjoy any of the privileges of legitimate combatants. In the interval he held a council of war, though much against his better judgement, at which General James McPherson, whom Grant held in high esteem, suggested that Grant offer to parole Pemberton's troops. Since even if Pemberton submitted to an unconditional surrender, Grant would face the burden of shipping Pemberton's thousands into captivity, Grant agreed and the proposition was sent into the fortress. Pemberton, whose starving soldiers were on the point of mutiny, accepted and on July 4 the garrison marched out to be paroled. Pemberton's officers were allowed to retain their swords and one horse cart. The other weapons and regimental colours were to be stacked outside the lines. Paroles were written and signed for the prisoners, 31,600 in number. Grant permitted them to return inside Vicksburg and then allowed them to drift away. As he was sure that, if left at liberty, they would return to their homes and not resume military service, he felt that this was a safe course of action. So, generally, it proved to be. The defeated Confederates were indeed content to find their own way from the battleground, a disturbing outcome of the Mississippi Valley campaign, with implications for the whole of the South. The occupation of the city that followed was notably good-natured, with Union troops distributing their rations to the emaciated survivors. The value of their victory perhaps disposed the victors to be generous. As Grant correctly observed, "The fall of the Confederacy was settled when Vicksburg fell."[1]

News of the surrender of Vicksburg caused General Frank Gardner, who commanded the garrison at Port Hudson, last of the Confederate blocking places on the Mississippi, to surrender on July 8. Port Hudson, very strongly fortified, controlled a bend in the river with twenty-one heavy guns. At surrender, the garrison numbered 6,340, but the soldiers were weakened by shortage of food. They had also been subjected to assault from land and water for many previous weeks. Surrender was a relief. As at Vicksburg, the incoming Union soldiers offered their rations to the starving defenders.

Not only did this place the line of the Mississippi under Union control, so that, in Lincoln's words, "the Father of Waters again goes unvexed to the sea," it also cut the Confederacy in half, slicing off the western half, including the whole of Texas and the territories of Nebraska, New Mexico, Nevada, Utah, Colorado, and what would be

Oklahoma from material and most other assistance from the Old South. Huge stocks of cattle, horses, and mules were lost to the Confederacy by the capture of Vicksburg and Kirby Smith, commander of the Western Department, was told by Jefferson Davis in the aftermath that thenceforth he would have to manage by himself.

After the capture of Vicksburg, Grant received the following letter from Lincoln:

My dear General,

I do not remember that you and I ever met personally. I write this now as a grateful acknowledgement for the almost inestimable service you have done the country. I wish to say a word further. When you first reached the vicinity of Vicksburg, I thought you should do, what you finally did—march the troops across the neck, run the batteries with the transports, and thus go below; and I never had any faith, except a general hope that you knew better than I, that the Yazoo Pass expedition, and the like, could succeed. When you got below, and took Port Gibson, Grand Gulf, and vicinity, I thought you should go down the river and join Gen. Banks; and when you turned Northward East of the Big Black, I feared it was a mistake. I now wish to make the personal acknowledgement that you were right, and I was wrong.

Yours truly,
A. Lincoln.[2]

CHAPTER THIRTEEN

Cutting the Chattanooga–Atlanta Link

T HE MIDSUMMER VICTORIES of 1863, at Gettysburg and Vicksburg, transformed the fortunes of the Union. In the East Meade's reluctance to compromise his great and unexpected success at Gettysburg deterred him from pursuing Lee as hard as Lincoln wished he would. Meade and Lee would confront each other across the Rapidan without seriously engaging each other for the next six months. In the West, the fall of Vicksburg allowed Union forces to campaign against the Confederate garrisons of Kentucky and Tennessee and opened up a line of advance into Georgia. Militarily, the situation in the border states was thoroughly confusing. Since February 1863 the states across the Mississippi had been organised by President Davis into the Trans-Mississippi Department, under General Edmund Kirby Smith, which he would run as a virtually independent fiefdom, "Kirby Smithdom." Davis had made it clear that Kirby Smith would need to manage on his own, which he did very well. He used the Trans-Mississippi's enormous wealth in cattle, horses, mules, and produce, together with the cotton crop, no longer transportable to the East since the loss of control of the Mississippi River, to set up a trading empire, with outlets in Mexico, the West Indies, and as far away as Europe. He also built his own arsenal at Tyler, Texas, and found ways of substituting for the military supplies from which he was now cut off. The Trans-Mississippi's self-sufficiency, however, could not translate into military success, since Kirby Smith lacked the troops and the battlefield talent to beat Union armies, which sensibly left him alone until the war was over.

In the summer of 1863, the main Union armies in the West, apart from those of Grant and Sherman, were in Tennessee and Kentucky. In

Tennessee, Rosecrans maintained a sizable Army of the Cumberland, with which he had driven off Bragg's Army of Tennessee from Murfreesboro at the battle of Stone's River at Christmas 1862. Since that success he had not been active. In June, however, Rosecrans had surprised Bragg by driving through gaps in the Cumberland Mountains and forced him to retire, via the Duck River valley, as far as Chattanooga. At the same time Burnside, with the Army of the Ohio in Kentucky, pushed forward to take Knoxville, the centre of Tennessee Unionism. The causes of Bragg's failure in Kentucky were manifold. He himself had come to despair of Kentucky Confederates' declarations of Southern patriotism. He repeated frequently to his principal staff officer that the Kentuckians, for all their protestations of belligerence, "had too many fat cattle and were too well off to fight." His retreat to Chattanooga marked the end of the Confederacy in Kentucky. Jefferson Davis was, however, determined to sustain Bragg, despite his manifest inability as a commander. Though Bragg was on bad terms with his subordinate commanders and not popular with his soldiers, Davis had him reinforced with troops from Johnston's army in Mississippi, tried to persuade Lee to join him with the Army of Northern Virginia, a move which Lee particularly resisted, and organised the transfer of Longstreet's corps from northern Virginia by train to Georgia, in a circuitous 900-mile journey over a dozen different railroad lines.

These reinforcements strengthened Bragg's army enough for him to contemplate going over to the attack. It was clear that the Union troops in Tennessee had as their aim to invade Georgia and to seize the vital Chattanooga–Atlanta rail link. Their route forward was a difficult one for the way into Georgia was blocked by the line of the Tennessee River and by the southern tail of the Appalachian Mountains, in particular the heights of Lookout Mountain and Missionary Ridge, which overlooked Chattanooga. Bragg's plan was to tempt Rosecrans into the mountains and then to fall on his columns as they emerged through the gaps. His first efforts to do so failed because of his subordinates' timidity in springing the trap. In mid-September, however, the arrival of Longstreet's reinforcements gave the Confederates superiority of numbers and emboldened the faint hearts. Four of the generals present had served in the same unit in Mexico. One of them, George Thomas, was Southern by birth but serving on the Union side. He was to play a critical role in the battle that was about to unfold. When Bragg made a heavy and concentrated thrust at the Union left on the morning of

September 19, Thomas's corps had just arrived in the theatre. Thomas himself was able to position such troops as he could find to stand, though fortunately the front at the point Thomas chose to defend had been strengthened with timber barricades during the night. One of the units deployed, the 39th Indiana Mounted Infantry, was armed with Spencer repeating carbines, which inflicted huge casualties on the weaker Confederates opposite. The Confederates had taken a position on the west bank of Chickamauga Creek, a small tributary of the Tennessee River running south of Chattanooga. Bragg's plan was to get around Rosecrans's left flank and to seize its communications with Chattanooga. Rosecrans frustrated this move by extending his line. By dawn, 60,000 Federals faced 62,000 Confederates and both sides were poised for battle.

THE BATTLE OF CHICKAMAUGA

What followed would develop into the bloodiest and bitterest of all battles fought in the western theatre. Local circumstances brought the fight on, since the brush and timber covering the banks of the creek meant neither side could properly see each other, close though they were. "The two armies came together like two wild beasts," recalled an eyewitness, "and each fought as long as it could stand up in a knock-down and drag-out encounter." By mid-morning the undergrowth was filled with clouds of dense gray powder smoke and the ground was covered with the bodies of the dead and wounded. The slaughter went on all afternoon "as if all the fires of earth and hell had been turned loose in one mighty effort to destroy each other." As dusk drew in, Patrick Cleburne's Confederate division, composed of Texas, Tennessee, Alabama, and Arkansas troops, launched a final attack which bent but did not break the Union line. The Northern soldiers built barricades of timber during the night and prepared themselves to withstand another Confederate assault.

The battle began again at 8:30 a.m. with a Confederate attack on the Union centre. Bragg still hoped to get round the Union left and cut its communications with Chattanooga but the attacks broke on the Union barricades. Rosecrans should have maintained his position without difficulty had he not made a grave and almost inexplicable mistake. One of his staff officers misread the battle line and told Rosecrans that there was a gap, where none in fact existed; the poor visibility on the battlefield may have been to blame. Rosecrans, however, without looking for himself, took a division out of the line to fill the supposed gap, thus creating a real one, into which charged Longstreet's corps, pushing the Union back nearly a mile at that point.

The effect was disastrous: panic took hold, shamefully affecting not only the rank and file but Rosecrans and several of his subordinate commanders as well, who made off for the safety of Chattanooga. The only senior officer of the Union left on the field was General George Thomas, who was a friend of his Confederate opponent opposite, James Longstreet. Thomas managed to rally some troops of his corps at Snodgrass Hill and form a line of defence. This line held for the rest of the day, preventing the Confederates from getting into the rear of the disorganised Union army and thus saving the day. Thomas, a quiet, slow-spoken man, was known forever after as "the Rock of Chicka-mauga" and came to be rated by Ulysses S. Grant as one of the few indispensable generals of the Union army. He saw his men ride out the attacks, which persisted all afternoon until, as evening came, he ordered their retreat to Rossville, a little short of Chattanooga on Mis-sionary Ridge, where Rosecrans was attempting to reorder his broken ranks. General Emerson Opdycke, who observed Thomas's conduct during the closing stages of the battle, wrote inspiringly of his direc-tion of the defence across the line of retreat. Only six divisions, Op-dycke saw, held the line. "In front stood the whole army of the enemy, eager to fall upon us with the energy that comes from great success and greater hopes. But close behind our line rode a general whose judge-ment never erred, whose calm, invincible will never bent; and around him thirty thousand soldiers resolved to exhaust their last round of ammunition, and then to hold their ground with their bayonets. Soldiers thus inspired and commanded are more easily killed than defeated."[1]

Thomas kept close to the battle line throughout, speaking fre-quently to his troops and encouraging them. Encouragement was needed, for the casualties rose to terrible heights: 2,312 Confederates killed, 14,674 wounded, 1,468 missing; 1,657 Union killed, 9,756 wounded, 4,757 missing. The battle was counted a victory by the Con-federacy though it could afford few more at that price. In the after-math, Rosecrans withdrew into the defences of Chattanooga, to which Bragg laid siege. He succeeded in drawing his siege lines tight, cutting off all supplies to the trapped Union soldiers except for what could be brought in by one narrow and awkward road to the north, which was frequently raided by Confederate cavalry at great cost in destroyed wagons and slaughtered horses and mules. Bragg's army took up positions on Lookout Mountain and Missionary Ridge, from which they commanded the Union line of retreat.

Halleck took steps to see that Rosecrans was not abandoned. In early October Hooker arrived in Chattanooga from Virginia with 20,000 troops. Hooker was sent by train, completing a journey of 1,200 miles in eleven days, a logistic movement not to be bettered until the twentieth century, and in mid-November Sherman brought 16,000 from Mississippi. Most important of all, Grant was appointed to command a new, all-embracing Division of the Mississippi, running from the river to the borders of Georgia, overseeing the armies of the Tennessee and the Cumberland. Rosecrans was relieved of command of the Army of the Cumberland and replaced by Thomas. Grant had already identified him as a battle-winning soldier, and his admiration would grow. Grant's first act was to open a line of supply into the city, known to the soldiers as the "Cracker Line" because down it came steady supplies of hard bread, as well as beef and "small rations"— which comprised coffee, rice, sugar, and desiccated vegetables. Grant noted their transforming effect: the disappearance of lassitude and the return of energy and good cheer.

The Cracker Line was open by October 28, and on November 23 Grant began the attacks on Lookout Mountain and Missionary Ridge which would raise the siege for good. While the reinforcements were arriving and Chattanooga was being resupplied with food and war matériel, Grant had put in hand a great deal of repair and rebuilding of the region's infrastructure. In their effort to deny the Union the chance to capture positions in the state of Mississippi and to conduct operations against their soldiers, the Confederate commanders had been forced to destroy a great deal of railroad line and stock and roadworks also. Grant was soon supervising a railroad-building business, constructing wagons and the tools with which to work. Fortunately he was able to find enough skilled men in his army who knew how, evidence of the extent to which the railroad boom had caught up the working population of the United States during the 1850s. In Chattanooga's hinterland, 182 bridges had to be rebuilt, including several spans a mile long. The workforce also constructed a large number of pontoons, for use both in the laying of bridges and as ferries.

The battle to capture Missionary Ridge and Lookout Mountain began with a secretive crossing of Chickamauga Creek in pontoons, rowed with oars that had been brought up by the wagonload and dumped beside them. The Union advance parties got across undetected under cover of darkness on the morning of November 23. By early afternoon they had captured a hill, Orchard Knob, on which they set up an artillery position. The assault on Lookout Mountain began the next day, that on Missionary Ridge on November 25. Both were formidable natural fortresses. Lookout Mountain culminates at an altitude of 1,100 feet, in a precipitous rocky platform, while Missionary Ridge has steep sides 500 feet high. Both features had been improved for defensive purposes by digging and were crisscrossed by trenches and lines of rifle pits. An entrenchment had also been dug to connect the two heights.

Grant began his grand assault on the mountain stronghold on November 25, following a preliminary success the day before on Missionary Ridge. Grant had now received the reinforcements brought from Mississippi by Sherman and had strength enough to press Bragg hard. Bragg's ability to hold the position was weakened by the deterioration of his relations with his subordinates, which, never good, now trembled on the brink of the mutinous. Jefferson Davis had been forced to come from Richmond to adjudicate between them, only to be met by demands that Bragg be dismissed and replaced by either Johnston or Longstreet. Johnston was not trusted by Davis, while Longstreet, as an officer of the Army of Northern Virginia, felt he lacked the authority to command western soldiers. So Bragg had been left in his post, with consequences he, the president, and the army would regret.

The consequences ensued soon after the opening of Grant's assaults on Missionary Ridge and Lookout Mountain, led by Hooker and Sherman. On November 24 Hooker's men got to grips with the Confederates on a narrow bench on the slopes of Lookout Mountain. The day was misty and the mist became thick fog, which made it difficult for the warring parties to see each other. As a result, the fight was broken off, though it would be known thereafter as "the Battle Above the Clouds." In the night that followed, the Confederate defenders slipped away to join those on Missionary Ridge. For November 25 Grant had made a new plan which required Sherman's corps to attack the Confederate right, Hooker's the Confederate left, while Thomas held the centre sector but did not attack. After a morning and early afternoon of heavy fighting Grant decided that neither Sherman nor Hooker could do any more and sent orders to Thomas to advance. The orders entailed an advance by 25,000 men across a mile of open ground from Orchard Knob into the enemy centre. Thomas's men were anxious to vindicate their performance at Chickamauga and advanced to contact in a head-strong mood calling out "Chickamauga! Chickamauga!" as they moved. They quickly took the line of rifle pits at the foot of Missionary Ridge and then began to move up its slopes, ignoring their officers' orders to halt and re-form. The supports and reserves joined in and soon all 25,000 were racing to storm the summit, driving the demoralised Confederates ahead of them.

Grant, who was watching the action with Thomas from the prominence of Orchard Knob, began questioning his entourage in a testy fashion, believing he had been disobeyed. "Thomas, who ordered those men up the ridge?" Thomas answered that he did not know and that it had not been he. Then to General Gordon Granger, commander of the Fourth Corps in Thomas's army, he said, "Did you order them up, Granger?" "No, they started up without orders. When those fellows get started, all hell can't stop them." Grant warned that if things did not turn out well, someone would suffer. General Joseph Fullerton, a staff officer of Thomas's army, then rode about to make enquiries, but also to give orders to push on if that were possible. General Philip Sheridan said, "I didn't order them up but they are going to take that ridge." He raised his canteen in salute, at a group of Confederate officers who were watching from a vantage point, and was fired on by Confederate artillery in response.

During the night, Bragg's army withdrew completely from the Chattanooga position and did not attempt to re-enter Tennessee. His vanguard was already thirty miles inside Georgia. Bragg wrote to Jefferson Davis to tender his resignation in recognition of the completeness of the defeat he had suffered and was replaced by Johnston, an unwilling change by Davis but he had exhausted his reserve of generals.

Given the intensity of the fighting on the two mountains, and the amount of ammunition expended, casualties, on both sides, were lower than might have been expected: 753 Union killed, 4,722 wounded, 349 missing; 361 Confederates killed, 2,160 wounded, 4,146 missing.

THE SIEGE OF KNOXVILLE

Knoxville was the major city of eastern Tennessee, the mountainous region for which Lincoln felt such concern as it was the centre of Union sentiment inside the Confederacy. From the beginning of the war, he was anxious to bring it under Federal control, and throughout 1862–63 he urged a succession of Union commanders to move against it. In March 1863 General Ambrose Burnside, who had been so heav-

ily defeated at Fredericksburg the previous December, was transferred
to the West. He was ordered to move against Knoxville as quickly as
possible, while General William Rosecrans was ordered to operate
against Braxton Bragg in what became the Tullahoma campaign. Burnside commanded the Army of the Ohio, Rosecrans the Army of the
Cumberland.

Burnside intended to advance from Cincinnati with two corps, the
Ninth and the Twenty-third, but lost the Ninth when it was given to
Grant for the campaign against Vicksburg. While awaiting the return
of the Ninth Corps, Burnside sent a brigade and some cavalry to
advance on Knoxville. During June, this force, led by General William
Sanders, destroyed railroads around the city, where General Simon
Buckner was in command.

In August Burnside began his advance on Knoxville. His direct
route ran through the Cumberland Gap, heavily defended by the Confederates. To avoid them Burnside made a flank movement to the
south, by forced marches through the broken country. As the Chickamauga campaign began, Buckner was ordered to take most of his
troops to join Bragg at Chattanooga and was left with only two
brigades, one in the Cumberland Gap, on the northeastern border of
the state, and another east of Knoxville. In these circumstances Burnside pressed forward and was able to send a cavalry brigade into
Knoxville on September 2. It was unopposed and found the city empty
of rebel troops. He was enthusiastically welcomed by the loyal population. Burnside arrived with his army the next day.

He then set about dealing with the Confederates at the Cumberland Gap in order to open up a more direct route to Kentucky. He had
two forces in position to confront the new Confederate commander,
General John Frazer; though outnumbered, Frazer refused to surrender. Burnside then led a brigade from Knoxville to the gap, making a
march of sixty miles in fifty-two hours. On his arrival, Frazer, accepting that he was hopelessly outnumbered, surrendered on September 9.
Burnside recruited new units of Tennessee volunteers and set about
clearing the roads and gaps leading northward towards Virginia.
Meanwhile, Grant, who had now captured Chattanooga, was preparing to fight at Chickamauga, to which Lincoln and Halleck ordered
Burnside to detach troops in order to support Rosecrans, who was in
difficulty. But, unwilling to surrender Knoxville, Burnside procrastinated; he was having difficulty supplying his troops in the desolate

country to the east of Knoxville. During September and early October he was forced to fight two small battles, at Blountsville and Blue Springs, both minor victories, which led to the reestablishment of Union authority in eastern Tennessee.

Braxton Bragg, fearing that Burnside might reinforce the Union troops at Chattanooga, asked Jefferson Davis to order Longstreet to concentrate against him. Longstreet objected, knowing he would be severely outnumbered, since large Union reinforcements were approaching Chattanooga to add to the imbalance. He also objected to the division of force involved, which, he said, would expose both Confederate commanders to defeat. He therefore resumed his preparations to move against Knoxville. The move was to be made by rail, but the journey proved difficult. The trains did not arrive on time, so that the advance had to begin on foot. When the trains did arrive, the locomotives proved underpowered, forcing the troops to dismount on the steeper gradients. They also had to collect wood for the engines. Food ran short. Longstreet's advance nevertheless cheered Lincoln, who, having previously told Burnside to leave Knoxville, now ordered him to stay and defend the city. Grant prepared to send reinforcements from Chattanooga, but Burnside now convinced him that he could detach sufficient troops to hold Longstreet at a distance. Grant willingly concurred. Next the Confederates attempted to encircle Knoxville with cavalry, but Union resistance thwarted their plan and the cavalry joined Longstreet in the north. Burnside manoeuvred outside the city and successfully reached a vital crossroads. Burnside won a brisk minor victory at this point, Campbell's Station, which allowed him to withdraw his strength inside Knoxville. On November 17 Longstreet laid siege. His assault on the defences was delayed, and Burnside took advantage of the opportunity to strengthen his earthworks. Longstreet eventually attacked a week after the siege had begun, at a point he judged weak, Fort Sanders, but which was deceptively strong. The Union had surrounded the earthworks with a network of telegraph wire strung between trees. The Confederate attack launched on November 29, 1863, was effectively checked by the defences and Union covering fire. There were 813 Confederate losses, only 13 Union.

The defeated Longstreet considered his options. He had been ordered to join Bragg, who had just been defeated at Missionary Ridge on November 25. He felt that move impracticable and told Bragg that he would withdraw with the Army of Tennessee to Virginia, but would keep up the siege of Knoxville as long as possible, to prevent Grant and Burnside concentrating against him. Longstreet's stubbornness had the effect of causing Grant to send Sherman with 25,000 men to raise the siege of Knoxville. Longstreet accordingly abandoned the siege on December 4 and retired northwards to Rogersville, Tennessee, where he prepared to go into winter quarters. Sherman left part of his force at Knoxville and took the rest back to Chattanooga. General John Parke, Burnside's chief of staff, pursued the retreating Confederates with 8,000 infantry and 4,000 cavalry, though he did not press the pace. Longstreet's route took him through Rutledge and Rogersville, followed by General John Shackelford with 4,000 cavalry and infantry. On December 9, he was near Bean's Station when Longstreet decided to turn and attack. The Confederates got Shackelford in a pincer movement but the Union troops defended so stoutly that they repelled all Confederate attacks until reinforcements joined in. Shackelford was then forced to withdraw to Blain's Crossroads. Longstreet followed but declined to attack their entrenchments. Both sides withdrew and left the area to go into winter quarters. Longstreet, who blamed subordinates for his failures in the campaign, asked to be relieved of command but was refused. His troops suffered in a severe winter, and he was unable to return to Virginia until the spring. His reputation and self-confidence were damaged by the campaign, while Burnside's reputation was restored. The campaign of Knoxville, together with Grant's victory at Chattanooga, returned eastern Tennessee to Union control for the rest of the war.

The battles of Chattanooga, Knoxville, Lookout Mountain, and Missionary Ridge had now altered the balance of advantage in Tennessee very much in the Union's favour. With Rosecrans in strength at Chattanooga, Burnside operating in upper eastern Tennessee, and Grant free to strike in several directions from Tennessee eastward or southward, Lincoln's long-cherished ambition, to liberate Unionist Tennessee from the Confederacy, could be safely regarded as achieved. Grant, as overall commander in the western theatre, was now at liberty to propose, if he so chose, a broad strategy for the Union's conduct of the war in the western theatre. In the spring of 1864 he did so choose. Grant did not affect to be a high-level strategic thinker. Nothing in his manner or appearance suggested that he was anything but a common-sense, down-to-earth fighting soldier. Common sense and down-to-earthness are among the most valuable qualities, however, that a strategist can possess and he possessed them in abundance. What is valuable to those who interest themselves in his career is that in his *Personal Memoirs* he describes with engaging frankness how he formed his way of thinking. Grant also preferred to attack, if possible. He was not a "wait and see," but a "go and see" general, as his conduct after Chattanooga showed. He then decided to lay plans before Lincoln for the next stage of the campaign in the West. He may have done so because he had at his headquarters a "special commissioner" from Washington, Charles Dana, formerly of the *New York Tribune*. Dana had been sent partly because a trickle of unflattering reports about Grant continued to reach Washington about his bad habits and Lincoln, who already wanted to promote Grant, sought his own source of information. Grant used Dana as a messenger to take his ideas for the West to Washington. He proposed leaving a reduced Army of the Tennessee to watch Bragg and to take the largest part down the Mississippi to New Orleans and then via the Gulf of Mexico to Mobile, Alabama, whence he would strike at important points in Alabama and Georgia. He had proposed such a scheme before and continued to believe in it. Those in power in Washington, however, did not. Lincoln, Halleck, and Stanton feared that if Grant's force was moved so far away, the rebels would reawaken the war in eastern Tennessee. Communication with Washington had the result, however, of involving Grant in high-level strategic discussion. Halleck explained to Grant that the president's anxieties in the West remained fixed on Tennessee and its Unionists, and that before any move was made elsewhere he wanted the surviving Confederate forces in Tennessee chased down and defeated; he also wanted the Confederate army in northern Georgia pushed far enough away from the Tennessee border to ensure that it could not intervene in the state; only when those things had been achieved would he consider approving wider operations in the West.

Grant's plan for an operation against Mobile was—surprisingly, given how clearly Grant thought—not a sound one. The Union lacked the troops in the West to mount two large operations at the same time. It could not move on Mobile and yet continue to menace the Confederates in Georgia. To attempt to find the necessary troops would inevitably result in weakening the position around Chattanooga and so encourage Johnston to strike into Tennessee. Chattanooga was that rare thing in strategy, a genuinely critical point. Held by the Union, it allowed the retention of Tennessee and the menacing of Georgia. Should it pass back into Confederate possession, Tennessee would be lost and so would the future dominance of Georgia. Halleck wrote to

Grant vetoing the plan, on the grounds that the president would not approve it, a perfectly legitimate thing for Halleck to say, so perfectly did he understand Lincoln's mind.

Later in January 1864, Grant wrote again to Halleck outlining a plan for the next stage of operations in the East. He proposed abandoning the direct advance upon Richmond for an indirect approach. The navy should embark 60,000 troops of the Army of the Potomac and land them on the coast of North Carolina, whence they could march to sever the Confederate capital's rail connection with the Lower South and so force Lee to abandon Richmond. Halleck answered Grant as he had done earlier in January: Lincoln would not approve, since the scheme would encourage Lee to move in force against any Union army in the Carolinas; moreover, it would weaken the defences of Washington. He pointed out to Grant that his scheme contained no plan to fight Lee's army, which should be the proper object of an eastern strategy, and was the president's favoured aim. The best way to defeat Lee, he insisted, was to fight him in the open field near Washington. He concluded his second letter to Grant, however, by hinting that he would soon have a hand in drafting strategy for the eastern theatre, a closer hint that Grant was about to be appointed to the supreme command.

There had been strong rumours circulating to that effect, of which Grant cannot have been unaware. In February Congress passed an act reviving the rank of lieutenant general. The Confederacy appointed generals in the rank of brigadier, major general, lieutenant general, and by 1864 (full) general. In the Union army, however, major general was the highest rank granted and most Union generals held the rank in the United States volunteers, as Grant had done until his victory at Vicksburg. Then he was made a major general in the regular army. The new rank of lieutenant general was open to regular major generals, so Grant qualified for the promotion. The law allowed the lieutenant general to be appointed general in chief. In early March, Grant, still in Tennessee, received orders to go to Washington, where he arrived on March 8. He stayed first at Willard's Hotel, where he received an invitation to attend a reception at the White House that evening. On his arrival there was a rise in the noise level. Grant knew almost no one in the capital, but since Vicksburg he was widely known there. The president recognised the signal and approached Grant with the words, "This is General Grant, is it?" After a few words, Grant was drawn away by the crowd, but later that evening Lincoln and Stanton took him into the Blue Room, where he was told that Lincoln would present him with his commission in the morning. The president also said that he would show him beforehand the draft of the short speech he would make. Lincoln may also have already known that Grant was tongue-tied and a hopelessly inept public speaker. He did, however, suggest that Grant should say something to forestall jealousy among other commanders and something to please the Army of the Potomac. It was entirely characteristic of Grant that when the time came he did neither. When nominated for the presidency, in 1868, his speech of acceptance ran to five words. On this occasion, when appointed by Lincoln in the White House room where the cabinet met, the president made a short but elaborate speech. "With this high honour devolves upon you also a corresponding responsibility. As the country herein trusts you, so, under God, it will sustain you. I scarcely need add that with what I here speak for the nation goes my own hearty personal concurrence."[2] Grant had an answer written on a half sheet of paper but read it so haltingly that his words were not recorded.

The day after his appointment the U.S. War Department announced the termination of Halleck's position as general in chief but his reappointment in the new office of chief of staff. Thus was inaugurated in the United States what would become the normal arrangement of a modern command system, with Lincoln as supreme commander, Grant as operational commander, and Halleck as principal military administrator. Over the course of the next century the high command structure of all large armies would be adjusted to conform, beginning with the Prussian, where, in 1870–71, Bismarck acted as supreme commander and Moltke the elder as chief of operations. The rationalisation of the Federal or, as Grant called them, the national armed forces was essential, for under him, on his assumption of the generalship in chief, there were seventeen different Union commanders overseeing 533,000 men. The most important was the Army of the Potomac, which still lingered in northern Virginia opposite Lee's army but was not at that time undertaking active operations. Elsewhere the military situation was determined by the Confederate deployments, which principally included that of Johnston's Army of Tennessee at Dalton, Georgia, on the Western and Atlantic Railroad, which ran from Chattanooga to Atlanta. The other large Confederate force in the West was the cavalry corps under Nathan Bedford Forrest, located in eastern Tennessee. Forrest was a potential threat since he might raid as far as Cincinnati but as long as he was detached from either of the big Confederate armies, Lee's and Johnston's, he did not really multiply Confederate power.

Grant, as general in chief, could now consider what large operations he might launch. His first act in high command was to return to the West, to confer with Sherman, who, at his behest, had been appointed to succeed him. Grant had already identified Sherman as the most competent of his subordinates, a true battle-winning soldier of indefatigable temperament. He had also secured the advancement of Sheridan, another western general who had won his good opinion, to come east as commander of the Army of the Potomac's cavalry, replacing Pleasanton, who was competent but lacked the aggressiveness by which Grant set such store.

On his visit to Sherman, Grant outlined his general philosophy for what he intended to be the closing stages of the war. It coincided with and may have been inspired by what was now Lincoln's fixed conception of strategy, formed by trial and error in three years of frustration. Lincoln in 1861 had known nothing of war, but harsh experience had now taught him some essentials which he held with the force of unshakable conviction. He had abandoned altogether the conventional thought that the capture of the enemy's capital would bring victory. Instead he now correctly perceived that it was only the destruction of the South's main army that would defeat the Confederacy and he had enlarged that perception to believe that it would be achieved by attacking the enemy at several points simultaneously.

This is what the French have called a "rich solution" to the problem of the Civil War, open only to the side with greater numbers and several armies, as opposed to the South's strategy of a "poor power" with weaker numbers and effectively only one or at most one and a half armies. Halleck, an extremely orthodox military thinker, had replied that the proper response to the rebellion was to concentrate the North's force at decisive points: "To operate on exterior lines against an enemy occupying a central position will fail, as it has always failed, in ninety-nine cases out of a hundred. It is undermined by every military authority I have ever read." Lincoln had read almost no military textbooks while Grant had profited from the notoriously patchy West Point syllabus by avoiding most of them also. It was a merit of West Point that its teaching, though dusty to a degree, was practical—mathematics and engineering—which were actually useful, particularly during his efforts to alter the geography of the Mississippi Valley in 1863. A doctrine that Grant might have imbibed but did not was that of the climactic battle, which at a single strike resolved a conflict and ended it. The doctrine has been called Napoleonic, and with reason. Napoleon was the master of the great battle and his name was associated with several which had ended conflicts and altered history. Lee aspired to fight such battles and to end the war with the Union by a single overpowering act, as Napoleon had ended the conflict with Prussia in 1806 by winning the battles of Jena-Auerstedt and had almost ended the war with Russia by fighting at Borodino in 1812. Ultimately Napoleon, however, had been the victim of his own method, Waterloo having been the outstandingly decisive battle of the Napoleonic Wars. Since 1815, moreover, there had been few, if any, decisive battles. Indeed the era of decisive battles was drawing to a close. There would be several during Prussia's wars of unification in 1866–71, notably the victory of Königgrätz-Sadowa against Austria, and Sedan against France in 1870. At the end of the era, states were learning to deny an enemy the chance of decisive battle by enlarging the size of their armies to a point at which it became difficult, if not impossible, to dispose of them in a single passage of fighting, while at the same time resorting to unorthodox tactics which would involve an opponent in guerrilla warfare or the tactics of protracted warfare should the main field army suffer defeat. France would cheat Prussia of a clear-cut decision in 1870–71 by resorting to a war in the provinces with irregular forces after the defeat of Sedan.

In mid-1863, the Union was approaching the point where it would have to decide by what military means the war was to be concluded: by pursuing the object of the final decisive battle or by some less direct method. Likewise, the Confederacy, which was rapidly losing the power to fight and win large-scale battles, would have to consider whether it should turn to protracted guerrilla tactics if it was to stave off defeat. The instructions Grant gave to Sherman on his visit to the western armies following his appointment as general in chief would soon confront the Confederacy with the necessity of fighting a small-scale, low-level war within its own territory, as opposed to a conventional army-to-army war on its frontier. Grant's written instructions to Sherman were "to move against Johnston's army, to break it up and to get into the interior of the enemy's country as far as you can, inflicting all the damage you can against their war resources." Sherman was perfectly willing to carry out such instructions since he had already formed the conclusion that the quickest way to break the Confederacy was to make its ordinary people suffer.

To Meade, commanding the Army of the Potomac, Grant sent the order, "Lee's army will be your objective point. Wherever Lee goes, there you will go also." Grant had already decided, with Lincoln's approval, to make his headquarters with Meade, while leaving him as much freedom of action as possible. That would require nice judgement, not always achieved. Meade would complain frequently in his letters to his wife that any achievement of the Army of the Potomac was credited by the press to Grant, any failure to himself. Still, Grant's intentions were fair and honest, and the two men would sustain an equable working relationship throughout the rest of the campaign in the East.

Meanwhile, in the West, Sherman was beginning what would become the culminating campaign of the war.

CHAPTER FOURTEEN

The Overland Campaign and the Fall of Richmond

OSIAH GORGAS MIGHT have sensed that the Confederacy was tottering after Gettysburg, but it was not racing to destruction. As Adam Smith might have phrased it, there is an awful lot of destruction in a country. America was still full of Confederate troops, who were armed and supplied with the necessities of war-making and whose morale, despite the loss of Vicksburg and the defeat of Gettysburg, remained high. Lincoln, anxious to see the Gettysburg victory completed, urged Meade to harry Lee's army to destruction but Meade missed his opportunity. His pursuit of the Army of Northern Virginia was lethargic. He should have backed Lee against the Potomac as he retreated to the Virginia line, but though the bridges at Williamsport had been destroyed, he hesitated to attack the enemy in his defended bridgehead, fearing fierce resistance, and allowed Lee sufficient time to improvise a bridge from the timbers of a dismantled warehouse, to cross and slip away during the night of July 13–14. Lee then withdrew to the Rappahannock, where he stood, watched by Meade, occasionally exchanging shots but not closing for battle, for the next five months.

"Soon after midnight, May 3rd, 4th [1864], the Army of the Potomac moved out of its positions north of the Rapidan, to start upon that memorable campaign destined to result in the capture of the Confederate capital and the army defending it," recorded Grant in his memoirs.[1] Though now general in chief, his headquarters were with the Army of the Potomac, whose commander, General George Meade, Grant had resolved to leave as far as possible in independence. It was inevitable, however, that Meade's freedom of action should be exercised in consultation with his superior and so proved to be the case. The course of the coming campaign was to be determined by Grant, as were the operations of the subordinate armies, Butler's on the James River, Sigel's in the Shenandoah Valley, and Banks's on the Gulf. Sherman, commanding the Union's other great army, was under less detailed supervision but the broad thrust of its drive was directed so as to further the main purpose of the 1864 campaign. Sherman, marching through Georgia and the Carolinas, would be heading to make contact with Grant, who would be fighting his way southward into central Virginia.

Yet, despite the absence of immediately bad consequences, in the wake of Vicksburg and Gettysburg, the rebel war clerk's judgement was correct. In July 1863 the war took a fatal turn for the South. In retrospect it is clearly visible what had happened. Two areas of vital importance to the South's survival had been lost or their defence compromised. The first of these areas was northern Virginia, which Lee's decision to invade Pennsylvania and Maryland had turned into a critical forward defence zone, or glacis, for the Confederacy. Its geography made it very difficult to use as an offensive campaigning ground by the Union; its narrowness and its plethora of short rivers flowing into Chesapeake Bay provided a defender with a succession of excellent lines of defence. McClellan, though he had not expressly voiced the perception, had correctly seen at the outset that to use the Army of the Potomac to butt its way southwards from one river line to the next would waste its strength and do the Confederates a favour. His scheme to bypass the region altogether by an amphibious but flanking movement to the Virginia Peninsula was strategically brilliant, and one for which he has never received correct credit. The withdrawal from Harrison's Landing after the Seven Days was consonantly a serious strategic mistake. Had the landing places been kept open, Richmond would have been kept under permanent threat, with highly beneficial consequences. Withdrawal provided Lee with the opportunity to stage his two invasions of the North and to recapture the ground which would have to be fought over at such cost and such delay during 1864.

Yet, even as he embarked on his advance into Virginia in May 1864, Grant maintained the healthiest respect for Lee's army. Though its commander had lost the most gifted of his subordinates, Grant doubted whether the Army of Northern Virginia could be pinned against an obstacle or denied a line of retreat. Lee was too skilful and his army too attuned to his methods to be trapped in the open field. Grant had decided that the only certain way of overcoming the enemy was by the relentless reduction of his fighting numbers. He had always been completely unsentimental about the nature of war, which he genuinely disliked. He had hated the Mexican War, which he thought an act of unjustified aggression. He had disliked everything about the Civil War so far, but had learnt to get on with it at whatever cost to his feelings. What sustained him was he disliked rebellion even more than bloodletting. If blood was the price of restoring the Union, then he would shed it. It was in that spirit that he set out south from the Rapidan in May 1864.

His first point of encounter with Lee ensured that the cost of battle would be high. The ground on which the two armies met was the dense woodland of the Wilderness, abandoned farmland gone back to secondary forest, where Lee and Hooker had clashed at the battle of Chancellorsville in 1863. Lee found Grant first and attacked. In the dense cover manoeuvre was difficult, though Longstreet delivered one dashing flank attack, and the fighting resolved itself into volleying whenever visibility offered a sight of the enemy. The conditions, which had led to Stonewall Jackson being shot by his own troops at Chancellorsville, now produced another similarly costly mistake. Longstreet was shot by Confederates, but though the wound was serious it did not prove fatal. The Wilderness was fatal to many others. Grant had hoped to cross it in a single day's march and press on to meet Lee in open country. Meade, however, was encumbered with the large transport train of the Army of the Potomac and, reluctant to be separated from it, made himself a target of Confederate attack.

Gettysburg had spelled the end of the use of northern Virginia by the Confederates as a strategic buffer zone. The loss of Vicksburg was worse. It inaugurated the hollowing out of the South, of the Union's capture of bases and lines of communication in the South's interior from which campaigns could be mounted to enlarge the void in the South's heartland and set about its destruction from within. It also spelled the end to the South's hope of mounting a strategic threat to the North equivalent to that staged by Grant when he embarked on his campaign to seize the line of the Mississippi and to bisect the Confederacy at mid-point. Its chance of so doing, given its relative weakness in numbers and resources, never equalled that of the North's bisecting the Confederacy.

Grant had been anxious to avoid fighting in the Wilderness, where the Union army had suffered so grievously the previous May. Lee, believing that his smaller army would be at less of a disadvantage in the tangled undergrowth of the forest, was prepared to risk a battle there. He recognised that the enemy was perilously close to Richmond and might, by successful manoeuvre, get past the Wilderness and into the open country which led across the little rivers of the Chesapeake shore to the capital's outskirts. In a day of heavy and confused fighting on May 5, the Union forces drove the outnumbered Confederates south and by evening had secured ground from which next day they might fall on Lee's right.

Lee planned an attack at the same time in the same sector. The Army of the Potomac, however, attacked first, driving the Confederate vanguard through the woods until both sides confronted each other across a small clearing where Lee had his headquarters. The circumstances of the battlefield were now chaotic, with the bush ablaze and threatening the many wounded with death. Union success had been partly due to the absence from the Confederate mass of Longstreet's corps, which was returning from Tennessee. In the nick of time its advance guard appeared; Lee himself tried to lead it into action. The Texans who formed the leading unit drove Lee back with shouts of dismay and as more of their comrades appeared the tide was turned. In two hours of fighting, Lee's men had driven Meade's units almost back to their starting point. The Confederates were assisted by knowledge of the ground. One of Lee's brigadiers knew of the existence of an unfinished railroad track, down which Longstreet directed four of his brigades in an attack on the Union flank. They achieved a successful surprise. In the fracas that followed Confederate units collided with one another unexpectedly, and just as had happened at Chancellorsville in 1863, a Confederate rifleman mistakenly hit one of his own comrades. Longstreet was struck in the throat and shoulder by a bullet which, though it did not kill him, severely incapacitated him and kept him out of action for several months.

Longstreet's wounding drew the fangs of the Southerners' attack, until Lee reorganised his entangled lines. In late afternoon one of his brigadiers discovered that Grant's right flank was exposed and, on his own initiative, won permission to launch an attack, during which two Union generals were captured. Grant, however, refused to be moved by the general turmoil. Instead he laid plans for a Union assault the following day.

In all previous battles in northern Virginia, the Army of the Potomac was accustomed to being led to the northern bank of one of the nearby rivers to establish a defensive position within which to rest and refit after a heavy engagement. In the aftermath of the Wilderness battle, which had cost 17,500 casualties overall (Confederate losses were 7,750), the soldiers were surprised to be overtaken by Grant and his staff, riding southward in order, as quickly became apparent, to resume the offensive. His objective, ten miles south of the Wilderness, was Spotsylvania Court House. If it could be seized, he would be closer to the Confederate capital than the Army of Northern Virginia would be and occupying a position Lee would either have to attack or retreat from. During May 7 the armies skirmished without serious fighting, while Grant sent his supply columns and heavy artillery to the rear; Meade had recently attempted to reduce the logistic train, but on the passage through the Wilderness it still consisted of 4,000 wagons. This overprovision assured that its soldiers were so well-fed that they could easily march on short rations for a few days without hardship. During the night of May 7, the fighting divisions were put on the road also. To their soldiers' surprise they found they were advancing, not retreating. Some began to sing. Despite the certainty of battle to come, they were exhilarated by the change of mood Grant's assumption of command had brought.

The infantry advance was complemented by a cavalry advance. Sheridan's 10,000 horsemen set off southward to harass Lee's line of communications. They were opposed by their old enemies, J. E. B. Stuart's cavalry corps, which challenged them to fight. Eventually they did, on May 11 at Yellow Tavern, after Sheridan had done a good deal of destruction to the local railroads and supply depots. The Union cavalry was now much better armed than their opponents, every man having a repeating carbine. The encounter at Yellow Tavern resulted in an easy success for Sheridan's men, who dispersed Stuart's horsemen in separate directions. During the firefight, Stuart suffered a mortal wound; his death was almost as grave a blow to Lee as that of Jackson a year before.

Meanwhile on May 9, the two marching armies had met at Spotsylvania. Grant's plan was to outflank Lee to the east and so get on the road to Richmond, now only forty-five miles distant, though still defended by several of the short rivers which had bedevilled campaigning in northern Virginia since the first days of the war. It was not water which was to form the critical obstacles at Spotsylvania, however, but earth. The Army of Northern Virginia had, as soon as it knew it would have to fight, fortified its front with entrenchments and timber obstacles. In the previous twelve months digging had become an automatic preparation for combat in both armies, though perhaps more so on the Southern side, which could afford the heavy casualties of close-range

rifle volleying less than the Union. Unusually, the tactics of entrenchment do not seem to have been imposed from above but to have been
adopted as a measure of self-protection by the rank and file. Pre-
existing obstacles had so obviously played a part in Confederate success at Fredericksburg: the stone-walled road at the foot of Marye's
Heights had held the Northerners at a distance while they were shot
down in hundreds. Deliberate digging on the battlefield had begun
earlier, however. Both sides had dug extensively during the Peninsula
Campaign. Some of the digging was to construct formal siege defences
around Richmond. Some, however, was "hasty" entrenchment, dug to
defend a position before a coming firefight. At Beaver Dam Creek
(Mechanicsville), Union troops had constructed timber barricades,
called abatis, to hold the Confederates at a distance, and extensive barricades were thrown up next day along Boatswain's Creek. It was an
enormous advantage to whichever side was defending that timber was
so abundant in nineteenth-century America. Even when battle was not
joined in woodland, as at Shiloh, Chancellorsville, and the Wilderness,
timber was still available. Field fences of the time were usually of the
split rail type, which had only to be pulled to pieces to yield the material for abatis, barricades, and chevaux-de-frise. American farmers were
profligate in their use of timber, which anyhow had to be cleared to
make fields. Their lumbering efforts provided huge quantities of
already worked wood which was immediately suitable for military
engineering.

Though the impetus to fortify implanted itself eventually among
ordinary soldiers, for the best of reasons, that of sparing their lives, it
was also part of the military mentality of the regular officer corps.
West Point was an engineering school and the professor of engineering, Denis Hart Mahan, father of the most important American strategist of the nineteenth century, Alfred T. Mahan, was an advocate of
engineering on the battlefield. A student of contemporary European
warfare, he drew from his studies the doctrine that the rising losses in
combat caused by long-range fire could only be stemmed if soldiers
dug. Some of his pupils took note. By 1864 they were digging, and
strengthening their diggings with cut timber, without any encouragement from higher up. At Spotsylvania, Lee's soldiers built the
strongest entrenchment yet to appear on any battlefield of the war.
Grant tried to outflank their defences on May 9 but failed. On May 10
he sent a stronger force to make yet another of his costly frontal as-

saults. The attack repelled on the enemy's left was more successful in the centre, where the young General Emory Upton ordered the assaulting force to try novel tactics. He formed his twelve regiments into four lines, with instructions not to fire their rifles until they were on top of the enemy trenches, which were to be carried by the bayonet. The succeeding regiments were to pass through the first to the next line of enemy trenches and so on, until a breach had been made and widened into the heart of the enemy position. Upton, though he could not know it, was anticipating a solution to the problem of carrying entrenched positions that would present itself on the Western Front sixty years later during the First World War. Upton's men took a thousand prisoners and opened a wide gap in Lee's front. Then the attack failed, for a reason often to be repeated in the First World War. The supporting division which was intended to exploit the success was slow coming forward and, when it did get into action, ran into massed artillery fire and retreated with heavy losses.

On May 11 Grant decided to make an all-out attack on the Confederate position, choosing as his centre of effort a salient known to the defenders as the Mule Shoe for its shape; its apex would become known as the Bloody Angle. During May 12–13, a ghastly eighteen-hour, close quarters battle ensued, neither side giving ground. Huge quantities of ammunition were expended at close range, the trenches filling up with the bodies of those killed and wounded and the soil turning red with blood. Not until darkness fell did the Confederates withdraw. In the week which ended on May 12, Grant's army had lost 32,000 killed, wounded, and missing, more than in any previous single week of fighting throughout the war. The Confederates, despite defending and from behind entrenchments, had lost over 18,000. Grant was accused by some of adopting the strategy of attrition—not yet a word in use—but that was not his intention. He was still striving to find a direct route to Richmond or open country in which to force Lee to fight in conditions where superior Union numbers would carry the day. Because Lee had skilfully met all his manoeuvres with counter-manoeuvres, he had been forced instead into pitched battles on Confederate terms. The frightful casualties of the second week of May 1864 were the inevitable consequence. It was not only the rank and file that paid the price. Lee lost twenty general officers in the twenty days that culminated at the Bloody Angle. James McPherson observes that the episode visibly marked those who survived to stay in the ranks.

They looked thin and pale; many exhibited the symptoms of what would be called shell shock in the First World War and combat fatigue in the Second.

Spotsylvania did not end the terrible ordeal of the Overland Campaign. More anxious than ever to reach Richmond, Grant sent his army onward from Spotsylvania to the North Anna River, a tributary of the Pamunkey, which flows round Richmond's northern approaches. Its meanders provided firm support for Lee's flanks; when Grant, following up Lee's retreat from Spotsylvania, appeared on May 23, Lee easily repelled his attacks. Grant's purpose in disengaging at Spotsylvania and marching southward was to bring Lee to battle in the open or, if battle was refused, to find his way round Lee's right flank and press forward towards Richmond down the narrow corridor between the Chesapeake and the James River. To start this episode in the Overland Campaign going, he sent Hancock's Second Corps, the strongest and best in the Army of the Potomac, forward along the highway known as the Telegraph Road. His calculation was that, once Lee became aware that a single Union corps was acting in detachment from the main body, he would bring his troops out of their earthworks, which, as was now standard, the Confederates had begun to dig along the far bank of the North Anna, and risk an encounter in the open. As soon as Lee got word of Grant's movement, he did indeed order the Army of Northern Virginia to leave Spotsylvania and start for the North Anna. He remained confident of his own and his army's ability to get the better of the enemy. He was too sanguine. His army's strength was dwindling and now amounted, after the awful losses at Spotsylvania, to only 40,000, though he was expecting reinforcements of 13,700 from Richmond. He had lost his trusted cavalry commander, J. E. B. Stuart, while his best subordinate, James Longstreet, was still recovering from wounds suffered at the Wilderness; worse, Lee himself was now showing signs of strain and exhaustion, unsurprisingly in view of the burden laid on him by the frequency of battle in this campaign, and anxieties about supply and manpower losses.

By the afternoon of May 22, 1864, the whole of the Army of Northern Virginia had taken station on the southern bank of the North Anna. That was not what Grant had hoped. He now had to drive the Confederates out of their position if he was to resume the advance on Richmond. During May 23 the Union troops, though at considerable cost, succeeded in crossing the North Anna at several points, but left much of the southern bank in Confederate hands. Unfortunately for Grant, Lee's chief engineer, General Martin Luther Smith, now persuaded him that a deteriorating situation could be saved if entrenchments were hastily dug along the river and across the Telegraph Road. The Army of Northern Virginia was now expert at rapid entrenchment and dug itself in during the night of May 23 so that on the morning of May 24 Grant was confronted by a new and difficult situation. Both Lee's flanks were refused, that is, turned away from the main line of the front on the river. Lee and Smith planned to inflict defeats on the Federals as they manoeuvred to attack the separate focus of the Confederate position and in so doing lost cohesion. The final stages of the battle of May 24 did indeed go badly for the Union. Units were thrown back and heavy losses suffered. The front became disorganised. On the afternoon of May 24, an opportunity was offered for the Confederates to deliver a concentrated counter-strike and halt the Union advance in its tracks. Regrettably for his army, Lee now succumbed to the strains of the campaign and retired to his sickbed. From it he railed at his subordinates, "We must strike them a blow . . . We must strike them a blow." He, however, was quite incapable of mustering the powers of command which would have made that possible, while none of his subordinates had the ability to do so. The battle began to flicker out. The rest of May 24 and the whole of May 25 was spent by the Confederates in mounting local counter-attacks at the positions taken by their much stronger enemy, while Grant organized probing movements to get around the Confederate earthworks to the east and resume the advance down the Telegraph Road. On May 27 Lee, still in a weakened physical condition, recognized that he had lost the chance of inflicting serious damage on Grant's army, and that his own could no longer hold the North Anna position. He ordered it to march out of its entrenchments and seek a new position, farther south, and ominously nearer Richmond, where he could stand across Grant's advance. The route chosen ran towards the crossroads of Cold Harbor.

The battle of the North Anna, though not costly by comparison with most of those in the Overland Campaign (2,100 Union casualties, 1,250 Confederate) was nevertheless crucially damaging to the South. By his failure to hold the river and inflict a serious reverse on the enemy, Lee had surrendered his last chance of keeping the Union at a distance from the defences of Richmond. At Cold Harbor, he would be fighting again on the terrain of the Seven Days' Battles of 1862.

Grant spent the rest of May trying to outflank Lee from the Tide-water side. Lee, though forced to surrender territory, fell back from one secure position on the Pamunkey to another on the Totopotomoy. These two little waterways would support Lee's flanks in the next, almost last stage of the Overland Campaign. Grant had fixed on a road junction known as Cold Harbor as the site of his next action. It lies close to Mechanicsville on the northeastern outskirts of Richmond, scene of one of the earliest of the Seven Days' Battles of 1862. Lee was ahead of him and, despite heavy skirmishing by Sheridan's cavalry, managed to entrench a position on a front of seven miles between the Pamunkey and the Totopotomoy. He had made good his losses but so had Grant, partly by remustering some heavy artillery regiments as infantry. Lee appealed to Richmond for reinforcements, but despite the failure of Sigel's campaign in the Shenandoah Valley and Butler's confinement in the Bermuda Hundred, none could be spared. Lee had to defend the Cold Harbor position with the troops on hand, now numbering, after receiving all available reinforcements, about 60,000. Grant had over 100,000 troops but his attack was disjointed. He shrank from ordering a frontal attack on what he recognised to be a very strong enemy position but he believed—wrongly—that the Army of Northern Virginia was nearly at the end of its tether and he hoped for a clear-cut victory to clinch the outcome of the impending presidential election. Grant began the attack in darkness on June 1, it was then bro-ken off for the day. At dawn of June 3, 1864, three corps of the Army of the Potomac attacked. The result was calamity, worse than Fredericks-burg. What thwarted Grant's hopes of victory were the preparations Lee's men had made to render their positions impregnable. The fight-ing in the first days of June had been so intense that the events of the battlefield had concealed from both Grant and Meade how skilfully the Army of Northern Virginia had prepared the ground it held. Heavy skirmishing at Haw's Shop, along the Totopotomoy, on the Matade-quin, at Bethesda Church, and at Cold Harbor itself, skirmishes that might realistically have been denoted proper battles in their own right, had not only checked Grant's advance upon Richmond but had solidi-fied the grip of the Confederates on highly defensible ground, a mud-dle of marshland, thickets, and ravines which had allowed them to dig in along a concave front, a curve including two subordinate concavi-ties, all covered by thousands of rifles and dozens of artillery pieces; the front was about seven miles long, resting at its ends on the Totopoto-moy and the Chickahominy, and so not susceptible to being turned. It could only be attacked frontally, though where to attack baffled the Union commanders seeking to glimpse what lay behind the screen of vegetation their troops faced. At the beginning of the Cold Harbor engagement a week before June 1, a Union soldier in the 110th Ohio Regiment had referred to the scene of action as "this wilderness looking place"; the poor worked-out farmland of Richmond's environs did readily recall that of the Wilderness, farther north, and though the line running across it had been dug largely with bayonets, mess plates, and drinking cups—spades were not a general issue in either army and the entrenching tool had not yet been invented—the soldiers of the Army of Northern Virginia had made themselves experts at sinking beneath the surface whenever serious battle threatened. Although Grant did not know what lay to the front, his orders for June 3 were that the Eighteenth, Sixth, and Second Corps were to advance at half past four in the morning and attack along the entire front.

The plan was for the whole of the seven-mile front to be attacked simultaneously, but because of its concave form the Union line was unable to exert an equal pressure at all points. The attack diverged. What made it even less concentrated was that the attackers could not see the enemy clearly, they being concealed by breastworks or by standing vegetation. Even the defenders lacked a clear view; Lee worked by hearing rather than sight. As the attack swelled in force, he remarked to a subordinate when the rattle of musketry swelled that that was what killed rather than the artillery, the roar of which was joining in. Confederate fire began to beat down the Union efforts to get onto the enemy position, efforts renewed in some places as many as fourteen times. The heavier and more frequently repeated assaults were made at the extreme right of the Confederates' line, delivered by Hancock's Second Corps against Marylanders and Alabamans dug in along Boatswain Creek. Defensive fire was so heavy that by six o'clock the ground in front of the Confederate earthworks was covered with the bodies of dead and wounded and the survivors were scratching the earth with spoons and fingernails to raise the slightest shelter. In places the Union troops got onto the enemy parapet and drove the Confederates out; but Lee, fearing weakness at this point, had positioned his only reserve to the rear, and the lost ground was recaptured, at even heavier loss to the Union. It was here that General Evander Law framed his later celebrated remark that the battle was "not war but murder." Union soldiers not killed or disabled took shelter behind the bodies of dead comrades and tried to wriggle their way backwards, but signs of movement attracted sharpshooter fire. Meade issued orders at quarter-hourly intervals for the attacks to be pressed but they could not be obeyed, if they even reached the men pressed to the ground by the weight of Confederate fire, and he had no fresh troops to reinforce the front. By ten o'clock it had become clear that the attack was a disastrous failure, clear to the tortured troops at the front, and dawningly so to Meade and other superiors in the rear. Meade continued to order an advance but it had no effect, and in some cases met flat refusals to obey. An estimated 3,000 to 7,000 Union soldiers had been killed and wounded, including a disproportionate number of officers; most of the losses had been suffered in the first hour of the Union assault. Four days after the battle opened, days spent in skirmishing and sniping, Lee and Grant at last agreed on terms for a truce to bring in the wounded and bury the dead. The Confederates, though so much better protected, had suffered 1,500 fatalities. In the interval a large number of the untended wounded had died of shock, loss of blood, or thirst.

Grant decided to terminate the offensive. He wrote later in his memoirs that he "always regretted the last assault on Cold Harbor." In truth, the whole battle was regrettable, since it hurt the Union more than the Confederacy and still left Richmond at a distance.

Grant had now to reconsider his strategy for bringing the campaign to a conclusion, which he wrongly believed might be done soon. What he could not afford, at least at this stage of the Overland Campaign, was another battle against entrenchments, since fighting behind earthworks favoured the defending Confederates, often in terms of casualties by a ratio of two to one or more. Accordingly, after Cold Harbor he decided to divide his efforts, which given his great superiority in numbers he could afford to do. He directed Sheridan to lead his cavalry on a raid into the southern end of the Shenandoah Valley, the source of much of the Army of Northern Virginia's food, to destroy its rail connections with Richmond. The Sheridan raid was only partly successful because he was intercepted by Lee's cavalry, now commanded by Wade Hampton, at Trevilian Station and because he then failed to join forces with General David Hunter's Union force in the valley. Hunter, harried by Confederate guerrillas, achieved little more than the destruction of the Virginia Military Institute at Lexington, where he burnt the buildings before beating a retreat across the mountains into West Virginia. His withdrawal was prompted by the appearance of Jackson's old valley army, now commanded by Jubal Early, who displayed remarkable initiative by using the valley, as Stonewall had done in his time, as an avenue of advance which would threaten Washington. Having clashed with Hunter at Lynchburg during June, Early turned about and crossed the Potomac in July, reached Frederick in Maryland, and proceeded to invest the defences of Washington, which had been stripped of their garrison to strengthen Grant's forces in Virginia. One Union contingent, the Sixth Corps, was hastily recalled and arrived just in time to deter Early from mounting an attack. There was scratch fighting nonetheless, witnessed by the president, his first view of the reality of the war thus far. As other Union troops marched to the rescue, Early found himself between two fires, so he prudently decided to retire into Virginia and got away scot-free. He had, however, reached as close as five miles to the White House, caused a sensation, and raised the spectre of a Southern military revival.

Such a reaction to what was only an impertinent raid was quite unjustified. It was the Confederacy which was now in danger, deadly danger, as Grant edged inexorably towards its capital. Lee had held him off so far by his unrivalled capacity to manoeuvre his pursuer onto ground where he could entrench and fight successful defensive battles. But he was running out of space in which to continue his game of evasion and delay, hemmed in as he now was between Chesapeake Bay, the lower courses of its rivers, and the fortifications of Richmond. On June 13 Grant disengaged his army from the Cold Harbor position and marched south, leaving Richmond to the west, until he reached the estuary of the James River, where he had arranged to be met by a pontoon-bridging train. What followed was an almost unprecedented achievement of combat engineering, made possible because Lee, short of cavalry, had temporarily lost touch with Grant and could not identify his whereabouts. While his military blindness persisted, the bridging column laid a span across the James, 2,100 feet long, and so got the Army of the Potomac across dry-shod, just east of City Point. The campaign had returned to the ground on which McClellan made his first attempt to take Richmond in 1862, with the difference that operations were now in the hands of a man who looked for reasons to press forward, rather than excuses to avoid action. Grant began to cross the James on June 14 and by June 15 was deploying the two most advanced of his five corps opposite the entrenchments defending Petersburg, Richmond's railroad town, through which ran five railroads. Its capture would cut Richmond off from communication with the rest of the South and so ensure the Confederacy's decapitation.

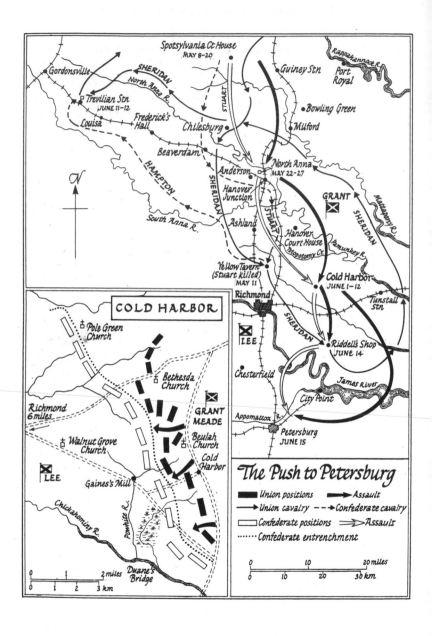

Spotsylvania Ct House
MAY 8-20

Gordonsville

SHERIDAN

Guiney Stn

Rappahannock R.

Port
Royal

North Anna R.

Trevilian Stn
JUNE 11-12

STUART

Frederick's
Hall

Louisa

Chilesburg

Bowling Green

Milford

Beaverdam

HAMPTON

Anderson

North Anna
MAY 22-27

GRANT

SHERIDAN

Mattapony R.

N

South Anna R.

Hanover
Junction

SHERIDAN

Ashland

STUART

Hanover
Court House

Totopotomoy Cr.

Pamunkey R.

Cold Harbor
JUNE 1-12

Tunstall
Stn

Yellow Tavern
(Stuart killed)
MAY 11

Richmond

LEE

SHERIDAN

Riddell's Shop
JUNE 14

Chesterfield

James River

Appomattox R.

City Point

COLD HARBOR

Pole Green
Church

Bethesda
Church

GRANT
MEADE

Richmond
6 miles

Walnut Grove
Church

Beulah
Church
Cold
Harbor

LEE

Gaines's Mill

Chickahominy R.

Powhite R.

Duane's
Bridge

Petersburg
JUNE 15

0   1   2 miles

0   1   2   3 km

The Push to Petersburg

▬▬ Union positions	➤ Assault
→ Union cavalry	- - → Confederate cavalry
▭ Confederate positions	⟹ Assault
⋯⋯ Confederate entrenchment	

0   10   20 miles

0   10   20   30 km

Grant recognised that. So did Lee, and he was determined to make the defence of Petersburg as tenacious as possible. Twenty miles separated the two cities, but because of the Army of Northern Virginia's extraordinary capacity to dig, acquired in the pitched battles fought during the Overland Campaign, it was quite possible to connect them with continuous earthworks which would protect the railroads and the outskirts of the capital itself. When the Union troops, who had crossed the James by the pontoon bridge, arrived in the vicinity of Petersburg in mid-June, they found the earthworks already complete over a distance of ten miles. The breastworks were twenty feet thick and the ditch to the front fifty feet deep. The works included fifty-five artillery positions full of cannon. Smith, the Union corps commander, did not appreciate that Beauregard, commanding the defences, had almost no troops with which to garrison them. Fearing a repetition of the losses suffered in earlier attacks on Confederate entrenchments, as at Cold Harbor, he declined to mount an assault until evening and, though his soldiers then took a mile of trenches, they did not progress further, allowing Lee the chance to bring up reinforcements from Richmond. During the next three days, both sides reinforced as Grant brought more of the Army of the Potomac across the James and Lee weakened the defences of Richmond to reinforce those of Petersburg. On June 18 General Meade lost patience with his subordinates and commanded a full-scale advance, but the men, also remembering Cold Harbor, were unwilling to face the risk. One of the heavy artillery regiments that had been re-formed as infantry did mount a charge across open ground at the breastworks, only to lose three-quarters of its number. Meade then called a halt, and was supported by Grant, who ordered the army to dig itself in until a weak spot could be found.

After this decision, the struggle for Petersburg and Richmond resolved itself into a stalemate which anticipated trench fighting on the Western Front sixty years later, and for the same reason: unsustainable casualties. Since early May, when the Overland Campaign had opened with the fighting in the Wilderness, the Union army had lost 65,000 men killed, wounded, or missing, a casualty rate equal to three-fifths of that it had suffered during the previous three years. Because of the North's superior manpower resources and the efficiency of its enlistment process, the losses could still be made good, as was decreasingly the case in the South. Nevertheless, such losses could not be sustained incessantly. The report of casualty figures in the newspapers encouraged time-expired regiments, those raised for three years' service in

1861, to insist on their right to muster out, while also driving up the desertion rate, which at its worst could reach a hundred a day. Unsurprisingly, the struggle to take Petersburg and Richmond declined after midsummer 1864 into siege warfare, with the Union forces seeking to envelop Richmond from the west and the defenders extending their entrenchments to prevent them. The Army of the Potomac also sought to cut the railroads into the city, and its cavalry tore up many miles of the Weldon and the South Side railroads. The cavalrymen were unable, however, to mount a permanent block of the lines of communication, as the Confederates brought the railroads back into service, a remarkable achievement given the shortage of almost every sort of railroad equipment and necessity, particularly rail and fixing spikes. The South was already cannibalising the less essential railroads to provide track for the vital links. There were other expedients. On one railroad in Texas which had worn out all its locomotives, traffic was maintained by harnessing oxen to pull the rolling stock. During nearly a year of siege in 1864–65, the railroads running into Richmond were kept open. Only when they were interrupted would the siege succeed. Between August and December 1864 the lines scarcely altered.

Grant had lived with the hope that by pressing the Overland Campaign he might end the war as soon as he reached the James River. It was probably not a realistic hope; but its dashing did not mean that the campaign had failed in its objects. At the outset, the Army of the Potomac stood on the line it had occupied at the beginning of the war and was separated from Richmond by over a hundred miles of highly defensible territory which included such water barriers as the Rappahannock and the Rapidan, the Totopotomoy, the Mattapony, the Pamunkey, the North and South Anna and the Chickahominy rivers. Between May 4 and June 15, 1864, the Army of the Potomac had retaken all the ground between the Rappahannock and the James, secured and bridged all the water obstacles, built roads and repaired railroads. Territorially, it was one of the largest successes of the war. The cost had been appalling. Grant's losses had been about 1,300 men a day, a total of 52,600 in forty days, in human terms a terrible price, though one that the Union could afford as the Confederacy could not. Lee's 33,000 casualties were a permanent debit. The moral effect on Grant's army was visible in the appearance of those who survived the ordeal to appear at the siege of Petersburg. As James McPherson describes, those who had fought the May to June campaign, with a battle almost every day, hard marching between engagements, and no relief from action, had grown thin and strained.[2] Observers remarked that the men of the Army of the Potomac had aged several years in a few months. Since the horror of the Mule Shoe and the repulse at Cold Harbor, they had also lost the appetite for attacking earthworks. It was for that reason, as much as any other, that Beauregard was able to hold the defences of Petersburg with so few men in the first days of the siege when they might have been captured by a single resolute stroke. The only Union unit which could be persuaded to attack was one of the heavy artillery regiments Grant had remustered as infantry. It paid a terrible price for its bald-headed assault on the earthworks, losing 632 men out of 850.

Although the discrepancy in numbers between defenders and attackers made it seem certain that Grant could bring the siege of Petersburg to a successful conclusion in a short time, all his efforts in the summer of 1864 foundered. The Union difficulty was that whenever they pushed their lines south and west of the Confederate defences, the Confederates always found the men to extend their line a little farther and to garrison the new works. In late June Grant attempted a new method. One of the besieging regiments, the 48th Pennsylvania, was recruited from coal miners. One of them suggested to their colonel, Henry Pleasants, a mining engineer, that the regiment could drive a shaft under the lines and blow up a Confederate fort that dominated one of the sectors. Pleasants got permission to try and in a month a 500-foot shaft had been dug and a chamber containing four tons of gunpowder excavated at the far end. Then the careful planning was overtaken by pettifogging disputes as to how to proceed. A Union formation was specially trained to exploit the devastation when the mine was detonated. As the formation consisted of black soldiers, however, it was decided at the last minute to substitute a white formation in its place. In the aftermath of the explosion, which blew a hole 170 feet long, 60 feet wide, and 30 feet deep, burying a whole Confederate regiment and artillery battery, the untrained white division, whose commander had remained behind, blundered about in the devastation, descending into the crater instead of negotiating the perimeter, and quickly fell victim to improvised Confederate defensive fire and then a well-executed counter-attack. The counter-attackers caught the black division, which had belatedly been sent forward, in an indefensible position and murdered many of its soldiers in the crater. When the fighting eventually ceased, over 4,000 Union troops had been killed or wounded and the Confederate line remained, apart from the enormous hole left by the explosion, intact.

After he was repelled from Washington in July, Jubal Early retired into the Shenandoah Valley, pursued by Sheridan, to whom Grant gave the additional instructions to lay the valley waste, to terminate for good the supply of provisions which reached the Army of Northern Virginia from it. Sheridan set about the laying waste energetically, in the process discovering that Early had retreated to Winchester, where his position seemed to be vulnerable. On September 19 Sheridan attacked and broke up Early's force, capturing thousands of prisoners. When Early retreated to Fisher's Hill, south of Strasburg, Sheridan attacked again on September 22 and drove them sixty miles into the mountains. Lee responded by sending Early an infantry division and a cavalry brigade. Despite news of this Confederate reinforcement, Sheridan left the army to go to Washington for a conference. While Sheridan was absent, Early concentrated his forces and attacked at dawn. He took the Army of the Shenandoah completely by surprise and drove it back four miles. Sheridan, however, had returned the previous evening, and when he woke to the sound of fighting, he jumped into the saddle and rode to the sound of the guns. Although Early had dispersed some of the Union force, the Sixth Corps was still intact and, shouting for the men to follow him, Sheridan gathered stragglers into a counter-attack force and caught Early contemplating what he believed to be a decisive victory. Sheridan, in what James McPherson calls "the most notable example of personal battlefield leadership in the war,"[3] managed to reorganise his troops as he advanced to contact and unleashed a counter-attack which caused Early's army to disintegrate in a rout to the south. Thus the battle of Cedar Creek, which had seemed to be a conclusive Confederate victory, ended as a Union triumph. With the valley pacified and stripped of all wealth, Sheridan was eventually able to withdraw the Army of the Shenandoah and rejoin Grant for the concluding stages of the siege of Petersburg.

Despite continuing good news from Sherman's army in Georgia, the failure before Petersburg brought about a severe decline in Northern morale during the summer of 1864. The peace party found a new voice while Republicans, including the president himself, grew increasingly pessimistic about the prospect of winning the presidential election in the coming autumn. Jefferson Davis made peace feelers, and Lincoln unwisely agreed to meet Southern representatives to discuss terms. Despite Lincoln's dread of bad war news and the personal agony brought by casualty reports, however, the South's insistence on being treated as a legitimate combatant entitled to independence continued to supply Lincoln, who himself was adamant on the issue, with the support necessary to hold out for eventual victory. The Southern peace mission failed, as did a Southern attempt to foment treachery in the Midwest, while Lincoln's electoral prospects improved as the summer drew out. Of cardinal importance to the presidential campaign was Sherman's capture of Atlanta in September, following Farragut's victory at Mobile, which decisively turned the tide of opinion. At the election Lincoln carried all but three states in the Union and won all but 21 of 233 votes in the Electoral College. His result was greatly assisted by the improvement of Union fortunes in Virginia, particularly the Shenandoah Valley.

By the fall of 1864, the military predicament of the South, combined with the fact of Lincoln's re-election as president, lent energy to the movements for a negotiated peace, of which there were many. Some were entangled with Southern attempts to foment dissent in the Midwest; the unveiling of the connection stifled their prospect of success. Peace efforts continued nonetheless, and grew in strength in the South, where there was much disappointment as news from the front worsened. One Southerner, Jefferson Davis, remained as fervent for war as ever. He came under increasing pressure in early 1865, particularly after the fall of Fort Fisher, at Wilmington, North Carolina, to seek terms. Lincoln, too, though in a much stronger position, was also lobbied by peace-seekers to enter into discussions with the South, a tricky undertaking since Washington had steadfastly repelled any dealing with Richmond throughout the war. In January 1865 the Washington political veteran Francis Preston Blair persuaded Lincoln to grant him a pass to visit Richmond, with the object of persuading the Confederate government to join with the Union in an expedition to expel the Archduke Maximilian from Mexico, a scheme Blair argued would result in the cessation of civil hostilities. Lincoln understandably thought the project nonsensical, but acquiesced in Blair's mission to see what came of it. Davis agreed to receive Blair, hoping that what he knew would be a restatement of Union demands for surrender and the abolition of slavery would reanimate Southern determination to fight for independence. Davis nominated three commissioners to meet the Northern delegation, including the Confederate vice president, the Speaker of the Senate, and the secretary of war. It was agreed that the two parties should see each other aboard the Union steamer *River Queen* in Chesapeake Bay. At the last moment Lincoln decided to join the Union delegation himself. He made it clear from the outset that surrender, disbandment of the Confederate army, and abolition of slavery were the only terms to be discussed and that they were non-negotiable. The delegates discussed points of detail inconclusively, and the talks relapsed into genial conversation about old political days in Washington, when they had been colleagues. The Southerners returned to Richmond without anything to offer to President Davis, who denounced the Northern party in contemptuous terms.

The *River Queen* episode occurred during the continuing stalemate on the Petersburg front, one of several long periods of quiescence in the eastern theatre. The first, between First Bull Run and the opening of the Peninsula Campaign, lasted nine months. The second, between Gettysburg and the Wilderness, lasted ten months. Grant, both by reputation and in fact so actively aggressive, allowed the Confederates to hold the Petersburg position without suffering a major attack between the Battle of the Crater in July 1864 and March 1865, a period of eight months. The reasons for these long pauses were various. After First Bull Run, McClellan delayed action because he was organising the Army of the Potomac and making plans, though at a luxuriously leisurely pace. After Gettysburg, Meade declined to attack Lee on the Rappahannock because he feared to compromise his great victory. Grant's acceptance of inactivity outside Petersburg after Cold Harbor was determined by the condition of his army. The almost continuous fighting from May to July between the Rappahannock and the North Anna rivers had not only killed or disabled many of his best soldiers; it had also left the survivors without eagerness to mount further attacks, particularly against entrenchments, which at Petersburg were visibly very strong. They also extended too far to the west to be outflanked, so Grant therefore decided to attempt to draw Lee's men out of the Petersburg lines, where they could be attacked and defeated in the open, without allowing them any opportunity to manoeuvre and escape towards Johnston's army in the deeper South. In order to make Lee move, it was essential to persist with the cutting of the Richmond–Petersburg railroads on which his supply depended. The most important of the railroads was the Southside, which followed the line of the Appomattox River, and the Weldon, up which supplies came from the south. In August A. P. Hill, commanding one of Lee's corps, managed to drive Grant away from the Weldon Railroad, and again on August 25. In September,

Wade Hampton relieved Lee's supply situation somewhat by capturing and driving into the lines 2,500 head of cattle. Grant ordered Meade to stage a major attack near Peebles' Farm; the battle lasted three days, until October 2, and resulted in the extension of the Union line a further three miles beyond Petersburg to the west.

Winter brought a pause, to add to Grant's frustration, but with the return of better weather in March he extended his siege lines again and interrupted the Boydton Plank Road, which brought supplies to Lee from the southwest. Grant's efforts to sustain pressure on Lee's communications were assisted by the return in March of Sheridan's cavalry from the Shenandoah Valley, now completely laid waste and empty of Confederate troops. Grant was certain that Lee would, as soon as opportunity offered, break out of the Petersburg line and move south to link up with Joseph E. Johnston's army, which was still operating in North Carolina. Before he did so, Grant wished to be certain that he had sufficient force in place to bring about Lee's destruction. That required the further extension of his own line to the west, so as to be certain of getting around Lee's flank as he moved out into open country.

Grant's lines were now nearly forty miles long, extending from east of Petersburg to thirty miles west of it. Manning the lines consumed much of his manpower, but the arrival of Sheridan's troops provided a mass of manoeuvre which he could use to advantage. On March 29 Grant started two corps westward towards Dinwiddie Court House; they were followed by three infantry divisions, while Sheridan's cavalry was sent on a wide westward sweep to cut for good Lee's surviving rail links with the South. Grant was sure that Lee would respond by bringing his troops out of the entrenchments. If he judged the Petersburg lines sufficiently weakened, he could assault them. In any case, once Lee was in the open, he would attack and bring about a clinching victory.

Lee, however, had plans of his own and hopes of securing sufficient advantage to make a clean break to join up with Johnston. His scheme was to attack Grant's entrenchments and so force him to shorten his line at the western end in order to reinforce the threatened point. When Lee attacked at Fort Stedman on March 25, although he achieved success, captured ground, and took many Union prisoners, he was swiftly counter-attacked, the lost ground was retaken and 2,300 Confederates made prisoner. Moreover, Grant did not shorten his lines. Instead, on March 29 he directed parts of the Army of the Potomac, the Army of the James, now commanded by General Edward

Ord, and Sheridan's cavalry to march westward round the end of the Petersburg entrenchments towards the road junction at Five Forks. Lee had two bodies of troops in the vicinity, a corps under General Richard Anderson and two divisions under General George Pickett, of Gettysburg fame. Sheridan fought and defeated them on April 1.

Next day, Grant judged that the Petersburg defences had been sufficiently weakened to risk an attack on the entrenchments. The Confederate defenders were swept aside in an hour's fighting, forcing Lee to recognise that he had no option but to leave the security of his positions and retreat westward. He gave orders to do so on the night of April 2, meanwhile sending word to Jefferson Davis that Richmond would have to be abandoned as well. The Confederates succeeded in extricating themselves from the entrenchments during the evening and by midnight were in retreat westward along the course of the Appomattox River. Lee had divided his remaining 30,000 men into two groups, marching parallel. They were pursued by Meade, leading the Army of the Potomac on the northern route, and Ord, leading the Army of the James behind them. The objective was the Richmond and Danville Railroad, which Lee had chosen as his route of escape south to join Johnston. Sheridan's cavalry, however, pressing forward, reached the railroad before the Confederates arrived. Lee turned west and then, at Amelia Court House, south again, but whatever his efforts to shake off the pursuit, he found all routes of escape blocked. There was a fight at Sayler's Creek on April 6 which resulted in heavy Confederate losses. Lee still had hopes of crossing the Appomattox and escaping to Lynchburg, in the Shenandoah Mountains, but the Union pursuers were able to prevent him, destroying the bridges behind him, and so terminated his last chance of delaying what was now inevitable. On April 7 Grant sent Lee a letter calling on him to accept what he could not now defer.

> The result of last week must convince you of the hopelessness of further resistance in the struggle. I feel that it is so and regard it as my duty to shift from myself the responsibility for any further effusion of blood by asking of you to surrender that portion of the C.S. Army known as the Army of Northern Virginia.[4]

CHAPTER FIFTEEN

Breaking into the South

S HERMAN, who had been left by Grant to command in the West—a term used during the war to signify the campaigns not fought in Virginia, Maryland, and Pennsylvania, but geographically in the beginnings of the Deep South—received on April 4 and 19 two letters in which Grant outlined his plans for the conclusion of the western campaign. Grant's order to Sherman and his armies in Tennessee for the campaign of 1864–65 had been to "move against Johnston's army, to break it up and to get into the interior of the enemy's country as far as you can, inflicting all the damage you can against their war resources."[1] In addition to the Army of the Potomac, Grant had three other armies to employ in 1864: those of Banks at New Orleans, Butler on the Virginia coast, and Sigel in West Virginia. Sigel was responsible for the Shenandoah Valley, from which Lee drew many of his supplies; Butler was to operate on the James River near Richmond, with the object of cutting the city's rail communications with the rest of the Confederacy; Banks, Grant hoped, would get into Mississippi and seize Mobile, an important naval and rail centre.

The key operation, however, was that of Sherman, who commanded, as a combined force, McPherson's own Army of the Tennessee (24,465), Thomas's Army of the Cumberland (60,773), and John Schofield's Army of the Ohio (13,559), total strength 98,797. Its task looked simple enough: to push forward from the neighbourhood of Dalton to Atlanta, ninety miles to the south, dispersing Johnston's Army of Tennessee, only 60,000 strong, and beating its component units as he went. Easier said than done. Part of Sherman's problem was his very long and attenuated line of communications, which stretched back along the Western and Atlantic Railroad 470 miles to his main base at Louisville, Kentucky, much of its length running through hostile or at least dangerous territory. Forward of Dalton, moreover, the defenders enjoyed the use of several strong defensible features, notably the Oostanaula, Etowah, and Chattahoochee rivers and the steep slope of Kennesaw Mountain. Johnston's favoured strategy, moreover, was perfectly suited to the terrain, since he believed in avoiding battle when possible and extracting advantage by manoeuvre.

Sherman began his advance into the South on May 4, 1864, leaving Chattanooga to confront Johnston on the route that led to Atlanta (not then Georgia's state capital, which was Milledgeville). The fighting opened on May 6 at Tunnel Hill, captured by Sherman the previous month. After some vigorous outpost skirmishing, Thomas, with General Oliver Howard, one of his corps commanders, spent May 7 and 8 trying to clear the Confederates off the high ground, so as to open a way forward. Johnston opposed him very effectively, until McPherson, whose corps was principally engaged, was forced to withdraw and wait between Sugar Hill and Buzzard-Roost Gap for a better opportunity. Johnston denied one until May 12, when, in what Howard called "one of his clean retreats," he left the way open. Sherman's men caught up with his at Resaca on May 14 and found that by entrenchment and barricading, Johnston had made the position as strong, in Howard's opinion, as Marye's Heights at Fredericksburg. While the army was advancing, Sherman, who had spent the night at his map table, took the opportunity to snatch a nap against a tree trunk. A passing soldier remarked, "A pretty way we are commanded." Sherman, who was less asleep than he appeared, called out, "Stop, my man. While you were sleeping last night, I was planning for you, sir; and now I was taking a nap." Least pompous of men, Sherman left the exchange there. He was sometimes mistaken for a young junior officer, since he stood less than five feet, six inches tall and weighed under 150 pounds.

The Confederate commander opposite at Resaca was Leonidas Polk, the Episcopalian bishop–turned–general. During the evening of May 14, he attempted to drive McPherson's men away, but his effort was defeated. The Confederates lost 2,800 men to the Union's 2,747 at the battle of Resaca. Sherman had a thoroughly realistic attitude towards losses: "A certain amount of . . . killing had to be done, to accomplish the end." At Resaca Sherman fought offensively, Johnston defensively, aided by earthen parapets. Johnston then fell back to Calhoun, Adairsville, and Cassville, where he halted for the battle of the

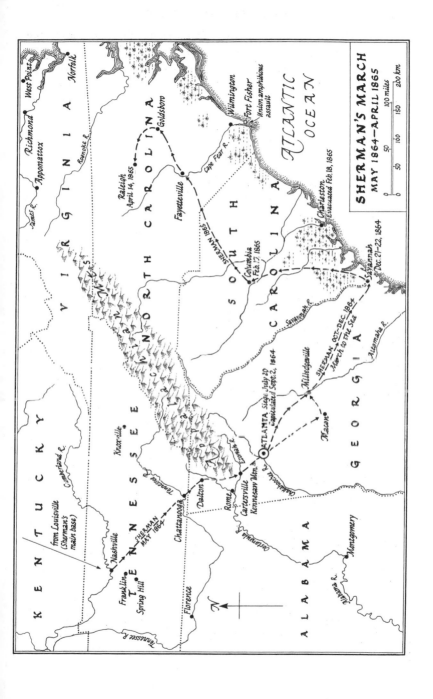

SHERMAN'S MARCH
MAY 1864–APRIL 1865

campaign, but then he continued his retreat beyond the next spur of the Appalachian chain to Allatoona.

Sherman, who knew Allatoona from a previous visit, decided not to fight there. After repairing the railroad he pushed on to Atlanta by way of Dallas. Johnston divined Sherman's intention and forced him to fight at New Hope Church on May 25–28, a slight Union victory. Sherman remarked that "the country was almost in a state of nature— with few or no roads, nothing that a European could understand."[2] Johnston continued to retreat, picking up reinforcements as he went to raise his strength to 62,000. His route took him to Marietta, between Brush Mountain and Lost Mountain. Johnston's line was too long for his numbers so he drew in his flanks and concentrated on Kennesaw. Sherman repaired the railroad up to his camp, awaiting a battle he knew must come. During the preliminaries, there was continuous skirmishing, with the batteries and line of battle pushed right forward. Sherman's effort to carry the Kennesaw position failed, however, with a Union loss of 3,000 to the Confederates' 630. Yet Johnston was so shaken that he abandoned his lines and retreated to the Chattahoochee River. After a skirmish at Smyrna Church, he was driven across the Chattahoochee on July 10. Sherman paid tribute to Johnston's conduct of the retreat, saying his movements were "timely, in good order and he left nothing behind."[3] The Union "had advanced into the enemy's country 120 miles, with a single-track railroad which had to bring clothing, food, ammunition, everything requisite for 100,000 men and 23,000 animals. The city of Atlanta, the gate city opening the interior of the important State of Georgia, was in sight; its protecting army was shaken but not defeated, and onward we had to go," illustrating the principle that "an army once on the offensive must maintain the offensive."

The fighting along the Oostanaula River was heavy. On July 15, Sherman committed the troops commanded by Hooker, who since being relieved of command of the Army of the Potomac had reverted to corps commander, with remarkable equanimity. After a heavy day's fighting, he carried most of the ground before him. Sherman committed cavalry and laid pontoons over the Oostanaula, thereby achieving superiority of numbers. During the night Johnston decided he could no longer hold the Resaca position and withdrew the Army of Tennessee. In the day following, the Confederates completed an extended withdrawal, to the line of Rome-Kingston-Cassville, along the Etowah River. Oliver Howard, with Sherman in his command party, pressed forward and was fired upon by rebel artillery, which killed several Union horses. The enemy, however, was now badly demoralised by the successful Union advance from Resaca. Howard captured about 4,000 prisoners, including a whole regiment.

His engineers were also energetically repairing the railroad running back to Nashville and Louisville. On the morning of July 18, word arrived by the repaired telegraph from Resaca that bacon, hardtack, and coffee, the essentials of the Union soldier's fare, were already arriving. The Confederates continued to fall back, all the more eagerly when Johnston, on the Etowah, discovered that the Union's advance guards were south of him in force at Cartersville and Kingston, where Sherman had set up his headquarters. General Howard found the countryside of farm and woodland about here so picturesque that it was as if there were no war, and the surroundings encouraged Sherman to give his troops three days' rest. Nevertheless, the abundance of timber allowed both armies to construct strong defences both in attack and defence and, when fighting broke out, to inflict heavy casualties on each other. It was in this region that, as Sherman pressed his advance towards Atlanta, Bishop Polk was shot through the body by an artillery round, dying instantly. By further disengagement, Johnston had now established his line on high ground at Kennesaw Mountain, one of the last peaks of the Appalachian chain, an obstacle which at last gave him a holding place Sherman could not turn. Sherman was in practice more concerned with Hood's suddenly evinced determination to cut the Army of the Tennessee's connection with its distant base, an aim that had drawn Nathan Bedford Forrest's cavalry into an attack on the Union's railroad link. Sherman had despatched a counter-attack force from Memphis to run Forrest down, angrily proclaiming that there would never be peace in Tennessee until Forrest was dead. The Memphis force brought Forrest to battle at Brice's Crossroads in Mississippi, where it was badly defeated. At a second encounter Forrest was defeated at Tupelo and wounded, but he did not die. There was a lot of life in the old hellhound yet.

Johnston's success in holding the Kennesaw position came, however, too late to save his own position. Jefferson Davis had an old grudge against him, over a trifling dispute about rank, but the real cause of his fall was popular dissatisfaction with his strategy of evasion and delay, which was almost universally misunderstood as reluctance to risk battle. He was now removed from command in the West and replaced by Lieutenant General John Bell Hood, who, by contrast, was aggressive, bold, and personally brave. Sherman, a friend and intimate of Grant's recorded his feelings as he embarked on his first major independent campaign:

> We were as brothers, I the older man in years, he [Grant] the higher in rank. We both believed in our hearts that the success of the Union cause was necessary not only to the then generation of Americans, but to all future generations. We both professed to be gentlemen and professional soldiers, educated in the science of war by our generous government for the very occasion which had arisen. Neither of us by nature was a combatative man [this was disingenuous of Sherman since the two were to prove themselves the most ruthless commanders of the whole war]; but with honest hearts and a clear purpose to do what man could, we embarked on that campaign which I believe, in its strategy, in its logistics, in its grand and minor tactics, had added new luster to the old science of war. Both of us had at our front generals [Lee and Johnston, then Hood, respectively] to whom in early life we had been taught to look up to,—educated and experienced soldiers like ourselves, not likely to make any mistakes, and each of whom had as strong an army as could be collected from the mass of the Southern people,— of the same blood as ourselves, brave, confident, and well-equipped; in addition to which they had the most decided advantage of operating in their own difficult country of mountain, forest, ravine and river, affording admirable opportunities for defense, besides the other equally important advantage that we had to invade the country of our unqualified enemy, and expose our long lines of supply to guerrillas of an "exasperated people." Again, as we advanced we had to leave guards to bridges, stations and intermediate depots, diminishing the fighting force, while our enemy gained strength, by picking up his detachments as he fell back, and had railroads to bring supplies and reinforcements from his rear. I instance these facts to offset the common assertion that we of the North won the war by brute force and not by courage and skill.[4]

Johnston's last act before his dismissal was to defend the earthworks he had built at the crossings over the Chattahoochee above Atlanta, which the Union overcame by finding crossings elsewhere, and then to withdraw into the defences of Atlanta itself. His conduct in the preceding weeks had been by no means contemptible; he had forced Sherman to spend seventy-four days in advancing a hundred miles, and was still in fighting form.

Hood's first battle as commander of the Army of Tennessee was at Peach Tree Creek, north of Atlanta, where he intended to carry out Johnston's plan to drive the Army of the Cumberland farther west so that Sherman could not concentrate his forces on Atlanta. Hood first came forward from the Peach Tree Creek position on July 20, and attacked the corps opposite, commanded by Hooker, which had crossed the creek on pontoon bridges. A bitter battle ensued, lasting five hours. The Confederates were driven back, leaving in the fields their dead and wounded, 4,796 altogether, to the Union loss of 1,710. Throughout the Atlanta campaign Confederate losses were to be much heavier than the Union's, a grievous disadvantage for the Confederacy, which could afford the losses much less. Hood fell back into his lines around Atlanta. Sherman closed up, and Hood, leaving half his force to defend the city, led the other half, under the cover of darkness, in a long, circuitous march through woodland, round Sherman's left flank. This led to what Sherman called "the hardest battle of the campaign."

The outer line of Atlanta's defences had now been reached. As Sherman recalled:

We feigned to the right, but crossed the Chattahoochee by the left, and soon confronted our enemy behind his first line of entrenchments at Peach Tree Creek, prepared in advance for this very occasion. At this critical moment, the Confederate Government rendered us most valuable service. Being dissatisfied with the Fabian policy of General Johnston, it relieved him and General Hood was substituted to command the Confederate army (near Atlanta), July 18. Hood was known to us to be a "fighter," a graduate of West Point of the class of 1853, No. 44 (in the order of merit), of which class two of my army commanders, McPherson and Schofield were No. 1 and No. 7. The character of a leader is a large factor in the game of war, and I confess, I was pleased at this change, of which I had early notice. I know that I had an army superior in numbers and morale to that of my antagonist; but being so far from my base and operating in a country devoid of food and forage, I was dependent on a poorly constructed railroad, back to Louisville, five hundred miles. I was willing to meet the enemy in open country, but not behind weak constructed parapets.[5]

Grant may have been exaggerating the value of the change of command. Johnston was not as averse to fighting as he made out, while Hood was a doughtier and cleverer opponent. He would not allow Atlanta to fall easily into Sherman's hands.

The battle of Atlanta began on July 22, when, believing that Hood had abandoned the city, the Army of the Tennessee advanced to the lines of earthworks the Confederate defenders had dug. At first they settled down, intending to harass the earthworks, to use them for their purposes, when in early afternoon Confederates appeared in large numbers and began to attack them. Hood had planned a complex offensive, sending part of his force to make a long flank march to take the enemy in the rear. The fighting soon became intense, as some of the Union troops found themselves attacked on three sides. Casualties quickly rose high, but the Union forces held their ground, greatly assisted by the presence in their ranks of two regiments of Illinois sharpshooters who had purchased, at their own expense, the Henry sixteen-shot breech-loading rifle. These two regiments inflicted terrible casualties on the Confederates they encountered, at a much smaller cost to themselves. The Confederates lost control of three of the four railroads leading into the city and suffered 8,499 casualties, to 3,641 on the Union side. Among the Union dead was General McPherson, who rode into Confederate lines whilst on reconnaissance, was called upon to surrender, but, tipping his hat to the enemy, turned his horse and was shot and killed as he rode away. His loss was deeply regretted by Sherman, who valued him highly. He was replaced temporarily by General John A. Logan, an Illinois congressman much valued by Lincoln as a political ally. He made an unforgettable impression on the battlefield, where he was temperamentally at home. Black-haired, with fiery eyes, he led by example, waving his sword overhead and shouting encouragement to his soldiers from the back of his warhorse. Unlike other notable mounts which had unmilitary names, such as Lee's Traveller and Jackson's Little Sorrell, Logan's was appropriately called Slasher. Command of the Army of the Tennessee was later given to General Oliver Howard.

In the later afternoon, Hood's men renewed their attack on the Union's advance lines in great force and with high ferocity. The fighting became very confused, with the Union jumping from one side to the other of the entrenchments that crisscrossed the battlefield, some Confederate, some Union. Hood's attack shook the Union lines, opening a wide gap which threatened to collapse Sherman's army. In this crisis, Logan, who had observed the disaster from a vantage point, turned his horse and galloped to intervene, leading a large reinforcement. As he approached the Union lines a cry of "Black Jack! Black Jack!" sped through the ranks. Inspired by Logan's arrival, and strengthened by the reinforcements he brought, the Union troops recaptured several guns the enemy had taken and turned them round against the attackers, who were quickly driven into retreat. During the fighting the Union forces were able to retrieve McPherson's body, sending a special detachment to do so. They also, at one stage of the fighting for the trenches, retrieved McPherson's hat, binoculars, and documents from Confederate prisoners who had taken them. At about six o'clock, with darkness drawing in, the battle of Atlanta reached its climax, leaving the field, littered with the dead and wounded, in Union hands. Sherman had scored a victory, though one of the most costly and hard-fought of his career as a general.

Sherman's troops now surrounded Atlanta, though they just failed to cut it off from contact with the outside world. A battle fought at Ezra Church on July 28 was again disproportionately costly to the Confederates, who lost 4,632 to the Union's 700, but it left them still protecting Atlanta from capture. Thereafter Hood contented himself with holding Atlanta's earthworks, and accepting siege, which was to last the whole of August.

Sherman spent August manoeuvring around the Atlanta defences with the object of severing the city's last railroad communications with Alabama. He also sent a large cavalry force, under General George Stoneman, on a raid to liberate the Andersonville prison camp. The raid was badly conducted, however, with the result that it not only failed but that Stoneman and 700 of his men themselves were taken prisoner and interned at Andersonville. Andersonville, a principal Confederate prisoner-of-war camp, had already become notorious in the North because of the very high death rate among its inmates. The prison camps of both sides had high death rates because they were vectors of disease. Disease at Andersonville was enhanced by malnutrition, though perhaps also by mismanagement. The commandant of Andersonville, Captain Heinrich Hartmann Wirtz, a native of Switzerland, was tried and executed on criminal charges after the war. He may have been overwhelmed by circumstances, but not even the most dedicated Confederates have ever tried to argue that he was unfairly treated.

Hood was so encouraged by the Union failure that he sent his 4,000 cavalry under General Joseph Wheeler on a raid of his own against

Sherman's principal supply link, the Western and Atlantic Railroad. Its apparent success led him wrongly to conclude that Sherman was giving up the siege of Atlanta. In fact the Union, which had gone off Hood's map, had placed themselves astride the railroad to Macon and thus cut off Atlanta from the outside world. During September 1–2, Hood therefore withdrew from Atlanta, correctly recognising that it could no longer be defended. Sherman telegraphed Lincoln on September 3: "Atlanta is ours and fairly won."

The sensation aroused in both North and South by the fall of Atlanta reinforced the equal sensation caused by the Union victory at Mobile Bay on August 5. Both Grant and Sherman had long sought to capture Mobile, as a means of opening up a local campaign in Alabama. When Mobile's fall came, it was as a result of a naval, not a land, battle. Mobile in August 1864 was one of the last active naval bases and blockade-running centres still open to the South, and home to some of the Confederate navy's most powerful ships, including the ironclad *Tennessee*. Admiral David Farragut commanded a sizable fleet in the Gulf, and in early August led it into Mobile Bay with the aim of destroying the forts and the Confederate fleet they protected. The anchorage was defended by belts of what were then called torpedoes and today would be called mines, barrels filled with gunpowder to be detonated by fulminate of mercury contact fuses. The Union's eighteen vessels, some ironclad, most wooden, advanced in pairs, lashed together, starting out early in the morning of August 5. They were brought under fire both by Fort Morgan and Fort Gaines, and by the Confederate fleet. Farragut had climbed the mainmast of his flagship, the USS *Hartford*, where the quartermaster had lashed him to the rigging. When the danger of the mines became apparent, Farragut uttered what were to become immortal words: "Damn the torpedoes! Full speed ahead!" A lively gun duel then opened up, causing heavy casualties on the Union ships. One Union seaman lost both legs to a conical shot, then throwing up his arms in agony, lost both arms to another. The *Tennessee*, which boldly took on the entire Union fleet single-handed, attempting to sink her enemies by ramming, made herself the target of its combined gunnery and had her rudder chains shot away as a result. Not answering her helm, she was surrendered under a white flag by her captain, and with her capitulation the rest of the Confederate ships gave up the fight. The Union troops in the vicinity then came up and secured the surrender of the forts, though the city of Mobile remained in Confederate hands until April 12, 1865.

The victories of Atlanta and Mobile had a crucial effect on the impending presidential election campaign of 1864. Both parties had already chosen their candidates; the Republicans, known for purposes of the election as the Union Party, had nominated Abraham Lincoln at Baltimore in June; the Democrats were running George McClellan. Frémont, the "Pathfinder," offered himself as a third-party candidate, tepidly opposed to the war, but made no showing and soon withdrew. McClellan, who had fought to preserve the Union without crushing the South, was identified as an anti-war candidate, though he wisely restored his pro-war position, saying that the sacrifices his comrades in arms had made could not be set aside for electoral purposes. During the Democratic Convention, held in Chicago, proceedings had been disturbed by the intervention of the long-term anti-war campaigner and troublemaker Clement Vallandigham, whose position was dramatised, though he did not deliberately encourage it, by an anti-war conspiracy based in Canada; arms were collected, and there were even some minor attempts at arson in New York and elsewhere, but the conspiracy failed to take fire. It was too blatantly pro-rebellion to win support among the partisans of peace. Nevertheless, at Niagara Falls, emissaries from Richmond hoped to manoeuvre the president into discussing familiar conditions for peace, including recognition, independence, and the continuation of slavery, but Lincoln issued a letter restating his inflexible commitment to restoration of the Union and abolition. At the same time the Republican Party weakly agreed to send its own peace mission to Richmond, with a letter from Lincoln offering peace upon the basis of the Constitution; Lincoln, however, recognised the pitfall, since the Constitution accepted slavery, and at the last moment declined to be caught. Nevertheless, he was, on the eve of the election, wholly uncertain of re-election, apparently believing that McClellan would win and that his last public duty would be to negotiate a way out of the war which would not compromise the Union.

In any event, what saved the Republicans from shaming concessions, besides Lincoln's unbending refusal to alter his position on the Constitution and slavery, was McClellan's retreat from an extreme anti-war position together with the news of victory from the fronts now opened within the Southern heartland, which greatly strengthened Lincoln's leadership. The anti-war movement was also seriously damaged by the violent activities of self-proclaimed anti-war campaigners in some of the border states, notably Missouri and Kansas, where groups calling themselves Sons of Liberty and the Order of American Knights attacked pro-Union people and, if they could get away with it, officeholders and uniformed Union defenders. The worst outrages occurred in Kansas, where a Confederate sympathiser (though probably a temperamental anti-authoritarian) called William Clarke Quantrill, whose band included the future gunfighter Frank James, brother of Jesse, took possession of Lawrence, a well-known centre of anti-slavery opinion, murdered 182 men and boys, and burnt 185 of the town's buildings. Anti-slavery activists in Missouri and Kansas, known as Jayhawkers, had added their own violent contributions to those states' sufferings before and during the war. They were multiplied by the enthusiasm with which local Confederate commanders attached terrorist bands to their units. Worst of these hangers-on was "Bloody Bill" Anderson, who attacked Centralia, Kansas, in September 1864, where he, with Frank and Jesse James, murdered 24 unarmed Union solders returning home on leave and killed 124 among the militiamen sent to chase them down. The leading sponsor of partisans among Confederate officers was General Sterling Price, who on the same day as the Centralia massacre fought a pitched battle at Pilot Knob, Missouri, which cost 1,500 Confederate casualties. Eventually Price and his men were driven out of the state, but it required the diversion of a regular Union infantry division to accomplish it. In the presidential election Lincoln took 70 percent of the vote in Missouri.

Voting was staggered in mid-century America, spread out in 1864 from September to November, when the result was declared. The election of 1864 was also complicated by the need to make provision for soldiers away at the front to vote. Some states allowed absentee voting, either by proxy or post; some did not, but insisted on the presence of the voter, which required commanders to permit soldiers to travel to their home states to register their votes. Despite the military difficulties this caused, most commanders were sensible enough of the importance of assisting Lincoln's re-election, if victory were to be assured, to facilitate their soldiers' participation. Research makes it possible to identify soldiers' votes on the returns from many states and reveals that soldiers voted overwhelmingly for Lincoln, probably in a proportion of 80 to 20. Soldiers' votes were decisive in several states, notably New York and Connecticut. On November 8, the official election day, Lincoln received 55 percent of four million votes cast, giving him 234 to 21 of the Electoral College votes. He carried every state still within the Union except for New Jersey, Delaware, and Kentucky. The Republicans also won the governorships and legislatures of all but those three

General Ulysses S. Grant, commander of the Union armies, 1863–65, and later president of the United States

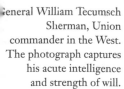

eneral William Tecumsch Sherman, Union commander in the West. The photograph captures his acute intelligence and strength of will.

General Robert E. Lee, commander of the Confederate Army of Northern Virginia

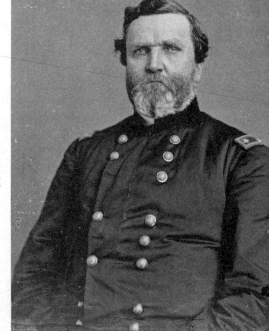

General George Thomas, "the Rock of Chickamauga"

Union engineers bridging the North Anna River, May 1864, Overland Campaign. The steep banks and depth of water show what serious obstacles the short Chesapeake rivers formed.

Union engineers destroying a Confederate railroad, Atlanta, 1864.
The rails are being heated for twisting, as the man in the foreground is doing.

Confederate dead gathered for burial, Gettysburg, July 5, 1863

The McLean house at Appomattox Court House, Virginia, where Grant and
Lee signed the surrender of the Army of Northern Virginia, April 9, 1865

The ruins of Richmond, 1865. The James River was in the background.

The gallows built in the Washington Arsenal for the execution of the conspirators in the assassination of Lincoln, 1865

Veterans of Pickett's charge on the field of action at the reunion for the fiftieth anniversary of the battle of Gettysburg, July 3, 1913

states. The presidential election of 1864 was thus a triumph not only for the Republicans and Lincoln but also for Lincoln's war policy.

Sherman's success in capturing Atlanta opened the way for a project close to his heart and increasingly to Grant's as well, which was to make the civilian population of the South suffer as long as resistance was sustained. On July 15, Grant wrote to Halleck, "Sherman, once in Atlanta, will devote himself to collecting the resources of the country." He was soon to do worse than that. Shortly afterwards his policy for dealing with the Southerners became even more radical. He began on September 8 by ordering the emptying of Atlanta of what remained of its civilian population. The women and children were loaded onto carts and wagons and sent south to the town of Rough and Ready, which had been fought over during his advance. "Then," recorded Sherman, "began the real trouble." Hood had retired from Atlanta, to Lovejoy's Station, thirty miles to the southeast of the city, on the Savannah railroad. His strength was 40,000, all seasoned troops, and he had a large supply train of wagons. On September 21, he shifted his base to Palmetto Station, twenty-five miles southwest of Atlanta on the Montgomery and Selma railroad and began systematic preparations for a campaign against Sherman's long line of communications, with the purpose of forcing him to abandon his conquests. As a result, Sherman was forced, during September and October 1864, into marching troops up and down the railroad to keep the line open. Hood was now visited by Jefferson Davis, who promised his army cooperation and made a speech threatening to make Sherman pay as dearly as Napoleon had in his retreat from Moscow. Sherman at once took precautions, sending one division westward to Rome, one to Chattanooga, and strengthening the detachments guarding the railroads. To keep Hood under such pressure that he could not interrupt supplies, General Thomas was sent back to the headquarters of his department at Nashville and Schofield to his at Knoxville, while Sherman remained with the Army of the Tennessee at Atlanta, and awaited Hood's move, which quickly followed. Hood, behind his cavalry, crossed the Chattahoochee River on October 1, with his main army at Campbelltown and then moved to Dallas, from which he destroyed the railroad above Marietta for fifteen miles. He then sent General French to capture Allatoona. Sherman followed Hood, reaching Kennesaw Mountain in time to see the attack on Allatoona, which was repulsed. Hood then moved westward, bypassing Rome, and by a flank march reached Resaca, which he summoned to surrender but did not attack, continuing up the railroad, destroying it as he moved to the tunnel at Dalton, where he captured the garrison. This was a complete reversal of the campaign which had led Sherman to Atlanta during May. Sherman followed to observe Hood's movements down the valley of Chattooga, where Sherman failed to intercept him. Hood escaped to Gadsden on the Coosa River. Sherman halted at Gaylesville to observe Hood's movements across the mountains to Decatur, which, since it was well defended, he avoided, finally halting at Florence, Alabama.

Sherman perceived that Hood's object was to harass and interrupt his communications, rather than to fight a major battle, which he was unlikely to win. Sherman accordingly made a redisposition of his forces to allow him both to restrain Hood and to prepare for a further march into the Southland. He sent Schofield with two of his six corps by rail to Nashville, gave Thomas the troops he needed to defend Tennessee, and began to concentrate, at Atlanta, the forces necessary for a major offensive into Georgia. Repairing the railroads, he assembled the food and transportation necessary for 60,000 men, sent to the rear all unnecessary baggage and equipment, and called in his detachments to Atlanta, where by November 4, he had had concentrated four infantry corps, a cavalry division, and 64 field guns, totalling 60,598 men. Hood remained at Florence, preparing either to invade Tennessee and Kentucky or to follow Sherman. "We were prepared for either alternative."

At the conclusion of the Atlanta campaign, Sherman was supremely confident and looked forward to the next and, he believed, final and decisive stage of the campaign and, indeed, of the war. In his survey of his operations, he quoted the great Napoleon "on the fundamental maxim of war, which was 'to converge a superior force on the critical point at the critical time.' " That meant, in 1864, on Lee's and Johnston's armies. He reflected that, had Lee abandoned Richmond before Sherman captured Atlanta, Grant would have advanced to meet him. As he had taken Atlanta first, the correct strategy was now to march his army to meet Grant. "The most practicable route to Richmond was a thousand miles in distance, too long for a single march; hence the necessity to reach the sea-coast for a new base. Savannah, three hundred miles distant, was the nearest point." " 'The March to the Sea' was in strategy only a shift of base for ulterior and highly important purposes."[6] It was the outcome of the battle and campaign of Atlanta which may thus be seen as one of the most crucial operations of the whole war.

Sherman's March to the Sea would make him the most hated Northerner in the Confederacy but also crush the South's spirit of resistance for good. He foresaw coordinating his advance on the ground with naval operations up the Savannah River so that he could "move rapidly to Milledgeville, where there is abundance of corn and meat and could so threaten Macon and Augusta that the enemy would doubtless give up Macon for Augusta; then I would move so as to interpose between Augusta and Savannah, and force him to give up Augusta with the only powder mills and factories remaining in the South."[7] He was actively contriving a scheme to make a war upon food resources turn into a war on industrial production. He was now certain that he could make the march to the sea and "make Georgia howl." After devastating Georgia he intended to turn on the Carolinas and thence to reach Virginia and Richmond. He now began to organise the troops he had around Atlanta into marching formations for the great advance. The force was divided into a right and left wing, commanded, respectively by General Oliver Howard and General Henry Slocum; the right wing consisted of the Fifteenth and Seventeenth Corps, the left wing of the Fourteenth and Twentieth Corps. There was also a cavalry division commanded by General Hugh Judson Kilpatrick. The army's strength totalled 55,000 infantry, 5,000 cavalry, and 64 guns. What opposed it was 3,500 of Wheeler's cavalry corps and 3,000 undertrained and poorly equipped Georgia militia.

The order of march arranged the corps on four parallel roads, and allotted a minimum of wheeled transport to each. The surplus and unnecessary were ruthlessly thrown away. Captain David Oakey, of the 3rd Massachusetts Volunteers, described the sorting out. "Each group of messmates decided which hatchet, stew pan or coffee-pot should be taken. The single wagon allowed to a battalion carried scarcely more than a gripsack and blanket, and a bit of shelter tent about the size of a large towel for each officer, and only such other material as was necessary for regimental business. Wagons to carry the necessary ammunition in the contingency of a battle and a few days rations in case of absolute need, composed the train of each army corps and with one wagon and one ambulance for each regiment made very respectable impedimenta, averaging about eight hundred wagons to a corps."[8]

The paucity of food carried was because Sherman had quite deliberately decided that the army should eat out the state as it advanced: "We were expected to make fifteen miles a day; to corduroy the roads where necessary; to destroy such property as was designated by our corps commander; and to consume everything eatable by man or beast." In Georgia, South Carolina, and, to a slightly lesser extent, in North Carolina when it was reached, Sherman's men found food in abundance, particularly sweet potatoes and hams, for which they developed a keen nose, usually accurate whatever trouble was taken by the inhabitants to hide the produce, often by burying it. The march into Georgia had begun on November 15. By early December, Sherman's Army of Georgia, as it was now officially known, was halfway to Savannah. A swathe of scorched earth had been driven through the state by the foraging parties which marched ahead of the troop columns, on whose flanks hung parties of "bummers" not under the control of the foraging officers; they were there simply to scrounge whatever they could. By December 10 the army was outside Savannah and poised to capture the city. Sherman wrote that it had pulled up a hundred miles of the three main Georgia railroads and, besides that, had also "consumed the corn and fodder of country thirty miles either side of the line from Atlanta to Savannah, as also the sweet potatoes, cattle, hogs, sheep and poultry and [had] carried away more than 10,000 horses and mules, as well as a countless number of slaves. I estimate the damage done to the State of Georgia and its military resources at $100,000,000. . . . This may seem a hard species of warfare, but it brings the sad realities of war home to those who have been directly and indirectly instrumental in involving us in its attendant calamities."[9]

Sherman also wrote, "War is war and not popularity-seeking. If they want peace, they and their relatives must stop the war." "You cannot qualify war in harsher terms than I will. War is cruelty and you cannot refine it; and those who brought war into our country deserve all the curses and maledictions a people can pour out."[10]

His march to Savannah brought maledictions in plenty. Before taking Savannah, Sherman had to overcome the defences of Fort McAllister, which guarded the bay. As the troops formed up, a Union gunboat, the USS *Dandelion*, appeared and signalled, "Is Fort McAllister taken?" and was answered, "Not yet, but it will be in a minute." Almost at once Hazen's Second Division, Fifteenth Corps, swarmed over the parapet and swamped the garrison of 200 men and their 24 guns. Following its fall and the arrival of the Federal fleet offshore, Savannah was evacuated on the night of December 20–21. Next day Sherman telegraphed to Lincoln, offering him the city, with 150 heavy guns and 25,000 bales of cotton, as a Christmas present.

The South was now running desperately short of soldiers, as desertion became endemic and widespread. By December 1864, manpower returns showed a nominal strength of 400,787 but only 196,016 actually present with the colours. The state's authorities, moreover, had generally ceased to run down deserters, who in many cases had formed themselves into armed bands to resist arrest and coercion back into the ranks. There were many reasons why men deserted. Concern for the welfare of their families was an overriding impulse, particularly where farms were falling out of cultivation for want of labour. Husbands and fathers also feared for their womenfolk's safety, though one of the few barbarities of which the marauding Union marchers were not guilty was rape.

After Savannah, Sherman was on the threshold of carrying his version of war-making into one of the states where slaves formed a majority of the population, South Carolina. It was also, in Northern eyes, the seedbed of the rebellion, and the region most deserving of harsh treatment. It was the home of several of the most fiery theorists of secession and the place where the first shots had been fired in 1861. Many in Sherman's army were eager to punish South Carolina and its people for their attack on the Union. Thus far, moreover, the state had escaped paying the cost of rebellion, except in the deaths of its sons on the battlefield. Now Sherman was determined to make it howl even louder than Georgia had done. But before the march into South Carolina began, there had to be a preliminary in Tennessee, where Thomas was charged by Sherman into dealing with Hood.

Sherman's departure into Georgia, which greatly reduced Union strength in the western theatre, prompted Hood to see a chance of reopening the campaign to seize Tennessee for the South. There was an element of fantasy in Hood's approach to war-making, since he consistently exaggerated his chances of success in whatever campaign he was fighting. Nevertheless, he possessed the valuable gift of boldness, and his courage was unquestionable. By the end of 1864 he was one of the most gravely injured senior officers in either army, having suffered disabling damage to his left arm at Gettysburg and having lost a leg at Chickamauga. Nevertheless he still rode a horse, in his own opinion quite as well as men fitter than himself. Hood was admired by his soldiers but had become a trial to the high command in Richmond because of his insistence on following his own whim and inclination in the conduct of campaigns. He was certainly to do so in the campaign of

Franklin and Nashville, where with only 40,000 men he set out to defeat 60,000 Northerners, partly by dint of hard marching, something which his army, much of which was shoeless, was unequipped to achieve. Yet Hood entertained the most extravagant of ambitions. He intended and believed he could break into Tennessee, then into Kentucky, where he counted on recruiting up to 20,000 fresh soldiers, though how they were to be trained and equipped was a matter he did not specify; with them he would complete the defeat of General Thomas and then march northeast, across the mountains, to join forces with Lee's Army of Northern Virginia and triumph over Grant and Sherman. Meanwhile, if comforted by fantasy, he was confronted by the demands of reality, which required him to defeat Thomas in the countryside between Franklin and Nashville, state capital of Tennessee. Thomas, whom he now challenged for control of Tennessee, was an old opponent.

Thomas's advance guard of 30,000 was commanded by General John Schofield, who had previously commanded Union troops in Missouri. Hood's plan was to get between Schofield at Pulaski, south of Nashville, where Thomas had another 30,000 troops. Schofield learnt of Hood's approach in time and took up a defensive position on the Duck River at Columbia, where Hood engaged his troops during November 24–27. Not wanting to risk a frontal assault on the Union's entrenched positions, Hood sent his cavalry, commanded by Nathan Bedford Forrest, and two of his infantry corps, now much diminished in strength, on a flank march against Schofield's rear. Schofield, however, detected the move and hastened two divisions to hold the threatened sector at Spring Hill. Confederate attacks on the position failed—here, as elsewhere all over the extended Franklin-Nashville battlefield, the Union troops threw up earthworks in haste wherever attack menaced, though the Confederates dug also. As Confederate attacks died away, Schofield withdrew his troops and led them back to join forces with Thomas at Nashville. Hood's men had suffered dreadfully, losing 7,000 killed, wounded, and missing, a casualty list as bad as any recorded in Virginia during the Overland Campaign. The colours of thirty-three Confederate regiments had been captured. Casualties among Confederate senior officers were exceptionally heavy. Fifty-four Confederate regimental commanders were hit, as were several generals, including Major General Patrick Cleburne and Brigadier General States Rights Gist, who had been at First Bull Run.

After disengaging at Franklin, Schofield fell back on Nashville, where General Thomas was preparing to attack the Confederates as they approached from a carefully dug line of earthworks crossing all the roads leading into the city from the south. Thomas had conducted the campaign faultlessly thus far, but not to the satisfaction of Grant in his faraway headquarters at City Point. Grant wanted victory and Thomas was not supplying it fast enough for his impatient superior. He had been bombarding Thomas with urgings and most recently with a threat of his removal, even with an actual removal order, which was fortunately delayed in transmission, for Thomas was just about to do all and more than Grant demanded. Thomas attacked the Confederate line on the morning of December 15. The Confederates, to Hood's disgust, had constructed earthworks as a defensive-offensive base opposite the Union line. Hood had formed the opinion that his army had lost its offensive spirit, but in action it showed no lack of aggressiveness at all, repelling all the Union attacks throughout the day. The attacks were renewed on December 16 and in mid-afternoon, supported by heavy artillery fire, carried a portion of the Confederate line on the left. The Confederates gave way, first at that point and then along the whole line. Hood was watching the action from horseback close in the rear. "I behold," he recorded, "for the first and only time a Confederate army abandon the field in confusion."

Worse was to follow. Hood soon discovered that "all hope to rally the troops was vain." The Confederate army pressed on southward, pursued by Thomas, until it at last was able to halt at Tupelo on January 10. Three days later, Hood wrote to the Confederate secretary of war, requesting to be relieved of command. On January 14 he met General Beauregard, who had arrived to assess the situation. Hood repeated to him his request to be relieved. He also wrote to Jefferson Davis, emphasising that the plan to invade Tennessee was his and his alone. He needed to concede responsibility. The Franklin-Nashville campaign had been a disaster, reducing the Army of Tennessee from a strength of 40,000 to less than 20,000, so rendering it effectively useless. As it had been the second largest in the South's order of battle, the Confederacy's force was now reduced to that of the Army of Northern Virginia, itself greatly diminished in number since the beginning of the Overland Campaign and shrinking rapidly as the siege of Petersburg was protracted.

Sherman started the Army of Georgia northward from Savannah on February 1. His march lay through what Carolinians called the Low Country, a zone of rivers and their many tributaries all swollen in that very wet fall by twenty-eight days of continuous rain in forty-five days of marching. General William Hazen, a commander in the Fifteenth Corps, counted thirty-six swamp crossings in his division's march through South Carolina, and fourteen river crossings. His men built seventeen miles of corduroy roads as well as bridges and fords. The local inhabitants and Confederate commanders believed that the terrain was impassable and made little effort to defend it. On February 22, however, Johnston was appointed commander of all Confederate forces in the Carolinas, and with 20,000 troops scraped together from the garrisons of Charleston and Savannah and Hood's Army of Tennessee, he organised defences for Charleston and Augusta, site of the South's most important armaments factories. Sherman, however, while disposing his troops on the line of march so as to appear as if he were threatening both, in practice kept away from them. His aim now was to get into North Carolina and from there to link hands with Grant in Virginia, so as to crush Lee between two Union pincer jaws. Charleston was evacuated on February 18, leaving Columbia, the state capital, the only place of importance in South Carolina still controlled by Confederate forces. By February 17, it too was abandoned, and that night Union troops entered it, finding the streets filled with bales of cotton, some of which were already alight. What followed remains a matter of dispute to this day. Liberated Northern prisoners, free blacks, and troops from Sherman's army roamed the streets; more cotton took fire, as did parts of the city. By the dark hours of the morning half the city was in flames. A great deal of drink had been consumed. Even so, officers and some of Sherman's soldiers tackled the flames and the fire did not get completely out of hand. Nevertheless, the burning of Columbia became a Confederate atrocity story and a difficult one for the North to refute, against the background of burning and looting in Georgia and the Carolinas which had been Sherman's deliberate policy.

The most important military operation in North Carolina during the closing phase of the war was not the work of Sherman's army but a deliberate and separate operation to close down the South's last large blockade-running port at Wilmington, on the Cape Fear River. The port was defended by a fortification built to a new engineering design intended to resist bombardment. Brick and masonry, as in the forts of the Third System, had proved vulnerable to gunfire. Indeed, Fort Sumter had been reduced to a pile of debris by 1863, largely as a result of the concentrated Union naval bombardment of that August and September. Fort Fisher, at Wilmington, was constructed on different principles: instead of being a rigid structure of stone walls and case-mates which shattered under gunfire, it was a timber framework, covered with turf and sand, which absorbed the impact of shot and could not be fractured, as the great Russian fortress of Bomersund had been by the British during the Crimean War. The Union eventually did not even try to batter Fort Fisher into submission but landed a large force of infantry to carry it by amphibious assault, which was achieved on January 15, 1865. Wilmington was then occupied and the Cape Fear River closed to blockade-running traffic.

After the occupation of Columbia on February 17, 1865, Sherman diverted his army towards Goldsboro, North Carolina, where he hoped to join forces with Grant, then still battling against the defences of Petersburg and Richmond. His advance, impeded by torrential rains, appeared to menace both Goldsboro and Raleigh, North Carolina's capital, and was opposed by most of the surviving Confederate hierarchy, including Johnston, Bragg, and Pierre Beauregard. Between them they had managed to assemble about 21,000 troops, deployed by Johnston at Fayetteville, North Carolina. Sherman accompanied his soldiers, who formed the Armies of Tennessee and Georgia, into action at Bentonville on March 19. Johnston, in opposition, put up a spirited performance. He was too heavily outnumbered, 80,000 to 20,000, to succeed, though Sherman, who was present, seems at this stage of the war to have lost the taste for bloodshed and did not press the issue. It was obvious to all, including most Southerners, in and out of the army, that the war was drawing to a close; only the self-deluding in the Confederacy continued to hope that it could be concluded on conditions that would soften Lincoln's terms of surrender and black emancipation. On March 25, Sherman left the scene of action in North Carolina and, by rail and then steamer, set out to meet Grant at City Point, Virginia, the Army of the Potomac's port on the James River, there to describe his march of 425 miles in fifty days, which ended resistance in Georgia and the Carolinas. It had been an extraordinary achievement, though it had inaugurated a style of warfare that boded the worst sort of ill for peoples unable to keep a conqueror at bay, as Hitler's campaigns in eastern Europe seventy-five years later would testify.

CHAPTER SIXTEEN

The Battle off Cherbourg and the Civil War at Sea

PARALLEL TO BUT quite detached from the land war, though potentially crucial to its outcome, was the Civil War at sea. It was a war that the North completely dominated, as could not otherwise have been the case. The United States Navy was an almost entirely Northern institution. Of its 7,600 seamen only a handful went south. The seafaring population of the United States was Northern, and provided the manpower of the country's merchant marine, an enormous resource of trained sailors which had no equivalent in the South. True, of the navy's 1,554 regular officers, 373 chose to side with the South; but their numbers could easily be made good from the ranks of the merchant service. At the outset, moreover, the South had almost no ships. Of the forty-two naval vessels in commission, almost all were either absent in distant waters or in Union ports. Those the North controlled were, it is true, almost all antiquated and at best obsolescent; but the South had nothing with which to oppose them. Stephen Mallory, the Confederacy's secretary of the navy, recognised from the outset that, lacking as it did almost all shipbuilding capacity, it would have to buy ships abroad, which effectively meant from England. For that purpose he sent the former U.S. Navy captain James Bulloch to Liverpool, where he set up business in June 1861. It was not difficult to place contracts with British builders; the difficulty lay in circumventing British neutrality law. Under the Foreign Enlistment Act, which had naval provisions, British builders would be prosecuted by their government for supplying ships to the rebellious subjects of a friendly foreign state. It would therefore be necessary to represent a Confederate-commissioned ship as a merchantman, to sail it from British waters to a neutral port, and to sail its armament separately. Bulloch quickly learnt the necessary tricks but was closely watched by

Union agents and diplomats, who attempted to prevent the delivery of suspected warships. The first vessel that Bulloch commissioned was launched as the *Oreto*, supposedly for the Italian government. The American embassy correctly identified her as identical to one of the propeller-driven steam gunboats currently being commissioned for the Royal Navy, but it failed to prevent her from leaving Liverpool. She was sailed in April 1862 to Nassau, in the British Bahamas, where she was joined by a merchantman, confusingly called the *Bahama*, carrying her guns and ammunition. The *Oreto*, now known as the *Florida*, was sailed to Cuba, where she met the *Bahama*. The Spanish colonial government refused to allow the warlike stores to be installed, some but not all having been taken aboard in the Bahamas, and the captain, Commander J. N. Maffitt, of the Confederate navy, determined to run the blockade and reach Mobile, Alabama. She was fired on by Union warships while penetrating the blockade but was not badly damaged and succeeded in getting to port in Mobile, where she stayed for the next four months.

In January 1863 she slipped out, evading the blockade, and got into the Atlantic, where she took a number of vessels, using them to unblock Southern shipping. After sinking fourteen, *Florida* was sailed for repairs to the French port of Brest. She then cruised in the Atlantic, destroying Union shipping, eventually going into port at Bahia, Brazil. There she was cornered by a Union sloop, which attempted to simulate a collision with her. Though the ruse failed, the sloop got possession of her, and she was taken to Hampton Roads and there sank, following an apparently genuine collision.

The Confederate Navy Department succeeded in acquiring several other commercial raiders, either by commissioning them to be built or by purchase abroad. They included the *Georgia*, originally the British-owned *Japan*; during her career as a cruiser she captured only eight vessels and was eventually taken to Boston by a U.S. Navy ship which had intercepted her outside Lisbon.

By far the most successful and best known of the Confederate cruisers was the CSS *Alabama*. She was built at Liverpool at the same time and under the same subterfuge as the *Florida*. In August 1862 she was sailed to the Portuguese Azores, where her guns and ammunition were transhipped, and she began her raids on United States shipping under the command of Captain Raphael Semmes. As a Union officer he had shared a cabin during the Mexican War with the future captain John Winslow, who would command the Union ship that sank the *Alabama* in battle at the end of her commerce-raiding career. Semmes was a sailor and leader of great ability. Soon after the start of his cruise he began to capture prizes, but while making for the entrance to New York harbour, the *Alabama* ran into heavy weather and suffered damage. He accordingly decided to sail to the Gulf of Mexico, where he got intelligence of a Union seaborne invasion of Texas and determined to intercept the enemy fleet. To his consternation, however, Semmes ran not into a large body of merchantmen but into a squadron of five U.S. warships and had to beat a hasty retreat. He was pursued by the USS *Hatteras* and brought to action but successfully defended himself, sank the *Hatteras*, and escaped first into the South Atlantic, then to the Pacific, where he successfully terrorised Northern shipping in that ocean. The *Alabama*'s operations in the Pacific caused all Northern shipping there to take refuge in local ports and so brought U.S. commerce in those waters to a standstill. *Alabama*'s eventual tally of prizes taken totalled sixty-four, one of the largest successes ever recorded by a commerce raider. Finding no more victims, Semmes therefore sailed the *Alabama* first to the East Indies, then to East Africa, and eventually to Brazil. He continued to attack Union shipping on the way. On arrival in Brazil, Semmes decided that his ship needed repairs, since her boilers were burnt out and she was shedding the copper from her bottom. Accordingly he proceeded to Europe, where in June 1864 he entered the French port of Cherbourg and secured permission for the *Alabama* to be docked. Soon afterwards his old shipmate Captain Winslow appeared in command of the USS *Kearsarge*. *Kearsarge* was almost the twin of the *Alabama*, same size, same horsepower, almost the same armament. Winslow declared his purpose to be the embarkation of the Union prisoners *Alabama* held. Semmes objected to *Kearsarge* getting permission from French authorities to do so, since she would thereby add to her crew. As *Kearsarge* left harbour, however, Semmes sent word that he would follow her and fight, apparently as a point of honour that he needed to demonstrate that *Alabama* was also a ship-of-war and not merely a commerce raider.

Alabama departed from Cherbourg on the morning of Sunday, June 19, and spotted *Kearsarge* lying about seven miles to the north. Semmes cleared for action and delivered a stirring address to his men in which he reminded them that they were about to fight in the English Channel, scene of so much naval glory of their race. By this he meant the English race; Americans commonly regarded themselves as sharing a common ethnicity with the English, even eighty years after the War of Independence. The two ships closed to a distance of about a mile and began to circle. The ships completed seven circles, keeping up a heavy fire. They were almost perfectly matched, the *Alabama* mounting one 100-pounder pivot gun, one 8-inch pivot gun, and six 32-pounders. The *Kearsarge* mounted, besides 32-pounders, two 11-inch pivot guns. Her advantage was that her hull was covered with chains, to serve as armour; these chains were concealed by pine planking. The *Alabama* had no armoured protection. Improvised as *Kearsarge's* armour was, it proved effective against the *Alabama's* shot and shell. *Alabama* suffered heavy damage when three 11-inch shells entered through a gun port. After over one hour's action, at just before one o'clock, the chief engineer of the *Alabama* reported to Semmes that the boiler fires were out; the ship was settling rapidly and was in a sinking condition. Semmes therefore ordered that the colours be struck and gave the order to abandon ship. Although *Kearsarge* had suffered only three casualties, the decks and below-deck spaces of the *Alabama* were crowded with dead and wounded. Winslow sent his two undamaged ship's boats to rescue men from the water. An English steam yacht, the *Deerhound*, commanded by John Lancaster, flying the ensign of the Royal Mersey Yacht Club, which had been watching the action at close hand, came down to pick up survivors also. News of the confrontation of the *Alabama* and the *Kearsarge* had brought by train hundreds of spectators from as far away as Paris. The crowd watching the sea battle from shore and headland was estimated at about 15,000.

Alabama was the most successful of the Confederacy's twelve commerce raiders. Collectively they inflicted about twenty million dollars of damage on Union shipping and permanently altered the balance in world trade to Britain's advantage. So high did insurance costs rise on U.S.-flagged ships that traders generally, and American exporters in particular, took to shipping cargos in non-U.S. bottoms, progressively reducing the size of the U.S. merchant fleet, until, from having been larger than and a vigorous competitor with Britain's, it ceased to be an important part of world commerce carrying. It never recovered from the damage done by the Confederacy's raiders.

The commerce-raiding campaign was a Confederate success, as was its blockade-running. The losses, however, made the effort too costly to be really worth the candle. The Confederacy's personnel, from Secretary Mallory to Semmes, were men of ability; to Mallory is due the credit of inaugurating ironclad warfare in world naval affairs. The base of the effort, however, was too small to have offered the Confederacy any prospect of success in offsetting the strategic balance.

The enormous length of the American coastline, the extent of its territorial waters, and the importance of seaborne trade to the American economy would have led to a pre-war appreciation that naval combat would play a crucial role in any war between North and South. So it did, to an extent. That extent, however, was limited, for simple reasons. The North was vulnerable to attack at sea, but the South's naval power was too small to do the necessary damage. The South was also vulnerable but succeeded in evading the North's much greater power by resort to irregular methods of sea warfare, commerce-raiding and blockade-running.

For such a small service with a short history, the United States Navy had already acquired a formidable reputation by 1861. Although it had only forty-two warships in commission, the fleet had won victories far from home in its seventy years' existence. Its frigates had triumphed in several notable single-ship actions against the Royal Navy during the War of 1812, and it had operated as far away as the Mediterranean in the campaign against the North African beys at the beginning of the nineteenth century. Its seamen were of outstanding quality and its officers equal in competence to those of the Royal Navy. Long ago its ships had been at the forefront of the builder's craft. Some dated from the eighteenth century. Almost all were sailing vessels, armed with broadside-firing cannon. The South's raising and rebuilding of the USS *Merrimack* as the armoured warship CSS *Virginia* revealed starkly how outdated all were. Only the almost miraculous appearance of the USS *Monitor* averted the Union fleet's complete destruction when the two ironclads met in Hampton Roads on March 9, 1862.

Riverine warfare, particularly on the Mississippi and its tributaries, was dominated by the North, which controlled and built the largest number of armed river craft. On the high seas, however, it was the South that was most active, because of its recourse to blockade-running and commerce-raiding, with fast ships built or bought abroad. Though it did not rescue the South from shortage, blockade-running was essential to its war economy. There were several thousand blockade-runners active during the war, of which 1,500 were captured by the several hundred U.S. Navy ships searching for them. Still, five out of six blockade-runners got through; it was very much in their captains' and crews' interests to take the risks, since the return on a successful voyage was enormous, several hundred dollars even for ordinary seamen. On the outward voyage the blockade runners shipped cotton, on the inward military supplies but also luxury goods, usually the private property of the captain. The danger of interception chiefly arose near the home port, of which the number open dwindled as the war drew out. The U.S. Navy became very skilled at setting traps for the runners, its task considerably eased because destinations were so predictable. The blockade-runners, with the assistance of shore parties, also became successful at avoiding interception. They made use of bad weather and the hours of darkness to run close inshore, where the removal of navigation markers and lights put their pursuers at risk.

As the blockade heightened, the South turned to active measures. At the outset the Richmond government had issued letters of marque, in effect licences to sail as pirates, to private shipowners. Twenty-four privateers sailed under the Confederate flag. Privateering, however, died out when the European powers closed their ports to them and their prizes. The privateering had the effect, however, of driving up maritime insurance rates to exorbitant levels and forcing U.S. shipowners to reflag their vessels under non-American flags. As privateering lost effectiveness, the Southern government, at the behest of Secretary Mallory, a pre-war chairman of the U.S. Senate's naval affairs committee, began to commission official commerce-raiders. The first was the CSS *Sumter*, commanded by Raphael Semmes. Beginning in June 1861, he captured six Northern merchantmen, which he took into ports in Cuba. His campaign, however, was frustrated by the Spanish colonial government, which returned the prizes to their crews. He was also hampered by Spanish restrictions on his freedom to refuel. He transferred to the coast of South America, where he was intercepted by the USS *Powhatan*, under Captain David Porter, and forced to flee across the Atlantic as far as Gibraltar. There he was blockaded by a Union squadron and obliged to abandon his command. He made his own escape to the South, having captured eighteen ships during his cruise in *Sumter*.

Other Confederate commerce-raiders were the CSS *Florida*, which captured thirty-five prizes but was eventually cornered in Brazilian waters in 1864 and towed to Hampton Roads. The circumstances of her capture were so clearly illegal that the Federal government agreed to return her to a Brazilian port, but she was, again illegally, disabled by a U.S. ship before she could depart. The CSS *Georgia* cruised in the Atlantic in 1863, reaching as far as Morocco, where she fought a ship-to-shore battle with Moors. She had captured nine prizes and was eventually decommissioned in Cherbourg. The CSS *Nashville* cruised off Britain during 1862, taking no prizes before being sunk by the USS *Montauk* in 1863. The CSS *Tallahassee* captured forty Atlantic prizes before taking refuge in Liverpool in April 1865 and being sold. The CSS *Shenandoah* had an adventurous career, sailing round the Horn to Australia in 1864, where she recruited many Australians. In early 1865 she made captures among the whaling fleet in the Bering Straits, off Siberia, but on hearing of the war's end she sailed for England and hauled down the Confederate colours on November 6, 1865. She had taken thirty-eight prizes. The CSS *Chickamauga* cruised in the Atlantic in late 1864, taking seven prizes, but was deserted by many of her crew in Bermuda and forced to return to Wilmington, North Carolina, where she was burnt to escape capture in February 1865.

The commerce-raiders destroyed about 5 percent of the American merchant fleet and, though small in number, severely disrupted the Union's seaborne commerce, with permanent effect. Because of reflagging and the sale of American merchantmen to foreign owners, the U.S. merchant marine, a potential rival to that of Britain, never recovered its place in world trade after 1865. The South's naval effort was remarkable. Yet the real naval achievement of the Civil War was the North's. By effectively closing down the South's maritime commerce, it not only denied the Confederacy the possibility both of resupplying and of funding its war effort, but it also denied Richmond the diplomatic recognition it craved.

The crux of the North's naval dominance was its imposition of blockade. Blockade had legal as well as military substance. To be recognised as having force in international law, blockade had to be effective. Mere declaration of blockade did not invest it with legality. It had to be demonstrated as working. The blockading squadrons of the U.S. Navy, therefore, had to actually be capable of closing the South's ports of entry. As the South had over 3,500 miles of coastline and hundreds of harbours large and small, the task of imposing effective blockade was considerable. Most of the South's harbours could, however, be ignored, since they were too small or deficient in lines of communication inland to be useful to blockade runners. In all there were only ten Southern ports sufficiently deepwater or with adequate facilities to count: New Orleans; Mobile, Alabama; Pensacola and Fernandina, Florida; Savannah, Georgia; Charleston, South Carolina; Wilmington and New Bern, North Carolina; and Norfolk, Virginia. Most of these places were taken early on, New Bern and Fernandina in March 1862, and Savannah was closed by the capture of its approaches in April. New Orleans was also taken in April 1862. Pensacola was abandoned, because the Federal fort guarding its entrance refused to surrender, in May 1862. By mid-1862 the only Atlantic ports left to the South were Charleston, Wilmington, and Norfolk. Norfolk, closely watched by the Northern fleet operating in Chesapeake Bay, was too well blockaded to be useful as a port of entry. Charleston was invaded from landward in 1865; eventually only Wilmington survived as a port of entrance and exit.

The Confederate naval effort was remarkable not for what it achieved but for what it attempted, with revolutionary naval means that permanently altered the nature of war at sea, not only with iron clads but also with "torpedoes," as mines were then called, and submarines. The Confederacy's first submarine was an experimental model, the *Pioneer*, built at New Orleans in February 1862. It was abandoned and sunk in Lake Pontchartrain the following month. The development team, including its leader, Horace Lawson Hunley, then transferred their work to Mobile, Alabama, where they built the *American Diver*. It was ready to make an attack on the Union blockading fleet by January 1863, but proved to be too slow for practical use, and after its failure, it sank in a storm in the mouth of Mobile Bay and was not recovered.

Very soon after its loss, Hunley began work on its replacement, which was to be known by his name. Earlier experiments with steam and electromagnetic propulsion were abandoned and it was built with a hand-cranked propeller shaft, turned by its seven-man crew. It was submerged by admitting water to its two ballast tanks.

Hunley was ready for trials in July 1863 and sank a coal barge in Mobile harbour. It was then sent by rail to Charleston, South Carolina, where it twice sank while undergoing trials in the harbour, drowning five of its crew in the first instance and the whole crew in the second, including its inventor. In each case it was raised and volunteers found to continue work. On the night of February 17, 1864, it attacked the twelve-gun USS *Housatonic*, five miles off Charleston, and sank her, by a spar torpedo rammed into her hull. The *Hunley*, perhaps herself damaged in the attack, sank afterwards, again drowning her crew. The wreck of the *Hunley* was discovered by divers in 1979 and raised on August 8, 2000. Postmortem examination of the crew's remains later revealed that four of the eight were American-born, four of European origin. They were buried, with military honours, in the Magnolia Cemetery, Charleston, on April 17, 2004, in the presence of a crowd of 35,000 to 50,000, in what was described as "the last Confederate Funeral." *Hunley* was to be remembered as the first submarine to commit an act of war in naval history. The Confederate navy was an insignificant strategic asset but one of the most innovative ever to have been organised.

Americans were the pioneers of submarine warfare, having constructed and operated an experimental submarine during the War of Independence. It was an understandable initiative by a people who were in rebellion against the world's foremost naval power and were unable to challenge the vast British surface fleet. It was also understandable that the Confederacy, lacking any hope of confronting the Union navy on equal terms, should have resumed the submarine experiment.

CHAPTER SEVENTEEN

Black Soldiers

INCOLN'S ambiguous declaration that the Civil War was "in some way about slavery" concealed a great deal more than it revealed. The most passionate anti-secessionists in the North were abolitionists; by no means all Northerners, however, were abolitionists, and few were emancipationist. Many regarded slavery, as long as it was confined to the Southern states, as an efficient and convenient means of controlling an alien population. The free blacks of the Northern states were not a welcome element. Some states indeed had enacted anti-black electoral laws, and a social prejudice against blacks was common and widespread, particularly among the poor, who competed with blacks for employment at the bottom of the economic heap. Segregation, in education and church membership, was the rule rather than the exception; few blacks enjoyed the right to vote, and extension of the franchise was not a cause espoused by many abolitionists; even equality before the law and free access to the courts was a step too far for many whites. Yet it was obvious to many in the North that abolition of slavery logically entailed emancipation. What to do with several million emancipated slaves was a problem to which few had an answer or seemed to want to find one. There was a widespread belief that liberated blacks would prefer to remain in the South, because of their familiarity with its environment and particularly its climate. Those not persuaded by such wishful thinking, though not only they, supported the idea of colonisation, that liberated blacks might be persuaded, or if not then coerced, to migrate to Central America and the Caribbean or to return to West Africa, where the territory of Liberia had been set up for the settlement of American freedmen and the British colony of Sierra Leone for British ex-slaves. As Frederick Douglass, the leading black spokesman for the cause of emancipation, harshly pointed out, however, there was little point in abolition if its end result was deportation of its beneficiaries.

Yet there was a practical solution to the problem, which recommended itself for other than social reasons in wartime conditions. And that was to enlist free blacks, including Southern runaways—or contrabands, as they were known—into the army, to fight the Confederacy at the front. Once the idea of black enlistment became current, the advantages seemed obvious. Enlisting blacks would not only add to the North's operational numbers but also deprive the South of their labour. At the same time it would enhance the North's reputation abroad, particularly in Britain, the country the North most wished to influence and one where opinion was most sensitive to the idea of emancipation. Britain had led the way in the suppression of the international slave trade, through the work of the Royal Navy's anti-slavery patrols, and Victorian Britons cherished their anti-slavery credentials. The South's persistence in the slave system was the principal obstacle to its diplomatic recognition by London in 1861–63. Thus there were both practical and political arguments for emancipation from the middle of the Civil War onwards.

There remained, nevertheless, strong objections to it. Beside racial prejudice, which in various degrees of intensity and for different motivations was almost universal in the North, there were also practical considerations. What was to be done with four million ex-slaves if they were to leave the plantations? How would they be employed, accommodated, and provided for? Enlistment would mop up a considerable number—eventually between 180,000 and 200,000 blacks served in the Union armies, two-thirds of them ex-slaves—in circumstances that promised control of their behaviour and freedom of movement. There were, however, all sorts of difficulties over their admission to the ranks. Frederick Douglass might argue that black freedom, unless fought for, was not worth having. Many white soldiers held that they were fighting a white man's war and that the enlistment of blacks would compromise the terms of the struggle. In the last resort, however, the difficulty came down simply to widespread Northern disbelief in the black soldier's combat value. Would the blacks fight? Or would they run away and leave the white soldiers in the lurch? Today, when black soldiers have won a sterling reputation as battlers in the modern republic's most bitterly contested wars, such a question seems not worth pondering. Indeed, the American black community's loss of enthusiasm for enlistment during the Iraq conflict sent waves of alarm through the

Defense Department, so heavily had the U.S. Army and Marine Corps come to depend on black recruitment to the combat formations, particularly the infantry, to guarantee essential numbers. In the mid–nineteenth century, however, Africans had not yet won the formidable military reputation they have subsequently attained. The Zulu kingdom was still scarcely known outside southern Africa. The French army, though it recruited from the same regions as the slave contingents had been drawn, did not use its black regiments outside West Africa. The British West India Regiment, though its membership was ethnically identical to the slave population of the South, was employed only as a colonial police force. So it was understandable that the white American should ask about black recruits, "Will they fight?," since few had done so in American experience. Black participants, on both sides, in the Revolutionary War, or the War of Independence as the English call it, had figured as individuals, not as members of formed black units. There were no black units in the antebellum army, while public policy in the antebellum South was to ensure that its black inhabitants were kept in a state of abject passivity.

Yet the first stirrings of black martiality during the Civil War took place paradoxically in the Southern states, not the North. The free blacks of Louisiana, the only part of the South to contain anything like an emancipated black community, formed and volunteered a militia unit, the Regiment of Free Men of Color, as early as May 1861. Its members wished to demonstrate their civic responsibility, but though the state governor appointed a colonel to command it, it provided its own weapons and uniforms and it was employed only on local guard duty. The Confederate government awarded it no recognition whatsoever. Also in May 1861 there occurred an event which would lead to a general enlistment of black soldiers. Three escaped slaves presented themselves at Fortress Monroe, announcing that they had been forced by their master to dig a Confederate battery. Shortly afterwards a Confederate officer appeared demanding that the runaways be returned, as was required under federal legislation. The fortress commander, Benjamin Franklin Butler, refused, giving as his reason the use to which the slaves' labour had been put, which made them, he said, legitimate contraband of war, and so legitimately to be confiscated. From this case derived the use of the term "contraband," which was henceforth to justify the taking into service of all runaways from the South. Soon the number of contrabands began to rise rapidly, as they defected to the Union enclaves established along the Atlantic coast as a result of the North's amphibious campaign to impose blockade. Several appeared near Charleston, South Carolina, while the black population of the Sea Islands consigned itself entirely to the Northern invaders. At first the contrabands were employed only as military labourers. Bit by bit, however, and with decreasing controversy as white losses in battle rose, military functions were extended to the blacks. After the promulgation of the Emancipation Act in September 1862, black enlistment was legally authorised and black regiments began to be formed, starting in Louisiana, where, after its capture by the Union army, the personnel of the free black militia regiments of 1861 approached the occupiers and asked to be mustered as Federal soldiers. On September 27, 1862, the 1st Louisiana Native Guard was formally admitted into the United States Army. It was shortly to be followed by many more; eventually 166 black regiments were formed, at first designated as "Colored" or "African Descent" as an appendage to the regimental title. Ultimately all became U.S. Colored Troops. The U.S. Army, though nearly 10 percent black by 1865, remained effectively segregated. There were less than a hundred black officers in the 166 black regiments and none of higher rank than captain; black soldiers were paid less than white.

At the very end of the war, as the clouds of defeat began to gather over the Confederacy, there arose a mood even there to make good its growing shortage of manpower by enlisting slaves. The proposal to arm and train slaves as soldiers, advanced by General Patrick Cleburne of the Army of Tennessee in January 1864, found favour with many of his senior subordinates, who accepted his argument that black enlistments would greatly expand the South's fighting strength. Others, however, violently disagreed. Cleburne's proposal simply caused division and ill feeling until Jefferson Davis forbade its being further discussed or even mentioned. By November 1864, however, Davis called on the Confederate Congress for permission to purchase slaves to be used as military cooks and transport drivers and went on to say, "Until our white population shall prove insufficient for the armies we require and can afford to keep in the field, to employ as a soldier the Negro would scarcely be deemed wise or advantageous. But should the alternative ever be presented of the subjugation or the employment of the slave as a soldier, there seems no means to doubt what would then be our decision." Congress, however, drew back at this point, with the former presidential candidate Howell Cobb stating, "You cannot make soldiers of slaves or slaves of soldiers. The day you make soldiers of them is the beginning of the end of the revolution. If slaves will make good soldiers our whole theory of slavery is wrong."[1] But policy in the North, where ex-slaves in tens of thousands had been enlisted since the Emancipation Proclamation of January 1863, proved that blacks made brave and efficient soldiers, which proved that the whole point of slavery was indeed wrong, for many other reasons as well. In February 1865 General Robert E. Lee had brought the weight of his enormous prestige to bear upon the matter, in a letter to a Confederate congressman in which he concluded that if the enlistment of blacks was the only means to avert defeat, then blacks must be accepted as soldiers. By March 1865, the Confederate Congress officially called on slave owners to make up to a quarter of the slaves in any one state available for military service. Eventually only two companies of black soldiers were enrolled, and they had taken no part in fighting before the Union army arrived in Richmond to impose surrender. Ironically many of the Union soldiers involved were black. Twenty-three soldiers of U.S. Colored Troops won the Congressional Medal of Honor before Appomattox. Thereafter the U.S. Army reverted to unequal treatment of its black soldiers, a policy not to be reversed until the presidency of Harry Truman after the Second World War.

By the end of the Civil War, the question of whether black soldiers could fight had been answered on several battlefields. They gave their first display of combat readiness at Port Hudson, near Vicksburg, on the morning of May 27, 1863. The black troops engaged belonged to the formerly Confederate Native Guard of Louisiana, now incorporated into Banks's U.S. Army of Occupation. The object of the operation was to break through to the town which obstructed Union use of the waterway. The approach to Port Hudson was defended by earthworks on a steep bluff behind the Little Sandy Creek, held by the 39th Mississippi Infantry Regiment and the 9th Louisiana Partisan Rangers, supported by six guns. They were outnumbered by the Native Guard, but the strength of the position and their supporting artillery made good the disparity. Most of the black soldiers, moreover, had only just been issued rifles and were inexperienced in their use. They nevertheless mounted three charges on the Confederate lines and suffered casualties of 37 killed and 155 wounded before the fall of darkness brought the battle to an end. The news of the Port Hudson fighting was widely reported in the North and cited as concluding the issue of whether black soldiers would fight. The *New York Times* wrote, "It is no longer possible to doubt the bravery and steadfastness of the coloured race when properly led." That was premature. Port Hudson was too small a battle to provide evidence for large judgements.

Shortly afterwards, however, and nearby, at Milliken's Bend, another battle occurred which gave a better verdict. Milliken's Bend, opposite Vicksburg, was one of Grant's supply points for his siege of the city before its fall. It was garrisoned by three black regiments raised by an enthusiast for black enlistment, General Lorenzo Thomas; the 9th and 11th Louisiana Infantry (African Descent) and the 1st Mississippi (African Descent). The local Confederates had decided to mount an attack on Milliken's Bend with General Henry McCulloch's brigade of three Texas regiments. Attacking on June 7, 1863, they advanced confidently to the assault and drove the Union troops back to their line of earthworks above the river's edge. The Texans, however, had paused to loot the Union encampment and were disorganised as a result. As they reached the river they came under fire from Union artillery and gunboats, the *Choctaw* and the *Lexington*, which drove them back. McCulloch was reinforced but agreed with the Union commander that it was futile to persist. Both Confederate forces withdrew. They had lost 44 killed, Union losses were 98 killed and 233 wounded. Charles A. Dana, the assistant secretary of war, who had been sent from Washington to observe Grant's operations, wrote that "sentiment in regard to the employment of negro troops has been revolutionized by the bravery of the blacks in the recent battle of Milliken's Bend. Prominent officers, who would in private sneer at the idea, are now heartily in favour of it."[2] A Confederate lady, Kate Stone, wrote in her journal that "it is hard to believe that Southern soldiers—and Texans at that— have been whipped by a mongrel crew of white and black Yankees. There must be some mistake."[3] There had been white soldiers at Milliken's Bend, a small detachment of the 23rd Iowa, but the overwhelming majority of the Union force had been black. No mistake about that.

Milliken's Bend preceded a whole series of operations by black soldiers against Confederate positions in the lower and seaboard South. One of the first was at Fort Wagner, at the mouth of Charleston harbour, on July 18, 1863. It was very strongly defended by four battalions of South Carolina infantry and copious artillery. The attacking force consisted of four battalions of white troops and one black, the 54th Massachusetts (Colored). The 54th had been raised by the fervently abolitionist governor of Massachusetts, John A. Andrews, in March 1863, immediately after the proclamation of emancipation. Because of the small size of the Massachusetts black population, he had to cast his net wide and many recruits came from elsewhere in New England, some, including the sons of Frederick Douglass, from New York. In the spring of 1863 it was deployed in small operations along the coast of South Carolina but in July was brought by ship to attack Morris Island, on which Fort Wagner stood. The purpose of its arrival was to take the fort and the island.

The attack began on the evening of July 18 after preparatory bombardment. The 54th advanced along the foreshore, at times having to wade in the shallows. Until the outworks of the fort were reached, the Confederates held their fire; then, as the black soldiers began their charge, they opened a violent bombardment and volleying which inflicted large casualties. The 54th nevertheless re-formed the gaps in its lines and pressed onward. The leading troops crossed the ditch, scaled the earthworks slope, and reached its crest. Some proceeded to enter the fort, but casualties were very heavy. Among those killed was Robert Gould Shaw, the 54th's abolitionist colonel. Fighting within the fort became hand-to-hand, and was quickly disfigured by Confederate atrocities, as enraged Confederates killed and wounded the black soldiers trying to surround them. Eventually there was a Union withdrawal, but not before Sergeant William H. Carney had so distinguished himself that he was later awarded the Medal of Honor, the first to be given to a black soldier. Many of the wounded were evacuated or managed to make their own way back to Union lines. Among those who had fallen in the shallow water, some were drowned as the tide rose. In the aftermath of the battle the Union began to sap towards Fort Wagner, digging further trenches until, in early September, the place was no longer defensible. On September 7, it and Morris Island were abandoned by the Confederates, the prelude to the eventual fall of Charleston itself. Ralph Waldo Emerson composed a threnody to the death of young Colonel Shaw, who became celebrated throughout the North, as did the 54th Massachusetts, which had lost 272 men killed, captured, or wounded.

In the aftermath of the attempt to capture Charleston, which would drag out into a long siege, only to be resolved by Sherman's invasion of the Carolinas in 1864, the Union decided on an invasion of the state of Florida. Very much a backwater of the Confederacy, with neither strong secessionist credentials nor a large contribution to the South's fighting forces, Florida had been isolated from the rest of the South by Union amphibious operations that had captured the naval bases of Fort Pickens, Key West, and Fernandina. The secretary of the Treasury, Salmon Chase, had fixed upon Florida as a means to further his ambition of running for the presidency in 1864. He believed that the state might be brought back within the Union if its Confederate defenders could be overcome and the population offered the chance to take the oath of allegiance, as Lincoln had proposed in the Proclamation of Amnesty and Reconstruction of December 1863, and Chase had adherents in Florida. He also saw an existing force available in the troops of the Charleston expedition. Their commander, General Quincy Gillmore, chief of the Department of the South, had achieved fame and advancement by his successful bombardment of Fort Pulaski in April 1862. Gillmore believed that he could enlarge the size of his forces by enlisting black soldiers from the slave population of Florida and thereby escape from the backwater in which the failure of the attack on Charleston had kept him. He persuaded Halleck to let him make the attempt. He received orders to take the 54th Massachusetts from Charleston and was given a number of both white and black regiments from further afield to mount the expedition. They included a number of units trained at Camp William Penn, Pennsylvania, specially established to enlist and train black soldiers. The 8th U.S. Colored Troops and the 1st North Carolina Colored Volunteers, together with the 54th Massachusetts, were sailed to Jacksonville, Florida, arriving on February 7, 1864. There, with a brigade of white New York troops, they formed for Gillmore a small army, which he led from Jacksonville towards Olustee on the headwaters of the St. Mary's River, which forms part of the boundary between Georgia and Florida. This army reached Olustee on February 20, 1864, and were confronted by Confederate earthworks dug into thick woods and held by 5,000 Georgia and Florida troops commanded by General Joseph Finegan, under the overall command of Beauregard.

Gillmore's cavalry ran into the Confederate outposts on the morning of February 20 and a confused battle broke out. The Confederate men were supplied with artillery which inflicted heavy casualties, but the Union mounted several charges. The line of battle swayed back and forth in the dense woodland. The 54th Massachusetts made a counter-attack, but by six o'clock in the evening the Union was in full retreat to Jacksonville, pursued by Confederate cavalry. One rebel soldier, meeting an officer, asked what was happening: "Shooting niggers" was the all-too-truthful answer. Dozens of black Union troops, wounded and unwounded, were shot or bludgeoned to death as darkness fell over the battlefield. The medical officer of the 8th U.S. Colored Troops saved many by filling ambulances with black soldiers in preference to white since, he said, he knew that white soldiers taken prisoner would survive but he feared that black soldiers would not. In all, 1,861 Union soldiers were killed and wounded at Olustee as against 950 Confederates. Olustee was an undoubted Union defeat, which brought to an end the overly optimistic attempt to take Florida back into the Union.

While the Florida campaign petered out, that in the Tennessee-Mississippi borderland flickered up. There were no large concentrations of troops in the area, only a scattering of Union posts and the standing cavalry force of Nathan Bedford Forrest, against whom the Union had never prevailed. Sherman had appealed to his troops to bring Forrest to surrender as a means of restoring order in the region. Forrest was not prepared to be tied down, and he decided to carry operations against Sherman's isolated outposts. The first on which he fixed in April 1864 was Fort Pillow, fifty miles above Memphis on the Mississippi. Sherman had ordered its abandonment, but the local Union commander, General Stephen Hurlbut, decided on his own authority to reoccupy it. Its garrison in April 1864 consisted of two regiments of coloured artillery and one of white infantry. Though entrenched, they were too few in number to defend the position. The cavalry that formed part of the garrison disliked the blacks: they were Tennesseans, and some were ex-Confederates who had changed sides. When Forrest, who had promised to "attend to Fort Pillow," turned up on April 12, his men swiftly overcame the resistance and then began imposing surrender, which had been his object from the outset. Surrendering both blacks, and whites, were shot down as they stood or knelt. The wounded were done to death. Confederate apologists later insisted that Forrest rode about trying to get his men under control. If so, it was with little effect. Sixty percent of the garrison, both white and black, were killed. Before his attack, Forrest had asked the Union commander to surrender but been refused. Two hundred and thirty-six of the garrison survived to be taken prisoner but of those only fifty-eight were black. The news of Fort Pillow sped rapidly and aroused anger in the North, though not in the South. Negro soldiers seem to have learnt that they risked all in going into battle against Confederates but decided to sell their lives all the more dearly. They continued to fight bravely when put to the test.

The Fort Pillow massacre encouraged Union efforts to hunt Forrest down, and in April 1864 General Samuel Sturgis arrived in Memphis with orders to pursue him. Many of Sturgis's soldiers were black, belonging to the 55th and 56th U.S. Colored Troops and the 2nd U.S. Colored Light Artillery of nine batteries. Sturgis led his force out southward towards Tupelo, Mississippi, with the object of destroying railroads supplying Forrest and so provoking an encounter. Forrest had two cavalry brigades and some artillery and so was outnumbered by Sturgis but nevertheless advanced to attack. The two forces encountered each other on June 10 at Brice's Crossroads, north of Tupelo. The developing battle went badly for the Union from the start, since Forrest's men found an unmarked road which led into Sturgis's rear. His supply train then got entangled with his fighting troops and in the confusion the Union column was forced into retreat. The retreat continued for several days, with Forrest in pursuit, until the Union troops eventually found refuge at Guntown, Tennessee. The battle of Brice's Crossroads greatly enhanced Forrest's reputation. It did not, however, tell against the military reputation of black soldiers, since it was rightly regarded as a failure of generalship by Sturgis, who was removed from command and not re-employed.

Black soldiers were also engaged in the unfortunate expedition to the Red River in Arkansas in 1864. Their most important field of engagement as the war drew to a close was in Virginia, to which large numbers were sent during the siege of Petersburg. Together they formed the Ninth Corps, almost completely composed of black soldiers, its original units having been broken up to provide garrisons for the West. The Ninth Corps, whose regiments had been raised and trained in Maryland, was sent to join the Army of the Potomac in early March 1864. It was the first black unit to march through Washington. On its way, one of its white officers recorded that, as it passed through Pittsburgh, Pennsylvania, "we was stoned by the low people." In Washington the regiment was reviewed by President Lincoln. The corps had been started forward into Virginia and was caught up in the fringe of the fighting at Spotsylvania but did not take part. A Massachusetts officer who witnessed the turmoil voiced what was still the all-too-common white opinion of black soldiers: "As I looked at them my soul was troubled and I would gladly have seen them marched back to Washington. . . . We do not trust them in the line of battle. Ah, you may make speeches at home, but here, where it is life or death, we dare not risk it."[4] In the fighting around Spotsylvania, the Ninth Corps protected the rear of Grant's army and skirmished against Confederate cavalry. Some black soldiers were taken prisoner. Unfortunately, the soldiers of the Army of Northern Virginia showed themselves as ready to kill captured blacks as their Deep Southern comrades.

As Grant prosecuted the Overland Campaign, the Ninth Corps took part in the effort to capture Richmond by direct assault. The effort was launched from the Bermuda Hundred, an enclave in a loop of the James River. It culminated in July 1864 in the most celebrated of all actions by black troops during the war, the assault on the Crater, which became notorious because of the mismanagement of the operation by Grant's commanders. Having undermined the Confederate earthworks defending Elliot's salient and exploded a gunpowder charge, the Ninth Corps then charged what remained of the Confederate position in an effort to break through. The Union orders given were lamentably confused. A black division was first selected to lead, but the commanders had second thoughts and a white division was substituted. It had not prepared or rehearsed, and when it got into the crater the explosion had created, it quickly fell into confusion. When the superseded black division then attempted to retrieve the situation, it fell victim to a strong Confederate counter-attack. The Confederates slaughtered the Union troops caught on the floor of the crater and killed prisoners wholesale. The survivors of the assault fled in terror to Union lines, but at least a thousand were trapped inside the crater and shot dead or bayoneted while trying to surrender. At the end of the day, it was found that 3,500 of the 15,000 Ninth Corps soldiers were dead. Seven black soldiers received the Medal of Honor for bravery shown at the Crater, out of 24,000 engaged altogether. In the aftermath, General Burnside was relieved of command. Grant's review on the operation was as judicious as could be: "General Burnside," he wrote, "wanted to put his colored division in front, and I believe if he had done so it would have been a success. Still I agreed with General Meade as to his objections to that plan. General Meade said that if we put the colored troops in front and it should prove a failure, it would then be said and very properly, that we were shoving these people ahead to get killed because we did not care anything about them."[5]

After the disaster of the Crater, black troops continued to take part in the siege of Petersburg and in other operations in northern Virginia and the Carolinas, including the assaults on Fort Fisher. They were principally involved, however, in operations along the Atlantic and Gulf coasts, where they had the satisfaction of taking part in the capture and occupation of Charleston in February 1865. Soon after, they joined other Union troops in taking possession of Petersburg. The pinnacle of their culminating operations, however, was to be their inclusion in the march into Richmond in April 1865. At first light on April 3, the Twenty-fifth Corps, now an all-black formation, left its lines and began to march on the city. The approaches were not defended, the Confederate troops having left under Lee's orders to retreat towards Appomattox. The 9th Regiment, U.S. Colored Troops (USCT), was the leading regiment and marched down the streets leading to the Confederate capital, singing "John Brown's Body." The route was lined by black residents of Richmond, cheering frantically to welcome their liberators, who were followed by more black and white soldiers, all with the certainty that the end of the war was at hand.

As peace returned, black soldiers were largely chosen to garrison the Southlands. A hundred black regiments were distributed across the former Confederate states. On May 13, 1865, the 62nd USCT took part in the last engagement of the war at Palmito Ranch, on the Rio Grande in Texas. In all 178,975 of the Union army in the Civil War were black, of whom 2,870 died in combat. When the peacetime army was reconstituted, two new infantry and two cavalry regiments were enlisted from blacks.

The war experience of black soldiers had been varied but difficult. Disfavoured, sometimes openly despised by their white comrades and commanders, they had from the outset fought on probation. They were not expected to perform well in combat, and they had been excluded from all of the war's great battles, most of which were over in any case before black troops were enlisted in large numbers, from 1863 onwards. The main feature of the war experience for black troops, however, was the reaction of white Confederates on meeting them in combat. There was undoubted Negrophobia in the mentality of many Northern soldiers, which weakened as the war progressed and the reputation of black soldiers improved. White Southerners simply hated black soldiers and were outraged at meeting their ex-slaves or supposed ex-slaves on the battlefield. They were commonly killed if taken prisoner. The survivors, if wounded, were taken out of hospitals to be shot or bayoneted. The danger of atrocity at the hands of the enemy might be supposed to have motivated black soldiers all the harder to avoid capture, but the reality seems to have been that the blacks were often terrified into passivity when confronted by the most black-hating Southerners, such as Texans and Mississippians. Fort Pillow was the worst of the Southern excesses but by no means an isolated one. Virginians proved as Negrophobic as their comrades from the Deep South.

By 1865 nearly one-tenth of the Union army was black. Psychologically the commitment of black soldiers enormously enhanced the Northern war effort. Yet despite their large numbers, black soldiers made disappointingly little material contribution. Faced by the ferocity of their Southern antagonists on the battlefield, they simply could not stand up to combat as white soldiers did. Forrest, their grimmest persecutor, was simply stating reality when he said that blacks could not cope with white Southerners, who, in the last resort, were fighting to preserve slavery as the mastery of the white over the black.

CHAPTER EIGHTEEN

The Home Fronts

THE NORTH, unlike the South, was an established and functioning state in April 1861, one on whose structures, resources, and machinery of government the war would exert unprecedented demands but which would continue to function, much as it had done in times of peace. The South, by contrast, did not exist as a state until the coming of the war. Almost everything necessary to wage that war had to be brought into being, if not actually invented, even while the first shots were being fired. The task would have proved impossible had not the existence of the United States and the political and legal habits of eighty years of independence provided a model which the secessionists could use to design their new polity. Thus the Confederacy, at the first meeting of the seceding states' representatives, held in Montgomery, Alabama, on February 4, 1861, adopted as a provisional constitution that of the Founding Fathers of 1787 almost in its entirety. The only changes were those that strengthened states' rights and reduced the power of central government and those making explicit the rights of slave owners and the legality of slavery. The provisional Confederate Congress remained at Montgomery until May 1861, when it transferred to Richmond. It was not an elected body, its members having been delegated by their states. There would be no elections until the autumn of 1861, though thereafter, despite low voter turnouts, it did assume a democratic character. A practical difficulty in investing the Southern Congress with a properly democratic nature was the absence of formal political parties in the South; there were at best remnants of the old Whig and Democratic parties, and these former party labels served to identify candidates. By 1861 former party affiliation had lost significance in the South, when adherence to secession overrode all other positions. Since the South insisted on the primacy of states' rights, it is not surprising that Congress and president were to experience a great deal of frustration at the hands of the eleven state legislatures, which remained energetic throughout the war. The states raised troops, produced military supplies, and furnished provender, often as they saw fit, rather than as the Richmond government required.

Jefferson Davis was a man of considerable talents who commanded, at the outset, general respect. Of all those available in the South to hold the office of president, he was probably as good as any other, but he was not of the first class as a politician. His vice president, Alexander Stephens, was a man of great ability, but he was a fanatic champion of states' rights, and devoted most of his efforts to supporting his state of Georgia against the central government throughout the war. Davis was also hampered by a dearth of good cabinet officers. The War Department frequently changed hands and never found a truly satisfactory head. The Treasury, of such key significance, was held by only two men, neither up to the extraordinary difficulties of making Confederate financial policy work. The best cabinet officer, Stephen Mallory, served as secretary of the navy, with great competence, but despite Confederate successes at sea, that theatre of war offered too little scope for his talents to achieve what they might have done in another department.

Manpower, munitions, and money are the lifeblood of war. Manpower was not a major Confederate problem until the last year of fighting. Volunteers and then conscription filled the ranks adequately until the onset of despair began to fuel desertion and absenteeism during 1864. Munitions supply was a Confederate success. Purchase abroad brought in great quantities of weapons in 1861–62, and thereafter improvised manufacture kept up the necessary flow. The Tredegar Iron Works at Richmond was a major industrial facility even by comparison with equivalents in the North. Tredegar produced 1,100 pieces of artillery during the war, vast quantities of ammunition, and the armour plate to protect the Confederate ironclads. Curiously, it did not produce any railroad track or locomotives, two items of supply of which the Confederacy was in desperate need throughout the war. Important manufacturers were established at Selma, Alabama, and a great powder mill at Augusta, Georgia. There were others at Macon and Fayetteville. Exploration concluded that there were more essential raw materials to be exploited in the South than had been recognised before the war.

Money, as many war-making states have discovered to their ultimate cost, is all too easy to improvise. America before 1861 worked on coin, minted in gold or silver. There was no official paper money. Indeed, Americans had a long and deeply held suspicion of paper money, and of bank investments and indeed of banks in general. At the start of the war there was only something between $25 million and $30 million in gold held in the South, by private citizens, banks, and financial houses, far too little to support the costs of the war. How were government purchases, expeditions, and soldiers' wages to be paid? Secretary of the Treasury Christopher Memminger was an intelligent man with orthodox financial views. The government, he decided, would have to subsist by levying taxes, selling bonds, and issuing paper money, in that sequence. Taxes never worked in the Confederacy. Prewar citizens had been taxed at a very low rate, and only on clearly definable transactions. Customs duties were the most common and acceptable, since imports were not run-of-the-mill commodities for most people. Memminger decided to enlarge the uptake by levying an export tax on cotton, at a time when cotton exporting had almost collapsed. He then tried levying a tax on property at one-half percent of value. The states, however, declared that their records were inadequate to assess such a tax, and most agreed to pay an estimated sum to the government, to be recouped later by applying the tax in the hope that their paperwork would improve. The eventual return was only 1.7 percent of the Confederacy's revenues.

Memminger had better hope for bond issues, in effect a government promise to pay a guaranteed rate of interest against a purchase of paper by a private buyer. Bond issues, if efficiently managed, are an ancient and effective way of raising money, if there is goodwill on both sides. Bonds have a long history, however, of renegotiation, on terms less and less profitable to the lender. So it proved with Confederate bonds. The Confederate Treasury began to accept purchase in the form of mortgages of future cotton crops. Not-yet-existent money was being used to secure a return on non-existent money, the face value of the bond. What began as an issue of $15 million was succeeded by an issue of $50 million and then $100 million. The final stage of the transaction was when planters refused to sell their cotton, hoping for better returns by export into the blockade-running traffic.*

---

* Confederate bonds were issued and sold successfully in Europe, particularly England, but were backed by cotton. When the Union blockade stopped cotton deliveries, the market in bonds collapsed, totally after 1864.

Failure to tax efficiently and the decline of the bond market drove the Confederate Treasury to the last recourse of a poverty-stricken government, the printing of paper money. The practice began even before war broke out, in February 1861. At first the issues were small, $1 million to begin with. By August 1861, however, the Confederacy had put $100 million into circulation and the amount grew. Bewilderingly, the notes were not legal tender, meaning that they need not be accepted as settlement of debt. Accepted the notes were nevertheless, and not only the Treasury's. Private businesses began to issue notes. The truth was that by 1863, if not earlier, paper money, even if without convertible value, had to be used. People spent in the knowledge that currency transactions were a sort of natural confidence trick made necessary by the absence of any other medium of exchange. By the end of 1863 more than $700 million in paper was in circulation, though the paper dollar had fallen in value to four cents in gold.

Depreciation was matched by runaway inflation. Between October 1861 and March 1864 prices rose on average 10 percent each month. By April 1865 average prices were ninety-two times higher than in 1861. In practice such calculations were difficult to make, since there were so many sources of issue, including the states and many towns and cities. Postage stamps were widely used as money. Confederate citizens were all too keenly aware of the level of inflation, since standard items of purchase rose inexorably in price. J. B. Jones, author of the celebrated *Rebel War Clerk's Diary*, noted the increasing cost of staples. By March 1864 he was paying $300 a barrel for flour and $50 a bushel for cornmeal; by October 1864 they had risen to $425 and $72. His income had risen to $600 a month but he felt poor and was oppressed by price rises and shortage of money. Jones, moreover, was middle class. Soldiers were paid $11 a month, skilled workers between $2 and $5 a day.

Inflation was deeply depressing to all within the Confederacy, particularly for parents. Its effect was heightened by the shortage of almost everything. While food remained plentiful in the countryside, difficulties of distribution eventually caused hunger in towns and cities. Almost all other necessities, particularly clothing, became difficult to obtain anywhere. Home weaving revived, as wives and mothers relearnt the skills of their pioneering ancestors to replace worn-out factory-made dresses and suits. Shoes fell to pieces. Luxuries disappeared. Shortage became part of the Southern way of life.

The shortages included shortage of labour. The ranks of the Confederate armies were filled to an overwhelming extent by young men from the countryside, which left farms to be run by older men, slaves, should any be owned, and by women. The place of women in Southern society has been heavily mythologised. There was little that was romantic about it at the time. For every brave beauty who assumed leadership on the plantation while the men were away at the war, there were hundreds of ordinary farmers' wives who simply added ploughing and reaping to the endless list of jobs they had always performed. War may have brought unaccustomed responsibility, but it also brought much extra work which taxed women very hard. Yet Southern women are a distinctive breed even today, admired for their femininity and outward-going personality. Their difference must surely be ascribed to the war, not perhaps so much to the work they were obliged to undertake as to the role they were forced to assume in the lives of their menfolk. To Europeans Southern women seem much more akin to European women than American women generally. The egalitarian qualities of American women are to Europeans one of their most striking characteristics. It is possible to believe that the femininity of Southern women derived from the parts they played as the war turned to failure and eventual defeat, in supporting and eventually comforting their men. Defeat is not part of the American way. American armies have an almost unbroken record of success. American women have traditionally welcomed their men home as victors. The exception is in the South, to which and to whose womenfolk the armies of the Confederacy returned beaten and dejected. Comforting beaten men, restoring their self-esteem, was a major part of the Southern women's work after April 1865. The experience helped to form the distinctive characteristics of Southern womanhood.

The Civil War for women was a significant moment in American history. Women in the 1860s were not recognised for their abilities outside the home, even though they had been working on their farms and in their family stores for generations as their husbands went pioneering out west. The Civil War forced recognition upon women who worked the land and kept their families together whilst their husbands were fighting. Some, like Pauline Cushman, an actress from New Orleans, risked their lives by offering their services as spies.

At least 250 and possibly as many as 1,000 women fought in the war on both sides, either dressing in the uniforms of their dead fathers, brothers, husbands, or sons or merely enlisting in order to fight alongside their menfolk, or to get away from the hard physical labour of farming and to earn more money. They evaded detection because, in most cases, the physical examination was so hastily administered that most women had no problem passing and went on to complete their enlistment; soldiers did not usually undress for bed; baths were few and far between; and the ill-fitting uniforms could disguise the female form. A woman who enlisted in either army masqueraded as a man by cutting her hair short, wearing men's clothing, binding her chest, and taking a man's name, and she tried to conduct herself in a masculine manner so as not to draw attention to herself. Sarah Emma Edmonds, using the alias Franklin Thomas, enlisted in a Michigan volunteer infantry company, successfully evading detection as a woman for a year. She participated in the battles of Blackburn's Ford and First Bull Run, the Peninsula Campaign, Antietam, and Fredericksburg. Sarah Edmonds also served as a spy, disguised as an Irish peddlar or as a black man, and provided valuable information on the enemy to the Union army.

Some women organised charity balls and functions in order to raise funds to supply the troops, and others provided meals for the troops coming through the towns and cities. Many women helped in the hospitals and tended to the wounded and sick soldiers. Clara Barton, a teacher from Massachusetts, established an agency to collect and deliver supplies to Northern troops around Washington. She was given permission, by General William Hammond, to ride in army ambulances to tend the wounded soldiers and was even authorised to travel behind the lines, where she served during some of the most horrifying battles and earned the nickname "the Angel of the Battlefield." In 1864 she agreed to serve as "head nurse" in the Army of the James. In 1865 President Lincoln placed her in charge of the search for the missing men of the Union army and whilst engaged in this work she traced the fate of 30,000 men. When the war ended, she was sent to Andersonville Prison, in Georgia, to set up and mark the graves of Union soldiers. This experience launched her on a nationwide campaign to identify all soldiers missing during the Civil War, and she set up a bureau of records. After the war she continued her humanitarian efforts with the International Red Cross. In 1881 Barton started the American Red Cross and devoted the rest of her life to it.

The other sector of society which was changed by the war was the black community, to which it eventually brought freedom. Many slaves took it for themselves, seizing the chance at the approach of the Union army once the territory of the South began to be penetrated, from 1863 onwards. Many Southerners feared that invasion would lead to black uprisings. In practice it did not. Runaway slaves were anxious above all to attach themselves to the Northern armies with which they sought to earn their keep by labouring or by performing menial tasks. The status of these "contrabands" caused Northern generals a succession of headaches. Some abolitionist generals seized slaves during incursions into the South as a means of impoverishing rebels. This practice was widespread during the fighting for the border states in 1861–62. It was, however, forbidden by the Northern government. The arrival of runaways in Union lines also brought with it the requirement to feed and shelter the incomers. Camps had to be built, and guarded, and army rations diverted to the camp kitchens. After the proclamation of emancipation in January 1863, runaways could be inducted as soldiers. That did not, however, altogether solve the problem, since many of the runaways were too young or too old or too feeble to serve in the ranks and many were women. The unwelcoming reception many received at the hands of Northern soldiers, which often amounted to downright mistreatment, did not deter blacks seeking freedom. They continued to run away at the approach of Northern armies, so that the upper fringe of Southern territory was in places denuded of black inhabitants.

Of all changes brought by war, and defeat, to the South, the end of slavery was the most profound. The South could never return to antebellum days now that the blacks were no longer tied to the soil but free to move as they chose, to pick their employers, and to work as hard or as little as they chose. In practice, of course, most blacks continued to reside in familiar surroundings with familiar white people and remained simple cultivators. Still, all was different. A million blacks had left their homes, to follow the Union armies and eventually to go north. The supervising class of the South had been decimated by the war; a quarter of the white able-bodied men had been killed or died of disease between 1861 and 1865. The South could never be the same again.

Defeat posed what many Southerners conceived of as an insoluble problem. Surrender was too bitter to be accepted at once, or even at all quickly. Southerners railed against the idea that the struggle for secession had all been in vain. A new idea took hold of the Southern imagination, that of the Lost Cause. Southernness was to be preserved by creating a New South, still distinctly different from the industrial, moneymaking North but enabled to survive and even to compete by adopting economically many of the North's strengths, including industrialism and financial independence. The conscious struggle for the New South was to persist for much of what remained of the nineteenth century. It was a hopeless undertaking. Even before the war the Southern economy was too small and too undercapitalised to sustain successful competition with the North; after 1865 the South was too impoverished by the costs of secession and military defeat to challenge its victorious neighbour. Growth was pitifully slow and revival would come only through the migration of Northern capital, a migration based on Northern need to seek opportunity for investments. It would take a century for a truly prosperous New South to arise on the ruins of defeat.

The interior life of the North was far less affected by the war than that of the South. The war brought increased prosperity to the North and much less intrusion into everyday life. Paradoxically, while the South championed the cause of small government, exigency obliged the government in Richmond to interfere at many levels in the social and particularly the economic life of the Southern people. The South really got the worst of two worlds: an attempt to run a command economy of price-fixing, requisition, and direction of labour which was at the same time inefficient. In the North, by contrast, the economy, left to itself by the Federal government, flourished, producing full employment and high wages, while delivering in abundance both the necessities of everyday life and the requirements of a war-fighting state. It did so, moreover, without succumbing to many of the normal faults of war finance, such as inflation, exorbitant taxation, or disabling public debt. The outbreak of war succeeded several years of economic downturn which the crisis threatened to exacerbate. Of particular concern was the cotton famine, which closed many New England textile mills or thrust them into working short time. The crisis was averted in an unexpected way. Poor harvests in Europe created a surge in demand for American grain, which thanks to contemporary improvements in agricultural practice the North was readily able to meet. The European trade also brought large payments in gold into American banks. At the same time, the demand for woollen uniforms to clothe Federal armies created a boom in sheep farming and also took up a lot of slack in the spinning, weaving, and garment-making industries. What had looked in 1861 to be a difficult period in Northern economic life turned by 1862 into a highly prosperous passage.

Building a wartime economy required, of course, the making of financial arrangements to pay for military expenditures. Before the war the government had spent very little. Civil servants were few and there were no large spending programmes. The army was tiny, most of the navy's ships antiquated to the point of obsolescence. Coastal fortification was costly but by 1861 most of the systems were complete. As a result the federal government of antebellum years found itself in the happy and unusual position of having a larger income than it needed. Most of its money came from customs duties. There were very few federal taxes and the government scarcely borrowed. Precisely because it had needed so little money before 1861, the government lacked the machinery and procedures necessary to rapidly enlarge its income when war came. How to do so caused much puzzlement and debate. Salmon P. Chase, the secretary of the Treasury, was a man of energy and ability, but not an experienced financier. He adhered, moreover, to shibboleths of American public finance, disliking debt and holding the banks in suspicion. He set out, therefore, to finance the war at first by taxation, but even when modest increases and new forms of tax were imposed, it was sufficient only to pay for normal expenditure, not for the exceptional costs of paying the soldiers and purchasing war supplies.

By the end of 1861 the Union's financial situation was becoming unsustainable. Chase believed sternly in the circulation of gold to pay for everything. There was, however, only $250 million in bullion in the Northern states, and as Chase postponed settlement of government debts to tide over the developing crisis, gold started to disappear, as it was hoarded by citizens and institutions alike. The immediate solution was to float a public loan, by issuing interest-bearing bonds, sold at below face value so as to offer an attractive rate of interest. The bond issue was an eventual success, but at the outset it did not solve the pressing problem of liquidity. With gold drying up there simply was not sufficient currency in circulation for either private citizens or institutions to meet their obligations. In February 1862, therefore, though only after heated debate, Congress authorised the issue of paper money, which came to be called greenbacks because of its colour. Paper money was regarded with deep suspicion in nineteenth-century America but necessity dictated terms and the first issue was for $150 million in notes, which were to be legal tender. Greenbacks caught on and there were two more issues in 1862–63. By the end of the war the total value in circulation was $431 million.

Against all prediction, paper money had not corrupted the financial system. It had, of course, caused inflation, but on nothing like the scale in the South. Taking the index in 1861 as 100, price increases at the height of inflation in the North in 1864 reached 182. Most working Northerners felt better off. There was a lot of money in circulation, a lot to spend and a reasonably ample supply of goods to purchase. It was, as always in inflationary times, those on fixed incomes who felt the pinch. The average spender managed and prospered. Evidence for the reality of the paper currency boom is supplied by expansion of settlement on new farming land released onto the market from government holdings, and by the continuing tide of immigration from Europe. The Homestead Act of 1862 gave title to farmers who worked a claim of 160 acres for five years. By 1865, 20,000 new farms had come into being. Few of the homesteaders were immigrants, since these lacked the capital to take and cultivate even free land. Immigration rose all the same, despite the danger of being conscripted into the army that immigrants faced on arrival. After a slump at the beginning of the war immigration rose during the conflict, exceeding 100,000 in both 1863 and 1864 and reaching a quarter of a million in 1865.

It was a Confederate allegation that the Federal government succeeded in filling the ranks of the Union army by impressing immigrants. That was certainly not the case. Almost half of the Union's soldiers were farm boys from New England and the Middle West. Moreover, the big cities in which immigrants congregated were hotbeds of hostility to the draft. Hostility did not take the form of rebellion, as it did in the South, where by 1864 large numbers of deserters had taken to the backwoods and organised themselves into armed bands which fought state militias sent to disperse and recapture them. Many Northerners did, however, forcibly oppose the imposition of the draft. In mid July 1863 there was a four-day riot in New York City, which caused 105 deaths, largely at the hands of Union soldiers sent to suppress the disorders, and there was widespread looting and burning.

Yet, remarkably, and despite resistance to or evasion of the draft, the most striking aspect of life on the home front in both North and South was how steadfast the populations remained in their support for the war. The anti-war movement in the North, though it grew in strength during the bad times of 1862 and after the onset of war weariness in 1864, never threatened to undermine Lincoln's authority. The normal processes of politics were maintained throughout the war years, with congressional and local elections held in 1862 and a presidential election in 1864. Though anti-war candidates and parties stood in all of them, and in 1862 made important gains, a serious anti-war movement never gained commanding influence in the North. That was due in large measure to Lincoln's extraordinary political talents, which allowed him to maintain personal control over individuals and factions in Congress, and to appeal directly and persuasively to popular opinion in the country. He took risks, particularly in insisting on the Emancipation Proclamation, but always avoided creating an effective internal opposition to his presidency and war policy.

In the South, though war weariness and loss of hope became almost tangible from 1864 onwards, it never coalesced into a defeatist movement. Jefferson Davis's worst difficulties were with uncooperative state governors, many of whom championed states' rights even as the experience of war demonstrated the growing necessity for centralisation of power. The belief in the fragility of Southern support for secession, which was so widely held in the North in 1861–62, was never substantiated.

CHAPTER NINETEEN

Walt Whitman and Wounds

THE LIKELIHOOD OF death or disfigurement on the battle-field was remote from the minds of the men of 1861 as they marched away. It became an all too urgent reality once the first shots were exchanged. The first battle of Bull Run left a thousand wounded on the field. By 1862 Union regiments were becoming accustomed to casualties of 30 percent in any engagement, of which the majority would survive to enter hospital. As quickly as Civil War soldiers learnt of the probabilities of death and wounding in action, however, they learnt to avoid, as far as possible, treatment by the regimental doctors, who acquired a reputation early on for incompetence and laziness. It was not understated; the staff of the pre-war medical department was ill-trained, rule-bound, and rarely abreast of modern methods. They were also poorly supplied with drugs or equipment. The first hospitals were improvised, often simply a few tents pitched on the outskirts of camp, attended by untrained men who acquired the reputation of shirkers.

Descriptions of the interiors of hospitals are among the most common pieces of reportage in Civil War writing, as are expressions of disgust at what was seen. The Union army had entered the war with entirely inadequate medical resources. The senior medical officer was eighty years old and his knowledge of medical practice of equal antiquity. The U.S. Medical Service possessed only twenty thermometers and lacked almost all other medical equipment. Surgeons were posted to regiments on a scale of one per unit, with an assistant surgeon as the only other trained man. In the field they took charge of the regimental musicians, who acted as litter-bearers. They were quite without medical training and earned a reputation as rough, incompetent, and often uncaring. There were at first no specialised ambulances to transport the wounded, who were jolted over rough ground to hospital on military wagons or requisitioned farm carts. The delay in evacuating the wounded was often extreme. After the second battle of Bull Run, 3,000 wounded still lay where they had fallen three days after the fighting ceased; 600 were found still alive five days after the battle. It was a week before the last survivors were got to hospital in Washington. It was often preferable to remain in a barn or private house, as many did, than to be taken to hospital, which were frequently sinks of infection, dirty, untidy, and overrun with parasites. Most soldiers were infected with lice but, while fit, were able to make some effort to rid themselves of the creepy-crawlies. In hospital they were dependent on others to delouse them, a duty not often undertaken. Many soldiers were brought in with their wounds crawling with maggots, stinking, and all too often gangrenous. Because of the prevalence of gangrene, amputation was the preferred surgical procedure. Many eyewitnesses recorded the sight of piles of severed arms and legs outside, and sometimes inside, hospitals. The frequency of amputation led soldiers to dread being taken to hospital, even though, surprisingly, anaesthesia, with chloroform or ether, was commonly available in Union hospitals. As the war progressed, its use grew rarer in the South, where the blockade cut off the supply of many essential medical stores.

As is commonly said, the Civil War occurred at a point of transition in scientific development, so that the armies had the use of some weapons of the future, such as breech-loading rifles, but, not others, such as machine guns. Military medicine was also very much at a point of transition. Doctors could administer anaesthetics, but they did not yet understand the germ theory of infection and so did not practice antisepsis. Surgeons commonly operated in old clothes stiff with blood or pus, dressing wounds with torn-up rags when bandages were not available, and they did not clean, let alone sterilise, their instruments and did not keep wards or operating theatres free of disease-carrying insects. Blood transfusion was unknown, as was blood-typing, and they would remain so until the end of the First World War. In the circumstances it was remarkable that as many wounded survived as did, given the nature of wounds suffered. The minié ball, fired from the Springfield and Enfield rifles—the main cause of wounds—was a conical lump of lead the size of a man's upper thumb joint and weighing two ounces. It penetrated the human body with ease, producing a comparatively benign injury unless it hit a blood vessel, but it frequently hit bone, which it tended to shatter, often a cause of amputation. Even worse was the wound caused by a fragment of artillery shell, which could remove a foot or hand or smash the ribcage. Worst of all was round shot, which could decapitate. A direct hit from a cannonball almost always meant death. Seneca Thrall, the surgeon of the 13th Iowa Infantry, wrote to his wife, "I have been hard at work today dressing wounds. The unutterable horrors of war most manifest in a hospital, *two weeks* after a battle, is terrible. It required all my will to enable me to properly dress some of the foul, suppurating, erysipelatous fractured limbs." Another letter to a wife, by the surgeon of a Kentucky regiment after the battle of Kennesaw Mountain in 1864, described how the wounded who had been out all day in the hot sun were covered with maggots by the time they were brought in. "You may well suppose that their suffering was immense, such as arms shot off—legs shot off. Eyes shot out—brains shot out. Lungs shot through and in a word *everything* shot to pieces and totally ruined for all after life. The horrors of this war can never be half told. Citizens at home can never know one fourth part of the misery brought about by this terrible rebellion."[1]

During 1862 the North urgently put in hand an effort to improve the quality of medical care offered to the wounded. As with other Civil War developments, the battle of Antietam, with its huge casualty list, was the spur. The decisive step had been the appointment in April 1862 of a new director of medical services, William Hammond. Young, energetic, and well educated, Hammond was supported by a voluntary organisation, the United States Sanitary Commission, which became a power in the land. Under the executive secretaryship of the formidable Frederick Law Olmsted, it coordinated the activities of thousands of civilian volunteers, collected medical supplies of all sorts, recruited several thousand nurses, and provided welfare facilities for soldiers, both sick and healthy, all over the Northern states. The Sanitary, as it was known, also acted as a pressure group, prodding Congress and the Union army into the provision of better care for the sick and wounded. There was similar voluntary effort in the South, where a Richmond lady, Sally Tompkins, set up a hospital on her own account and was commissioned a Confederate captain, so valued were her services by President Davis.

William Hammond was responsible for widespread reform and for choosing able men to fill surgical and medical appointments throughout the Union army, among whom was a contemporary, Dr. Jonathan Letterman, appointed chief of medical services in the Army of the

Potomac. Letterman expanded and reorganised the ambulance corps. The first results were seen after Antietam, when the wounded were moved from the battlefields according to a rational and disciplined schedule. Letterman also introduced carefully designed and prefabricated hospitals, the Letterman hospital, which was to remain in use up to the First World War. Modelled on the wooden "balloon" house then springing up in all American industrial cities, it grouped single-storey wards around a central complex of operating theatres and dressing stations, and was properly ventilated and heated. He also insisted on strict standards of hygiene. An important aide in Letterman's drive to impose correct standards of hygiene and order was Dorothea Dix of the United States Sanitary Commission, who took up work as early as April 1861. The commission was modelled on that of Florence Nightingale, during the Crimean War. Dix had visited the British commission and seen Nightingale's hospitals. Soon she was active in the dozens of hospitals which began to be opened all over Washington, which was close to most of the major battlefields. Some were improvised in the capital's public buildings, such as the Patent Office. Others were accommodated in schools and colleges, including Georgetown University. Wooden hospitals were built wherever space was available, until more than fifty were in operation in the capital. One stood on what is now the site of the Smithsonian Air and Space Museum, another on the south lawn of the White House.

The original hospitals, since Washington had almost none of its own, were groups of tents, as used by regimental medical teams in the field. They were only slowly replaced by more solid constructions. Either too cold or too hot, depending on the season, they were open to the public, which wandered in and out at whim.

An early visitor was the poet Walt Whitman, who came to Washington following the evacuation of his brother George Washington Whitman from the field of Fredericksburg. Whitman was a New Yorker who was trying to set up as a professional writer. He did not serve in the army, though another brother did; he was never present at a battle and visited the armies only twice. Nevertheless, the war was to possess Whitman. After finding his brother, he decided to devote himself to the welfare of the wounded; he took a clerical job in the army paymaster's office and spent the small salary he earned on tobacco and other comforts for the patients, to whom he devoted his time. He wrote copiously during his four years as a self-appointed hospital visitor. By his own reckoning, he attended at the bedsides of 80,000 casualties. He believed that his visits were beneficial and recorded that "the doctors tell me I supply the patients with a medicine which all their drugs and bottles and powders are helpless to yield." That medicine was kindness and cheerful attention, particularly in writing and sending letters to the soldiers' families.

Whitman, who was to become America's leading poet of the nineteenth century, was of humble origins and simple nature. He was temperamentally egalitarian and might, had his bent taken him that way, have become a leader in the socialist movement. He was also deeply humanitarian with a heartfelt belief in the greatness of his country and its people. Besides his openhearted goodness, he also had a deep love for the beauties of the American landscape and skies, about which he wrote memorably in his first and best-known collection of verse, *Leaves of Grass*. The war moved him greatly, at first by its drama and display, then by its tragedy, which he was to express in deeply moving lyrical terms. One of his war poems, published in the collection *Drum-Taps*, is undoubtedly one of the greatest works of literature the war was to inspire and one of the finest war poems ever written. It came from his experiences as an army hospital visitor.

Come Up from the Fields, Father

Come up from the fields, father, here's a letter from our Pete;
And come to the front door, mother—here's a letter from thy dear son.

Lo, 'tis autumn;
Lo, where the trees, deeper green, yellower and redder,
Cool and sweeten Ohio's villages, with leaves fluttering in the moderate
*   wind;*
Where apples ripe in the orchards hang, and grapes on the trellis'd vines;
(Smell you the smell of the grapes on the vines?
Smell you the buckwheat, where the bees were lately buzzing?)

Above all, lo, the sky, so calm, so transparent after the rain, and with
*   wondrous clouds;*
Below, too, all calm, all vital and beautiful—and the farm prospers well.

Down in the fields all prospers well;
But now from the fields come, father—come at the daughter's call;
And come to the entry, mother—to the front door come, right away.

Fast as she can she hurries—something ominous—her steps trembling;
She does not tarry to smoothe her hair, nor adjust her cap.

Open the envelope quickly,
O this is not our son's writing, yet his name is sign'd;
O a strange hand writes for our dear son—O stricken mother's soul!
All swims before her eyes—flashes with black—she catches the main
*   words only;*
Sentences broken—gun-shot wound in the breast, cavalry skirmish,
     taken to hospital,
At present low, but will soon be better.

Ah, now, the single figure to me,
Amid all teeming and wealthy Ohio, with all its cities and farms,
Sickly white in the face, and dull in the head, very faint,
By the jamb of a door leans.

Grieve not so, dear mother, *(the just-grown daughter speaks through*
*   her sobs;*
The little sisters huddle around, speechless and dismay'd;)
See, dearest mother, the letter says Pete will soon be better.

Alas, poor boy, he will never be better, (nor may-be needs to be better,
*   that brave and simple soul;)*
While they stand at home at the door, he is dead already;
The only son is dead.

But the mother needs to be better;
She, with thin form, presently drest in black;
By day her meals untouch'd—then at night fitfully sleeping, often
*   waking,*
In the midnight waking, weeping, longing with one deep longing,
O that she might withdraw unnoticed—silent from life, escape and
*   withdraw,*
To follow, to seek, to be with her dear dead son.

What makes this poem of Whitman's so heartrending is that everything in it is entirely genuine. Whitman knew what happened to boys

shot in the chest; he knew how such news affected families, since he often met them on their visits to the hospitals; he knew what terrible truths the consoling letters sent to families concealed, since he had often written such letters himself. Even though he was not a witness of battle, he knew what results battles caused, since he saw them on the hospital wards. Whitman was a great poet of the Civil War, because he understood the purpose and nature of the war, which was to inflict suffering on the American imagination. The suffering was equally distributed between the two sides, and was felt particularly by those not present. The whole point of the war was to hold mothers, fathers, sisters, and wives in a state of tortured apprehension, waiting for the terrible letter from hospital that spoke of wounds and which all too often presaged the death of a dear son, husband, or father. It was a particular cruelty of the Civil War that because neither side had targets of strategic value to be attacked—not, at least, targets that could be reached by the armies in the field (until Sherman took the war to the Southern people by marching into their homeland)—its effect had to be directed principally, indeed for years exclusively, at the man in the field and at the emotions of those who waited at home. Torturing the apprehensions of the non-combatants was a new development in warfare, produced by the rise of an efficient postal service. Before the days of rapid and reasonably certain postal communication, soldiers could be banished to the mind's recesses after they marched away, because the nearest and dearest knew that they would receive no news of their fate until the war was over, if indeed then. The only certain news of a soldier on campaign came by default, when he did not return. Whitman caught at the truth in an entry in one of his notebooks. "The expression of American personality through this war is not to be looked for in the great campaign and the battle-fights. It is to be looked for . . . in the hospitals, among the wounded."

Whitman's words would have carried an even stronger ring of truth had he written, "The expression of American national emotion." Whitman's keen sense of the national character might have encouraged him to emphasise explicitly the strength and importance of family feeling in nineteenth-century America and the degree to which the brutalities of the Civil War played upon those feelings. He touched on those truths in his great elegy for President Lincoln, which is also an epitaph for the war itself, "When Lilacs Last in the Door-yard Bloom'd":

I saw the debris and debris of all the dead soldiers of the war;
But I saw they were not as was thought;
They themselves were fully at rest—they suffer'd not;
The living remain'd and suffer'd—the mother suffer'd,
And the wife and the child, and the musing comrade suffer'd,
And the armies that remain'd suffer'd.

CHAPTER TWENTY

Civil War Generalship

MERICA WAS AWASH with generals in 1865, or at least with men who held that title. It could not have been otherwise, since the armies of both North and South had swollen to comprise dozens of corps, scores of divisions, and hundreds of brigades, command of any of which carried the title. In 1861, however, there had been almost no generals on either side. The only men holding rank as generals were a few ancients who had risen to their rank during the Mexican War or survived from even earlier conflicts. The most important in the hierarchy was Winfield Scott, general in chief of the republic and holding the rank of lieutenant general, previously only held by George Washington. He was an experienced operational commander. By 1861, however, he was seventy-five years old and too stout and feeble to mount a horse. Though his brain was keen and active, he was unable to take the field or indeed to stray far from the invalid chair in his Washington office. As the victor of the war against Mexico in 1846–48, Scott was an experienced military campaigner who also possessed, for a soldier, a high degree of political understanding, having run as the Whig candidate for the presidency in 1852. His main contributions to the conduct of the war were to counsel and encourage Lincoln, which he did with great sympathy and beneficent effect in the opening months and to frame what would become the North's fundamental strategy, later called the Anaconda Plan. Designed to profit from the geographical advantage the North enjoyed, it envisaged cutting the Confederacy off from contact with the outside world by naval blockade, and bisecting the Confederacy by seizing control of the Mississippi River. Excellent in conception, it suffered from the defect—which was also a defect of Scott's mind—that it fell short of promising to deliver victory. A blockaded and bisected South would be a poor

South but not necessarily one deprived of the power of resistance. Scott could not accept that this constituted a fundamental weakness of his planning, since, like many Northerners, he shrank from the idea of shedding the blood of fellow Americans, nor did he want to inflict disabling damage on the economy or society of the southern states.

At the outset Lincoln shared many of Scott's views, and himself lacked any conception of how to transform his desire to crush rebellion into military reality. His first attempt to frame a scheme of decision was far too moderate to have produced a result. It envisaged holding Fortress Monroe, the great fortified place at the tip of the Virginia Peninsula, organising blockade, and then mounting a seaborne expedition to attack Charleston, South Carolina. What he needed and begged for from Scott were suggestions as to how to proceed. What he wanted were generals who would give him sound advice and then put plans successfully into action. At the outset, however, he had the greatest difficulty in finding any generals who displayed the least competence or resolution. He promoted dozens of men in 1861, though without confidence that any of them were good leaders, and often because their promotion would strengthen his political position. As a result, many of the first to put stars on their uniforms were local political bigwigs, representatives of European immigrant groups, or state officials, including governors. As he shortly discovered, however, none could offer worthwhile advice and some could not be trusted to command the formations to which they had been appointed.

The procedure for appointing generals was strangely unsystematic. Because promotion to general's rank lay in the hands of Congress, those chosen were normally made brigadier or major generals of U.S. volunteers, which were organisations of the states, rather than in the regular army, which was a federal institution. As they took the field and if they proved their worth, they might be given regular rank, which was greatly esteemed. Grant, for example, began his general's career as a brigadier of Illinois volunteers but was then given a commission as major general in the regular army until, in March 1864, he assumed the appointment of general in chief and the rank of lieutenant general.

As the war drew out, it became easier for Lincoln to identify which of his appointments were good ones and which merited further promotion. What Lincoln looked for in his generals was the ability to achieve results without constantly requiring guidance from Washington or reinforcement by additional troops. The war produced far too few such men. Lincoln's first choice, Irvin McDowell, had excellent paper qualifications. He had been to a French military college, had served a year with the French army, until 1870 thought the best in the world, and had served as a staff officer under Scott in Mexico. McDowell, had he been given a properly trained army, might have proved a competent officer. In 1861, however, there were almost no properly trained soldiers or units anywhere in America and those McDowell led to drive the Confederates out of Manassas and away from Washington in July were particularly ill trained. There was nothing wrong with McDowell's plan of action or with his execution of the opening stages of the battle. What went wrong for the Union is that its untrained soldiers panicked, after failing to carry the position held by more determined if not better trained Virginia troops, then initiated a stampede to the rear and abandoned the field to the Confederates.

McDowell, for all his credentials, could not survive such a disgrace and was swiftly removed, to be replaced by George McClellan, who had recently won a few very small battles in the western Virginia mountains. McClellan shared some of McDowell's experience. He had been to Europe to observe the Crimean War and had also served with distinction in the Mexican War. He had more ability than McDowell, particularly in the training of troops, at which he excelled. The Yankee soldiers' first favourite, though he never served in the West, the "Young Napoleon" was an excellent organiser and a master of the details of logistics. His armies were always well-fed and supplied and his soldiers held him in high esteem despite his insistence on strict discipline. McClellan was always popular with the troops. That was partly due to his defects as a commander. Because he did not believe in inflicting heavy costs on the enemy, his soldiers were often not pressed in battle to the point of suffering heavy losses. He also, at first, got on well with Lincoln, who admired his intellect. The era of good feeling did not last. Civilian though he was, Lincoln knew what he wanted from a principal military adviser and McClellan quickly revealed that he was not the man to supply it. Appointed to command the Union troops defending Washington in July 1861, and then promoted general in chief in November, he dissipated his and his subordinates' energies in discussion of projects and in reorganisation during his first nine months of authority. When, in April 1862, he eventually embarked on action, he at once began to exhibit symptoms of caution and defeatism, which proved to be fundamental qualities of his character and which unfitted him for high command of any sort, let alone supreme command. The first stage of his grand strategic idea, the transshipment of the Army of the Potomac by sea and river to the Virginia Peninsula, was inspired and ought to have led on to great results. As soon as his army landed in enemy territory, however, McClellan began to torment himself with fears of being outnumbered. He also failed to do what he could easily have done had he begun forcefully and at once. Confounded by enemy entrenchments across the peninsula, he declined to storm the defences, which were weak and lightly garrisoned. Instead he began to await reinforcements from Washington. When at last the enemy abandoned his positions and began to retreat towards Richmond, McClellan followed lethargically. Though managing to achieve a small victory at Williamsburg, he eventually arrived outside the defences of Richmond in July having scarcely damaged the enemy at all. What followed was even worse than his failure to press his advance up the peninsula. He began to fight, in what would become known as the Seven Days' Battles, but halfheartedly, so that what should have been victories ended as indecisive defeats, disabling to neither side but fatal to McClellan's plan of defeating the Confederacy by capturing its capital. Throughout the Seven Days, he pestered Washington with requests for reinforcements, predicting disaster unless he was given more troops. Eventually, he was ordered by Halleck, his successor as general in chief, to withdraw the army by ship from the peninsula and bring it back to Washington. Once arrived he persisted in his distaste for decision by failing to come to the support of General John Pope, who was thereby exposed to defeat at the second battle of Manassas. In its aftermath Lee resumed his advance northwards until brought to battle at Sharpsburg, or Antietam Creek. Antietam was a battle McClellan should have won, since he outnumbered Lee several times. He frittered away the advantage, however, in piecemeal attacks, and although the result was a sort of Union victory, McClellan's refusal to pursue the badly shaken Confederates resulted in their escape. Antietam was the end of McClellan's military career. In November 1862 he was removed from command.

McClellan's failure in generalship cannot be ascribed to the actions of the enemy but to his own defects of character. His was a curious mixture of high self-regard and disabling anxiety. However many troops he was given he always chose to believe that the enemy had more and was receiving reinforcements which exceeded in number any he was offered. This was a form of moral cowardice. But it was also an effect of his professionalism. His armies were so well organised that he shrank from exposing them to anything that would disorganise their perfect order, as battle was bound to do. Convinced of his personal superiority over all others on the Union side, including the president, he took his failures as proof of their failure to support him. McClellan, a brilliant organiser who retained to a surprising degree the confidence and affection of his men, may be thought the worst general of the war and his reputation has suffered greatly in the war's aftermath, yet his is one of the most interesting psychological cases in military history: a first-class military mind capable of achieving great results at leisure but utterly incapable of overcoming difficulty, even, perhaps particularly, imagined difficulty. Without being wholly incompetent, he threw away any chance he was given, wasted time when circumstances were in his favour, and shrank from delivering decisive blows in battle even when events were running his way. It is fortunate that he was never asked to exercise authority in the West, since he was constitutionally incapable of achieving such victories as those at Forts Henry and Donelson, let alone of recovering from a setback such as the first day at Shiloh.

He is most obviously contrasted with Thomas "Stonewall" Jackson, who possessed the qualities he lacked and though indeed often outnumbered had the gift of compensating for numerical weakness by striking savage and unexpected blows. Jackson's virtues are easy to enumerate. He had an acute topographical sense, enabling him in the complex geography of the Shenandoah Valley to read the lay of the land as if by instinct. He also had an empathetic understanding of how his enemy would react and how his movements would conform to the geographical accidents of the campaign theatre. His philosophy of war was to establish psychological superiority by surprising, mystifying, and misleading his opponent, which he succeeded in doing on occasion after occasion. He succeeded because he was utterly without fear or self-doubt. He was not, however, without faults, notably those of aloofness and secretiveness. He did not explain himself to his subordinates or take them into his confidence, with the result that, when he was not present in person, his plans could miscarry. Generally reckoned the war's supreme practitioner of battlefield command and an undoubted master of manoeuvre in small theatres of action, he was not really a general of the highest gifts. His talents were for operations outside the centre of events. Moreover, he was a bad subordinate, sometimes, as at the opening of the Seven Days' Battles, declining to obey orders or to coordinate his movements with those of his superior. He also preferred improvised arrangements to conformity to a system. Thus, before Chancellorsville, he used a clergyman as his chief of staff, without broadcasting the appointment to his subordinates, an obvious recipe for confusion and misunderstanding. A deeply devout Christian and member of the Presbyterian Church, he was Calvinist in his outlook, both as an individual and as a military commander, since preordination influenced all his judgements. When slightly but painfully wounded at First Manassas, he revealed to a subordinate who was sympathising with him about his injury but also questioning him about the wellsprings of his evident courage that he refused to fuss about the risks he ran in the presence of the enemy because he said the time of his death was fixed by God and that there was therefore no point in feeling fear. He said he felt no more fear on the battlefield than he did settling to sleep in his own bed, and that all men should feel the same, in which case all would be equally courageous. Jackson's supreme lack of anxiety, both under fire and in decision-making, assured him a unique place among Civil War generals, indeed among generals of any army or nationality. He was certainly a very great general, if of a somewhat limited sort.

Of the South's other generals, few deserve great reputation. Beauregard was a reliable commander of the middle rank. Braxton Bragg, despite his notorious bad temper and general unlovability, was at about the same level. Joseph Johnston was the superior of both in intellect but, though he proposed a grand strategy for the South which was conceded by Grant to have offered the chance of prolonging the successful defence of the Confederacy's land area, did not bring and could not have brought the South victory. Johnston advocated fighting defensive battles and surrendering territory if attacked in such force as to threaten heavy casualties. When in command in Georgia in 1864 he practised what he preached. The defect in Johnston's otherwise sensible scheme was that the South had a finite amount of territory to surrender and that, if adopted, the plan would eventually have transferred the territory of the Confederacy to the Union armies without cost. Though not the author of any strategic plan, Bragg must be recognised as a considerable military intellect. Had he possessed a more cooperative character, instead of always getting onto bad terms with subordinates, equals, and superiors, he might have achieved much for the South.

The North never produced an equivalent to Jackson, which was one reason for the psychological dominance he consistently exercised over his opponents. No Union general ever matched him in his ability to inspire his soldiers or win their affection, which allowed him to extract from them feats of endurance unequalled by any other units or formations, North or South. Jackson had little or no strategic vision and poor powers of analysis, but in a small theatre whose geography he understood he was almost invincible. Unlike Sherman, however, he bequeathed no legacy of generalship. His talents were too personal and too momentary in effect to be formalised into an operational system and though he was to be imitated and admired for generations to come, his achievements could not be turned into lessons or methods for would-be imitators.

Jackson was the complement to Robert E. Lee, whom he served with great loyalty, perhaps because he was impressed, as a deeply devout Christian, by Lee's purity of character. Even as war broke out, Lee was regarded in both North and South as the most eminent soldier in the country. This was due in large measure to his character and personality, as a great southern gentleman, as head of one of the First Families of Virginia. Lee was offered command of the Union army but chose instead to lead Virginia's troops. He had been an outstanding cadet at West Point and a successful engineer officer and had served with distinction in Mexico. Curiously, he did not enjoy a successful start in the Civil War. He was nevertheless chosen to replace Joseph E. Johnston, wounded in the Seven Days' Battles as President Jefferson Davis's principal military adviser, and given command of the Army of Northern Virginia, which he held to the war's end, then with the additional title of commander in chief. Lee's great talents were as a tactician rather than as a strategist. His strategic views were rather narrow. He really had only one stroke of strategic inspiration throughout the war, which was to carry the war onto Northern soil in 1863, with the objects of relieving Virginia of the burden of being fought over, profiting from the supplies which were to be captured, and raising Southern spirits and depressing those of the North. Lee's generalship, like Jackson's, was too personal to be formalised as an operational method. Moreover, it was derivative, based on Napoleon's achievements; Lee believed that the pursuit of victory was the true strategy and that victory was best attained by inflicting crushing defeats on the enemy in the style of Austerlitz or Jena, Napoleon's great victories over the Austrians and the Prussians. Those were the victories taught and studied at West Point, and Lee was responsible for achieving at least two in that pattern, Chancellorsville and Second Manassas. Though Lee was a "creative" imitator of Napoleon, he cannot really be credited with any originality. On a battlefield, by contrast, Lee fizzed with ideas which he conceived at high speed and carried out with extreme despatch. That was particularly evident at Chancellorsville, his military masterpiece, where he deliberately broke several fundamental rules of generalship and yet achieved a striking victory.

Lee's greatest gifts of generalship were quick and correct decision-making in the face of the enemy, exploitation of his enemy's mistakes, and economic handling of the force available to him. His defects were excessive sensitivity to the feelings of his subordinates and a failure to insist upon his own judgement, both of which emanated from his breeding as a Virginia gentleman. His defeat at Gettysburg stemmed largely from his failure to give direct orders to Longstreet and to insist on their being carried out. Lee was undoubtedly a very great soldier and a formidable opponent. He was also, however, a great gentleman and an indulgent colleague, qualities which could detract from his powers of will and decision.

Lee's generalship was enhanced by the inferiority of his opponents during the first two years of war. McClellan simply was not his match in mental firmness or power of decision. In Meade, who commanded the Union forces at Gettysburg, he met a man who equalled him in efficiency, if not in imagination or daring, but it was not until Grant came east in 1864 that he was challenged by someone of equal, indeed superior, quality. Grant was the greatest general of the war, one who would have excelled at any time in any army. He understood the war in its entirety and quickly grasped how modern methods of communication, particularly the telegraph and the railroads, had endowed the commander with the power to collect information more quickly and the means to disseminate appropriate orders in response. Once his qualities became apparent, as they had by 1862, he rose very quickly, to the surprise of his West Point contemporaries. Nothing in his earlier life had marked him out as exceptional; indeed the contrary was the case. The son of a moderately prosperous Illinois family, he was nominated to West Point against his will, and while a cadet he followed with hope and interest a congressional debate on closing the academy down. He excelled at his studies, particularly in mathematics, and hoped on graduation to find employment as a professor, but academy routine carried him into the army, in which he served successfully in the war against Mexico, of which he strongly disapproved, believing it to be an aggressive and immoral conflict. After the war he was posted to California, where, separated from his beloved wife, Julia Dent, he took to drink and disputation with his seniors, which led to his resignation from the army. He was unsuccessful in civilian life, failing as a farmer and in commerce and being reduced eventually to working as a clerk in his father's tannery.

Redemption came with the outbreak of the Civil War. Grant's military training and experience proved to be in demand, and enlisted by the governor of Illinois to help organise the state's volunteers, he got command of a regiment, which he commanded successfully in local action. Grant proved an efficient organiser of men, then in an early action a decisive and successful commander with remarkable intellectual powers, including the gift of dictating clear orders without hesitation in a steady stream. He was quickly advanced from colonel's to brigadier's rank and given larger powers in the campaign on the lower Mississippi. His victories at Forts Henry and Donelson brought him to the attention of Lincoln and ensured the acceleration of his career. By 1864, when he had overseen a string of western victories, including Shiloh and the capture of Vicksburg, he was widely recognised as the best Union general, brought to Washington, and appointed general in chief, thus embarking on a new passage, against Lee and the Army of Northern Virginia. Lincoln had decided he was indispensable. To a critic, the president riposted, "I need this man; he fights."

In the West, Grant won success by risk-taking and unceasing aggressiveness, but his soldiers paid the price. Most of Grant's battles were costly in casualties. He retained nevertheless his men's confidence and devotion, and eventually he came to be almost venerated by his soldiers, who would gather in silent groups to watch him walk past. Grant seemed at home in the West. He applied his keen sense of topography to its sinuous rivers and jumbled hills and mountains and never seems to have been confused by their complexity. He certainly did not allow difficulties of terrain to interfere with the supply of his troops, which was never interrupted even during the most difficult passages of his campaigns. In the struggle to capture Chattanooga, the key railroad junction that was vital to the South to maintain communication between the southwestern and northeastern regions of the Confederacy, when for a time the Union army was constricted in its line of supply, Grant succeeded in rapidly opening the "Cracker Line" to furnish his troops with basic necessities and then in restoring supply in amplitude. Grant had a philosophy of war, which was to keep the enemy under relentless pressure at all points and to fight whenever opportunity offered. This style of generalship tried his men very hard. Indeed, without the assurance of frequent reinforcement, Grant would have had to desist from his desire to destroy the Army of Northern Virginia before its destruction was achieved. Grant's reputation was made late.

It was greatly to Grant's advantage that he was served by subordinates of talent, with whom he established cordial personal relations. That was particularly so with Sherman and Sheridan. Sherman was a sort of *alter* Grant, having the same aggressiveness and relentlessness, though he went even further than Grant in his belief in the moral effect of offensive force on the enemy's will to resist. Sherman resembled Grant in his originality; his determination to attack the spirit of the Southern people was an entirely novel approach to war-making and anticipated the technique of psychological warfare as employed by twentieth-century European commanders fighting against national liberation movements in post-1945 colonial campaigns. Sherman came to believe that the South could only be beaten if its people were made to suffer both in body and spirit. By destroying their source of wealth and ruining their means of livelihood, he convinced himself, and eventually his superiors and his own soldiers that the rebels would repent and relapse into inactivity. Sherman applied his philosophy of destruction and spoliation first in Georgia, then in the Carolinas, and it worked as he believed it would. It is not surprising that he has been made the object of study by modern strategic analysts in America and abroad. He also showed something of Grant's gifts of communication, quickness of decision, and ruthless analysis of the military situation. Though not as gifted a writer as Grant, Sherman composed several aphorisms about war which have passed into the anthologies. His most considered statement of his beliefs was "we are not only fighting hostile armies but a hostile people, and must make old and young, rich and poor, feel the hard hand of war, as well as the organised armies."

Sherman and Grant were the two outstanding generals of the war. Sherman's legacy was the more lasting since his style of war-making, brutal and decisive, was highly imitable. As a battlefield commander, however, Grant was the more able, with higher achievements and more decisive victories to his credit.

Sheridan, Grant's cavalry commander in the East during the last year of the war, owed much to Grant's sponsorship and, like him, had an unpromising start. His first appointment was as a quartermaster officer, but he excelled at the unglamorous duties of supply in a war where supply was of paramount importance. He also later demonstrated unequalled powers of leadership, by personal example and vivid inspiration, as during the campaign against Early in the Shenandoah Valley in 1864.

Grant even succeeded in keeping on terms with General Meade, a notoriously cantankerous man with reason for dissatisfaction, after Grant ranked him as general in chief and then established his headquarters with Meade's personal command, the Army of the Potomac. Thereafter Grant was consistently credited with successes that rightly belonged to Meade, causing disgruntlement that the latter regularly communicated to his wife. Meade could not, however, be deprived of the credit for having won Gettysburg, a distinction which perhaps supplied the basis on which they maintained their equable relationship. Meade was not a great general, but he was sound, and efficient.

In panoramic view, it remains remarkable that, out of a body of trained officers not more than 3,000 strong, America should have produced between 1861 and 1865 two unquestionably great soldiers, Grant and Sherman, of whom Sherman was also a visionary. Just below their level it also produced a gifted battle-winner in Lee, who would have shone in any of the contemporary European wars of manoeuvre. Not far below them in workaday talent belonged the resolute George Thomas and such exotics as Nathan Bedford Forrest, the self-taught genius of cavalry raiding, J. E. B. Stuart, Philip Sheridan, and the Cromwellian Stonewall Jackson. The American Civil War continues to provide a wealth of material for the study of generalship of the highest order.

Temperament, a factor in human affairs widely ignored by professional historians, was of the greatest importance in distinguishing the good from the bad, the effective from ineffective, among generals of the Civil War.

It was most notable in the case of McClellan, who provides material almost for a clinical study in the psychology of generalship. He was an extraordinary mixture of timidity and overweening self-importance, always overcome by self-doubt and anxiety in the face of the enemy, combined with tiresome belief in his superiority over all the colleagues with whom he worked during the war, from Lincoln downwards. He was not alone in his capacity for self-doubts. Halleck, too, found his enthusiasm for battle strongly diminished the closer he approached the enemy. Hooker suffered from the same disability. In the opinion of Professor T. Harry Williams, an excellent judge of the Civil War generals' characters, Hooker lacked the ability to make war "on the map." He functioned well only as long as his troops were under his eye. Once they moved beyond his field of vision, he lost the power to visualise their whereabouts. A contrast to Hooker was William Rosecrans, who also failed when action promised. His fault, however, was not timidity, but overexcitement. A great talker, he would work up a head of steam while he outlined his plans; his excitement grew as he listened to himself so that he lost his composure and, with it, his ability to implement his plans. He was successful as a junior commander of small forces, but in a major command he never brought off a great project. John Pope, too, was a great talker, who greatly impressed the world of Washington in 1862. Pope was always promising to fight and looked as if he would, being tall and of impressive appearance. But he too was afflicted by ineffectiveness; a later fault of Pope's was quarrelsomeness. He got on the wrong side of McClellan, his direct superior in Virginia in 1862, and never re-established good relations. Pope was not as quarrelsome as Don Carlos Buell, who differed with any colleague he had and also failed in all his enterprises. Curiously, he was liked by McClellan, perhaps because he never threatened to be a rival in any respect.

The two consistently successful generals of the war, Grant and Sherman, were blessed with equable temperaments. Close friends, they cooperated admirably and avoided quarrelling with others. Grant even kept his temper with McClernand, who, in his egotism, would have tried the patience of a saint. In his frenzy to have the reputation he thought he deserved, he tried to intrigue his way into command on the Mississippi. He magnified every encouragement Lincoln gave him until he eventually overstepped the boundary of military propriety and gave Grant incontestable grounds to remove him for insubordination, thus sparing Lincoln, who valued his political connections in the Midwest, the need to do so.

Lincoln, a totally inexperienced commander in chief, was confronted from the onset of his presidency by a kaleidoscope of temperamental difficulties among his military helpmeets which would have brought down a lesser person. The verdict on the military leadership of the Union during the Civil War is that there was too much personality in play and far too little talent. Only Lincoln showed greatness from beginning to end. It was a war caused by his election and ultimately won by his capacity for compromise, an unexpected strategic skill.

CHAPTER TWENTY-ONE

Civil War Battle

BATTLE WAS THE defining characteristic of the Civil War. Some authorities count as many as 10,000 battles fought between 1861 and 1865. It is easy to reckon up between 200 and 300 named battles familiar to a general reader. Such a number, compressed into four years of warfare, speaks of a quite remarkable intensity, compared, say, to the experience of Wellington's army in Spain and Portugal in 1808–14, when one major battle a year was nearer the norm. Civil War armies appear to have fought all the time, at very short intervals, so that it was not uncommon for individuals to have taken part in dozens of battles. It is the frequency of battle which makes the Civil War distinctive. There was no gradual intensification. Americans fought each other as if imbued with deadly mutual hatred from the outset. First Bull Run was as hard-fought as Second Bull Run a year later, which was as hard-fought as Gettysburg. It is difficult to define why this should have been so. Americans in 1860 did not hate each other as Spanish workers and the Spanish middle class did before 1936. Though identifiable sections existed in the United States before 1860, "sections" referred to geographical areas of the country, of which the cotton-growing South was one and the industrialising North another. But the sections were not homogeneous. There were notable internal divisions. In the South the most important division was that between the large landowning regions and those of subsistence farming, from which the Confederate army was to draw most of its recruits. Particular sections were the Low Country of the Carolinas, where the first large concentrations of black slaves were established and which became in consequence hotbeds of Confederate patriotism, and Tidewater Virginia, homeland of the state's political class. Virginia was socially the most distinct of the colonies and later of the states, because it was deliberately set up in imitation of the English landed counties by its mid-seventeenth-century governor, Sir William Berkeley. Berkeley recruited the younger and therefore landless sons of English landowning families, which bequeathed all to the eldest, with the promise that in the New World they would be able to set up as landed gentlemen themselves. He succeeded perhaps better than he hoped. As early as 1660 every seat on the ruling Council of Virginia was held by members of five interrelated families, and as late as 1775 every council member was descended from one of the 1660 councillors. As Berkeley had endowed many of the settlers he attracted with large grants of land, the families were not only politically powerful but rich. They remained so and their names were to become celebrated in American history, the Madisons, the Washingtons, the Lees. They supplied the young United States with many of its Founding Fathers and the Confederacy also with many of its leaders. The strength and extent of the Virginia oligarchy helps to explain the speed and completeness of the Confederacy's establishment. The old families, who were also large plantation holders and slave owners, felt the most threatened of all Southerners by the rise of anti-slavers to political power in the North and in Washington during the 1850s and, by their legal and social dominance, easily carried the majority of the population with them in 1861.

The speed with which the Confederacy took off and the attraction that the Confederate idea exerted in the border states, which were not cotton-growing or slaveholding, greatly divided opinion in the North. It was also to present the Union with its principal military problem, which was how to achieve victory in the conflict. Many Northerners persuaded themselves that secession, leaving the Union, was repugnant to many Southerners and that if the right overtures were made to the people below the Mason-Dixon line, the errant population could be brought back into the fold without fighting, the prospect of which was abhorrent to many in the North. While it was true that there were important areas in the secessionist states, notably western Virginia and eastern Tennessee, which were at the outset hostile to the Confederacy and remained so, their people lacked the means to alter opinion in the larger South or to influence the rebel government in Richmond. The Confederate leaders were quite as prepared to coerce anti-secessionists as the Union was to suppress rebellion within its own territory. Thus from the beginning it became obvious that the conflict between North and South was destined to be a struggle for minds. Indeed, though the truth was not perceived until much later in the war, and then only by a few professional Northern soldiers of brutal imagination, the Southern mind was the only profitable target in the Confederacy. Just as all the rich material objectives in the North—the Atlantic seaboard cities and the industry of New England—lay at too great a distance from the Confederacy's northern border to be attacked, so the South was not materially vulnerable to the North, though for a different reason. It had no great industries or financial centres against which the Northern armies might have marched. Its only store of wealth, the cotton crop, the North had devalued by imposing blockade. As a result there was nothing for the North to ruin—except the South's stock of fighting men. That fact explains the relentless recurrence of battles between the two armies, and the determination of the war's great generals to fight for victory on the battlefield.

At the beginning of the war, there arose a belief in both armies and both governments that the war could, indeed should, be won by a single great victory. This belief owed its origins to the prevailing power of the Napoleonic legacy. Napoleon owed his rise to imperial dominance to his ability to win battles, which he did with dispiriting regularity. His great victories were taught to the West Point cadet, whose professors extolled the virtue of seeking decision by blows of crushing force, as delivered at Austerlitz and Marengo. President Lincoln, but also Jefferson Davis, the new Confederate president, both hoped for an American Austerlitz, to end the conflict in a single day of violence. In the first seasons of campaign the hope was futile, for neither side yet possessed trained soldiers or weapons in sufficient quantity to inflict decisive blows. Even as they grew stronger, decisive victory continued to prove elusive. Victories there were, as at Chancellorsville and Fredericksburg, but though sometimes spectacular they achieved no destruction of the enemy. The reasons for that seemed obscure at the time and remain so. One was that the Confederates possessed commanders, notably Stonewall Jackson but also their supremo, Robert E. Lee, who were unfailingly daring and attacked even in the teeth of apparently overwhelming odds, achieving a moral effect which time and again carried the day; another was that neither side fielded cavalry in sufficient numbers to perform the battle-winning role it had traditionally done in Europe. Cavalry in the great European campaigns broke up the large formations of infantry and then pursued the fugitives to destruction. America did not possess either a cavalry tradition or the sort of soldiers who might have established one. The battles of the Civil War were almost exclusively infantry struggles, in which casualties were inflicted by rifle fire at ranges from fifty to a hundred yards or more, but because of the efficiency of the Springfield and Enfield rifles they were very costly to combatants.

The casualty figures pose what is perhaps the supreme mystery of the war: why did the common soldier of both sides bear the loss of comrades in such large numbers and the fear of the battlefield experience and yet return again and again to the fray to continue fighting as if bolstered by the effect? Eighteenth-century armies recognised a mass reaction to extreme fear, called by the French *panique-terreur*. *Panique-terreur* does not seem to have afflicted the Americans of the Civil War. That may have been because, since it was a civil war, the soldiers surrendered to each other, their English-speaking fellow inhabitants of the same landmass, with relative ease. This was not the case, however, with black Union soldiers, who following massacre at Fort Pillow and the Petersburg Crater were understandably not prepared to entrust their lives to white Confederates and fought fiercely to avoid capture.

The nature of the terrain in the theatres of war helps to explain why battles occurred as often as they did. In the two great corridors of conflict—one formed in the east by the Appalachian chain and the Atlantic; the other in what is loosely called the "West," formed again by the Appalachians and the Mississippi—the barriers to left and right forced the armies, once set in motion, into frontal contact with each other, as long as they could be supplied, which ease of access to river lines of communication, supplemented by the railroads, assured that they could. Neither side lacked for men. Numbers compressed by geography ensured that as long as there was the will to fight, and the will held up throughout the war, battles would take place. Indeed, one of the most consistently surprising factors of the war was the readiness of both sides to expose themselves to the risks of combat and to return to the fight even after suffering heavy losses.

The armies' readiness for battle is all the more extraordinary given their almost total lack of experience of warfare. Both sides had to learn as they went along, leaders and led alike. Memory of America's wars of the past, written accounts of wars in Europe, particularly those of Napoleon, supplied the uninformed with almost their only notion of what a battle should be like. The nature of battle was scarcely understood, hence the belief, which persisted long after the first encounters, that one great engagement would settle the issue.

Perhaps the first reality that had to be grasped was the necessity of massing firepower. There past American experience did not assist, for Europeans had identified from King George's War and the French and Indian War a style of fighting they called "American" or "Indian" war, in which armies did not form ordered masses as they did on the open battlefields of the Old World, but skirmished behind tree cover and sought to take the enemy by surprise. "American" warfare was individualistic, not ordered, and fighting in such conditions typically took the form of ambush or surprise attack, as at the battle of the Monongahela in 1755, where a small French army with numerous Indian allies had overwhelmed the redcoats of Edward Braddock's army in the preliminaries to what would become known as the French and Indian War. The armies of 1861, recognising that "American" warfare would not win them this conflict, had to learn, by reference to the available drill books, how to organise themselves for Old World fighting. It had taken European armies long years of trial and error to learn that the fire of gunpowder muskets was effective only if those who carried them stood shoulder to shoulder and fired in unison. While knowing that such tactics were correct, the soldiers of 1861 had to teach themselves to do likewise, since the requirement defies nature. Instinct drives men who are fired upon to seek cover, either by lying down or by finding shelter behind a natural obstacle, the antithesis of battle-winning procedure. Many inexperienced Civil War regiments did indeed give way to instinct at the first onset of battle, running away or breaking formation at the first exposure to fire.

The obsessive repetition of drill movements, taught from books by officers or sergeants who were themselves only a page ahead of their pupils, was thus exactly the correct way of preparing the innocents of 1861 for battle. The drill books, almost always translations from the French or rewritten versions of French originals, laid down that the regiment of ten companies should form most of them into a line of two ranks; three had been earlier ordered, but the practice abandoned because of the danger to the front rank from bullets fired by the third. Even so, the front rank was regularly singed and deafened by the rifles of the second. Live firing practice was a rare event. Many soldiers did not fire their weapons for the first time until they met the enemy. There was, however, a great deal of practice in the seventeen separate movements necessary to load and level the rifle, extracting the paper cartridge from the pouch, tearing it with the teeth, pouring the powder down the barrel, spilling the bullet after the powder, crumpling the paper into a wad, ramming home with the ramrod, placing the percussion cap on the nipple, and bringing the butt to the shoulder. Speed and dexterity in loading did not, however, exhaust the requirements of the drill master. It was also necessary to mass the effect of discharge, by training the soldiers to stand shoulder to shoulder and perform the drill movements simultaneously; otherwise the impact of the volley was diminished, while accidents would occur if loading and aiming were mistimed.

Regiments advanced to contact in columns, their officers hoping to successfully deploy from column into line at optimum range from the enemy, perhaps a hundred or two hundred yards. Changing formation or direction on the battlefield was an invitation to disorder but was essential if the regiment were to damage the enemy, and could be achieved even by inexperienced troops if they had been sufficiently exercised in foot drill. The ideal was for the regiment to make the approach to contact in column, then deploy into line, at which point the regimental skirmishers would move to the front and flank to bring individual fire against the enemy's front. What followed was rarely as prescribed in the drill book, which expected the battalion line to deliver a succession of volleys until the enemy drew back or it essayed a charge, with or without fixed bayonets. In practice, once a regiment had delivered its first volley, firing tended to become individual. The bayonet charge was rarely practised. The proof of that, Civil War observers believed, was because of the very low proportion of bayonet wounds displayed among the wounded brought to hospital. The low incidence of such wounds has been noted in many conflicts at different times and places but is not proof that the bayonet was not used; it may have been that bayonet wounds were so often fatal that the victims died on the spot, and were not collected for treatment. Nevertheless, it does seem the case that the bayonet was rarely used in Civil War battles. The charge of the 20th Maine at Little Round Top, after it had exhausted its ammunition, was an exception to the rule that Civil War battles were largely fought with the rifle.

That this should have been so was made the more likely because of the confidence the soldier had in his firearm. The Springfield and Enfield rifles were a great technological advance over the smoothbore musket. They were more accurate, carried to a greater range, and, being ignited by a percussion cap, rarely misfired. Firing was still a complicated and time-consuming business, leading to eccentric results when a novice rifleman, for example, would ram home the contents of several cartridges but forget to place the percussion cap on the nipple. With such a weapon in his hands, the soldier was naturally tempted, once the firefight began, to stand and deliver shot after shot, even if they fell short, than to take the risk of closing the distance with a charge, during which he could not reload. Hence the descriptions of regiments standing opposite each other for long periods during which they fired off all the ammunition in their pouches. But the armies of the Civil War soon became accustomed to rifle firefights and adept in the rifle's uses. Lee certainly esteemed the rifle more than the artillery gun as a battle-winner, and he did not notably employ artillery to decisive effect in any of his battles. That may have been because his great skill as a commander was in the rapid manoeuvre of infantry units in the face of and in direct contact with the enemy; infantry was easier to manoeuvre than artillery. Indeed, there was no outstanding artillery general on either side.

Prolonged firing could result in one side overcoming the other and advancing to occupy its ground. A shaken or beaten regiment, though, should have been replaced or stiffened by reserves appearing from the rear, as it often was. The outcome of Civil War battles was often decided by reinforcement or the movement of reserves to the front at a critical moment. As has been often observed, outcomes were not usually influenced by the intervention of cavalry or even by the effect of artillery. Cavalry simply did not play a decisive or even particularly noticeable role between 1861 and 1865. Cavalry conducted many daring and successful raids into enemy territory, spreading alarm, destroying matériel, and capturing valuable supplies. It almost never charged infantry on the battlefield, or artillery; during the great battles of the war, it suffered negligible casualties. There are a number of reasons for the ineffectiveness of Civil War cavalry. One was that the terrain was not suited to cavalry, which required wide, uncluttered spaces in which to gather and deploy. Another was that there was no cavalry tradition in the pre-war American army, no group of leaders committed to its use. Cavalry was expensive to maintain and difficult to train, and there was no pool of skilled horsemen to enlist. The result was that neither side formed large bodies of cavalry.

The diminished role of artillery is more difficult to explain. During the Napoleonic Wars artillery had dominated battlefields and been widely regarded as the decisive arm. Napoleon's Grand Battery of 100 guns at Waterloo had caused Wellington severe concern. In 1861 both armies suffered from a shortage of field artillery, which was only slowly repaired. By mid-war, however, both armies fielded guns in European proportions, about four guns per thousand men, quite enough to decide battles if properly used. Yet such was rarely the case. At Malvern Hill, outside Richmond, in 1862 the Union artillery inflicted very heavy casualties, as the Confederate artillery did at Fredericksburg. The reason in both cases seems to have been that the terrain suited the gunners. At Malvern Hill there were wide, long fields of fire; at Fredericksburg the Confederate guns occupied commanding positions overlooking open ground. The guns could do their worst. More often, however, the field of fire was obscured by trees or broken ground and very often by the interposition of ranks of friendly troops. That could have been avoided had the guns been pushed right forward and manoeuvred as horse artillery during fluid moments of the battle. However, there was a reluctance by commanders on both sides to risk the capture of their valuable guns by placing them in exposed positions, and there was also a general shortage of horse artillery.

Much debated is the question of whether infantry, armed with the new rifle, and so able to engage targets as far distant as 300 yards, were enabled to defend themselves against enemy artillery by targeting the batteries with aimed fire. Artillery usually fired at infantry at ranges of a thousand yards, though less if it were using canister, case shot containing packed musket balls, which was very destructive against massed formations of infantry. The conclusion of experts is that infantry fire rarely forced artillery to retire from its positions and that artillery rarely suffered heavy casualties from rifle fire.

The effect of fire, whether from rifles or cannon, was heavily moderated by the digging of entrenchments, which began early in the war and became general practice as the war lengthened. That was a departure from the habits of the dynastic armies of the eighteenth century and the Napoleonic Wars. In those wars, once battle was joined, protection against casualties was held to reside in the return of fire, the use of artillery, or the unleashing of cavalry to drive the enemy away. Soldiers rarely dug in. There were exceptions, however. Entrenchment was known even as early as the War of the Spanish Succession. The French partially entrenched their positions at the battle of Ramillies in 1706. In general, however, it is true that eighteenth-century armies did not, except during sieges, dig.

European practice was a strong influence on Civil War armies, so much so that, despite West Point's emphasis on the teaching of engineering and fortification, most Civil War commanders began at the outset without any thought of setting their soldiers to dig. They sought to win by the practice of manoeuvre. As the war progressed, however, and casualties rose until 30 percent killed and wounded became the normal casualty list in infantry regiments in large battles, soldiers began to dig anyhow, whether encouraged to do so by their generals or not. They dug to protect themselves if ordered to hold a position in defence. They dug when the enemy's fire began to tell during an advance to contact. After 1863 digging was a feature of all battlefields, and on those where the defender was given warning of impending action, battlefield entrenchments became very elaborate. Some of the complex lines that sprang up around Petersburg in 1864 were begun as "hasty" entrenchments against Grant's constant efforts to outflank the Confederates to the south and west.

The practice of entrenchment, apparently a soldier's exercise rather than one imposed from above, at least at the outset, helps us to answer the most obvious question about Civil War battle, which is this: how did the ordinary mortals in blue and gray sustain the fear and horror that close-order fighting engendered? Frightened men run away or, if they cannot, hide themselves or fling themselves flat. Civil War soldiers of both sides did all those things and also offered themselves as prisoners, hence the surprisingly large number of prisoners taken by both sides during the war. But Civil War soldiers also did *not* run away or take cover or freeze or cry "surrender" but stood their ground, fired, reloaded, and fired again, often minute after minute until they overcame the men opposite. What held them to their soldierly duty? There are a number of factors that explain steadfastness in all wars, including the example of leaders, the coercion of junior leaders, Dutch courage, and the undesirable consequences of cowardice. Coercion does not seem to have played a significant role in the Civil War. Americans are not accustomed to threatening their fellows or being threatened. It is not the American way. Although there are instances of Civil War soldiers turning their weapons upon comrades who showed cowardice in the face of the enemy, they are not commonly found in the records. There are by contrast many instances of soldiers recording the admiration they felt for the courage of their officers and drawing inspiration from it; sometimes they wrote of the contrary also, as when an officer was found hiding in a hollow tree at Shiloh or another was observed applying cosmetic marks of battle to himself at a safe distance from the enemy. Dutch courage was in common use; the canteen full of whisky was greatly appreciated and not much disapproved of. Generals who became drunk during battle were, however, usually removed from command. It was also often remarked that flight was too dangerous when in close proximity to the enemy and that it was safer to stay and attempt to return fire. Moreover, and this underlay the whole Civil War experience of combat, men did not run because they were motivated by what James McPherson characterises as "cause and comrades." Men on both sides had gone to war because they believed passionately in their reasons for doing so: to preserve or restore the Union, if they were Unionists; to defend states' rights and the Southern way of life if they were Confederates; and in both cases because their standing in the eyes of their brothers in arms meant a great deal to them—indeed, at the time probably more than anything else. Both armies had intensely masculine identities, in which to be thought manly was the overriding value and to be thought a coward the supreme devaluation.

In nineteenth-century America religion was a powerful motivation of many, both in peace and war. In many ways the Civil War was as much a religious war as a political one, since abolitionists held their beliefs with religious fervour while Southern rustics, who may not have been able to articulate any coherent political view, identified their Southernness with their membership in their Baptist and Methodist meetinghouses and took their beliefs with them into the ranks.

Ultimately, Civil War battles came to be characterised by heavy rifle fire, by the absence of significant quantities of artillery, and by the prevalence of earthworks. Fire between the lines could continue for long periods without movement by one side or the other, in the hope that volume of fire would eventually persuade the enemy to retire. Hence the phenomenon of large-scale exchanges at medium range resulting in very few casualties. Heavy casualties, of course, were also a feature of Civil War battles but were usually explained by troops finding themselves confined by local terrain features in a position from which it was difficult to escape and within which it was difficult to manoeuvre. Such was the case at Antietam, and on parts of the field of Gettysburg. Woodland, so frequently present, also contributed to heavy casualties, since troops came upon each other by surprise in the poor visibility and then found it difficult to disengage because of the density of vegetation.

The nature of battle in the Civil War has been much debated and strong views are held by historians. It cannot be disputed, however, that Civil War battle was very largely rifle battle, with cavalry playing almost no part in the clash of major armies, and artillery fulfilling a subordinate role. Firepower was not the main cause of death. The Union's total of fatalities amounts to 110,000 battle deaths, the Confederacy's to 94,000 battle deaths; twice as many as died on both sides, but were the victims of disease, still the greatest killer of soldiers, as would remain the case until the First World War.

CHAPTER TWENTY-TWO

Could the South Have Survived?

THE QUESTION OF WHETHER the South could have won has become one of the most popular of post-conflict questions. The answer is almost certainly not. Material disparities in numbers of men and in industrial output make it most unlikely that the Confederacy could have prevailed over its stronger northern neighbour, though at the outset there were many in the South who believed and proclaimed that what were seen as critical advantages, particularly European dependence on the South's exports of cotton, made it certain that expenditure on that raw material would, if supply were interrupted or denied, compel Europe's industrial states—which were also its great powers, Britain foremost but France as well—to recognise the Confederacy as a legitimately independent state and to intervene in its support, breaking the North's blockade and supplying necessities, including credit, which would nullify the North's economic advantages. As we now know, prudence deterred the South's putative supporters from offending the United States, even when provoked as Britain was during the *Trent* affair.

Though the question persists, it is not therefore pursued with much diligence. Even the most disgruntled Southerners came to accept, almost in the war's immediate aftermath, that the South had been beaten fair and square and that indulgence in daydreams about a different outcome was profitless. A great deal of the credit for the fact that the South accepted defeat so quickly and completely belongs to Robert E. Lee for his unyielding opposition to all suggestions that, after Appomattox, or instead of Appomattox, the remnants of the Confederate States Army should have taken up guerrilla warfare. Lee's commendable decision derived from his admirable constitutionalism and respect for law, both the common laws of war and those of his country, but also, as he made clear, to his determination to spare the South the horrors of irregular warfare within its own territory. The sufferings of those parts of the South, particularly the Shenandoah Valley of his beloved Virginia, during the campaigns of depredation conducted by Union armies had convinced him that prolonging the conflict simply out of a refusal to accept its result as determined on conventional battlefields would not be in his fellow Southerners' interest. Instead of irregular resistance to the results of the war, the South instead consoled itself with resort to an idealised version of Confederate history, which became known as the Lost Cause. Fortunately for Americans, the Lost Cause took the form of a legend rather than a political movement, a highly romanticised legend which eventually resolved itself into a depiction of the antebellum South as a land of magnolia blossoms, white-pillared mansions, pretty damsels of the plantation, and contented slaves, which reached its apotheosis in the best-selling novel *Gone with the Wind*, later made into an enormously successful Hollywood film. Eventually *Gone with the Wind* became in a way the South's revenge on the North for the popularity and influence of *Uncle Tom's Cabin*. Just as Harriet Beecher Stowe ("the little woman who made this great war") had succeeded in making the South appear populated by selfish, heartless, and cruel slave owners, Margaret Mitchell succeeded in reworking the picture as one in which Southern beauties and their gallants presided over chuckling old black retainers who gave as good in banter as they got by way of servitude. The result was that, over time, *Gone with the Wind* has become better known than *Uncle Tom's Cabin* and had greater lasting effect.

Gone with the Wind may even have influenced the way in which the Civil War is seen. Its memorable depiction of the battle of Atlanta and the spoliation of the Tara plantation certainly fed the loyal of the Lost Cause in emphasising the story of Southern bravery and of a war lost in a less than fair fight. If it were a reader's only source it would certainly raise the issue of how a people so resolute lost the war they fought to defend their way of life, and so whether, given appropriate alterations in the course of events, the Confederacy could have survived. Were such a reader to turn to the military history of the war in search of illumination, he or she would almost certainly and promptly conclude that no other outcome than the one delivered by the war's events was possible.

The first set of events pointing to the inevitability of the actual outcome, leaving material disparities in the strength of the combatants out of account, was the progress of the imposition of blockade. At the outset, the South's access to supply of military essentials was unimpeded; indeed, in the first months of the war, the Confederacy succeeded in purchasing abroad and in importing very large quantities of war materials. By August 1861 the South had brought 50,000 European rifles into the country, despite the fact that the blockade had been declared and was being enforced by the United States Navy, which had nearly a hundred vessels at a time when the South had no navy at all. The blockade proceeded relentlessly as the Union, by action at sea and by landing troops on the coast, took possession of the South's ports and coastal waters. By April 1862 the whole Atlantic coast of the Confederacy, with the exceptions of Wilmington, Charleston, and Savannah, was in Union hands, and the Union army could land troops wherever it chose, to garrison, if so wanted, several large enclaves it had established ashore.

The loss of the Confederacy's coastline presaged doom, since it undermined the South's claim to be sovereign and independent by cutting it off from the outside world. The next progressive stage in its isolation, an internal rather than foreign isolation, came with the capture of the shorelines of the western rivers, first the Cumberland and the Tennessee following the taking of Forts Henry and Donelson in February 1862, which rapidly led to the capture of most of the length of the Mississippi (less Vicksburg). The isolation of this area, which eventually became known as Kirby Smithdom, was not fatal to the South's survival, since the region contained no great centres of population or manufacturing but it was weakening nevertheless since it did contain the largest concentration of livestock in the South and was an important source of agricultural produce. The fall of Forts Henry and Donelson inaugurated the North's domination of the Mississippi Valley and of the sequence of Northern offensives in Tennessee and then Georgia which weakened the Confederacy both materially and morally. Grant's campaign in the Mississippi Valley was to unfold as one of the most complex of the war, both geographically and in its sequence of events. Vicksburg, because of its location on high ground, and because of the girdle of its encircling waterways, was almost impregnable. Grant's success in tempting Pemberton, the Vicksburg commander, out of his fortifications to do battle in the open was a brilliant achievement. Grant's western campaign of 1863 defeated all hope of further Southern success in the border states, consolidated Union dominance over the Mississippi Valley, and secured the platform for

Sherman's invasion of Georgia and the inauguration of his war against popular morale inside the South.

Eastern successes in 1863, at Gettysburg in particular, brought to an end for good the Confederacy's freedom to mount invasions of the North. Events in 1864, particularly the Overland Campaign, with its appalling toll of casualties, shook the resolution of the North again, but the Union's will to fight on revived and once the siege of Petersburg began, the determination to see the war out to victory persisted undimmed to the very end.

By that stage of the war, the overthrow of the Confederacy was unavoidable. The strength of its armies was in irreversible decline; its currency had lost all value, and so isolation from the outside world was complete. Important areas of the South were no longer under Richmond's control, and some had already been laid waste, a process which was to continue.

In retrospect and in the light of its progressive material weakening, what stands out as remarkable about the Confederacy's conduct of the war is Southern resilience. Just as the North recovered from psychological setback, such as invasion of its borderland and defeats such as Fredericksburg, so the South made recoveries also. It seemed not offended at all by the early loss of New Orleans, its largest city, or by such terrible slaughters as at Shiloh. It was undoubtedly cast down by Gettysburg and even by the loss of Vicksburg, on the same day, but a month afterwards it was tussling as hard as ever. At no point in the war, until Davis's flight from Richmond in April 1865, did the South publicly disclose a loss of the will to resist. It was astonishing that it contested the onward march of the Union army on both the day before the surrender at Appomattox and the day before that. On April 7, two days before he met Grant to capitulate, Robert E. Lee was still denying that resistance was pointless.

The continuation of the war after that date was certainly impossible, since Lee was outnumbered several times over and had no rations with which to feed his troops. It seems probable, however, that had food been available and if numbers had sufficed, he might well have gone on resisting, as would many of his men. In that sense the South could have survived longer than it did.

CHAPTER TWENTY-THREE

The End of the War

L EE, whose retreat towards Lynchburg continued, managed to remain ahead of the Union pursuit during April 8 but by then it was clear to both Union and Confederate headquarters that the arrangement of a formal cessation of hostilities could not be long delayed. The Northern army dominated the field of operations. The Southern army was urgently in need of sustenance which only the enemy could supply. Lee sent another letter, asking Grant to meet him but disdaining any intention to surrender, and asking for a statement of terms. Grant, for once, did not, as he had during the Henry and Donelson campaign and at Vicksburg, insist that the terms be unconditional. An uncharacteristic tenderness informed the letters he began to exchange with Lee. Lee asked Grant to meet him between the two armies' picket lines, but Grant, emphasising that he had no authority to negotiate peace, refused. Lee kept the rendezvous, but finding Grant absent returned to Appomattox. Meade, meanwhile, was forming the Army of the Potomac into line of battle, for a final and conclusive attack. Grant was with the other column. The impending clash was averted when Meade was informed by one of Sheridan's officers that the two supreme commanders were closeted at Appomattox. Grant, who was suffering from an acute headache, spent the night of April 8 in a farmhouse at Curdsville. When he rose, still in pain, he joined his staff to ride to the nearby village of Appomattox Court House, where Lee and his headquarters was known to be. Riding into the village street, they were told that Lee was in a house fronting the street; he had arrived a little earlier, and one of Lee's officers had told a resident whom he met in the street that he wanted the use of a house in which to meet General Grant. Wilmer McLean had moved to Appomattox Court House from Manassas after the battle there, in the hope of avoiding further disturbance by the war. He now showed Lee into the front room of one of the village houses, but Lee deemed the premises too cramped and undignified for the business that had to be done. McLean therefore took him into his own front room. The McLean house was a roomy, double-fronted dwelling with a pillared verandah, built in Federal style. It had a driveway round it and a yard at the rear in which, when Grant and his staff arrived, Lee's famous horse, Traveller, was tethered. The other officers held back while Grant entered the front room to introduce himself to Lee. They then entered to find seats or to arrange themselves standing. Grant's opening words to Lee were, "I met you once before, General Lee, while we were serving in Mexico, when you came over from General Scott's headquarters to visit Garland's brigade, to which I then belonged. I have always remembered your appearance, and I think I should have recognised you anywhere." "Yes," replied Lee, "I know I met you on that occasion, and have often thought of it and tried to recollect how you looked but I have never been able to recall a single feature."[1] The exchange reflected their different appearances. Lee, six feet tall and with classical good looks, stood out in any company. The much shorter and undistinguished-looking Grant was at a physical disadvantage, which was quite cancelled out at this meeting by his status as the victor and Lee's as the vanquished.

Lee opened the proceedings by asking, "I suppose, General Grant, that the object of our present meeting is fully understood? I asked to see you to ascertain upon what terms you would receive the surrender of my army." Grant answered that the terms were as already stated, that those surrendering should be "paroled and disqualified from taking up arms again until properly exchanged, and that all arms, ammunition and supplies to be delivered up as captured property." Lee nodded his agreement and Grant expressed the hope that there should be an immediate suspension of hostilities to avoid any further loss of life. Grant then called for his message book so that he could write out a draft of terms. To them he added as an afterthought that the personal weapons and baggage of officers were not to be surrendered. Lee then mentioned that in the Confederate army horses and mules were usually the private property of the soldiers. Grant declared that he was unfamiliar with that custom but accepted that many in the Confederate army, being small farmers, would need their horses and mules to put in a crop to see their families through the next winter. He declined to alter the wording of the surrender document but gave Lee his assurance that he would instruct the supervising officers to allow men to take animals they claimed to own. Lee said, "This will have the best possible effect upon the men. It will be very gratifying and will do much toward conciliating our people."[2] Grant next presented his officers, whom Lee acknowledged formally. He was taken aback to be confronted by a man of dark complexion, apparently taking him for a Negro. He was in fact Colonel Ely Parker, a Native American who was reigning chief of the Six Civilized Nations. As the group started to disperse, Lee asked for rations for his men and Grant agreed, after a discussion about numbers, to send what was available; 25,000 rations were distributed. The meeting was courteous on both sides, though Lee had said beforehand that he would have rather died a thousand deaths than meet Grant to arrange surrender. As soon as Lee left the room, the members of Grant's staff began to bargain with Mr. McLean for mementos. George Custer paid twenty dollars for the table at which Lee had sat; Grant's table fetched forty. By the time the party left, the room was bare of furniture.

When Grant returned to camp, his staff gathered round expecting him to discuss the surrender. Instead Grant asked General Rufus Ingalls, "Do you remember that old white mule so-and-so used to ride when we were in the city of Mexico?" The old white mule remained the subject of conversation for some time. Not until after supper would Grant discuss the surrender and then not for long. He shortly announced his intention to leave for Washington next day. In practice, he did not depart until the day after. In the interval he had ridden into the lines of the surrendered army, where he and Lee exchanged salutes and then returned to sit on the verandah of the McLean house and receive visits from old friends in the Confederate ranks, including Longstreet, who had been at his wedding, and Pickett, among others. When, at noon, Grant rode off to take the train to Washington, Lee departed for Richmond. Grant had forbidden demonstrations of rejoicing, sending a message to his soldiers stating "The war is over, the rebels are our countrymen again and the best sign of rejoicing after victory will be to abstain from all demonstrations in the field."[3]

While Lee rode to Richmond, Jefferson Davis, with his cabinet, was travelling south, first by train, then, escorted by a troop of Tennessee cavalrymen, on horseback. He went first to Danville, Virginia, where he learnt of Lee's surrender, a bitter blow. He went next to Greensboro and Charlotte, in North Carolina, then to Abbeville,

South Carolina. His flight was to last thirty days and cover 400 miles, culminating at Irwinville, Georgia, where on May 10 he and his wife and what remained of his entourage were captured by men of the 1st Wisconsin and 4th Michigan Cavalry. Disrespectfully, for he maintained his dignity to the end, he was mocked and jeered by his captors as they rode him away to imprisonment at Fortress Monroe, where he would spend two years, the first weeks in chains. Lincoln, brought to Richmond by ship, sat in Davis's office only forty hours after he had left it.

John Wilkes Booth, a successful and well-known actor but a fanatical devotee of the Confederate cause, had, with others, spent much of March and April 1865 plotting to do harm to President Lincoln. They first thought of kidnapping him and holding him to ransom for the sake of concessions, then realised that a kidnap attempt would fail and decided on assassination. There were half a dozen conspirators, mainly misfits and dropouts. Booth was by far the most impressive of the gang, a strikingly handsome twenty-seven-year-old actor who was earning $20,000 a year on the stage.

On the evening of April 14, Good Friday in 1865, Booth entered Ford's Theatre, six blocks from the White House, where the well-known comedy *Our American Cousin* was playing. He found his way to Lincoln's box, where Lincoln and his wife were sitting close together, and, drawing a pistol, shot the president in the back of the head. Then shouting, "*Sic semper tyrannis*" (So perish all tyrants), a familiar Latin tag which happened to be the motto of the Commonwealth of Virginia, he leapt twelve feet to the stage and hobbled off. He had broken his leg, but having a horse tethered nearby, he made his escape, bluffed his way past a sentry on the Potomac bridge, and escaped into the Virginia countryside. There during the next twelve days he passed from the house of one Confederate sympathiser to another, not all of whom knew he was the hated assassin, until on April 26, while taking refuge in a tobacco barn on the farm of a family named Garrett on the Rappahannock River, he was run to earth. Found by questing Union cavalrymen, he challenged them to a shoot-out but their officer threw in a burning twist of hay which set fire to the whole building. While Booth hobbled about inside, one of the soldiers outside fired a shot which mortally wounded him.

One of Booth's accomplices had tried and nearly succeeded in murdering Secretary of State Seward. The vice president, Andrew Johnson, survived, because his nominated assailant lost his nerve. It was estimated that seven million people lined the track of the train carrying Lincoln's body, which had lain in state in the White House, back to Springfield for burial in Illinois. The death of Lincoln, mourned as a national tragedy and a sort of martyrdom, left the government in severe disarray, with a host of problems unresolved. For several years there had been much debate in the North over Reconstruction, or how the South should be treated after the Union was restored. Reconstruction did not mean, as it might to modern ears, the physical rebuilding of the war-ravaged states. There was no thought at all, nor would there have been support for, a financial programme to restore the South's economic life. Reconstruction meant the rebuilding of the Union, a subject on which Northerners held very varied ideas. Lincoln had wanted to begin by pardoning, after they had taken an oath of loyalty, all Southerners, who would thus preserve their rights of property except in slaves. Excepted were those who had held office in the Confederate government or high military rank. The state governments were to be reconstituted by election, the right to vote going to those who had sworn loyalty, so long as they numbered 10 percent of the electorate in the last pre-war election of 1860. These provisions were incorporated into a peace convention which the officers of the federal government correctly condemned as a little better than a peace treaty. Jefferson Davis, in refuge at Goldsboro, North Carolina, was not unnaturally only too willing to accept these terms, but Washington repudiated them all. The war had not been fought to end in what was virtually a recognition of Southern sovereignty.

Some experiments in restored state governments were made before the end of the war, in those states wholly occupied by the Union, such as Louisiana and Arkansas. In some states the suffrage was extended to blacks, though with great reluctance. Over the coming years it was almost everywhere withdrawn by the passage of what became known as "Black Codes."

Blacks obtained less from Reconstruction than Lincoln had intended, particularly economically. Among the freed slaves there was a universal hunger for land, which they almost always lacked the money to purchase. On the other hand, their former owners needed their labour to bring farms and plantations back into cultivation. The solution to the impasse proved to be the sharecropping system, by which owners leased land in return for a portion of the crop. Because it entailed the commitment of the following year's crop against credit, the system effectively reimposed that binding of the black to a particular plot under a particular master which had been almost the most hated feature of plantation slavery. Northern opinion never really concerned itself, however, with the ex-slaves' economic lot. Far more important in the eye of Northern reformers was the establishment of their electoral rights. Northern Republicans, overwhelmingly the controlling faction in the occupied regions, wanted to be assured that blacks would be allowed to vote, though at home they showed little enthusiasm for the admission of blacks to the electoral process. In the South, assuring that the blacks would not exercise decisive electoral power, or even any power at all, became an object that united almost all white Southerners.

Andrew Johnson, Lincoln's successor as president, was a Southerner who scarcely troubled to disguise his sympathy for the defeated. His insistence on attempting to rescue members of his race from the consequences of rebellion provoked in 1866–68 a political crisis almost as great as that which had led to rebellion in 1861. The president and Congress were at loggerheads. Congress, though by no means as benevolent as its most radical members claimed it to be, fundamentally disapproved of Southern resistance to Reconstruction and of the president's efforts to further that resistance. The most important evidence of Congress's reformism was its promulgation of the Fourteenth Amendment to the Constitution in 1866. It was effectively a bill of rights, guaranteeing the new black citizens their political and legal equality. Johnson urged the Southern states not to ratify it, a requirement if it were to become law, and they followed his bidding. This, however, was only a delaying measure. The amendment was later ratified and became law. Presidential opposition so outraged Congress, however, that in March 1867 it passed a Reconstruction Act that imposed its desired version of a post-war settlement on the South by diktat. Ten former Confederate states (Tennessee, always strongly Unionist, had been readmitted to the Union in 1866) were grouped into five military districts each ruled by a military governor with extensive powers. When law and order had been assured, states were to organise conventions to amend state constitutions so as to conform with the Constitution of the United States, including the incorporation of the Fourteenth Amendment. When these stages had been completed, the conforming state could be readmitted to the Union and to representation in the federal Congress. Faced with a process that threatened black intervention in state politics, most Southern states demonstrated their readiness to persist with their provisional governments, hastily established after the surrender and in effect continuations of the Confederate regimes. As a result, Congress had to empower the military governors to impose its will. It was grudgingly accepted and between 1868 and 1870 all ten former Confederate states still outside the Union were readmitted. In 1869, to confirm the progress thus achieved, Congress passed the Fifteenth Amendment, which in brief but unambiguous terms stated that citizens' rights were not to be limited by "race, color or previous condition of servitude." Within five years of the end of the war, it might therefore have appeared that the purposes for which the war had been fought, including emancipation as well as restoring the union, had all been achieved.

Such, however, was not the case. The South had been beaten but had not been fundamentally changed. Anti-black feeling was a universal emotion and state localism more powerful than loyalty to the union. Almost none of the former Confederate states were under the government of men who accepted Congress's desire for equality and the untrammelled rule of law. Ingenious political minds, of which there were a plethora in the South, soon found ways to preserve white supremacy and deny black rights without formally transgressing the dictate of Congress. This informal secession was to persist for a century, and result in a rigidly segregated society, until the rise of the civil rights movement in the 1950s.

The Civil War at its start was a unique conflict, in which the combatants tried to do their worst to each other by drill-book learning. The wonder is that they could function at all. They scarcely could; the early engagements of the war justified the contemptuous dismissals of European observers, who viewed them as conflicts between armed mobs. What lent purpose was the determination of the men in the ranks to turn themselves into soldiers, by sheer effort of will. The process was slow and laborious. As late as Gettysburg, there were few regiments on either side that knew how to fight effectively. The performance of the 20th Maine at Little Round Top, though it changed position under fire, was due to the dynamic leadership and force of character of its commander, Joshua Chamberlain, but Chamberlains were few. Their numbers were diminished, moreover, by the startlingly high casualties, particularly among officers, always inflicted in battle. Civil War armies were destroyed almost as fast as they were formed. The 7th New York Heavy Artillery, one of several heavy artillery regiments converted to infantry after the Army of the Potomac's disabling losses in the Overland Campaign, lost 291 men killed and 500 wounded in its last stages. So high was the fatality rate, and that of wounding, that it is a rational enquiry to ask how the Civil War soldier sustained his courage, suppressed his fear, and returned to combat. James McPherson, the Civil War's leading contemporary historian, has devoted one of his studies of the war to that subject. In *For Cause and Comrades* (1997), McPherson separates the questions into three: What impelled a soldier to enlist? What motivated him to fight? What sustained his steadfastness? The first question is the easiest to answer. The Northern volunteers of 1861–62 joined up because they were outraged by the South's assault on the integrity of the republic, a motive which most retained throughout their service, even though it was undermined by combat fatigue and homesickness as the war protracted. An impressively large proportion of the early volunteers served throughout the war if they escaped wounds or capture. Such emotions were offset by what Professor McPherson identifies as the sentiments of "duty, honor, country," very much like those that underlay enlistment in the first place. Such motives were reinforced by the recognition that, having journeyed through the war thus far, their sacrifice would be nullified if they gave up before the decision had been achieved. Persistence was always attacked, however, by the brute facts of battle when the stress of battle supervened. Then the men in the ranks overcame their fear by sensing the greater fear of being thought a coward. In letters home almost all soldiers tried to explain how they bore the terror of facing the enemy and why they refused to seek a way out, emphasising their horror of being thought a coward, particularly by comrades known to their families. It is exactly true that of the Civil War soldier, as of most soldiers in most wars, his greatest fear was of fear itself. Primary fear was entirely rational, since the risk of death or wounding in battle was very high. One in ten Union soldiers was wounded, one in sixty-five killed, while one in thirteen died of disease. Confederate figures were similar but less than those of the Union, because of the South's lack of white numbers. As long as the war persisted and casualties were inflicted at that rate, Northern victory was foreordained. Certainty, however, was prejudiced by the effect of military losses and occasional setbacks.

The war had inflicted more than a million total casualties, of whom 200,000 had been killed in battle. The total exceeds that of the American fatalities of the Second World War and bears comparison only with the European losses of the Great War and Russia's in the Second

World War. In many respects the Civil War was and remains America's Great War, in the way it is commemorated nationally in so many towns and battlefield cemeteries and subjectively and collectively in the American consciousness. Just as even at the beginning of the twenty-first century most Europeans, certainly most people in Britain, know and remember the identities of family members who were killed on the Somme or at Passchendaele, so living Americans remember ancestors who died at Gettysburg or Cold Harbor. The links remain startlingly close. An American neighbour, married to an Englishman, never ceases to surprise me by remembering that both her grandfathers fought in the Confederate army, one at Gettysburg. There is this difference between the Civil War and the Great War, however. The Great War is always spoken of with regret in Europe. It is the Continent's tragedy, the cause of many of its persisting troubles, the war without justification or point. No such regrets attach to the Civil War, which is remembered as the struggle which completed the Revolution and made possible the realisation of the ideals on which the Founding Fathers launched the republic in the 1770s. The memory of the war, of the terrible casualties of its costliest battles, strikes a chill, naturally. It also, however, brings a glow of pride, at the sacrifice a previous generation was ready to make in the cause of ideals held central to its life by modern America; equality, human freedom, the rights of the individual before the law. Such reaction comes more readily to Northerners than to Southerners. Southerners, however, have found ways, consistent with American values, in honouring their Civil War generation, the bravery and patriotism, which somehow overlies the Confederacy's commitment to the preservation of slavery.

Indeed, the causes of the war are now its least remembered ingredients. What persists are the values and qualities which animated those who fought; and, as with so many other wars which are central to the national life of the countries that fought them, the thrill and romance of the events of the war, seen as a historic drama. There is much to fuel the imagination in the Civil War so remembered. Wars usually and by obvious mechanisms lose their horrors in imaginative retrospect. The sufferings of those who experienced wounds are easily forgotten, submerged under the supposed sensation of charge and counter-charge. This seems particularly the case with the Civil War, perhaps because it was being romanticised even in the lifetime of the survivors. Pickett's charge at Gettysburg was re-enacted by a gray-headed contingent of participants on the battlefield at a convention of veterans, both North and South, held in 1913. The meeting went entirely without recrimination. Lack of recrimination was equally characteristic of the literature of the war that began to appear in its immediate aftermath and has never ceased to do so.

The first task was to tell the story of the war, an enormous undertaking in itself. Soon, however, narrative was overtaken by the urge to interpret. What had the war been about? Southerners, from the start and until modern times, had no difficulty in demonstrating that it had been about states' rights, Northerners that it had been about preserving the union and suppressing rebellion; it could not be forgotten, however, that Lincoln's opinion was that the war had "in some way been about slavery," a point of view which grew in strength the more often expressed. Eventually, except in the South, the belief that the war had been fought to abolish slavery came to dominate interpretation. In parallel with discussion of cause, there arose another strand of interpretation: what had the war been like, as a human experience? As the war receded in memory and those who had fought reached the end of their lives, the nature of the war became the matter of overriding interest and the urge to re-create its realities came to possess the writers of the great popular histories of the war which appeared as the centenary approached.

American writers naturally chose to argue that the war was unlike any of the other great wars of history. They had reason to do so. The Civil War was and remains the only large scale war fought between citizens of the same democratic state. It was as a result the most important ideological war in history. That quality lent particular fascination to the story of its battles. Both sides at Gettysburg were animated by belief in the justice of their cause and fought with the greater determination because of that. A strong cause, in the sense of the reason for fighting, was necessary because of the extreme danger on Civil War battlefields, where close-order ranks, meeting at short range, were subjected to firepower of an intensity not previously encountered in war. To an extraordinary degree, the Civil War was a war of battles—frequent, bloody, but yet not decisive. Both sides at the start expected and sought a great battle that would determine the outcome and end the fighting. No such battle was fought, even as the end approached. The cycle of battles kept on unfolding even within sight of Appomattox, where the war was terminated by surrender.

Yet though the threat and reality of battle determined the character of the war, it was not ultimately the opposition of the enemy ranked for combat which prolonged the struggle. There was another element of resistance that had to be overcome and which never relented. That was the military geography of the war. It supplied the South with its most formidable ally and the North with its most unyielding opponent. Time and again, in almost every account of the conduct of campaigns, the obstacles which most hampered the North's armies in their pursuit of victory were terrain and landscape, the enormous distances to be traversed, the multiplicity of waterways to be crossed, the ubiquity and impenetrability of forests, the gradient and contour of mountain ranges. In a real sense, the North was fighting the country itself in its struggle to overcome the South. Certainly, whatever else the student of the Civil War will learn from following its unfolding story, the facts of American geography will imprint themselves on his consciousness. It is that which lends the war its continuing fascination. Those who fought the war are now all dead. The causes for which it was fought have been settled, but the determining facts of its scenes of action remain, as dominating and impressive as they ever were. As long as the Mississippi flows and the great American forest spreads, the Civil War remains with us and so will never be forgotten.

THE LEGACY OF THE CIVIL WAR

The Civil War left a patchwork legacy, both at home and abroad. In Europe, and particularly among European soldiers, the military significance of the war, though it was the largest and costliest of the nineteenth century, was largely ignored. Europe had its own nineteenth-century dispute about the value of volunteer armies. The professionals, both for military and political reasons, deprecated the raising of and depending upon volunteer armies, because of the danger they saw to established order of arming the masses. This attitude was particularly strong in Prussia, Europe's leading military nation, because Prussian officers, who affected an aristocratic manner not always founded on social reality, feared that a people's army could also be a democratic army, at a time when democracy was held to threaten the supremacy of king and property. Curiously, the same officers did not oppose the raising of conscript armies from the mass of the population, as long as recruitment was tilted towards the countryside and command and leadership was firmly attached to the landowner-officer class. The German and French armies in consequence declined to see any value in the study of Civil War campaigns, or Civil War generalship, or Civil War mobilisation of national resources. The British, who did not follow the view of Europe into the practice of conscription, but retained a small volunteer army with a class-based officer corps, took more interest and a British regular officer, Colonel G. R. S. Henderson, wrote the first objective biography of Stonewall Jackson. In a later generation, the British military radical Basil Liddell Hart would write equally influentially about Grant and Sherman.

At home, the legacy of the Civil War was naturally far stronger and more immediate. Several Civil War leaders continued their army careers in the Indian wars on the high plains in the 1860s and 1870s, notably Sherman and Custer. Much that the Department of the Army had learnt in 1861–65 was incorporated into its policies and procedures. The remarkable United States mobilisation for the Great War in 1917–18, which produced an army of five million in less than a year, owed a lot to what had been learnt in 1861–65, while its involvement in arms procurement led eventually to the creation of the Industrial College of the Armed Forces after the First World War. In other less predictable ways, the legacy of the Civil War was surprisingly limited. While the Great War of 1914–18 inspired or at least motivated an extraordinary literary movement in England which in some ways persists to this day, it had no counterpart in America. The Civil War left no equivalent of Robert Graves, Siegfried Sassoon, or Wilfred Owen. Many veterans wrote their war memoirs, but typically they were more like war diaries or recollections of battle than literary achievements. As the American celebrator of English Great War literature Paul Fussell has pointed out, that brilliant literary flowering was the product of the impact of terrible loss of life and suffering on a highly educated officer class, drawn from the public schools and ancient universities, where the young men had been exposed to Greek and Latin literature and the lyrical and romantic verse of the great English poets. Nineteenth-century America had no such literary tradition of its own and no such literary class. Civil War–era America was a literate country, the most literate in the world, but not a literary one. Americans were therefore not drawn to write of their experience of the war in poetic or psychologically explorative terms, and there was no school of literary realism to guide American Civil War writers into the right emotional and psychological path if they were to produce an explicitly imaginative narrative of the war. Edmund Wilson, the great American literary critic, alludes to that state of affairs in his essay on John De Forest in *Patriotic Gore*, his survey of the literature of the Civil War. De Forest was a man of independent means who had travelled in Europe and the Middle

East before 1861. He returned to the United States precisely because of the war and raised an infantry company in his hometown, New Haven, Connecticut. De Forest spent forty-six days under fire and so, when he came to write his memoirs about the war, knew what he was describing. In 1867 he published *Miss Ravenel's Conversion from Secession to Loyalty*, which contained striking passages of description of battle. Edmund Wilson recognised in De Forest's approach what he called "the birth of realism" in American writing.

> The unusually horrible clamor and the many-sided nature of the danger had an evident effect on the soldiers, hardened as they were to scenes of ordinary battle. Grim faces turned in every direction, with hasty stares of alarm, looking aloft on every side as well as to the front for destruction. Pallid stragglers who had dropped out of the leading brigade, drifted by the Tenth, dodging from trunk to trunk in an instinctive search for cover, though it was visible that the forest was no protection but an additional peril. Every regiment has its two or three cowards, or perhaps its half dozen, weakly hearted creatures whom nothing can make fight and who never do fight. One abject hound, a corporal with his disgraced stripes on his arm, came by with a ghastly backward glance of horror, his face colourless, his eyes protruding and his chin shaking. Colburne cursed him for a poltroon, struck him with the flat of his sabre, and dragged him into the ranks of his own regiment; but the miserable creature was too thoroughly unmanned by the great horror of death to be moved to any show of resentment or even of courage by the indignity; he only gave an idiotic stare with outstretched cheek to the front, then turned with a nervous jerk like that of a scared beast and rushed rearward.[4]

Later De Forest would write that he "did not dare state the extreme horror of battle and the anguish with which the bravest soldiers struggle through it."

Despite his diffidence, De Forest undoubtedly did succeed in conveying the extreme horror of battle, particularly Civil War battle, because he was one of the sources used by Stephen Crane in writing *The Red Badge of Courage*. Since his great book appeared in the 1890s, Crane has always been regarded as the supreme fiction writer of the Civil War. What is even more remarkable is that, as is widely known, Crane, who was in his twenties when *The Red Badge* appeared, had not only not fought in the Civil War but had never been a soldier and knew nothing of war but what he read. He himself admitted that he based his accounts of the emotions of battle on football games at Yale. However, one of his schoolmasters had served in the same regiment as De Forest and may have told war memories to Crane. Whatever Crane's sources and given that Whitman's were wounded soldiers, it remains the case, remarkably, that the two greatest writers of the war had not been in it and had entirely secondhand and detached exposure to its reality.

Whatever the reasons for the absence of a literary legacy of the Civil War from its veterans, there were, nevertheless, vivid and imaginative records in the memories of its survivors. Several hundred thousand young Americans had experienced the fear and exhilaration of battle between 1861 and 1865; tens of thousands of them carried into later life the marks of battle, scars, and missing limbs. When he died in 1914, Joshua Chamberlain, the hero of Little Round Top at Gettysburg, succumbed to the effect of a bullet wound received at Petersburg fifty years earlier. But beside physical marks there were internal, psychological scars that entered the American psyche. Most of the Civil War's soldiers, North and South, served as combatants, usually in the infantry, and therefore most took part in battle. As a result, hundreds of thousands of Americans of the 1870s and 1880s, the "Gilded Age," had seen horrors at first hand, dismembered bodies, decapitations, files of corpses ranged so close in roadways or trenches as to make stepping on them unavoidable. There were the horrors of the other senses, splashes of blood or brains from a neighbour wounded in the ranks and, so often recorded, the nauseous smell of decomposing bodies. Whole battlefields stank, if not from human remains, then from those of dead horses and mules, so often the casualties of war in the age before internal combustion. And the horror not only of smells but of the cries and groans of the untended wounded who often lay uncollected for days after the fighting was over. These terrible sensations inhabited the minds of a whole generation of Americans of postbellum North and South, to be taken back to civilian farms and streets after the guns fell silent. These awful sensations, not to be obliterated by conscious effort, lingered and festered to return unbidden as nightmares or waking horrors, for years afterwards. That was a dimension of the war never to be commemorated. Walt Whitman wrote that "the war we had never got into the books." He might better have written "the real memory of the war." In Britain after the Great War, the real memory was painfully resurrected by veterans who, assisted by the new movements in psychology pioneered by Freud and his followers, had persuaded their generation to face their worst and most damaging memories and so perhaps overcome them. There was no such catharsis after 1865.

British Armistice Day, which takes place every year on the Sunday nearest November 11, invites the countrymen of the dead to an act of remembrance. The South could not agree on a memorial day and so for years recognised three days separately. Though the Northern states eventually agreed to commemorate the war annually on May 30, Memorial Day, it never achieved the status of a national act of reconciliation, as Remembrance Day was to do in Britain after the Great War.

The most important literary memorial of the war would be the *Personal Memoirs of U. S. Grant*. After his retirement as president in 1877, he was swindled out of his money. To provide for his family, he devoted his last year to writing. He was simultaneously diagnosed with cancer of the throat but, in a supreme act of determination which was his principal mark of character, concluded the book a week before he died. It sold 300,000 copies in the first year of publication and so rescued his family from penury. Its concluding words are "I feel that we are on the eve of a new era, when there will be a great harmony between the Federal and the Confederate. I cannot stay to be a living witness of the correctness of this prophecy, but I feel within me that it is to be so." The harmony has come to pass but the memory of the great conflict remains.

By common computation, about 10,000 battles, large and small, were fought in the United States between 1861 and 1865. This enormous number of battles, seven for every day the war lasted, provides the principal key to the nature of the war. Americans fought as frequently as they did in the Civil War because they could find no other way to prosecute the conflict. Economic warfare, excepting blockade, was not an option. Nor was attack on the civilian population, since the deeply Christian character of nineteenth-century American society forbade atrocity. Indeed, from the outset, the two most prominent Northern commanders, Winfield Scott and George McClellan, expressed their principled hostility to making civilians the object of attack, even to the infliction of hardship. That was to be changed by Grant and Sherman, when they began to destroy property and the means of livelihood in their western campaigns. But their war against the people did not begin until 1863 and was not deliberately prosecuted until 1864. Economic warfare was not feasible until the North was able to penetrate the South's outer crust and find factories and mills to destroy. The South was unable to reciprocate, except patchily during its two invasions of the North, because the Union's economic and manufacturing centres lay too distant from its borders to be reached. Moreover, the value of taking or damaging economic targets seemed dubious, since the capture in 1862 of New Orleans, the South's largest city and the principal point of exit to the outside world, had no appreciable effect on its war-making capacity at all. The capture of Augusta, Georgia, the South's centre of gunpowder manufacture, would have been a disaster for the Confederacy but its remoteness preserved it from danger until the end of the war.

In the absence of economic targets, it was inevitable that the enemy's army should form the principal object of military operations. Interestingly, Lincoln, completely untutored as he was in military science, quickly came to see that in northern Virginia, Lee's army, rather than Richmond, the enemy capital, should be the Army of the Potomac's main target. Lee had no real alternative, since attractive though the idea was to attack Baltimore or Philadelphia, the objective of one of his forays into the North, both lay too far from his start line to be attainable.

The bellicosity of Civil War armies led to the expectation that a clear-cut result would terminate the war sooner than actually happened. Yet Civil War battles, fought so fiercely though they were, were strangely inconclusive. That was not because the soldiers were half-hearted. On the contrary, they fought with chilling intensity. What robbed their efforts of result was the proliferation of entrenchment, thrown up on the battlefield at high speed in the face of the enemy. First appearing in 1862, by 1863 hasty entrenchment was an automatic response to enemy fire, and a very effective one. But entrenchment had a stalemating effect. By 1864 entrenchment had imposed a universal stalemate, a veritable state of siege, combined paradoxically with a huge toll of casualties, in an anticipation of the stalemate of the First World War. As in 1914–18, the combination of immobility and high losses could be overcome by reinforcement, at which by 1864 the North easily outdid the South, at least in availability of replacements. As for the management of replacements, the North never hit upon the right method; it allowed regiments to decline in numbers until they became ineffective and then raised new regiments to keep up total strength. It was not an efficient system since it did not preserve the cohesion and esprit de corps of experienced and successful units. Unit for unit, and perhaps man for man, the Confederate army exceeded that of the Union in quality, so that the Union triumphed in the end only because of larger numbers and greater wealth of resources.

Greater numbers and greater resources assured that the North would win most of the war's battles, at least the battles that counted. The frequency and intensity of battles determined the war's character. Battle also determined the war's outcome. Antebellum America was a country, not a state. Political America impinged too little upon its citizens to confer a sense of common purpose or of belonging. As is often remarked, the only contact with the state experienced by most antebellum Americans was a visit to the post office. The Civil War changed that. There was no more graphic means of apprehending the power of the state than to stand in the line of battle, a voluntary act with unintended consequences. Men who performed the act and survived the consequences were transformed as citizens. Their understanding of "duty" and "sacrifice" were thereby revolutionised. Men who had stood shoulder to shoulder to brave the volleys of the enemy could not thenceforth be tepid or passive citizens. They became pillars of the republic and pillars of their communities. It is often overlooked that hundreds of thousands of Americans of the Gilded Age had been touched by fire and hardened by it. Antebellum America had been a gentle society. Postbellum America was a nation as well as a society and one hardened by the Civil War to embark on a rendezvous with greatness.

The experience of battle, so widely diffused, may have had another effect on postbellum America. The American historical profession has laboured hard and long to explain why the United States alone among major industrialised countries failed to produce a domestic socialist movement. It gave birth to powerful trade unions, such as the American Federation of Labor (AFL), and its splinter group, the Congress of Industrial Organizations (CIO), but neither adopted a socialist ideology as their European equivalents did. It was not for want of trying by the ideologues. Karl Marx, himself a passionate student at a distance of the Civil War, believed and argued that it should inaugurate a new social order. In January 1865, he wrote, "The working men of Europe feel that as the American War of Independence initiated a new era of ascendancy for the middle class so the American anti-slavery war will do for the working classes. They consider it an earnest of the epoch to come that it fell to the lot of Abraham Lincoln, the single-minded son of the working class to lead his country through the matchless struggle for the rescue of an enchained race and the reconstruction of a social peace."[5] Lincoln had already stridently rejected Marx's vision of the future in words that encapsulated the American dream and anticipated the brunt of American historians' attempt to explain why socialism failed to find rooting ground in his country. In 1864 he wrote, "None are so deeply interested to resist the present rebellion as the working people." Then, in a reference to the draft riots in New York of 1863, he went on: "It should never be so. The strongest bond of human sympathy, outside the family, should be one uniting working people of all nations and tongues and kindreds. Nor should this be a war upon property—property is desirable—is a positive good in the world. That some should be rich shows that others may become rich and hence is a just encouragement to enterprise and industry. Let not him who is houseless pull down the house of another but let him labour diligently and build one for himself, thus by example assuring that his own shall be safe from violence when built."[6] In those last three sentences, Lincoln set forth the idea of individual effort on which the rise to prosperity of late Victorian and twentieth-century America was built. It was an idea perfectly acceptable to the thinking classes of the epoch in Europe but also in America, who had decided to give their allegiance to the state and to collective activity and many of whom found their inspiration in the ideology of the left in all its varieties. Karl Marx, who captured the imagination of so many on the left, argued that the working class should re-organise itself for its advance to capture the necessary resources on military principles. In the *Communist Manifesto* he urged the working class to "form industrial armies." The American working class, though it unionised enthusiastically, consistently opposed the appeal to revolution. American intellectuals struggled for generations to understand the American worker's antipathy for radical and violent change. The American worker, had he been able to articulate his feelings, might have said that his country's first revolution, as he called the War of Independence, had fulfilled many of his aspirations by founding his republic and that the second revolution, which was the Civil War, had completed the first. He had no desire to form industrial armies, having in his hundreds of thousands already formed and served in real armies and learnt by his experience that armies brought hardship and suffering. One experience of army life was enough for a lifetime and not only for an individual lifetime but for a national lifetime as well. American socialism was stillborn on the battlefields of Shiloh and Gettysburg.

NOTES

CHAPTER ONE

1. U. S. Grant, *Personal Memoirs of U. S. Grant* (New York, 1885–86), p. 22.
2. John M. Gould, *The History of the First—Tenth—Twenty-ninth Maine Regiment* (Portland, Maine, 1871), pp. 613–64.
3. Bell Irvin Wiley, *The Life of Billy Yank* (New York, 1952), pp. 303–4.
4. Ibid., pp. 304–5.
5. Ibid., p. 356.
6. Ibid., pp. 360–61.

CHAPTER TWO

1. Carl Sandburg, *Abraham Lincoln* (New York, 2002), p. 228.

CHAPTER THREE

1. Bell Irvin Wiley, *The Life of Billy Yank*, (New York, 1952), p. 20.
2. James M. McPherson, *Battle Cry of Freedom* (New York, 1988), p. 325.

CHAPTER FOUR

1. T. Harry Williams, *Lincoln and His Generals* (London, 1952), p. 20.

CHAPTER SIX

1. Bell Irvin Wiley, *The Life of Billy Yank* (New York, 1952), p. 119.

CHAPTER SEVEN

1. *Richmond Examiner,* September 27, 1861, quoted in McPherson, *Battle Cry of Freedom* (New York, 1988), p. 337.
2. Abraham Lincoln, *Speeches and Writings, 1859–1865* (New York, 1989), vol. 2, p. 302.
3. Earl B. McElfresh, *Maps and Mapmakers of the Civil War* (New York, 1999), passim.

4. T. Harry Williams, *Lincoln and His Generals* (London, 1952), p. 5.
5. Ibid., p. 24.
6. Allen Tate, *Stonewall Jackson* (Nashville, Tenn., 1991), p. 86.
7. Ibid., p. 88.

CHAPTER EIGHT

1. John C. Waugh, *The Class of 1846: From West Point to Appomattox; Stonewall Jackson, George McClellan and Their Brothers* (New York, 1994), p. 332.
2. Ibid., p. 362.
3. T. Harry Williams, *Lincoln and His Generals* (London, 1952), p. 14.
4. Ibid., p. 21.
5. Ibid., p. 16.
6. James McPherson, *Battle Cry of Freedom* (New York, 1988), p. 396.
7. U. S. Grant, *Personal Memoirs of U. S. Grant* (New York, 1885–86), p. 311.
8. Abraham Lincoln, *Speeches and Writings, 1859–1865*, pp. 323–24.
9. Williams, *Lincoln and His Generals*, p. 109.

CHAPTER NINE

1. R. U. Johnson and C. C. Buel, *Battles and Leaders of the Civil War* (New York, 1884–88), vol. 3, p. 68.
2. James McPherson, *Battle Cry of Freedom* (New York, 1988), p. 550.

CHAPTER TEN

1. R. U. Johnson and C. C. Buel, *Battles and Leaders of the Civil War* (New York, 1884–88), vol. 2, p. 662.
2. Ibid., vol. 3, p. 682.

CHAPTER ELEVEN

1. R. U. Johnson and C. C. Buel, *Battles and Leaders of the Civil War* (New York, 1884–88), vol. 3, p. 161.
2. Ibid., vol. 3, p. 196.
3. Ibid., vol. 1, p. 249.
4. James McPherson, *Battle Cry of Freedom* (New York, 1988), p. 651.
5. Abraham Lincoln, *Speeches and Writings, 1859–1865* (New York, 1989), vol. 2, p. 464.
6. T. Harry Williams, *Lincoln and His Generals* (London, 1952), p. 211.
7. McPherson, *Battle Cry of Freedom*, pp. 655–56.
8. Johnson and Buel, *Battles and Leaders*, vol. 3, pp. 387–90.

CHAPTER TWELVE

1. U. S. Grant, *Personal Memoirs of U. S. Grant* (New York, 1885–86), p. 281.
2. Abraham Lincoln, *Speeches and Writings, 1859–1865* (New York, 1989), vol. 2, pp. 477–78.

CHAPTER THIRTEEN

1. R. U. Johnson and C. C. Buel, *Battles and Leaders of the Civil War* (New York, 1884–88), vol. 3, p. 671.
2. U. S. Grant, *Personal Memoirs of U. S. Grant* (New York, 1885–86), p. 469.

CHAPTER FOURTEEN

1. U. S. Grant, *Personal Memoirs of U.S. Grant* (New York, 1885–86), p. 117.
2. James McPherson, *Battle Cry of Freedom* (New York, 1988), pp. 733–34.
3. Ibid., p. 779.
4. EyeWitness to History, "Surrender at Appomattox, 1865," www.eyewitness tohistory.com (1997).

CHAPTER FIFTEEN

1. R. U. Johnson and C. C. Buel, *Battles and Leaders of the Civil War* (New York, 1884–88), vol. 4 p. 250.
2. Ibid., p. 252.
3. Ibid.
4. Ibid., p. 256.
5. Ibid., p. 253.
6. Ibid.
7. William T. Sherman, *Memoirs of General William T. Sherman* (London, 1975), p. 112.
8. Steven E. Woodworth, *Nothing but Victory* (New York, 2005), p. 539.
9. Sherman, *Memoirs*, p. 173.
10. Ibid., p. 852.

CHAPTER SEVENTEEN

1. H. Cobb, quoted in James McPherson, *Battle Cry of Freedom* (New York, 1988), p. 835.
2. N. A. Trudeau, *Like Men of War* (Boston, 1998), p. 326.
3. Ibid., p. 416.
4. Theodore Lyman, *Meade's Headquarters*, ed. George R. Agassiz (Boston, 1922), p. 102.
5. McPherson, *Battle Cry of Freedom*, p. 759.

CHAPTER NINETEEN

1. Steven E. Woodworth, *Nothing but Victory* (New York, 2005), p. 518.

CHAPTER TWENTY-THREE

1. James McPherson, *Battle Cry of Freedom* (New York, 1988), p. 849.
2. Ibid.

3. Ibid., p. 850.
4. Quoted in Edmund Wilson, *Patriotic Gore* (New York, 1994), p. 685.
5. Saul R. Padover, *Karl Marx on America and the Civil War* (New York, 1972).
6. Ibid.

BIBLIOGRAPHY

Alexander, Bevin. *Robert E. Lee's Civil War.* Holbrook, Mass., 1999.

Atkinson, Rick. *The Long Gray Line.* London, 1990.

Black, Robert C. *The Railroads of the Confederacy.* Chapel Hill, N.C., 1952.

Boritt, Gabor S., ed. *Why the Civil War Came.* New York, 1996.

Catton, Bruce. *The Centennial History of the Civil War.* New York, 1961–65

Cornish, Dudley Taylor. *The Sable Arm: Negro Troops in the Union Army, 1861–1865.* New York, 1956.

Crane, Stephen. *The Red Badge of Courage.* 1895; New York, 1962.

Cunliffe, Marcus. *Soldiers and Civilians: The Martial Spirit in America, 1775–1865.* Boston, 1973.

Davis, George B., Leslie J. Perry, Joseph W. Kirkley, and Calvin D. Cowles. *The Official Military Atlas of the Civil War.* New York, 1903.

Donald, David H. *Lincoln.* New York, 1995.

———. *Why the North Won the Civil War.* Baton Rouge, La., 1960.

Dyer, F. H. *A Compendium of the War of the Rebellion.* New York, 1953.

Esposito, V. J. *The West Point Atlas of American Wars.* Vol. 1. New York, 1959.

EyeWitness to History. "Surrender at Appomattox, 1865." www.eyewitnessto history.com, 1997.

Faust, Drew Gilpin. *The Creation of Confederate Nationalism.* Baton Route, La., 1998.

Fox, Stephen. *Wolf of the Deep: Raphael Semmes and the Notorious Confederate Raider CSS Alabama.* New York, 2007.

Freeman, Douglas S. *Lee's Lieutenants.* New York, 1942–44.

———. *R. E. Lee: A Biography.* New York, 1934–35.

Furgurson, Ernest B. *Not War but Murder: Cold Harbor, 1864.* New York, 2000.

Garrison, Webb B. *Atlanta and the War.* Nashville, Tenn., 1995.

Genovese, Eugene D. *Roll, Jordan, Roll: The World the Slaves Made.* London, 1975.

Gould, John M. *The History of the First—Tenth—Twenty-ninth Maine Regiment: In Service of the United States from May 3, 1861, to June 21, 1866.* Portland, Maine, 1871.

Grant, U. S. *Personal Memoirs of U. S. Grant.* New York, 1885–86.

Griess, Thomas E., ed. *The American Civil War.* Wayne, N.J., 1987.

Griffith, Paddy. *Battle Tactics of the Civil War.* New Haven, Conn., 1989.

Hattaway, Herman, and Archer Jones. *How the North Won: A Military History of the Civil War.* Urbana, Ill., 1983.

Henderson, G. F. R. *Stonewall Jackson and the American Civil War.* New York, 1900.

Herman, Marguerita Z. *Ramparts: Fortification from the Renaissance to West Point.* New York, 1992.

Hess, Earl J. *The Union Soldier in Battle.* Lawrence, Kans., 1997.

Hicks, Roger W., and Frances E. Schultz. *Battlefields of the Civil War.* Topsfield, Mass., 1989.

Johnson, R. U., and C. C. Buel. *Battles and Leaders of the Civil War: The Century Magazine.* 4 vols. New York, 1884–88.

Jones, Archer. *Civil War Command and Strategy: The Process of Victory and Defeat.* New York, 1992.

Jones, John B. *A Rebel War Clerk's Diary.* New York, 1958.

Katcher, Philip. *The American Civil War Source Book.* London, 1992.

Kennedy, Frances H., ed. *The Civil War Battlefield Guide.* Boston, 1990.

Kerby, Robert L. *Kirby Smith's Confederacy: The Trans-Mississippi South.* New York, 1972.

Liddell Hart, B. H. *Sherman: Soldier, Realist, American.* New York, 1958.

Lincoln, Abraham. *Speeches and Writings, 1859–1865.* New York, 1989.

Livermore, Thomas L. *Numbers and Losses in the Civil War in America, 1861–5.* Boston, 1901.

Lyman, Theodore. *Meade's Headquarters, 1863–1865: Letters of Colonel Theodore Lyman from the Wilderness to Appomattox.* Edited by George R. Agassiz. Boston, 1922.

Lytle, Andrew Nelson. *Bedford Forrest and His Critter Company.* Nashville, Tenn., 1984.

McElfresh, Earl B. *Maps and Mapmakers of the Civil War.* New York, 1999.

McFeely, William S. *Grant: A Biography.* New York, 1981.

McPherson, James M. *Battle Cry of Freedom: The Civil War Era.* New York, 1988.

———. *For Cause and Comrades: Why Men Fought in the Civil War.* New York, 1997.

McWhiney, Grady, and Perry D. Jamieson. *Attack and Die: Civil War Military Tactics and the Southern Heritage.* Tuscaloosa, Ala., 1982.

Miller, Willam J. *Mapping for Stonewall: The Civil War Service of Jed Hotchkiss.* Washington, D.C., 1993.

Mitchell, Joseph B. *Decisive Battles of the Civil War.* New York, 1962.

Mitchell, Reid. *Civil War Soldiers.* New York, 1988.

Nevins, Allan. *The Ordeal of the Union.* 4 vols. New York, 1947–71.

Oates, Stephen B. *With Malice Toward None: The Life of Abraham Lincoln.* New York, 1977.

Parish, Peter J. *The American Civil War.* New York, 1975.

Potter, D. M. *The South and the Sectional Conflict.* Baton Rouge, La., 1968.

Pullen, John J. *The Twentieth Maine: A Volunteer Regiment in the Civil War.* Philadelphia, 1957.

Reid, Brian Holden. *The Origins of the American Civil War.* New York, 1996.

Rutledge, Archibald, and Richard Rollins, eds. *Pickett's Charge: Eyewitness Accounts at the Battle of Gettysburg.* Mechanicsburg, Pa., 2005

Sandburg, Carl. *Abraham Lincoln: The Prairie Years and the War Years.* New York, 2002.

Sears, Stephen W. *Landscape Turned Red: The Battle of Antietam.* New Haven, Conn., 1983.

———. *To the Gates of Richmond: The Peninsula Campaign.* New York, 1992.

———. *George B. McClellan: The Young Napoleon.* New York, 1996.

Sherman, William T. *Memoirs of General William T. Sherman.* London, 1975.

Smith, Robin. *American Civil War: Union Army.* Brassey's History of Uniforms. London, 1996.

Sommers, Richard J. *Richmond Redeemed: The Siege at Petersburg.* New York, 1991.

Stevens, Joseph E. *America's National Battlefield Parks.* Norman, Okla., 1990.

Tanner, Robert G. *Stonewall in the Valley.* Mechanicsburg, Pa., 1996.

Tate, Allen. *Stonewall Jackson: The Good Soldier.* Nashville, Tenn., 1991.

Thomas, Emory M. *Robert E. Lee: A Biography.* New York, 1995.

Trudeau, N. A. *Like Men of War: Black Troops in the Civil War, 1862–1865.* Boston, 1998.

Turner, G. E. *Victory Rode the Rails.* New York, 1953.

U.S. War Department. *The War of the Rebellion.* 36 vols. Washington, D.C., 1880–1901.

Ward, Geoffrey C., and Ric and Ken Burns. *The Civil War: An Illustrated History.* New York, 1998.

Waugh, John C. *The Class of 1846: From West Point to Appomattox; Stonewall Jackson, George McClellan and Their Brothers.* New York, 1994.

Weigley, Russell F. *History of the United States Army.* New York, 1967.

———. *A Great Civil War: A Military and Political History, 1861–1865.* Bloomington, Ind., 2000.

Wiley, Bell Irvin. *The Life of Johnny Reb: The Common Soldier of the Confederacy.* New York, 1983.

———. *The Life of Billy Yank: The Common Soldier of the Union.* New York, 1952.

Williams, Kenneth P. *Lincoln Finds a General: A Military Study of the Civil War.* 5 vols. New York, 1950–59.

Williams, T. Harry. *Lincoln and His Generals.* London, 1952.

Wilson, Edmund. *Patriotic Gore: Studies in the Literature of the American Civil War.* New York, 1994.

Winik, Jay. *April 1865: The Month That Saved America.* New York, 2001.

Woodward, C. Vann. *Mary Chesnut's Civil War.* New Haven, Conn., 1981.

Woodworth, Steven E. *Nothing but Victory: The Army of the Tennessee, 1861–1865.* New York, 2005.

ACKNOWLEDGEMENTS

It is fitting that my first debt of gratitude goes to Bill Coolidge. It was through his philanthropic enterprise that I and many other Balliol men and women were introduced to the United States. In 1957 I became a Coolidge Scholar and embarked on a tour of the country, primarily to visit some of the Civil War's most important battlefields.

Twelve years before I undertook that journey, hundreds of thousands of American men were returning from fighting in the twentieth century's most terrible conflict. Their not-so-distant Union and Confederate relatives must have experienced the same emotions as they, too, were reunited with their families after surviving what remains to this day the United States' most costly of wars.

So it is natural that my second debt of thanks goes to the people of the United States. To arrive in post-war America as a twenty-three-year-old Englishman was to step from the shadow of European reconstruction into the light of a nation determined to realise its own interpretation of a democratic society. Since then I have been fortunate enough to have made numerous return journeys to the United States and witness that ongoing ambition. There are countless individuals and institutions who have so generously played host and to list them all after my fifty-year association would constitute a book in itself. But I would like to thank staff at West Point, Vassar College, and Princeton University and the U.S. Army Center of Military History, including General John Foss, who was the first of the post-war West Point liaison officers at the Royal Military Academy Sandhurst and finally a four-star general, and Professor James McPherson of Princeton University. I owe special thanks to the thoughts and suggestions provided by my numerous friends and colleagues, including former Senator Paul Sarbanes, Tom Clancy, and George Thompson, who assisted me so kindly during my last visit to the United States.

I must single out my publisher at Knopf, Ash Green, for his stoic faith in this book and for the unrelenting support he has so generously given. George Andreou, who succeeded Ash during the final editing, has graciously carried on that baton of encouragement.

In England my gratitude goes to my agent Anthony Sheil who has, as ever, paid such careful attention to the project. Anthony Whittome, my editor at Random House, deserves special praise for his patience and encouragement during the time I spent writing this book, as does my picture editor Anne-Marie Ehrlich. I owe a lifetime of gratitude to two great British institutions: the Army and the Royal Military Academy Sandhurst, from where so many talented soldiers and academics have emerged. In particular I must thank Field Marshall Sir John Chapple, General Sir John Wilsey, Major-General Charles Vyvyan, Colonel Mike Dewar, and Lieutenant Colonel Richard Hoare. From Sandhust I have received great support from my former colleagues Duncan Anderson, Christopher Duffy, and Ned Willmott. I also wish to acknowledge the support of *The Daily Telegraph* and in particular Con Coughlin, Simon Heffer, David Twiston-

Davies, and Pat Venter. I would also like to thank Professor Robert O'Neill and Professor Hew Strachan, the past and present Chichele Professors of Military History at Oxford University.

I would not have able to undertake this book without the love and support given to me by my family. My wife, Susanne, has been, as always, a tower of strength, as have been our children and children-in-law, Lucy and Brooks Newmark, Tom and Pepy, Matthew and Sharon, and Rose and James McCarthy. Their wonderful children, Benjamin, Sam, Max, Lily, Zachary, Walter, Martha, and Mamie have all helped make the passage of this book easier to navigate. I would also like to thank friends in Kilmington, who include Nesta and Michael Gray, Shirley Thomas, and Eric Coombs. And finally thanks to my assistant Lindsey Wood, to whom this book is dedicated. Her tolerance and hard work in difficult circumstances were central to its completion.

INDEX

Page numbers in *italics* refer to maps.

ILLUSTRATION CREDITS

Abraham Lincoln: Photograph by Anthony Berger. Library of Congress. Prints & Photographs Division, Civil War Photographs, LC-DIG-ppmsca-19305.

Jefferson Davis: The Art Archive/Culver Pictures

Thomas "Stonewall" Jackson: The Art Archive/National Archives, Washington, D.C.

George McClellan: The Art Archive/National Archives, Washington, D.C.

Former slaves: Library of Congress. Prints & Photographs Division, Civil War Photographs, LC-USZ62-118354.

Company E, 4th U.S. Colored Infantry: Photograph by William Morris Smith. Library of Congress. Prints & Photographs Division, Civil War Photographs, LC-DIG-cwpb-04294.

Zouave Company: Library of Congress. Prints & Photographs Division, Civil War Photographs, LC-DIG-cwpb-03688.

A cavalry repeating carbine: © The Board of Trustees of the Armouries

A Springfield percussion rifle-musket: © The Board of Trustees of the Armouries

David Farragut: The Art Archive/National Archives, Washington D.C.

Officers of the USS *Monitor*: Library of Congress. Prints & Photographs Division, Civil War Photographs, LC-USZC4-7979.

The Confederate ram *Stonewall*: Library of Congress. Prints & Photographs Division, Civil War Photographs, LC-DIG-cwpb-04311.

Improvised Union hospital: Library of Congress. Prints & Photographs Division, Civil War Photographs, LC-DIG-cwpb-00202.

Basic amputation set: © Dr. Michael Echols/www.braceface.com/medical

Confederate dead in a ditch at Antietam: Photographs by Alexander Gardner. Library of Congress. Prints & Photographs Division, Civil War Photographs, LC-DIG-cwpb-01100.

Dead Confederate infantrymen in the Devil's Den: Photograph by Alexander Gardner. Library of Congress. Prints & Photographs Division, Civil War Photographs, LC-DIG-cwpb-03701.

Ulysses S. Grant: The Art Archive/Culver Pictures

William Tecumseh Sherman: Library of Congress. Prints & Photographs Division, Civil War Photographs, LC-DIG-cwpb-07314.

Robert E. Lee: Library of Congress. Prints & Photographs Division, Civil War Photographs, LC-DIG-cwpbh-03116.

George Thomas: Library of Congress. Prints & Photographs Division, Civil War Photographs, LC-DIG-cwpbh-03123.

Union engineers bridging the North Anna River: Library of Congress. Prints & Photographs Division, Civil War Photographs, LC-DIG-cwpb-03568.

Union engineers destroying a Confederate railroad: Library of Congress. Prints & Photographs Division, Civil War Photographs, LC-DIG-cwpb-00391.

Confederate dead gathered for burial: Library of Congress. Prints & Photographs Division, Civil War Photographs, LC-DIG-cwpb-00907.

The McLean house at Appomattox Court House, Virginia: Library of Congress. Prints & Photographs Division, Civil War Photographs, LC-DIG-cwpb-03957.

The ruins of Richmond, 1865: Library of Congress. Prints & Photographs Division, Civil War Photographs, LC-DIG-cwpb-02696.

The gallows built in Washington Arsenal: Photograph by Alexander Gardner. Library of Congress. Prints & Photographs Division, Civil War Photographs, LC-DIG-cwpb-04198.

Veterans of Pickett's charge: Pennsylvania State Archives, RG-25 Records of Special Commissions, Fiftieth Anniversary of the Battle of Gettysburg, Pickett's Charge of July 3, 1913

ALSO BY JOHN KEEGAN

FIELDS OF BATTLE
The Wars for North America

From Wolfe's siege of Quebec to Custer's downfall at Little Big-horn, John Keegan revisits the critical American battles of two centuries. He shows us how Washington was able to overwhelm British fortifications at Yorktown, and why the Union offensive collapsed during the Seven Days campaign. Combining masterly scholarship with the fresh eye of a latter-day de Tocqueville, Keegan gives Americans a brilliant reassessment of their military heritage.

History/978-0-679-74664-5

A HISTORY OF WARFARE

In this encyclopedically learned and immensely gripping book, one of our foremost military historians demolishes the famous dictum that war is the continuation of policy by other means. Analyzing centuries of conflict in societies from the Amazon to the Balkans, waged by nomadic horsemen, peasant guerrillas, and superbly disciplined regiments, John Keegan unveils the deepest motives behind humanity's penchant for mass bloodshed.

History/978-0-679-73082-8

ALSO AVAILABLE
The Battle for History, 978-0-679-76743-5
The First World War, 978-0-375-70045-3
Intelligence in War, 978-0-375-70046-0
The Iraq War, 978-1-4000-7920-9
War and Our World, 978-0-375-70520-5